Political Change in Central America

Also of Interest

†*FOREIGN POLICY on Latin America, 1970–1980,* edited by the staff of *Foreign Policy*

†*Latin America and the U.S. National Interest: A Basis for U.S. Foreign Policy,* Margaret Daly Hayes

†*Latin America, Its Problems and Its Promise: A Multidisciplinary Introduction,* edited by Jan Knippers Black

Controlling Latin American Conflicts: Ten Approaches, edited by Michael A. Morris and Victor Millán

The Venezuela-Guyana Border Dispute: Britain's Colonial Legacy in Latin America, Jacqueline A. Braveboy-Wagner

Revolutionary Cuba: The Challenge of Economic Growth with Equity, Claes Brundenius

†*The Caribbean Challenge: U.S. Policy in a Volatile Region,* edited by H. Michael Erisman

U.S.-Panama Relations, 1903–1978: A Study in Linkage Politics, David Farnsworth and James McKenney

†*Latin American Foreign Policies: Global and Regional Dimensions,* edited by Elizabeth G. Ferris and Jennie K. Lincoln

†*The New Cuban Presence in the Caribbean,* edited by Barry B. Levine

Development and the Politics of Administrative Reform: Lessons from Latin America, Linn Hammergren

Colossus Challenged: The Struggle for Caribbean Influence, edited by H. Michael Erisman and John D. Martz

†*Revolution in Central America,* edited by the Stanford Central America Action Network

†*The End and the Beginning: The Nicaraguan Revolution,* John A. Booth

†*Revolution in El Salvador: Origins and Evolution,* Tommie Sue Montgomery

PROFILES OF CONTEMPORARY LATIN AMERICA:

†*The Dominican Republic: A Caribbean Crucible,* Howard J. Wiarda and Michael J. Kryzanek

†*Honduras: Caudillo Politics and Military Rulers,* James A. Morris

†*Mexico: Paradoxes of Stability and Change,* Daniel Levy and Gabriel Székely

†*Nicaragua: The Land of Sandino,* Thomas W. Walker

†Available in hardcover and paperback.

Westview Special Studies on
Latin America and the Caribbean

Political Change in Central America: Internal and External Dimensions
edited by Wolf Grabendorff, Heinrich-W. Krumwiede, and Jörg Todt

Recent events in Central America have been seen as constituting a major regional crisis in international politics. Their impact not only has been endured by the suffering peoples of Central America but also has led to a complex web of activities by various international actors who have made their presence strongly felt. This book looks at the regimes in Nicaragua, El Salvador, and Guatemala and at conditions and strategies for regime transformation in those countries. The authors focus also on the reasons for the internationalization of the Central American crisis, as well as on the strategies and policies of the actors involved. Supporting the urgent need for more tolerance toward the process of revolutionary change in Central America, the authors argue for a less security-oriented and more developmental approach to the region.

The book results from two international conferences sponsored by the Friedrich Ebert Foundation in Bonn, at which an effort was made to bring together the viewpoints of all parties involved in the process of change in Central America.

Wolf Grabendorff, of the SWP–Research Institute for International Affairs, Ebenhausen, and **Heinrich-W. Krumwiede,** of the University of Mannheim, are political scientists specializing in Latin America. **Jörg Todt** is a development economist with the Friedrich Ebert Foundation, Bonn.

Published in association with the
Friedrich Ebert Foundation

Political Change in Central America: Internal and External Dimensions

edited by Wolf Grabendorff,
Heinrich-W. Krumwiede,
and Jörg Todt

Westview Press / Boulder and London

Westview Special Studies on Latin America and the Caribbean

Published in 1984 in the United States of America by Westview Press, Inc., 5500 Central Avenue, Boulder, Colorado 80301; Frederick A. Praeger, President and Publisher

Library of Congress Cataloging in Publication Data
Main entry under title:
Political change in Central America.
(Westview special studies on Latin America and the Caribbean)
"Published in association with the Friedrich Ebert Foundation"—Prelim. p. iv.
Includes index.
1. Central America—Politics and government—1979- —Addresses, essays, lectures. 2. Central America—Foreign relations—1979- —Addresses, essays, lectures. 3. Revolutions—Central America—Addresses, essays, lectures. I. Grabendorff, Wolf, 1940- . II. Krumwiede, Heinrich-W., 1943- . III. Todt, Jörg. IV. Friedrich-Ebert-Stiftung. V. Series.
F1439.5.P65 1984 972.8′052 83-19883
ISBN 0-86531-609-0

Printed and bound in the United States of America

10 9 8 7 6 5 4 3 2 1

Contents

Introduction

Wolf Grabendorff
Heinrich-W. Krumwiede
Jörg Todt

Until recently, Central America was unknown territory for Europeans—far more so than for North Americans. Since the Sandinist victory in Nicaragua in 1979, however, this situation has changed completely. Increasingly, West Europeans are coming to view Central America as an important Third World region in which the superimposition of the East-West conflict upon the North-South conflict has created a cauldron of international crisis. For the most part, Western Europe is critical of the Reagan administration's reaction to the revolutionary challenge laid down in Central America. Because the Central American conflict serves as an example for the relationship between the First World and the Third World, West Europeans now feel obliged to participate in the search for solutions to conflicts in a region previously considered to belong exclusively to the United States' sphere of influence.

In answer to this newly recognized obligation, the Friedrich Ebert Foundation, a private, independent foundation in the Federal Republic of Germany, organized two international colloquiums—one in fall 1980 and one in spring 1981—on the problems and perspectives for Central America following the national uprising in Nicaragua. By including scholars and politicians from Central America, the United States, and Western Europe, special emphasis was placed on creating a dialogue in which the divergent viewpoints and interests could be discussed. Because of the special importance of regional powers to finding a constructive solution to the conflicts in Central America, experts from Mexico and Venezuela were also included in the dialogue. Several of the contributions to this book are based on the papers presented at these two conferences. They were revised and updated for this publication. Also included are contributions by other authors whose work complements the theme of this book.

This volume is consciously limited to a discussion of the political dimensions, narrowly defined, of change in Central America. Equal emphasis is placed on the endogenous and exogenous factors of crisis development as well as on the possibilities for exercising control over these factors. Of special interest is the analysis of the interrelationship of these factors. Particular attention is paid to Nicaragua, El Salvador, and Guatemala, the three Central American states in which the problem of regime transformation and regime stability was or still is of primary importance. Here the deep-reaching social-revolutionary processes of change have already been completed or at least have become clearly evident.

The book is divided into two parts that describe the internal and external dimensions of political change in Central America. Each part begins with an introductory essay by one of the editors, which presents an overview of the problems to be discussed in the following chapters.

In the first chapter, which is more theoretical than descriptive, Heinrich-W. Krumwiede discusses two main problems from a comparative Central American perspective. These problems are either directly or indirectly addressed in each of the following chapters of Part 1. First, why have social revolutionary mass movements developed in several Central American countries and under what circumstances have they been politically successful? Second, what form of government and government transformation holds the most promise for political stability in Central America given the challenge laid down by the social revolutions in the region?

In Chapters 2 and 3, Richard L. Millett and Donald Castillo Rivas analyze the many factors—national and international, "objective" and subjective, structural and conjunctural—that determined the success of the Sandinist revolution in Nicaragua. They indicate that the Sandinists enjoyed more favorable circumstances for their revolutionary takeover than seemed to be the case for the other revolutionary movements in Central America. Both authors stress the extent to which national and international factors interacted with one another. As in the other articles in the "domestic" part of the book, it is remarkable—and thus certainly not just accidental—how much emphasis is placed on foreign-policy factors, in particular the attitude of the United States.

In Chapter 4, Heinrich-W. Krumwiede describes the structures and the developing trends of the Sandinist provisional regime. He is most interested in the possibilities that a regime could be established in Nicaragua that would be acceptable to Western industrialized states because it conforms to a sufficient extent to democratic-pluralist norms or differs to a sufficient extent from the communist state-party model.

The civil war in El Salvador is the main theme of the two following chapters. Harald Jung concentrates on the genesis and development of the civil war from a historical perspective. He thereby comes to the conclusion that the systematic prevention and delay of social-reform policies and the discrimination against and repression of social-reformist parties and groups laid the groundwork for the social-revolutionary mass movement. Cynthia J. Arnson presents an analysis of the political behavior of the Salvadoran military, in particular since the coup d'etat on October 15, 1979. Here she places special emphasis on the struggles between rival factions within the military as well as on the relationship of the military to the United States. She also discusses the possibility of bringing an end to the civil war through negotiations.

In Chapters 7 and 8, Edelberto Torres-Rivas and Piero Gleijeses survey the political characteristics of the different counterrevolutionary regimes in Guatemala since the overthrow of the Jacobo Arbenz Guzmán government in 1954. They analyze the constant political advances of the military and the importance of political violence as a means of maintaining control and ask whether, given the destruction of the political center and the strength of the socialist forces, only a regime more or less to the left could offer some promise of permanent stability.

In the last chapter of Part 1, Margaret E. Crahan analyzes the trends toward change and continuity in the political attitudes and political behavior of the Catholic church in Central America. She points out that only a minority of the clergy identifies itself with the revolution and holds clearly socialist positions, whereas the institutional church assumes a moderate or, rather, conservative political attitude.

Part 2 of the book deals with external interests and strategies in Central America. In Chapter 10, Wolf Grabendorff focuses upon the internationalization of the Central American crisis and touches upon the topics that are dealt with in more depth in the following chapters. Among them are the changes of the foreign-policy postures toward the region from the Carter to the Reagan administration and the interests of the regional powers (Mexico, Cuba, Venezuela, and Colombia) as well as the extraregional actors (Soviet Union, Israel, Libya, the socialist bloc, and the West European countries). He finds three international tendencies: The status quo alliance, the social-change alliance, and the revolutionary-change alliance compete with each other for influence upon the outcome of the crisis developments in the region.

Richard E. Feinberg and Robert A. Pastor deal with the options of U.S. policy and the U.S. national interests in Central America in Chapters 11 and 12 respectively. Both put the discussion of U.S. national interests in Central America into the context of a general sense of frustration about the decline of U.S. power and see the policy of "reassertionism" of the Reagan administration evolving from the determination to transform Central America in a "test case" of halting or even reversing such a process of decline. Pastor stresses the effects of the "Caribbeanization" of the United States as an important factor for the long-term U.S. involvement in the region and suggests six ways in which U.S. influence should be more clearly demonstrated, assuming that the United States first recognizes that it cannot control developments in the region.

As the "Cuban threat" is seen by the U.S. administration as well as by most Central American regimes in power as the principal source of instability in the region, Carla A. Robbins looks critically at the evidence available to support such charges. Considering Cuba's record so far she finds that the Cubans played only a limited role in the Sandinist revolution in Nicaragua and that Havana has been urging a negotiated settlement in El Salvador for a long time. She even expects Cuba to exercise only a very limited role in the region in the future.

In Chapter 14 Henrik Bischof traces the activities of other socialist countries in Central America, stressing the point that it seems impossible to find any Soviet initiative to implement communism in Central America. Nevertheless the aid to Nicaragua from the socialist countries has been considerable and is seen as likely to increase. Although the Soviet Union showed little interest in the Sandinist revolution from 1979 to 1981, since 1982 it has upgraded its attention to Central American developments in general.

Demetrio Boersner's and Bruce Michael Bagley's chapters deal with the policies of the principal regional powers, Venezuela and Mexico, respectively. Both countries have been involved in the process of political change in Central America very openly at least since 1978 and collaborated in the case of the Nicaraguan revolution, whereas in El Salvador their political interests at times have differed widely. But both countries have recently joined forces again to seek negotiated settlements for the many-sided conflicts in the region. Bagley argues strongly that Mexico might have reached the limits of its regional-power status and will in the future not be able to form a political counterweight to U.S. policies in the region. This is mainly because it lacks the economic and financial resources it was able to muster in support of its foreign policy before 1982.

In the last chapter Wolf Grabendorff compares the general perceptions of the Central American crisis in Western Europe and the United States by asking if the situation constitutes a North-South problem or an East-West rivalry, if the Atlantic alliance cohesion is the issue at hand or rather the problem of Third World accommodation for the West European states. And finally he looks at the divergent instruments and strategies put forward on both sides of the Atlantic: Social and Christian Democrats seem to prefer party diplomacy in influencing political change in Central America, whereas the U.S. administration seems to rely mainly upon national-security considerations in addressing the problems in the region.

If certain lessons are to be learned from the analysis of political change in Central America during recent years, they will have to include the following points.

1. The attitude of Western industrialized states toward Nicaragua, El Salvador, and Guatemala is an important indicator of the extent to which these industrialized states are willing and capable, either individually or collectively, to seek constructive political solutions for those Third World countries in which, as the result of oligarchic and repressive as well as antireformist and antidemocratic regimes, the political center has been weakened and the social-revolutionary movements have gained mass support.

2. In order to achieve long-term stability in such societies, it is essential not only to tolerate but in some cases even to encourage political solutions that guarantee social-revolutionary movements direct, or at the very least indirect, access to political power.

3. In such countries of upheaval, the social credibility of Western democracy is put on trial. From the viewpoint of the social-revolutionary movements and the social-reformist parties in these countries, this credibility is measured against the performance of the Western industrialized states. To what extent do they recognize demands for fundamental reform regarding the distribution of wealth? To what extent are they willing to tolerate noncapitalist or only partially capitalist economic development models? To what extent do they refrain from flatly claiming that social revolutionaries are remotely controlled by "international communism"? To what extent do they accept political solutions that guarantee social-revolutionary movements a share of power? Finally, to what extent are they willing to recognize that freedom from degrading need is one of the most elementary of human rights?

4. By championing social justice in these countries, the Western industrialized states will be in a better position to demand respect for and the realization of pluralistic democracies in the countries of Central America.

5. Even in the medium term, any support for rightist regimes like that in Guatemala could be far more problematic for the Western industrialized states than would be support for leftist regimes like that in Nicaragua. Given the process of social-revolutionary change spreading throughout the Third World, an alliance strategy that concentrates

primarily on the rightist military, the entrepreneur, and parts of the middle class is unlikely to encourage long-term stability. Particularly in Central America it has yet to be proved that Western industrialized nations can demonstrate the same kind of flexibility toward leftist regimes that they have often shown toward rightist regimes. Only those groups and political currents in the Western industrialized states that seek a positive arrangement with the social-revolutionry movements and their allied social-reformist parties and that do not automatically label these as "enemies of the West" have any chance of exercising a moderating influence on the future developments in Central America.

6. Western industrialized states have employed direct or indirect destabilizing tactics in order to avoid undesirable developments and to enforce internal and external satisfactory conduct from postrevolutionary regimes by means of economic and military pressure. Such attempts can only lead to a deepening of the crises in the region—and in the long run can cause considerable damage to Western interests.

Part 1

Regimes and Regime Transformation

1
Regimes and Revolution in Central America

Heinrich-W. Krumwiede

Social-revolutionary mass movements that began to take shape in the 1970s in Nicaragua, El Salvador, and Guatemala exposed the deep cracks in the foundations of the then-existing political regimes. In 1979 the social revolutionists seized political power in Nicaragua. Since 1980, El Salvador has been in the throes of a civil war. There the situation has developed into a stalemate: The leftist front seems too weak to win the military-political battle, but is obviously strong enough to prevent the military from "pacifying" the country. Guatemala finds itself in a prerevolutionary state in which the ruling regime is attempting to stifle the development of the social-revolutionary movement in the country by waging a kind of "civil war from above."

This chapter is introductory in nature. It analyzes, from a comparative perspective, two central political problems that are themes in all of the following chapters dealing with each country individually. For reasons to be explained later, Honduras will be included as both a comparative and a contrasting case. The two basic questions to be discussed are:

- Which factors presumably determine the chances for success of the social-revolutionary movement in Central America?
- Given the challenges laid down by these social revolutions, what kind of regime transformation promises the greatest degree of political stabilization?

The discussion of the second question will deal primarily with El Salvador. The trends of development in Sandinist Nicaragua are analyzed in Chapter 4.

CENTRAL AMERICA AS A LABORATORY FOR THEORIES OF REVOLUTION

The reader should attempt to envisage Central America as a kind of "laboratory for theories of revolution."[1] This method of observing the political processes in Central America may appear particularly heartless to a reader interested in normative political statements. And those readers fascinated only by realpolitik, who as "pragmatists" have an aversion to "gray theory," may harbor the suspicion that the following analysis will use an approach of interest only to the so-called academic world. I hope that the following contribution will demonstrate the fertility of the comparative-theoretical approach and allay the suspicion that such an approach is remote from reality. The pragmatist should be aware of the fact that all political actors of relevance for Central America, be they internal or external, can also be seen as "practicing theorists of revolution." Their political behavior is based on certain assumptions or hypotheses about the causes, developmental possibilities, and chances of success of social-revolutionary movements, as well as about the possibilities for counteracting such movements. The actors are "testing" these hypotheses in everyday practice at the cost of much and often unnecessary violence. Thus, for example, the Salvadoran *campesinos* (small farmers and farm laborers) must suffer violent death in the name of the "domino theory" and/or the "theory of popular revolution."

It thus seems methodologically justified to speak of Central America (or, to be more exact, Nicaragua, El Salvador, Guatemala, and Honduras) as a "laboratory of revolution theory," because these four countries to a considerable extent are distinguished by a mixture of commonalities and differences that can be considered desirable and useful for comparative studies of revolution.

A Specific Type of Revolution or Attempts at Revolution

Many theories of revolution suffer by using a very broad and thus diffuse concept that includes in the term *revolution* a large number of quite different phenomena. The resulting attempts to explain these phenomena are then similarly diffuse, trivial, and often tautological. An effort at explaining everything runs the risk of explaining nothing.

In attempting to determine the preconditions for the success of revolutions in the case of Central America, I hope to be able to avoid such a pitfall because *that which is to be explained can be precisely defined.* I shall ask which factors most influence the chances that more or less Marxist-oriented groups, through the use of force, will succeed in acquiring political power and in changing the basic structure of a regime according to their goals.

I propose using a *graduated concept* of revolutionary success. If one recalls that the revolutionary struggle in Central America began with very small guerrilla groups (called *revolutionary elites* in the following discussion) that, as in other Latin American countries, for years often remained relatively isolated and were forced to sustain heavy losses, then the creation of a social-revolutionary mass movement must be considered a success. In this chapter, particular attention is paid to the problem of determining under which circumstances a social-revolutionary elite can succeed in creating this precondition for further achievements. And in the final section I shall show in some detail why the existence of a social-revolutionary mass movement in El Salvador and Guatemala seems to require the development of a special logic of regime transformation.

The following can be considered further stages of success: gaining a share of governmental power; assuming power by overthrowing a regime; establishing a revolutionary regime; consolidating a revolutionary regime. Such a differentiation of the definition of "success" also seems to be useful because in certain circumstances different combinations of factors could prove optimal for the individual stages.

Necessary Conditions for the Emergence of a Revolutionary Situation

Social Dissatisfaction

Since social-revolutionary mass movements can develop only when social dissatisfaction is widespread and intense among the lower classes, only those countries with a large potential for social dissatisfaction can be considered candidates for social revolution. Nicaragua (unless otherwise stated, this always means Somozist Nicaragua), El Salvador (this refers to the situation until late 1979, if nothing else is indicated), Guatemala, and Honduras were or are marked by socioeconomic structural and procedural conditions that make possible the development of a powerful potential for social dissatisfaction. "Life chances" in the sense used by Max Weber—that is, land ownership, income, wealth, educational opportunities, chances for social advancement, and so on—were or are extremely unevenly distributed. The majority of the population participated not at all or only marginally in the occasionally impressive growth of the national product and still lives in a state of poverty. For decades the governing regimes had pursued a policy of socioeconomic modernization according to the motto "growth without equality-oriented development," which forced primarily the lower classes to carry the burden of economic "progress." Significant structural reforms with a redistributive character, such as agrarian reform, were never initiated. Since the four societies may be defined as "posttraditional," it can be assumed that the disadvantaged will no longer accept the predominant state of social inequality as God-given and unchangeable.

Costa Rica, because of its considerably higher standard of living and its far more advantageous distribution of "life chances," is not a candidate for the development of a revolutionary situation and can therefore be excluded from the following study. The fact that there is a stable democratic regime in Costa Rica and that no large social-revolutionary movement exists that could threaten the political system coincides with standard assumptions, verified in correlation studies, that there is a connection between socioeconomic structural and procedural conditions and democratic political stability.[2]

Because Panama's per capita income exceeds the regional average, it can be compared to Nicaragua, El Salvador, Guatemala, and Honduras only to a limited extent. However, it is excluded from the following comparative study primarily because of the special case presented by the Canal Zone.[3]

Weak Political Legitimacy

The "hammerblow of revolution" can only destroy a regime that is already crumbling. Regimes that enjoy only limited legitimacy or can count on only weak "diffuse support" from the general population are more susceptible to overthrow attempts, including social-revolutionary ones, than regimes enjoying strong legitimacy. Weak political legitimacy (or, to put it in procedural terms, the rapid decay of legitimacy) is thus a necessary—if by no means sufficient—condition for the development of revolutionary situations (this will be discussed further in the section on causes for the success of social-revolutionary movements).

Although in Costa Rica a democratic political system enjoying strong legitimacy continues to survive, in Nicaragua, El Salvador, and Honduras the authoritarian or semiauthoritarian regimes of the 1970s were marked by considerable deficits of political legitimacy. It seems reasonable to assume that the great majority of the population not only never identified itself with these regimes, but also was more or less intensely antipathetic toward them.

Various Cases of "Revolutionary Success"

Only those hypotheses can claim to have an explanatory power that are able to explain not only the success of revolutions but also the failure, the partial success, or the absence of revolutions. It is therefore methodologically impermissible to examine hypotheses about the causes and conditions for success of revolutions solely on the basis of countries in which a revolution was successful.

The proposed group of countries offers a double methodological advantage. On the one hand, in all four countries the necessary basic conditions exist for the development of a social-revolutionary situation. On the other hand, social-revolutionary movements were, or probably will be, successful to varying degrees. The social-revolutionary movement in Nicaragua succeeded in overthrowing the ruling regime and in establishing a revolutionary regime; it is now struggling with the problems of consolidating its revolutionary regime. In my opinion, the social-revolutionary movements in El Salvador will not be able, in the foreseeable future, to achieve more than an institutionalized share of power. Pre-revolutionary Guatemala can serve as a "test case" for the predictive efficiency of hypotheses. Honduras is simultaneously a "comparative case" and an important "contrasting case" since no social-revolutionary popular movement so far has developed in that country; indeed, radical social reformists have not even been able to win a large following.

Commonalities and Differences

The four countries are comparable because of the following commonalities: They are small states; they are at a similar level of socio-economic development and have similar social structures; they enjoyed a common history (in the 1820s and 1830s they were even part of a federal state); they were and are confronted by the same hegemonic power, the United States. The commonality of their political-cultural and political-institutional characteristics (an authoritarian tradition that remains strong) becomes particularly evident when they are compared with Costa Rica.

These common characteristics simplify the task of analyzing the conditions for the success of revolutions for two reasons. On the one hand, they permit us to exclude certain factors that could be responsible for unusual findings. Thus, we can omit the question of the extent to which differences between large and small states affect attempts at revolution. To offer another example: If we were to include Asian states as objects of comparison, conclusions would always be open to the question of to what extent the success or failure of revolutions must be attributed to completely different cultural frameworks.

On the other hand, the selection of these countries offers the advantage that the large number of existing commonalities makes it possible to examine closely which differences, or changes in which factors, are particularly responsible for the different chances of success of social-revolutionary movements. My assumption is that given certain conditions (common socioeconomic and other conditions, the existence of a large potential for social dissatisfaction, and weak political legitimacy), it is political factors (in the narrow sense, such as the kind of regime and regime policy, the behavior of external actors, and the strategies of revolutionary movements) that are responsible for the success or failure of revolution.[4] Accordingly, the rest of this chapter deals almost exclusively with such political factors.

CAUSES FOR THE SUCCESS OF SOCIAL-REVOLUTIONARY MOVEMENTS IN CENTRAL AMERICA

As the individual case studies in this book demonstrate, the chances for success of social-revolutionary movements in Central America are determined by a large number of different factors. Analytically, one can differentiate between national and international, structural and conjunctural, objective and subjective factors.

In order to simplify the analysis, the factors will be divided into clusters. Making the plausible assumption that a social revolution has particularly good chances for success when a *strong social-revolutionary movement* is struggling against a *weak regime* in a *favorable international environment*, I shall differentiate among three clusters:

- the weakness of the existing regime (in particular: "structural vulnerability," crisis-accelerating factors, crisis-creating behavior of the ruling elite)
- the strength of the social-revolutionary movement (in particular: structural and procedural conditons for its growth, strategies for gaining power)
- the international context (in particular: degree of external dependence, behavior of the most important international actors)

My primary goal is to point out interdependencies within and among the factor clusters. Structural factors, that is, those that can be considered especially "objective," will receive particular attention.

Included on the list of important factors is the behavior of relevant national and external actors. It is possible to reconstruct revolution-conducive and revolution-obstructive modes and logics of behavior. Naturally, the problem remains that the political behavior of the actors does not necessarily follow any particular logic, but rather can frequently be characterized as relatively irrational—that is, destructive of professed goals. Thus there are clear limits to any prognostic theory of revolution, be it predictive or "postdictive." To mention one example: It seems probable that the Sandinists could not have come to power in Nicaragua if Anastasio Somoza Debayle had bowed to pressure from the United States and the "bourgeois opposition" and had stepped down in 1978. It is questionable whether the Salvadoran leftists would have risked the civil war had they not been encouraged by the success of the Sandinist revolution in Nicaragua.

In order to gain a tangible and graphic picture of the problem the reader should recall that very small guerrilla groups initiated the revolutionary struggle in Central America. For example, in 1977 the Sandinist Front of National Liberation (Frente Sandinista de Liberación Nacional—FSLN), was still so weak that it could be considered to be but one of the many unimportant guerrilla groups in Latin America with absolutely no prospects for success. Against this background, questions such as the following gain importance that is to a certain extent dramatic. Under what conditions can a social-revolutionary elite succeed in gaining mass popular support? Which weaknesses of a regime make it particularly vulnerable to social-revolutionary attempts to overthrow it? To what extent and at what stage in their conflict are the regime elites and the social-revolutionary elites dependent on foreign support?

In the following analysis, particular emphasis is placed on the relationship between social-reformist and social-revolutionary forces. Here, the basic thesis, which will be dealt with more fully later, is: The rise of social-revolutionary forces can only begin when the belief is widely shared among the population that social-reformist attempts at peaceful transformation have failed.

To contribute to a greater understanding of the postulated connection between social reform and social revolution, it is important to note that only social dissatisfaction that has been politicized can cause problems for a regime, because it breeds the expectation that the common person's situation will be improved through political means. In contrast, non-political and certainly common reactions to social dissatisfaction, such as resignation, apathy, and fatalism, do not confront a regime with such expectations of change and improved performance.[5] The politicization of social dissatisfaction can occur in two forms. The social-reformist one seeks to achieve improvements in general living conditions through gradual reforms and peaceful regime transformation. The social-revolutionary form attempts to achieve social improvements by toppling repressive regimes (with violent means, where necessary) and introducing radical redistributive measures.

It is assumed—probably realistically—that the socially disadvantaged usually prefer the social-reformist alternative because it is associated with smaller risks. Social revolutionists thus find themselves in an unfavorable competitive situation with social reformists. Therefore one must ask in what political context and with the help of which strategy can social revolutionaries shift this competitive situation in their favor.

Recognizing the Emergence of a Revolutionary Situation

Weak and Deteriorating Political Legitimacy

Weak or deteriorating political legitimacy can be considered a necessary precondition for the emergence of a revolutionary situation. One must ask, however, whether the usual analytical concentration on problems of legitimacy and legitimation, so often found in diverse theories of crisis and revolution, is really capable of producing more than conventional wisdom regarding the causes and chances of success of revolutionary processes. On the one hand, for example, even regimes with little legitimacy can enjoy long periods of considerable political stability. On the other hand, not every type of political instability can be considered conducive to revolution; one should focus instead on one very specific type. An analysis of Central American political developmental processes supports this assessment.

If one accepts a close connection between weak political legitimacy and regime instability, it seems astonishing that the Somoza regime survived for more than forty years and became seriously threatened only during the last two years of its existence. The Somoza regime was supposedly the weakest in terms of political legitimacy of all Central American regimes. In contrast to the oligarchic-military regimes of El Salvador and Guatemala, which enjoyed, or enjoy, the support of the upper class and large parts of the middle class, in Nicaragua even a large part of the "bourgeois camp" was always opposed to the Somoza clan and its regime.

It is telling that the first Somoza (Anastasio Samoza García) described the strategy of his regime for ensuring stability without referring once to the problems of legitimacy and legitimation so favored by many social scientists:

> *plomo para los enemigos* (bullets for the enemy)
> *palo para los vacilantes* (the stick for the vacillators)
> *plata para los amigos* (money for friends)[6]

The support of the hegemonic power, the United States, for a regime professing to be anticommunist; the monopoly over the institutions of repression (national guard); a policy of divide and conquer, which combined the use and threat of force against the radical opposition and the class enemy (in particular the organized lower class) with the systematic tactic of corrupting and co-opting the moderate opposition, the "class allies" (the bourgeois camp), and the coalition partners (in particular the national guard): All this proved sufficient to keep alive a regime rejected by the majority of the population.

In general, Przeworski is probably correct in stating that a regime is threatened only when the opposition has discovered a *realistic* alternative to the ruling regime: "What matters for the stability of any regime is not the legitimacy of this particular system of domination but the presence or absence of preferable alternatives. A regime does not collapse unless and until some alternative is organized in such a way as to present a real choice for isolated individuals."[7]

The Somoza regime faced its first serious—and final—crisis only after U.S. support during the Carter administration became doubtful and the bourgeois opposition gained the impression that, with the help of the United States, it would be possible to replace the Somoza regime with a parliamentary-democratic system free from repression and corruption. In other words, the existential crisis of the Somoza regime only set in when a realistic alternative to the regime began to take shape.

Donald Castillo Rivas in Chapter 3 and, in particular, Richard L. Millett in Chapter 2 describe in detail how and why this gradual, more or less peaceful alternative for transforming the Somoza regime failed. Only when it became clear that this alternative would not work (Somoza prevented its realization by refusing to step down) did the FSLN become the dominant force in the opposition camp. The viewpoint of the FSLN that the Somoza regime could be overthrown only by force appeared more attractive and plausible not least because all other alternatives for transformation of the system seemed to have failed.

Shrinking Coalition, Deserting Elites

It has been argued here that it is possible for regimes quite weak in political legitimacy to remain stable for long periods of time. They are threatened only when realistic alternatives become visible. How long a regime is able to survive depends to a great extent on the *breadth* of the coalition supporting that regime. Thus is seems plausible that the Somozist Clan regime was more vulnerable to overthrow attempts than the rightist regimes in El Salvador and Guatemala because it could draw on considerably less support from the upper and middle classes.

In assessing the probable stability of a given regime, however, the *composition* of the coalition supporting that regime may be more important than its breadth (measured, for example, by the percent of the population that, for whatever reasons, supports the regime). Even a very narrow coalition can ensure stability if it includes highly politically influential groups, that is, groups with important political resources (means of repression, wealth, organizational skills, conflict capabilities). Examples are the security and military forces, the business associations, the church, the most important mass media, some middle-class organizations, and some labor and *campesino* associations (loyal to the regime because they receive favors from the regime).

In the final analysis, a regime's *ruling techniques* determine whether it can successfully maintain this coalition (for instance through co-optation, corruption, and clientelism), defend itself against real opposition (through force) or potential opposition (through co-optation and/or threat of force), and neutralize the "vacillators" (through a combination of different measures). In this sense I have already referred to the Somozist technique of ruling. Harald Jung, in Chapter 5, deals at some length with the Salvadoran ruling technique, which he says consisted, among other things, of a "policy of selective social reform and repression serving to divide the middle and lower social sectors."

A regime will be decisively weakened if important groups withdraw from the regime coalition ("desertion of the elites") and renounce their loyalty to that regime. If these groups go so far as to join the revolutionary coalition challenging the regime, the chances of success of a revolution increase considerably.

It goes without saying that a regime—given the existence of a strong revolutionary movement—becomes particularly vulnerable to overthrow attempts when the loyalty of the military and security forces becomes doubtful, or at least when some of them are no longer willing to defend the existing regime and possibly even join the revolutionary opposition. Since the Russian Revolution, at least partial "desertion" of the military has been considered a prerequisite for the success of any revolution (in part it is seen as a necessary condition for success).

Central America conforms only partially to the expectations of this model. In Nicaragua, no important member of the regime coalition, except for the Catholic church, ever defected. The hopes of the Sandinists that at least a part of the national guard would defect were not fulfilled. In spite of many factional struggles, the Salvadoran military is following an antirevolutionary course; so far only a few officers have joined the revolutionary left (see Chapter 6 by Cynthia Arnson). The Guatemalan military, for the most part, also seems to be loyal to the regime (see the chapters by Edelberto Torres-Rivas and Piero Gleijeses).[8] In addition, there is little hard evidence of a drastic reduction in upper- and middle-class support for the Salvadoran and Guatemalan regimes.

For the maintenance of a regime, and this is particularly true for small states such as those of Central America that are dependent on foreign powers, the *external* coalition partners are at least as important as the internal partners. Thus the dissociation of the Carter administration from the Somoza regime was a basic precondition for the success of the revolution; and today the support of the Reagan administration for the existing regime in El Salvador is preventing the militarily not impossible victory of the leftist front. All chapters in this book, not only in Part 2 but also in Part 1, document the importance of an analysis of the behavior of the external actors in order to understand the domestic processes in Central America. Accordingly, coalition building must be analyzed as both a national and an international process.

The Central American case points to the necessity of analyzing the effects of the "defection of the elites" not only in terms of the behavior of the regime coalition but also in terms of the behavior of the *moderate* regime-critical opposition. It seems useful to study the behavior of the pluralistic-parliamentarian, more or less social-reform–oriented regime-critical opposition, regarding it as a "crisis indicator" for an authoritarian or semiauthoritarian regime. Such an approach is to be recommended particularly where a regime's vulnerability to social-revolutionary movements is to be assessed.

It can be argued that the moderate regime-critical opposition can serve completely unwillingly—as stabilizer of an authoritarian or semiauthoritarian regime and can protect it from the threat of social revolution. It performs this function most effectively when the population believes that this opposition embodies the *real* possibility of peaceful regime transformation and of a reshaping of the society through social reforms. As long as this belief prevails, the drawing power of the riskier social-revolutionary transformation alternative, which is bent on using force to gain power, is limited. The existence of a moderate regime-critical opposition has proved particularly valuable on the international level for maintaining a regime. The United States normally prefers to support those states that at least give the appearance of being democratic, even if they are not in fact. Particular importance is placed on holding elections even where these elections are fraudulent or where large parts of the political spectrum do not participate (for example, the elections to the constitutive assembly in El Salvador in 1982). The mere participation of the moderate regime-critical opposition in elections, as fraudulent as they may be, can be interpreted as an indication that the country is semidemocratic, or at least on the way to becoming democratic.

An authoritarian or semiauthoritarian regime loses, both nationally and internationally, an important line of defense and a certain protective covering when large parts of the regime-critical moderate opposition defect. The intensity of the "defection" can vary from revocation of its willingness to participate in "elections" and to serve as an involuntary and indirect provider of legitimacy for the regime to attempts, with the help of friendly military factions, to come to power by way of a coup d'etat, with the idea of establishing a pluralistic social-reformist regime after a certain transition phase, and finally to the willingness to form an indirect or direct coalition with social-revolutionary movements and to support indirectly or directly the armed revolution.

The bourgeois anti-Somozist opposition went through the various phases of such a "defection" and thereby decidedly increased the chances of success of the FSLN: Confident of the support of the Carter administration, it challenged the Somoza regime, thereby further weakening the regime's already crumbling national and international legitimacy. By pursuing the overthrow of the Somoza regime through peaceful means such as strikes and protest marches, at times in coalition with the FSLN, and then by seeking a "negotiated settlement" with Somoza that finally failed, the bourgeois opposition contributed, in the eyes of the *national* and *international* public, if not to a legitimization, then at least to a *destigmatization* of the FSLN and its strategy of gaining power by force. Both domestic and foreign moderate political forces lost their fear of the FSLN. It was increasingly seen less as a Marxist guerrilla movement and more as a particularly determined part of a general, society-wide, democratic, anti-Somozist opposition movement and thus also won a following among moderate, social-reformist forces.

In a similar way, the decision of the social-democratic party and sections of the Christian Democrats in El Salvador in early 1980 to cancel all cooperation with the military and to join the revolutionary camp contributed at least in part to a "democratic legitimization" or "Marxist destigmatization" of the guerrillas united in the Frente Farabundo Martí de Liberación Nacional (FMLN). Conversely, the faction of the Christian Democratic party under José Napoleón Duarte serves as a particularly important "democratic legitimizer" of the existing regime. In the years to come, the behavior of the Social Democratic and Christian Democratic parties in Guatemala will similarly serve as an indicator of the vulnerability of the regime to social-revolutionary movements.

The Strength of the Social-Revolutionary Movement

An important indicator of the weakness of a regime and of its "social-revolutionary vulnerability" is, naturally, the strength of the social-revolutionary movement. An open revolutionary situation can be said to exist where the social-revolutionary movement has gained such strength through military successes and territorial gains that it has created a state of "dual sovereignty." This is clearly the case today in El Salvador.

The "strength" of a social-revolutionary movement is determined by many factors (I will discuss these in a later section). Suffice it here to say that one characteristic of the strength of a social-revolutionary movement, namely its *size* (measured by the number of its followers), is of decisive importance for Central American revolutions. In Central America, as shown by Nicaragua and El Salvador, only social-revolutionary *mass* movements can be successful. The Cuban revolution, in which a small guerrilla group, in the style of a coup d'etat, took over power "surreptitiously" more than by open fighting, could not and cannot be repeated in Central America for several reasons: Central American and Latin American governments and military forces in general have demonstrated that they, like the United States, have learned certain "lessons" from the Cuban experience and are quite willing and able to eradicate small guerrilla formations through counterinsurgency measures. Only powerful social-revolutionary movements are therefore in any position to pose a serious threat to a regime. Indeed, it seems possible to formulate the speculative thesis that each successful revolution in Latin America increases the requirements for the next social-revolutionary movement wanting to take over power and that the degree of "necessary strength" grows. Thus, in order to be successful, the Salvadoran revolutionists must recruit more followers and mobilize more political and military resources than the Nicaraguan Sandinists had to.

Given this problem, the following section deals with the question of under what conditions a social-revolutionary elite can win a mass following.

Political Conditions in Which a Social-Revolutionary Elite Can Win a Mass Following

In the following discussion, I will differentiate among three political arenas: the political-party arena, the interest-group arena, and the political-ideology arena. I proceed on the assumption that vacant political arenas provide new political movements, including social-revolutionary movements, with more opportunity to develop than do arenas that are already occupied. I also assume that social revolutionists are in constant competition with social reformists and can gain a mass following only in competition with or at the cost of the social-reformist groups.

Parties

In Honduras, the possibilities for development available to social-revolutionary movements are severely limited since the political-party arena is already completely occupied by the two traditional parties, the National party and the Liberal party. Throughout the *whole* population, including the lower classes, historically strong ties to the two traditional parties have developed that, as the latest elections again demonstrated, still exist today. In contrast, intense party identification is far less widespread in Nicaragua, El Salvador, and above all Guatemala, with its extremely low voter participation. Thus, in these countries there are far larger arenas open to the social-revolutionary movements.

However, since social-revolutionary movements, in their efforts to occupy political arenas, must face the competition with the social-reformist parties, the key question is: Under which political conditions does the competitive situation shift in favor of the social revolutionists? The following may be stated as a general hypothesis: The authoritarian or semiauthoritarian regimes that provide a social-revolutionary elite with good opportunities for recruiting support are those that offer the regime-critical, moderate, more or less social-reformist opposition at least limited opportunities for political articulation, organization, and mobilization and concede to it the right to participate in elections, but that then systematically prevent, through election fraud and other means, this peaceful transformation alternative from gaining power and translating its program into reality. Under such conditions, which clearly demonstrate the impotence of peaceful transformation alternatives, the probability grows that social-reformist–oriented elements will become dissatisfied and then radicalized and will, to an ever greater extent, move from the social-reformist camp to the social-revolutionary camp. In such a political context, the conviction that even rather modest social reforms can be pushed through only by means of revolution easily spreads.

In Somozist Nicaragua, in El Salvador (particularly until late 1979), and in Guatemala, regimes governed or govern that foster such a radicalization of the potential for social protest. It is possible, at least at a certain stage of development, to characterize such regimes as *demo-authoritarian.* They can pass as *partially democratic* insofar as they permit a multiparty system, normally legitimize their political rule through elections, and basically concede the articulation, organization, and representation of pluralist interests. But they are clearly *authoritarian* to the extent to which they systematically subject the opportunities for political selection, election, and influence and the processes of articulation, organization, and representation of diverse interests to drastic legal and extralegal limitations, controls, and often extensive and bloody repressions. The state that operates on the basis of legal norms finds itself constantly restricted by the state that operates on the basis of political expediency. As to their social character, these regimes might be labeled *rightist class regimes:* "Democracy" is limited, in particular for leftist ("left" in the broadest sense of the word) parties, trade unions, *campesino* associations, and other organizations. In these countries, the military functions as the strongest "party" with a hegemonic claim to power (the Somoza Clan in some respects represented as exception).[9]

El Salvador is a particularly clear-cut example of the possible radicalizing effects of a rightist demo-authoritarian regime. In the 1960s, the Salvadoran regime did permit the creation of important regime-critical, social-progressive opposition parties. But in the 1970s, after this opposition had gained strength, the regime made certain, through both systematic election fraud and repression, that this peaceful social-reformist transformation alternative could not gain power through elections. In the 1972 presidential elections, the candidate of the opposition coalition, José Napoleón Duarte, was robbed of victory by election fraud. It was certainly no coincidence that, following these elections, masses of people thronged to the leftist radical "popular movements" such as the Bloque Popular Revolucionario (BPR) and the Frente de Acción Popular Unificada (FAPU) and to the various guerrilla organizations; the largest social-revolutionary mass movement in Central America began to take shape.

For similar reasons, the social-revolutionary camp in Guatemala seems to be growing constantly at the cost of the social-reformist camp (the role of violence in Guatemala will be discussed later). In regard to Nicaragua, I have already pointed out the connection between the failure of the attempt by the bourgeois opposition to force Somoza to resign in order to establish a moderate regime and the ascent of the Sandinists to the dominant position within the opposition camp.

Rightist demo-authoritarian regimes also enhance indirectly the drawing power of the social-revolutionary movements, not only because they expose the political impotence of social-reformist parties and movements but also because they are able, in both crude and subtle ways, to discredit them and to contribute to their loss of prestige. A purely authoritarian regime—such as that in Honduras during the 1970s, where the military regime did not even bother to seek legitimation through "elections"—may offer a party-based political opposition certain advantages, if not in the short term, then perhaps in the medium term. Under the military regime, the two traditional parties were not severely discredited, and they suffered no loss of prestige as civilian alternatives to military rule; the reverse actually seemed to occur.

Under demo-authoritarian regimes, however, the moderate party-based regime opposition must decide before each election whether or not even to participate. Its members have no real chances to gain power, and in addition the regime misuses them as domestically and internationally important democratic providers of legitimacy. But if they follow certain "rules of the game," the regime can also occasionally offer certain compensations: for example, the guarantee of a certain quota of parliamentary seats (as in Somozist Nicaragua); the award of some cabinet seats (as in Guatemala); recognition of an election victory by granting them important secondary political positions, such as that of mayor of the capital city (as in El Salvador and Guatemala). Demo-authoritarian regimes thus constantly force the moderate regime-critical opposition to choose between honorable noninfluence on the one side or limited—that is, concessionary and compromised—influence on the other side, which could damage its credibility and attractiveness to voters. The Guatemalan Partido Revolucionario (PR) serves as an example of a formerly regime-critical social-progressive party that conformed to the system's "rules of the game" and was thereby transformed into a pronounced regime party. It thus has won a certain limited influence within the regime but lost credibility and voter sympathy. Similarly, the Conservative party in Nicaragua lost prestige by vacillating between energetic regime opposition and a policy of entering into pacts with Somoza. It remains to be seen what effect, in the medium term, the willingness of the Christian Democratic party in El Salvador to cooperate with the military and rightist parties will have on its voters and supporters.

Interest Groups

In the four countries analyzed here, in which the majority of the working population is employed in the agricultural sector and in which industrialization has just begun, the *agrarian conflict*—the conflict between *latifundistas* (large landowners) and *campesinos* for wages, rents, and land-ownership rights—is the central class conflict. It is particularly liable to be politicized because a redistribution of land, which offers the only hope for effectively improving the *campesinos'* situation, can be accomplished only by political means through massive agrarian reforms.

The question arises whether the creation of a social-revolutionary mass movement in Nicaragua, El Salvador, and Guatemala can also be explained by the fact that the organization of the rural lower classes into interest groups was forbidden or severely suppressed. This opened up an important source of recruits for the social-revolutionary movement. It is no wonder that particularly in El Salvador a social-revolutionary movement could win mass support in the countryside. Due to the high population density, the agrarian conflict is even more important here than in the other three countries. In addition, the regime's constant promises of agrarian reform in the 1970s, which were not carried out, probably also contributed to the radicalization of social dissatisfaction in the countryside.

In general, it is possible to formulate the thesis that the institutionalization of class conflicts contributes to their "regulation" and thus to their defusion. Just as El Salvador provides a negative example of this thesis, Honduras can serve as a positive illustration. In Honduras, the rural class conflict was not suppressed; rather, the most powerful *campesino* organizations in Central America were allowed to be formed. These organizations were able to function relatively freely even under the military regimes of the 1970s. Moreover, the military did introduce agrarian reform, if only with very modest results. It would appear that in their attempt to recruit a mass following, the social-revolutionary elites meet with rather large obstacles among those lower-class groups that are permitted to organize into interest groups and whose daily experience demonstrates that social progress—however limited—can be achieved through social-reformist organizational efforts.

In contrast to agrarian conflict, *industrial conflict* between urban blue- and white-collar workers and the entrepreneurs in the four countries is of only secondary importance. Because of the relatively small number of people employed in the industrial sector, this type of conflict is easier to manipulate than agrarian conflict. Here selective social-political concessions are possible. With the help of corporatist and/or "divide and conquer" practices (targeted support for trade unions loyal to the regime; control or suppression of trade unions critical of the regime), the blue- and white-collar workers can be pacified for quite long periods of time. In addition, the industrial conflict is not as apt to become politicized as is the agrarian conflict. Whereas the agrarian conflict over the redistribution of wealth develops into a typical zero-sum conflict (the land gains of the *campesinos* are the land losses of the *latifundistas*), in times of economic growth the income of both the entrepreneurs and the blue- and white-collar worker also grows, although usually in different proportions.[10]

Only at times of a prolonged economic crisis, as seen in Nicaragua, do the social revolutionists seem able to find large support among the urban workers and low-level employees. In particular the violent and almost terrorist suppression of even moderate trade unions, as practiced for some time now in Guatemala, appears to have a radicalizing effect. Such a policy is particularly well suited to transforming social reformists into social revolutionists.

A special study would be required of the service sector, which plays a significant role in all four countries, but because of its heterogeneity is very difficult to analyze. Suffice it to say that a public policy of social discrimination and repression, as practiced against certain middle-class organizations such as teachers' associations, has given new impetus to radical tendencies.

Social-revolutionary movements have enjoyed fairly broad latitude among the urban *marginados* (slum dwellers). The Sandinists seem to be the first Central American social revolutionists to attempt to organize this sector. They succeeded in communicating a belief in revolutionary success to this presumably unstable group of supporters, and thus, to a great extent, in mobilizing them for the "people's revolt."

Ideologies

The chances for a social-revolutionary movement to recruit supporters grow when existing institutions and organizations are willing, under certain circumstances, to recognize the legitimacy of social-revolutionary ideas and actions and thus contribute to overcoming the ideological isolation of the social revolutionists.

From this viewpoint, the politico-theological process of change within the Latin American Catholic church following the Second Vatican Council is of extreme importance. It is true that in the three Central American revolutionary countries—Nicaragua, El Salvador, and Guatemala—only a minority of the clergy and lay people identifies with social-revolutionary positions and that the bishops overwhelmingly take a cautious, moderate, social-progressive stand (see Chapter 9 by Margaret Crahan). Nevertheless, it is important to note that the church's teachings after Vatican II offer not only social-reformist but also social-revolutionary Christians legitimizing points of reference and contact. And only a few radical leftist priests and leftist bishops (like the murdered Salvadoran Archbishop Oscar Arnulfo Romero y Galdámez) are needed to serve as objects of identification with a Catholic-inspired or -legitimized social revolutionism. Perhaps the social revolutionists in those three countries could win mass support only when the church and Catholicism opened up to the left and when, in turn, the originally purely secular social-revolutionary movements opened up to the church and Catholicism. The church is also important because it offers a certain protection to the regime opposition, including social revolutionists; and because several Catholic organizations have permitted themselves to be infiltrated by social revolutionists. One can find in Central America that several Catholic organizations, originally social-reform–oriented, have in the meantime turned toward the social-revolutionary camp.

It is also easier for social-revolutionary movements to recruit followers when they can refer to a national revolutionary tradition. The FSLN could refer to the continuity of historical Sandinism; the Guatemalan left to the "revolutionary period" under Arévalo/Arbenz; and the Salvadoran left to the *campesino* revolution of 1932.

Repression

It seems that when governmental repressive violence becomes excessive, it no longer efficiently performs its intended function of eliminating and deterring opponents of the regime. It is difficult to determine at what level officially sanctioned repressive violence ceases to ensure stability (in the sense of a brutal but efficient ruling technique) and becomes counterproductive. It seems plausible that *undirected* governmental repression that can strike regime opponents, neutrals, and even regime supporters alike has not only a deterrent but also a radicalizing effect. A regime that intentionally makes social-reformist forces an object of government-initiated or -tolerated terror is likely to encourage mass support for social-revolutionary movements. It generally holds true that the more a regime seeks refuge in illegal violence as a means of governing, the more revolutionary violence will be regarded as justified.

The undirected annihilating behavior of the national guard in 1978 and 1979 probably won the FSLN new support. And similarly, the undirected *counterinsurgency* measures of the Salvadoran military and security forces seem to have contributed to the growth of the fighting forces of the revolutionary left. Since the 1960s, governmental repression in Guatemala has been particularly sweeping and brutal (see the chapters by Edelberto Torres-Rivas and Piero Gleijeses). Since 1978 in particular, the regime has attempted to decapitate and decimate not only the social revolutionists but also the social reformists. Under the current president, Gen. Efrain Rios Montt, even great numbers of the Indian population have fallen victim to governmental violence. Given this policy, it is no wonder that Guatemala in particular is becoming increasingly polarized and that a civil war is in the offing, which in its severity will probably widely surpass those in Nicaragua and El Salvador. During the 1970s, the military regime in Honduras exercised far less repressive violence against regime opponents than did the regimes of the other three countries.

Strategies of Revolutionary Elites for the Takeover of Power

It is possible to analyze both the disintegration of power and the takeover of power in terms of coalitions.[11] The chances of overthrowing an existing regime grow when the reduction in the size of the regime coalition corresponds to an expansion of the antiregime coalition.

The strength of a social-revolutionary movement is determined by the number of its supporters, the strength of its arms, and its military and political organizational skills. Of perhaps decisive importance, however, is its *ability to form coalitions.* It is imperative to realize that for a revolutionary elite, the overthrow of a regime is not an end in itself, but only a means to an end. In order to ensure that it can later establish a governmental and social system consistent with its own goals, a social-revolutionary elite must attempt, beginning during the phase of power takeover, to achieve a *hegemonic* position within the camp of regime opponents. A social-revolutionary movement can achieve such a hegemonic position primarily under two conditions.

- It wins mass support and gains control over important organized groups or groups capable of organization (hegemony in the field of mass political mobilization).
- It succeeds in convincing the opposition camp to pursue a strategy of politico-*military* takeover of power. Since it holds the monopoly over armed force within the opposition camp, it is then able to play a key role.

The Nicaraguan example suggests that a social-revolutionary movement that is organized in the form of a militarized cadre and avant-garde party and based on political mass mobilization is in a good position to exploit the weakness of an authoritarian or demo-authoritarian regime, to win mass support, to achieve a hegemonic position within the opposition camp, and finally to take over governmental power.

The FSLN demonstrated considerable virtuosity in combining military and political forms of combat. Through sometimes spectacular military actions it succeeded in convincing the national and international public that the Somoza regime was "vulnerable." At the same time, by creating its own organizations and systematically infiltrating existing organizations, the FSLN managed to occupy political arenas left unoccupied by the regime. Not least on account of its organizational abilities and its skills at mass mobilization, the FSLN finally turned to its own advantage a previously adverse competitive situation within the opposition camp. In the process of gaining power, the FSLN followed the classic rule of revolution: Although it was possible for a small flock of Sandinist *militants* to accept a more or less Marxist program, a broad following (*simpatisantes*) could only be gained by propagating a *leftist integration ideology* that, in principle, was also acceptable to social reformists. It very cleverly elected the popular hero Augusto César Sandino as a symbol of integration, a man attractive to many different groups. Thus it also was able to play on the anti-U.S. sentiments widespread throughout the whole population.

The FSLN proved particularly adept in its coalition policy. It fully exploited the special opportunities offered by the regime of the Somoza Clan for creating a very broad antiregime coalition. By adopting a pluralistic social-reformist governing program, rather than a Marxist social-revolutionary program, the FSLN became worthy of coalition even in the eyes of Nicaraguan business interests. By adopting an intelligent foreign policy based on a broad alliance (here the Group of Twelve was particularly important), it succeeded in isolating the Somoza regime, mobilizing international support for the revolution, and averting the major threat of military intervention.

The coalition question is a constant source of controversy among social-revolutionary elites. They are faced with a problem that might be characterized as *"the dilemma of the revolutionary minimum winning coalition."* The dilemma for social revolutionists is that on the one hand normally only a broad—that is, quite heterogeneous—coalition of political and social groups, which for various reasons are dissatisfied with the existing regime and therefore expect different improvements from the establishment of a new regime, is in a position to overthrow a regime—particularly when the latter enjoys the unflinching support of the military and security forces. Revolutionists know that after the takeover of power, the broad revolutionary coalition, which had been united by the negative consensus that the existing regime must be overthrown, will sooner or later disintegrate because of differences of opinion over the configuration of the new order. Therefore, they are also aware that the coalition for the establishment and the consolidation of power has a narrower base than the coalition for power takeover. At the same time, however, social revolutionists also must face the problem that their claim to hegemony during the period of power takeover is threatened when they cooperate with a broad and heterogeneous coalition of many groups. And the broader and more heterogeneous the revolutionary coalition is, the greater could be the compulsion to compromise during the phase of power establishment and power consolidation following the overthrow of the regime. Purist social revolutionists therefore plead for a "long people's war," which alone is to bring to power the "proletariat" and its political-military avant-garde, in order to assure that the maximal revolutionary program can be fully translated into reality. More pragmatically oriented social revolutionists count on a broad coalition to assist them in exploiting the auspicious historical moment.

Within the social-revolutionary movements, the problem of adopting a policy of coalition leads not only to power conflicts but also usually to the formation of factions and to internal ruptures. This was also the case within the FSLN; however, the faction of the Terceristas, which supported the formation of broad national and international alliances, was able to prevail. Depending on one's perspective, it is possible to view the Terceristas as a "moderate" or as a particularly intelligent, because realistic, Leninist faction within the FSLN (both views are probably correct).[12]

In El Salvador and Guatemala, the possibilities for the social revolutionists to gain a mass following were or are perhaps even more favorable than in Nicaragua. But from the start their chances of forming a national coalition were more limited (the whole upper class and important parts of the middle class supported and support the regime; since 1980, the Christian Democrats, who form the most important social-reformist party, have identified with the Salvadoran regime). Also, since President Ronald Reagan took office in the United States, the opportunities for the Salvadoran leftists to enter into international coalitions have narrowed considerably; Part 2 of this book takes a closer look at this development. Finally the Sandinists' loss of "democratic credibility" (see Chapter 4) has had a negative impact on the ability of the Salvadoran leftists to form international coalitions.

It is not possible to discuss here the military-strategic problems of revolutionary takeovers. Suffice it to say that the Salvadoran leftists do not have access to the terrain for military retreat and redeployment that the FSLN enjoyed during the Nicaraguan revolution. Also, the ability of the FSLN to stimulate the population to a real "people's revolt" seemed to be directly related to the fact that the actual civil war could be won within a few months, thus keeping awake the revolutionary élan, the belief among the population in revolutionary success. In contrast, the long "war of attrition" in El Salvador seems to have sobered the general population, which has become increasingly tired of war. Since significant military successes by the leftists in El Salvador would probably lead to military intervention by the United States, a military victory by the leftists seems to be precluded, even if they should surpass the Salvadoran armed force in military strength. The only possibility for the Salvadoran leftists to attain a share of power seems to be by way of negotiations (see the section on regime transformation and stabilization). The urban masses in El Salvador do not, however, appear all too willing to fight to the death for such a negotiated solution.

The International Context

The example of Central America proves that every analysis of revolution, particularly in small and dependent states, must deal with the limitations imposed by domestic- and foreign-policy factors. Since the internationalization of the Central American crisis and the significance of the most important international actors for the political development process in the region will be carefully analyzed in Part 2 of this book (see Chapter 10 by Wolf Grabendorff for an introduction to the problems), and since all contributions to Part 1 also deal at some length with the international dimensions, further comments here are unnecessary.

It is enough to point out that the "string-pulling theory," which seeks to locate the causes for social-revolutionary movements primarily in the international environment ("subversion of Central America by international communism"), should not be taken seriously. The chapters on the individual countries demonstrate in some detail that the social-revolutionary movements in Nicaragua, El Salvador, and Guatemala were the product of social, economic, and political structures as well as the results of regime policies in each of the countries. The United States has been partially responsible for the development of such social-revolutionary mass movements because it has supported regimes that fostered, and in part still foster, the development of such movements. On the other hand, it is of course also correct that as soon as social-revolutionary *mass* movements have been established and are strong enough to challenge the ruling regimes, the possible impact of communist states as regionally influential actors begins to grow. They are indispensable to Salvadoran leftists as suppliers of weapons. Their importance in Nicaragua is growing, not only as weapons suppliers but also as providers of economic aid. In addition, communism, in its Cuban variant, serves to some extent as a model for the social-revolutionary leftists in Central America.

The "diffusion effect" of the Nicaraguan revolution, which could be included in this section, will be discussed in the next section.

PROBLEMS OF REGIME TRANSFORMATION AND STABILIZATION IN THE FACE OF SOCIAL-REVOLUTIONARY CHALLENGES

Problems of regime transformation and stabilization in Central America must be discussed not from an isolated national perspective but rather from a regional perspective. For one thing, the small Central American states form a regional subsystem in which national political developmental processes are closely interrelated. It is also true that important international actors treat Central America as a *region* and consider only *regional* strategies for solving the problems of instability.

The Nicaraguan revolution had a strong "diffusion effect." It became the model for the Salvadoran revolutionary leftists, who attempted, with limited success, to copy the Nicaraguan example. And it had a "deterrent effect" on the United States, which wants to prevent in El Salvador the creation of a "second Nicaragua" (in the eyes of the Reagan administration, this would be tantamount to a "third Cuba").

Given this political context, a negotiated solution in El Salvador, which would put an end to the civil war, probably is possible only if the Sandinists are willing and able to convincingly dispel the suspicion that they aim for a communist system of government and membership in the communist bloc. It seems feasible that an arrangement could be found whereby the Sandinists, in return for a guaranteed share of power for the revolutionary left in El Salvador, would accept a system of government that places limits on their claims to power and on their plans for social reorganization and that grants the domestic opposition more rights than it now has. Bearing this situation in mind, I will concentrate in Chapter 4 on the question of what the probabilities are that a system of government can be found for Nicaragua that the Western industrialized countries, including the United States, might consider "sufficiently democratic" or "sufficiently noncommunist."

One possibility for "regime stabilization" in El Salvador would be the military annihilation of the revolutionary leftists. Given the stalemate that has developed in the civil war, the costs of such a "military solution" to the conflict would probably be extremely high. The former U.S. ambassador to El Salvador, Robert White, estimated that such a solution would require the extermination of one-fourth of the population. The leftists in El Salvador could probably be defeated only if the United States intervened directly with its own troops. In such a case, however, the conflict would most probably become regionalized and the danger of a "Vietnamization" or "Lebanonization" of Central America would become acute.

The proregime forces in El Salvador as well as the Reagan administration reject the demand for a negotiated solution as proposed by the Salvadoran leftists and other important international actors; instead, they regard *elections* as the most suitable *political solution* for the conflict. The revolutionary leftists were consequently urged to lay down their arms and to participate in the March 1982 election of a constitutive assembly. A similar call was issued for the forthcoming presidential elections. The social revolutionists' reluctance to participate in elections is interpreted as proof of their supposedly antidemocratic, totalitarian political orientation. This argument can hardly be called very realistic.[13] Rather, one wonders if the strategy of the Reagan administration to press for elections in El Salvador while simultaneously rejecting any initiative for negotiation cannot be interpreted as an attempt to create the conditions that would provide the Reagan administration with the necessary legitimation for a *military* solution (mobilization of public and congressional opinion in the United States for a crusade against "communist" and "antidemocratic" forces in El Salvador).

A realistic *military-political* argument has to acknowledge that the Salvadoran revolutionary left, united in the FDR/FMLN (Frente Democrático Revolucionario/Frente Farabundo Martí de Liberación Nacional), is not willing to lay down its arms. Given the historical experience that elections in El Salvador do not settle the question of who will have the power to govern, but rather that it is primarily military power that guarantees political power, this stand is understandable. Experiences regarding massive governmental violence and the constant breaking of legal norms by organs of government have shown the revolutionary left that for purposes of mere survival it would be well advised not to lay down its arms and to demand a negotiated settlement that would guarantee it a *share of power,* ensuring its continued existence. Once such a settlement could be achieved, the FDR/FMLN seems willing to participate in elections in order to determine the precise distribution of political power.

Given the fact that on both the right and the left the armed forces hold the real political power, any compromise over the division of power presupposes agreement on the distribution of military power between military and security forces on the one hand and the guerrilla forces on the other. Spanish-type models for a liberal-democratic transformation of an authoritarian regime obviously have only limited relevance for countries such as El Salvador. Here an armed, combat-ready, social-revolutionary mass movement already exists. A compromise over the future form of government must be found that includes not only the military but also the armed left. Only those political solutions are viable that take into consideration the institutional survival interests of both the rightist and leftist "military." They will both demand at least political veto power in the new regime, regardless of what kind of elections formally legitimize that regime. In order to reduce feelings of insecurity on both the right and the left, concordant-democratic or consociational-democratic arrangements seem to make the most sense, at least during a transition period (see in Chapter 4 analogous thoughts on compromise over a form of government acceptable to all relevant actors in Nicaragua). Whether a negotiated solution should guarantee the left an equal or only an "appropriate" share of power depends on the national and international distribution of power; thus at present it can only be the object of fruitless speculation. It is, however, difficult to imagine that a negotiated solution can be successful if it is limited to an agreement on political institutions and processes. Both a political-procedural and a political-substantive consensus on the basic form of the economic and social order appear necessary. The statement of the FDR/FMLN expressing its satisfaction with the reform program of the junta of October 15, 1979, seems to demonstrate its relative willingness to compromise.

Both parties to the conflict might be prepared to accept various and to a certain extent "enlightened" versions of a political-strategic settlement; this would seem to demonstrate that a negotiated solution could be found. Representatives of the FDR/FMLN probably do not argue in favor of a negotiated solution only because they expect it to bring the civil war to an end. Rather, they likely hope that a negotiated settlement will create favorable conditions for a later transformation of the governmental and social order in accordance with their objectives. On the other hand, one might argue from the perspective of an intelligent policy of containment (see in particular Chapter 12 by Robert Pastor) that negotiations would expose the great heterogeneity in the leftist camp and that serious negotiations would result in a split between forces amenable to democracy and compromise and those that pursue an orthodox Leninist model for state and society. It is obvious that such a negotiated solution will be difficult to achieve because it requires of both parties a great willingness to compromise. However, given the alternatives, everything speaks for such a solution.

An arrangement between Western industrialized states and the social-revolutionary left in Nicaragua and El Salvador as outlined in this chapter and in Chapter 4, could have particular relevance for Guatemala. I believe it to be completely improbable that the Guatemalan regime will be successful in its attempt to destroy the social-revolutionary movement in its country by waging a "civil war from above." Due to the policy of terror pursued by Efrain Rios Montt, we will probably see, in the medium term and perhaps even in the short term, an even greater strengthening of the already powerful social-revolutionary movement in that country; Indios, too, in ever greater numbers, will probably join the movement. In coming years, a Salvadoran-type negotiated settlement could spare that country what would probably be the most severe and bloodiest civil war in Central America.

Notes

1. It is not possible to include here a detailed discussion of the various approaches to theories of revolution that I have studied in the course of my work. For an introductory survey, see: Thomas Greene, *Comparative Revolutionary Movements* (Englewood Cliffs, N.J.: Prentice-Hall, 1974); Charles Tilly, "Revolutions and Collective Violence," in Fred I. Greenstein and Nelson W. Polsby, eds., *Handbook of Political Science*, vol. 3 (Reading, Mass.: Addison-Wesley, 1975), pp. 483–555; and Ekkart Zimmermann, *Krisen, Staatsstreiche und Revolutionen. Theorien, Daten und neuere Forschungsansätze* (Opladen: Westdeutscher Verlag, 1981). The theory-oriented literature on authoritarian regimes, the collapse of democracies, and the problem of redemocratization of authoritarian regimes proved quite stimulating for this analysis. For an introduction to the literature, see: Juan J. Linz, "Totalitarian and Authoritarian Regimes," in Greenstein and Polsby, *Handbook of Political Science*, vol. 3, pp. 175–411; Juan J. Linz and Alfred Stepan, eds., *The Breakdown of Democratic Regimes* (Baltimore/London: Johns Hopkins, 1978); and Workshop Papers of the Woodrow Wilson Center, Washington, D.C., for meetings in 1979, 1980, and 1981 on "Prospects for Democracy: Transitions from Authoritarian Rule." I do not include references to the literature on the individual countries. For an introductory survey of the countries included

here, see: Thomas P. Anderson, *Politics in Central America: Guatemala, El Salvador, Honduras and Nicaragua* (New York: Praeger, 1982).

2. See, for example: Edward N. Muller, "Economic Development and Democracy Revisited," paper for a panel on "Conditions of Regime Stability and Change," Annual Meeting of the Midwest Political Science Association, Milwaukee, April/May 1982. The following data for 1978 from the Comisión Económica para América Latina (CEPAL) compare Costa Rica with the other four countries and Panama.

	Per Capita Income	Coefficient of Income Concentration	Percent of Poor in Population
Costa Rica	US$883.80	.42	24.5
El Salvador	463.30	.60	68.1
Guatemala	517.80	.55	79.0
Honduras	290.00	.45	60.9
Nicaragua	412.10	.51	63.7
Panama	913.80	.58	58.1

[a]From 1970 [b]Capital City Area

Costa Rica's special situation is clearly demonstrated by the data. Honduras has quite a favorable distribution of income. However, if one takes into consideration the large proportion of poor, then the conclusion that Honduras has a far-lower potential for social dissatisfacton than the three revolutionary countries is questionable. Comisión Económica para América Latina (CEPAL), "La pobreza y la satisfacción de necesidades básicas en el istmo centroamericano (avances de una investigación regional)," *CEPAL/MEX/SEM* (Mexico, D.F., March 31, 1981), pp. 13, 15, 23.

3. Guatemala potentially poses the greatest problem for a comparison because of the large proportion of Indios (barely half of the population). However, since the Indios have been until now more objects than subjects of the country's politics, it is perhaps not necessary to discuss this special problem further.

4. Technically, the research design can be described as follows: if one set of independent variables (here: socioeconomic and other variables) is kept constant while variation is introduced into a second, theoretically important set of independent variables (here: particularly in the narrow sense, political variables), what effect does this have on the variation of those dependent variables in need of explanation (here: the success of revolution at various stages)?

5. A discussion of the question of under what conditions social dissatisfaction becomes politicized and radicalized can be found in: Heinrich-W. Krumwiede, *Politik und katholische Kirche im gesellschaftlichen Modernisierungsprozess. Tradition und Entwicklung in Kolumbien* (Hamburg: Hoffmann und Campe, 1980), chap. 2.

6. Quoted from: Bayardo Arce, "Unidad para proteger la revolución nicaraguense," *Nueva Sociedad,* no. 48 (May/June 1980), p. 17.

7. Adam Przeworski, "Some Problems in the Study of the Transition to Democracy," paper for the meeting on "Prospects for Democracy: Transitions from Authoritarian Rule," Woodrow Wilson Center, Washington, D.C., September 25–26, 1979, p. 10.

8. There is, however, a decisive difference between the Nicaraguan national guard and the Salvadoran and Guatemalan military: The Nicaraguan national guard saw itself as a kind of praetorian guard of the ruling family clan and suspended all fighting as soon as the dictator had left the country. It thus significantly facilitated the Sandinist victory. Similar behavior cannot be expected from the Salvadoran and Guatemalan military forces, which are far more intent on gaining institutional autonomy and do not consider their existence dependent on the survival of a clan or a social class (for example, the "oligarchy"). See on this problem: Alfred Stepan, "The Military and Regime Transformation in Central America: Some Notes," paper for the second conference sponsored by the Friedrich-Ebert-Stiftung on "Zentralamerika: Perspektiven nach dem Volksaufstand in Nicaragua," Bonn, March 1981.

9. I propose using the term *demo-authoritarian regime* because these countries are ruled by a special kind of regime that is not discussed in the literature on authoritarianism although it is quite obviously relevant to the problem of regime transformation.

10. The fact that until now revolutions were successful only in agrarian societies can be explained by pointing out that agrarian conflict—contrary to classic Marxist assumptions—is far more likely to become radically politicized than is industrial conflict.

11. See also: Peter Waldmann, "Vergleichende Bemerkungen zu den Guerrilla-Bewegungen in Argentinien, Guatemala, Nicaragua und Uruguay," in Klaus Lindenberg, ed., *Lateinamerika. Herrschaft, Gewalt und internationale Abhängigkeit* (Bonn: Neue Gesellschaft, 1982), pp. 103–124.

12. See in this connection the very interesting document: Frente Sandinista de Liberación Nacional (FSLN), Dirección Nacional, "Circular Interna," Algún Lugar de Nicaragua, April 1978.

13. See here, in greater detail, Heinrich-W. Krumwiede, "Zur innen- und aussenpolitischen Bedeutung der Wahlen zur Verfassungsgebenden Versammlung in El Salvador vom 26.3.1982," *Zeitschrift für Parlamentsfragen* 13, no. 4 (1982), pp. 541–548.

2
From Somoza to the Sandinistas: The Roots of Revolution in Nicaragua

Richard L. Millett

The flight of Nicaraguan dictator Anastasio Somoza Debayle to Miami on July 17, 1979, and the entry into Managua two days later of the forces of the Frente Sandinista de Liberación Nacional (FSLN) marked the first success of a social-revolutionary movement in Latin America since Fidel Castro took power in Cuba over twenty years earlier. The revolution not only ended the rule of Latin America's longest-lasting family dictatorship, it also totally destroyed the regime's armed forces, shattered the image of U.S. control in Central America, and brought to power a young, Marxist-influenced government determined to transform the nation's economic and social structure. The significance of this event reaches far beyond Nicaragua, and an understanding of how and why this revolution took place is vital to any analysis of it.

Any discussion of the causes of the Nicaraguan revolution must take into account a multitude of factors, both foreign and domestic. Such an analysis needs to address two different questions: Why did the Somoza dynasty fall after over forty-two years in power and why did the FSLN replace it? This obviously assumes that the Sandinistas, in and of themselves, were not the basic cause of the regime's collapse and that there were other alternatives to their assuming power.

The Somoza Dynasty

To understand why Gen. Anastasio Somoza Debayle fell from power in Nicaragua it is first necessary to examine how his family managed to control that nation for more than four decades. The Somoza dynasty rested on three basic pillars of support: complete control over the Guardia

Nacional (Nicaragua's combined military and police force), maintenance of the image of U.S. support, and the reality of U.S. support.

Control of the Guardia Nacional

Control over the Guardia Nacional was maintained by an extreme degree of paternalism and isolation. Actual command of the force was always exercised by a Somoza. In the last years of the dictatorship, when Gen. Anastasio Somoza Debayle acted as both president and Guardia commander, his half-brother José Somoza was inspector-general and commander of the armored units and his son, Anastasio Somoza Portocerrero, ran the infantry training school that produced the Guardia's best troops.

Paternalistic favoritism (often administered by José Somoza), isolation, alienation from the public at large, and opportunities to exercise petty tyrannies and profit from corruption helped ensure the loyalty and dependence of the enlisted men. Officer loyalty was maintained by a system of indoctrination that indentified the Guardia with Anastasio Somoza Debayle and all opponents with communism, by promotions and appointments to key posts based on personal loyalty to the Somozas, and by careful assignment of only the most trusted, least independent officers to command of combat units. Identification of the Guardia and of Somoza with the United States was also used to foster loyalty, inculcate anticommunism, and help maintain at least a modicum of combat efficiency. By the 1970s the key to this system was the retirement each year of a large number of senior officers, thus regularly opening up to those below new posts with profitable opportunities for corruption. Those retired continued to draw full pay, but this was only a fraction of what they previously received. Somoza, therefore, found himself forced to give them other jobs in the government or in his family-owned businesses or to help them go into business for themselves. All of these measures eventually helped undermine the dictatorship.

The Image of U.S. Support

The image of U.S. support also was maintained through a series of complex, interrelated tactics. All members of the ruling family spoke excellent English, with legitimate sons being sent to the United States for high school and college. General Somoza Debayle himself was a West Point graduate, a tie he constantly stressed to enlist support in the United States. He made it a point to attend his West Point class reunions and utilized the influence of such former classmates as Congressman John Murphy of New York. His older brother Luis Somoza Debayle, who died in 1967, had also been educated in the United States. So had their father, the founder of the dynasty, Anastasio Somoza García.

For the Somoza family a key tactic had long been to be more gringo than the gringos, conveying an identification not only with U.S. policies, but with American culture, sports (they actively promoted baseball as the national sport), and life-style.

Throughout their tenure in power the Somozas sought to promote the image of their identification with the United States both in Nicaragua and in Washington, D.C. In the latter case a variety of tactics was used. U.S. positions in the United Nations (UN) and Organization of American States were virtually always supported. The Somozas provided support for the 1954 CIA overthrow of the Arbenz government in Guatemala, the 1961 Bay of Pigs invasion of Cuba, and the 1965 intervention in the Dominican Republic. Anastasio Somoza Debayle even offered to send a token contingent of the Guardia to fight in Vietnam. U.S. investments were encouraged, and official visitors were always given a red-carpet treatment. Richard M. Nixon reportedly retained fond memories of Nicaragua as one of the few nations where there were no hostile demonstrations against his 1958 Latin American tour. In his last years in office, Anastasio Somoza Debayle began spending large sums of money to employ a Washington, D.C., public relations firm to spread propaganda on his behalf.

Equal effort was expended within Nicaragua on maintaining this image of close identification with the United States. History had convinced most Nicaraguans that, in the words of former U.S. under-secretary of state Robert Olds, "those governments which we recognize and support stay in power, while those we do not recognize and support fall."[1] In these terms the long survival of the Somoza dynasty was, in and of itself, proof of U.S. support. The Somozas took every opportunity to reinforce this perception. Trips by government leaders to Washington, D.C., or visits by U.S. officials to Nicaragua were given maximum publicity in the family-owned newspaper, *Novedades*, and on radio and television. Special efforts were made to publicize contacts, both official and social, with the U.S. ambassador. One ambassador's picture was even placed on the twenty-cordoba bill.

Economic and military ties were also the subject of a constant publicity barrage. Most of the Guardia Nacional received at least some training in the United States or in the Panama Canal Zone. Most uniforms and equipment came from the United States, and the role of the U.S. Military Group was stressed and exaggerated. Economic assistance, especially that received after the 1972 earthquake, was presented as evidence both of the dictator's influence in the United States and of U.S. support for the dynasty. To most Nicaraguans the message was clear: The United States supported Anastasio Somoza Debayle and any effort to topple him would probably produce prompt intervention.

Weaknesses of the Dynasty

This image of U.S. support was an important source of strength for the dictatorship, but it also contained some serious potential weaknesses. To maintain this perception, Somoza had to limit overt repression of educated elites and allow them limited press and political freedom. Expressions of Washington's concern over internal conditions often elicited at least cosmetic reforms. There was always an effort to portray any disputes as simply lovers' quarrels and to actively discourage any speculation that they might be the preliminary steps leading to an ultimate divorce. The Somozas faced the constant danger that their cultivation of the idea that U.S. support meant that no change in government would be tolerated could be turned against them. If the relationship ever began to seriously deteriorate and that deterioration became public knowledge, Nicaraguans would interpret that as a sign that Washington wanted a new government. Many would then rush to distance themselves from the Somozas and get in line for succession.

In the words of a former U.S. military attaché, middle- and upper-class loyalties were ensured by "giving them a piece of the pie, but not of the action." This meant that they could maintain or even improve their economic status if they accepted Somoza domination over the nation. They received prosperity but no power, stability in exchange for dignity. A certain degree of opposition politics was allowed these classes, but they never had an opportunity to gain control. They could even engage in minor plots and uprisings. When caught they might be beaten, imprisoned, and/or exiled briefly, but their property was usually left intact, their families were not molested, and eventually they themselves were allowed to return to their previous pursuits. Only those within the Guardia faced summary execution for joining revolutionary movements.

Another effective Somoza tactic in dealing with the traditional sources of internal opposition—such as the newspaper *La Prensa,* the Conservative party, labor movements, university students, and the business community—was to divide and conquer. Pacts would be made with various sectors. Offices, favors, and economic opportunities were bestowed in return for gestures of support or even a moderating of opposition. The ultimate tactic for keeping most of the upper and middle classes in line was to present the Somoza family as the only alternative to communism, a tactic made more credible as years of co-optation, acquiescence, and humiliation undermined the prestige and credibility of the traditional opposition.

Always shaky, Somoza Debayle's support among middle and upper classes began to weaken seriously following the 1972 Managua earthquake. The resultant corruption, inefficiency, and incompetence of the regime angered and disillusioned many who had previously convinced themselves that the benefits of stability outweighed the costs of the dictatorship. Younger technocrats began to abandon the regime, often seeking new jobs abroad. In addition, General Somoza Debayle, propelled in part by the ever-growing need to find places for the hosts of retired, corrupt, and often not too competent former Guardia officers, used the earthquake to extend his interests into new areas of the economy, notably construction and banking. This increased his competition with both the oligarchy and middle class, who saw their own economic future threatened.

A final factor in this growing process of alienation was the developing generational split among many elite families. Often sent abroad for education, younger members of the elite were increasingly disenchanted with conditions in Nicaragua and came to view the Somoza dynasty as an oppressive, corrupt anachronism. They were disillusioned with the efforts of traditional opposition groups, efforts that usually ended with the dictatorship co-opting their leaders in return for a small share of political offices and patronage. The massive corruption following the 1972 earthquake had also dashed the technocratic hope of some young, educated Nicaraguans that the regime would provide a stable framework for steady economic progress and gradual political liberalization. As the 1970s progressed, the gap between the regime and middle- and upper-class youth constantly widened. Many left the country, and others continued to seek moderate political means to oppose the regime, but increasing numbers were attracted to the FSLN, seeing it as the only force with a long-range, coherent program for ending the rule of the Somoza dynasty.

In the mid-1970s the Roman Catholic church, long politically dormant, began to join the opposition to Somoza rule, thereby threatening the regime's legitimacy. Led by Archbishop Miguel Obando y Bravo, the church became increasingly critical of existing economic and political conditions. Foreign missionary priests played a prominent role in this criticism, a development that had a significant impact in the United States.

Growing Strength of the FSLN

At first, the FSLN showed little capacity for taking advantage of the growing strains within the Nicaraguan political system. Although it had existed since 1963, the Frente's efforts were generally ineffective until December 1974, when a spectacular seizure of high government officials refurbished their image, exposed the unpopularity of the regime, and gained the release of several prominent FSLN leaders. The following year renewed guerrilla operations produced a major Guardia response. The brutality of Guardia counterinsurgency efforts inflicted heavy casualties on the Sandinistas but also further undermined the regime's legitimacy. Church protests rapidly widened the gap between that institution and the government. Public opinion in the United States, responding in part to congressional investigations and to a series of anti-Somoza columns by Jack Anderson that characterized Nicaragua's dictator as "the world's greediest ruler," also became increasingly critical of the situation.

The FSLN was going through a critical period at this time. Its members had suffered serious losses, including their founder and leader Carlos Fonseca Amador, in the Guardia operations of 1975 and 1976. Internal divisions had produced three separate tendencies; the Tendencia Proletária (TP), the Prolonged Popular War (Guerra Popular Prolongada—GPP) and the Insurrectional Tendency (popularly known as the Terceristas). The GPP represented much of the original Sandinista leadership, including the last surviving founder, Tomás Borge. Its basic approach was a slow, wearing campaign against the Guardia in the mountains while it gradually built up human resources in the rest of the nation. The TP was impatient with this approach and stressed the importance of urban organization and the formation of a worker-based Marxist-Leninist party. Efforts to moderate this dispute actually helped produce the third faction, the Terceristas, led by the Ortega brothers. They were at first the weakest in terms of influence upon Nicaraguan student groups and lacked the military strength and leadership of the GPP. But their tactical approach, formulated and enacted in 1977 and 1978, soon made them by far the largest and strongest of the tendencies. They emphasized the necessity of a mass, popular uprising against the dictatorship. To bring this about they sought alliances with other disaffected groups in Nicaragua, including sectors of the middle class and the traditional opposition. They also promoted international contacts with anti-Somoza and antiimperialist forces, most notably those associated with the Socialist International.[2]

To promote this strategy Humberto Ortega Saavedra met in June 1977 with a group of prominent, publicly nonpolitical Nicaraguans, including Maryknoll priest Miguel D'Escoto Brockman; ex-director of Nicaragua's National University, Carlos Tunnermann; writer and educator Sergio Ramírez Mercado; lawyer Joaquín Cuadra Chamorro; and leading businessmen Emilio Baltodano Pallais and Felipe Mántica. The major result of this meeting was the creation of the group known as Los Doce (the Twelve)—twelve prominent Nicaraguans not publicly identified with the FSLN—who would play a key, intermediate role between the FSLN and the middle-class opposition to Anastasio Somoza Debayle. The role of the FSLN Tercerista faction in the creation of Los Doce was never revealed before the fall of Somoza, a fact that added to their credibility.[3]

The first public statements of Los Doce were timed to coincide with a series of FSLN attacks on the Guardia in October 1977. In this manifesto they called for the removal of Anastasio Somoza Debayle, declared that no dialogue was possible with the dictator and that no political situation could be reached without including the FSLN, and concluded that if Somoza could not be pressured out of office, a national uprising was the only alternative left for the Nicaraguan people. This approach changed the basic orientation of Nicaraguan political opposition to the dynasty. The tradition had been to ignore the FSLN and to try to negotiate with Somoza. The public response to the manifesto of Los Doce and to the October attacks shook the dictatorship. Numerous business and civic leaders endorsed the statement and even Conservative party members of Congress began to defend the FSLN. Pedro Joaquín Chamorro, leader of the traditional political opposition combined into the Democratic Liberation Union (Unión Democrática de Liberación—UDEL), met in Mexico with Miguel D'Escoto Brockman, agreed with him not to participate in any dialogue with Somoza, and showed interest in establishing contacts with the Frente.[4]

Collapse of the Somozas

By the end of 1977 the support system for the Somoza dynasty, carefully erected and maintained over several decades, was beginning to collapse. The inauguration of Jimmy Carter as president of the United States produced an increased emphasis upon human rights and contributed to a steady deterioration of close U.S. support for the Somozas. The growing political and military strength of the FSLN had begun to undermine the dictator's claim that he offered an effective bulwark against communism. Constantly increasing corruption and deteriorating international economic conditions had slowed economic growth and contributed to a rapid rise in the external debt. The middle class and the church had not only become increasingly vocal in their opposition, they had also shown signs of moving away from their traditional hostility to the Frente. Even Somoza's own supporters were beginning to have second thoughts about the dynasty's long-range practices, especially after the dictator suffered a heart attack in July 1977. Traditional family cronies, like congressional leader Cornelio Hueck, began to maneuver for the succession or for access to other potential successors. Only the Guardia, where the dictator's half-brother and eldest son held key posts, showed no signs of weakening its support.

In this context the January 1978 murder of Pedro Joaquín Chamorro provided the spark needed to ignite what *New York Times* reporter Alan

Riding aptly described as a "national mutiny." Although direct responsibility was never traced to the government, the Somozas were universally believed to have been implicated in the killing. This broke the last strands of the arrangements between the regime and its traditional opponents, who reasoned that if Pedro Joaquín Chamorro could be murdered then the life of no opponent of the dynasty's was safe. A national strike was called, and many businesspeople even paid their employees wages while they were on strike. Church criticism of the dictator mounted, Venezuela cut off petroleum supplies, and even the United States demonstrated its displeasure by suspending military assistance. The Carter administration began to realize that the Somoza dynasty was becoming nonviable and began to look for some sort of "moderate" successor regime. Popular uprisings, notably in the Indian barrio of Masaya known as Monimbo, gave a greater urgency to this task. Until August, however, the prevailing attitude was that Somoza could hold on for a while longer and that the emphasis should be on pressuring him to step down when his term expired in 1981 and allow a relatively free election of a successor.

Somoza Debayle, of course, had no real intention of giving up power, but he was alarmed by the strength of the internal opposition and by his weakened international position. In an effort to deal with the growing threat, he resorted to a mixture of tactics traditionally employed by his family. Steps were taken to shore up Guardia loyalties, including promotions, pay raises, and the expansion of specially trained combat troops from the new Basic Infantry School (EEBI) commanded by his son, Anastasio Somoza Portocarrero. All available forces were used in an effort to defeat the rising tide of FSLN attacks and popular uprisings. Efforts were made to appease the United States and domestic elite opponents with a series of concessions, none of which threatened the fundamental basis of Somoza power. Press censorship was lifted, the state of siege in force since 1974 was ended, reforms were promised, and calls for a national dialogue were issued. General Somoza Debayle publicly pledged that he would locate and punish Chamorro's murderers, and that neither he nor any relative would run for president. Strong international pressure even forced him to allow Los Doce to return to Nicaragua in July and to permit them to openly campaign for the ousting of his administration. But in responding to demands for his own resignation, for a purge of the Guardia's high command, or for a removal of his relatives from key positions, the dictator's opposition remained adamant. Believing time was on his side he hoped that delays, minor concessions, and promises of future changes would mollify the United States, divide and weaken elite opposition, and isolate the FSLN. For a time these tactics seemed to be having some degree of success. Business opposition showed signs of weakening, Somoza's hypocritical pleas for a national dialogue appeared to have a chance of dividing the opposition, and President Carter sent the general a letter congratulating him on the improvements made in his human-rights record.

Actual support for the dynasty within the world community, however, remained extremely limited, and within Nicaragua the bulk of the population fervently desired the dictatorship's fall. Whatever prestige the government retained crumbled when the FSLN seized the National Palace in August 1978 and then followed this with a series of uprisings in Nicaraguan cities. A plot within the Guardia was defused and the uprisings put down, following several weeks of bitter fighting, but the brutality of the Guardia, the evident popular rejection of the regime, and the arrogant attitude of General Somoza Debayle combined to produce a worldwide wave of revulsion. Panama, Costa Rica, and Venezuela openly sided with Somoza's opponents; press coverage was overwhelmingly unfavorable; and church criticism of the government became even stronger. Even the Carter administration appeared to decide that the time had arrived for Somoza to go.

The Overthrow of Somoza

In October 1978 the major issues seemed to be when Anastasio Somoza Debayle would go and what type of government would succeed him. Prospects that the FSLN would defeat the Guardia and that Nicaragua's next government would be Sandinista-controlled seemed highly unlikely. To understand why what seemed unlikely in October 1978 became reality in July 1979, four basic factors must be examined: the character of the Somoza regime in its last months, the international opposition to Somoza, the nature and tactics of the non-Sandinista opposition within Nicaragua, and, of course, the strategy of the FSLN itself.

Somoza's Attitude

It now seems evident that neither the fate of Nicaragua nor even that of his supporters in the Guardia was a major concern of General Somoza Debayle during his final nine months in office. Maintaining power and destroying or at least humiliating his opponents was of much greater importance. It took the Nicaraguan dictator a long time to appreciate the seriousness of the threat he faced. Decades of family rule had produced a contempt for the opposition, a conviction that U.S. pressures could always be outwaited or diverted, and an assumption that time was on his side. The major task seemed to be to maintain

Guardia loyalty until the United States and the traditional opposition became convinced that Somoza's fall would produce an FSLN victory.

Somoza placed too much faith in the ability of his allies in the U.S. Congress and elsewhere to use the fear of communism to undermine democratic opposition to him. He underestimated the degree of international opposition and the strength of the domestic rejection of his government's legitimacy. The impact that a staggering economy, U.S. pressures for an arms boycott, and popular resistance would have on the Guardia's capacity to maintain control over the situation was also badly underestimated. After September 1978 Somoza could continue to rule, but he could never again effectively govern Nicaragua. He could maintain himself in office a while longer, but he could not regain legitimacy, effectively address any of the pressing national problems, or forge any viable coalition willing to acquiesce in his retention of power. By seeing negotiations not as a way of peacefully transferring power, but rather as a way of buying time until his opposition weakened and divided, the Nicaraguan dictator merely strengthened the FSLN's claim that they represented the only viable alternative. Although not totally contrary to his own tactics, such an impression would ultimately play a major role in Somoza's final fall.

International Opposition

International efforts to oust the Somoza dictatorship ultimately played a major role in bringing about the revolution. This opposition had begun to solidify during the September fighting. Venezuela, Panama, and Costa Rica played leading roles and in the months that followed began to funnel arms to the FSLN. In November the Inter-American Commission on Human Rights issued a report that strongly condemned the Nicaraguan government's massive violations of human rights, and the following month the United Nations General Assembly passed a resolution condemning the Somoza regime by a vote of eighty-five to two. Solidarity movements sprang up throughout Latin America and Europe, and groups such as the Socialist International and Amnesty International played major roles in mobilizing world opinion against the Somozas.

The key to effective world pressure, however, remained the position of the United States, and throughout early 1979 this appeared equivocal. The United States had strongly condemned the Somoza regime in January when the OAS mediation effort broke down, had withdrawn its military mission from Managua, and had expelled the last Nicaraguan students from U.S. military schools, but this was not accompanied by any effective economic sanctions. As late as May 1979 the United States, following sharp internal debate within the Carter administration, decided not to oppose a sixty-six-million-dollar International Monetary Fund (IMF) credit to Nicaragua. Carter administration officials continued to refuse to meet officially with FSLN representatives and even made some efforts to limit the support given the Sandinistas by other Latin American nations.

There were a host of reasons for the total ineffectiveness of Carter's policies. First, the Iranian crisis acted to divert attention away from Nicaragua and increase pressures to try to keep the lid on that situation, at least for the time being. Second, key members of Congress, notably Democrats John Murphy of New York and Charles D. Wilson of Texas, continued to support Somoza. Murphy even threatened to hold up enabling legislation for the Panama Canal treaties if too much pressure was put on the Nicaraguan dictator.[5] This had a paralyzing effect on the administration that was further compounded by a lack of effective input from the embassy in Managua. U.S. Ambassador Mauricio Solaún left Managua in February and shortly thereafter resigned. His replacement, Ambassador Lawrence Pezzullo, did not arrive in Managua until late June.

The Carter administration was also hampered by its own commitment to nonintervention as an aspect of the human-rights policy, an aspect strengthened by post-Vietnam reactions against the use of military force abroad. Limitations on CIA capacity for covert action and lack of effective influence within the Guardia Nacional also reduced the chances for promoting an anti-Somoza coup within that body. But most importantly, the United States was still determined to find a formula for replacing the Somozas with a coalition of "moderates" (defined as pro-American and anticommunist) who would be able to exclude the FSLN from any effective share of power and maintain a reorganized Guardia Nacional as the dominant military force within Nicaragua. The net result of these factors was that even though Carter was determined not to support Anastasio Somoza Debayle, he was unable to find any effective means of exerting pressure on the regime or of strengthening any alternative forces acceptable to Washington.

Non-Sandinista Opposition

These forces, composed chiefly of business interests, traditional opposition politicians, and a few discontented Guardia officers, lacked effective support within Nicaragua and pinned their hopes of eventually achieving power through U.S. support. They supported the U.S.-organized international mediation process that was conducted under the cover of the OAS from October 1978 through January 1979, confident that through this mediation Somoza would be ousted and Washington would then install a new government of its own choosing. Throughout the process they minimized cooperation with the FSLN and agreed to make concessions to Somoza that cost them internal support. When Los Doce, representing the Frente, withdrew from the mediation, most of these "moderates" remained, further weakening their image within Nicaragua. When the mediation collapsed, so did much of their remaining prestige and influence. Like the United States, they were left without any effective policy. A few, such as Alfonso Robelo Callejas, joined with the Sandinistas. Others continued to hope that the United States would eventually find some means of removing Somoza Debayle and continued their verbal and economic opposition to the regime. To the dictator's surprise, virtually none made any effort to reach an accommodation with him, despite his repeated overtures. Realizing the depths of popular rejection of the regime and knowing that the dictator's days were numbered, the middle and upper classes for once refused to let their fears of the left drive them back to the fatal embrace of the dynasty. Infuriated at this betrayal of class interests, Somoza turned his military force against their industries, shopping centers, and warehouses in the last weeks of the war. Already weakened by the near collapse of the national economy, the traditional elites were in no position to oppose these assaults. When Somoza finally fled to Miami he left behind a traditional opposition that was splintered and discredited and was suffering acute economic problems. Although they were important to the economic recovery process, opposition members lacked the power, influence, and leadership necessary to play a decisive role in Nicaragua's immediate future.

The FSLN

The FSLN, meanwhile, had been steadily strengthening its own position. Courage, self-sacrifice, and dedication were important elements in laying the groundwork for its ultimate triumph, but alone these elements were not sufficient to allow the Sandinistas to take power. An effective military strategy was also important to the Frente's success, but this too was secondary. The basic reasons for the phenomenal growth of the FSLN in the early months of 1979 and for its ultimate success were political. There were three major elements to this; the mobilization of internal support, the strengthening of international assistance, and the unification of the three tendencies within the FSLN. The last was the easiest to achieve. With the direct participation of Fidel Castro, the leaders of all three groups met and worked out a program of unity. Basic agreement was worked out by December 1978, and a joint public document was issued the following month. Shortly thereafter combined military operations were begun, and the unification process was completed with the formation of a nine-member National Directorate—three members from each tendency—in March 1979.

The unification of the FSLN accelerated the process of popular organization and mobilization within Nicaragua, a process already well advanced by the end of 1978. This involved several distinct elements. While the traditional opposition parties were bogged down in the mediation process, the FSLN was busily engaged in promoting mass organizations among labor, women, students, peasants, and other groups. These were then integrated into the United Peoples Movement (Movimiento Pueblo Unido—MPU), a political support organization for the Frente. In February 1979 the MPU joined with several other groups, including the Social Christians and the Independent Liberal party, to form the United Patriotic Front (Frente Patriótico Nacional—FPN). This provided the FSLN with a relatively broad-based coalition on the left to offer as an alternative to both the Somoza regime and the U.S.-supported Broad Opposition Front (Frente Amplio de Oposición—FAO). As this latter group's ineffectiveness became increasingly apparent, support for the FPN increased steadily, making it by the late spring of 1979 the dominant political force opposed to the dictatorship.

In order to increase its internal and international support, the FSLN also modified some of its rhetoric and programs. Emphasis was now placed on unity of all patriotic forces. Antiimperialism and an end to all relics of Somocismo were the dominant themes in most public pronouncements. Elements of the middle class were invited to join with the FSLN and were promised that they would be included in any post-Somoza government. Stress was placed on economic and social reforms, establishment of democratic institutions, respect for human rights, and maintenance of political and economic pluralism. The Sandinista leadership's commitment to Marxism and expectation that ultimate power in post-Somoza Nicaragua would rest with the FSLN directorate, not with the formal governmental structures, were deliberately downplayed. The results were highly effective. Popular support for the Sandinistas grew rapidly as more and more Nicaraguans came to visualize them as the only viable alternative to the dictatorship. Concerns over their ultimate aims were submerged in a wave of patriotic, antiimperialist sentiment.

Somoza Debayle's own efforts at polarization played into the hands of the FSLN, helping to convince many Nicaraguans that the Frente really was the only alternative to continued Somoza rule. His arrogance and brutality also persuaded many that only violence could remove him and that the FSLN was the only force available and capable of undertaking this task. Finally, the Guardia's tactic of executing young men found in areas recaptured from Sandinista control made it clear to many that if the Sandinistas withdrew from an area they would to be wise to join with them. Otherwise they might expect a summary execution by Somoza's troops.

A final factor was the massive, effective international campaign launched in favor of the FSLN and against Somoza. This proved most crucial in Latin America and in Western Europe. Los Doce played a key role here, lending prestige, credibility, and a vital organizational framework to contacts at high governmental levels. Their efforts helped isolate Somoza and produced vital diplomatic support for the Sandinistas.

Venezuela, Panama, Costa Rica, Mexico, and Cuba played the most important roles within Latin America in bringing about the downfall of Somoza. For Omar Torrijos of Panama and Carlos Andrés Pérez of Venezuela this effort, at times, assumed the dimensions of a personal crusade. They were persuaded to provide arms and other material support to the FSLN. Panama helped organize an international brigade to fight alongside the Sandinistas in the final stages of the war. All of this not only aided the FSLN's military efforts but also undercut Somoza's efforts to portray the Sandinistas as tools of Cuba.

Costa Rican support was absolutely crucial, since without this it would have been much more difficult for outside supplies to reach the Frente. The Costa Rican people, especially after the September 1978 uprisings, were united in their hatred of Somoza. The FSLN was able to operate almost openly in Costa Rica, especially in the last months of the war. Relations were broken with Anastasio Somoza Debayle and Costa Rican president Rodrigo Carazo Odio also helped convince Mexico to later take the same step. Ultimately, the FSLN-sponsored Junta of National Reconciliation was openly established in Costa Rica, negotiations between the FSLN and the United States were conducted there, and the town of Liberia became the supply and staging base for much of the final offensive of June and July 1979.

Cuba had long been the major international supporter of the FSLN, but during the critical months of September 1978 until May 1979 it took a back seat, allowing other nations to take the lead in opposing the Somozas and supporting the Frente. Cuban support became much more important in the last weeks of the war, but by then the dictatorship was in a state of virtual collapse and the major effect was to simply speed up the process.

The effectiveness of FSLN diplomatic efforts to rally opposition to Somoza and at least tolerance, if not open support, for their own cause became apparent in the emergency OAS session on Nicaragua held in June 1979. U.S. efforts to prevent a Sandinista victory by sending an OAS peacekeeping force to the region encountered virtually no support. Instead, international sentiment concentrated behind demands for Somoza's ouster and for the establishment of a new government independent of his influence and including the FSLN. Panama recognized the Frente-created junta set up in Costa Rica, and other nations, notably those of the Andean Pact, granted belligerent rights to the FSLN. U.S. efforts to force a broadening of the junta and to salvage the Guardia Nacional encountered almost no effective international support. So overwhelming was the combination of international and internal support that even the military governments of Guatemala, El Salvador, and Honduras, themselves fearful of the consequences of a Sandinista victory, refused to listen to Somoza's frantic pleas for support during his final weeks in power. At the end only Paraguay and Israel could be identified as offering any international support for the collapsing dynasty.

Conclusions

The Somoza dynasty collapsed because of internal contradictions and a growing inability to adapt to a changing world. It had become an anachronism, embarrassing even to the United States and humiliating to Nicaraguans with any sense of national pride. Internally, it had become an instrument of economic destruction and political polarization. Total dependence on the Guardia for regime survival further alienated the bulk of the population and eventually undermined Guardia morale. Internationally, the regime's own excesses, the ineptitude of U.S. policies, and the success of FSLN propaganda efforts had made Nicaragua the ultimate pariah state. Even the dictatorships in Guatemala and El Salvador saw Somoza's fall as the only hope for restoring any measure of regional stability. The character of Anastasio Somoza Debayle also further weakened the regime and helped ensure that any efforts to promote a peaceful transition of power to a new government would fail.

The FSLN took power because it was able to project itself as the only viable alternative to the dictatorship. It effectively mobilized anti-Somoza, antiimperialist sentiment both within and outside of Nicaragua, forging an overwhelming national coalition in the process. By subordinating ideology to nationalism, the FSLN even convinced much of the middle and upper classes that FSLN triumph was preferable to a continuation of the Somoza dynasty. Alternative forces proved inept, divided, and unable to mobilize effective domestic or international support. Both the traditional opposition and the United States also suffered from their long association with the dictatorship and from their efforts to reach a compromise agreement with Somoza Debayle during the mediation process. When the dynasty finally collapsed, only the FSLN, with the vital support of Los Doce and the National Patriotic Front, was in a position to establish an effective claim to the popular support, unity, will, and dedication needed to confront the massive problems that would face post-Somoza Nicaragua. The military success of the FSLN contributed greatly to this, but the basis of that success was political and its roots lay deep in the history of Nicaragua.

Notes

1. Confidential memorandum by Under Secretary of State Robert Olds, February 2, 1927, Record Group 59, Decimal File 817.00/4350, National Archives, Washington, D.C.

2. For descriptions of the three tendencies and their tactics, see George Black, *Triumph of the People* (London: Zed Press, 1981), pp. 91–96; and Adolfo Gilly, *La nueva Nicaragua* (Mexico, D.F.; Nueva Imagen, 1980), pp. 107–109.

3. For details on the creation of Los Doce, see the interview with Sergio Ramirez in Pilar Arias, *Nicaragua Revolución: Relatos de combatientes de Frente Sandinista* (Mexico, D.F.: Siglo Veintiuno, 1980), pp. 129–136.

4. Ibid., p. 152.

5. In November 1982 a State Department official in a conversation with me still defended this policy, arguing that the treaties were much more important than events in Nicaragua and that President Carter simply could not risk their disruption.

3
Reasons for the Success of the Nicaraguan Revolution

Donald Castillo Rivas

Alike even in the diversity of their specific contradictions, the countries of Central America cannot be understood unless they are viewed by the light of their historic experiences, especially those of their recent past. Economic crisis, political violence, and the options brought about by the transition toward a new sociopolitical model turn out to be inseparable common elements in the short- and long-term analysis of these countries.

Nonetheless, it would seem hardly feasible to infer that these factors, in being common to the countries of this region, could initiate a replay of the social struggles—their experiences and results—in all the Central American region. Also, judging by the facts of the present situation, it would seem that the power structures are being arranged into a hierarchy in the entire Central American area and the Caribbean, with exogenous factors acquiring greater relevance for the final solution of conflicts in local processes.

A hypothesis, in order to explain the nature of the generalized violence in the region, must necessarily consider the characteristics and conditions under which the economic development model was implemented during the last twenty years.

One central element—the accelerated modernization of Central American societies—should be underlined independently from such well-known conditions as the concentration of income and the regressive and exclusive character of wealth distribution, chronic unemployment, absolute misery thresholds, scant participation of most of the population in the decision making concerning their vital interests (economical, cultural, social, and political), generalized repression of any dissident activity, and the progressive loss of autonomy. Induced in great measure from outside so as to cater to the expansive needs of transnational capital, modernization took place under circumstances that generated a profound discrepancy between the growing expectations of the population and the limited possibilities of improving living conditions for most members of these societies.

This is particularly valid for Nicaragua, where an accelerated urbanization process in twenty-five years has transformed the demographic profile of the country. The urban population, 19 percent of the total population in 1950, had grown to more than 50 percent in 1975. This would not, by itself, reveal much of the social tensions accumulated in a society, but considering that in Nicaragua growth and modernization were not in accordance with the transformation of structures whether economic (especially in the agricultural field), social (creating enough jobs and social security), cultural (access to schools and universities), or political (democratic participation), this adds new angles to the analysis of violence and to many characteristics of the popular rebellion.

Did this have anything to do with the fact that in Nicaragua a popular rebellion starting from an epicenter in the marginal neighborhoods of the great urban concentrations grew to be a nationwide insurrection? Was it the crucial factor that the population, excluded from the benefits of modernization, rebelled when it realized its expectations had been frustrated? Is it sheer coincidence that the insurrection did not break out among the *campesinos* (small farmers and farm laborers) who, after all, were given maximum priority in the strategy of the revolutionaries during many years?

The questions raised highlight only a few structural elements of prerevolutionary Nicaraguan society in their complex articulation. An objective reconstruction of the various factors that helped to give the Nicaraguan process its present sociopolitical dimension may today be more important than ever, but the following discussion will be limited to bringing into systematic order those elements that contributed to the success of the popular insurrection. For the time being, the projection of those circumstances in the context of the sociopolitical model that is taking shape will be left aside.

Internal Factors

The long period of dynastic dictatorship that the succession in power of the Somoza family brought to Nicaragua reflects, beyond all its negative aspects, a particularly important fact: Somoza, in the specific framework of prerevolutionary Nicaragua, was a guarantee of stability and consequently of the capitalist development model, at least while that model brought accelerated modernization with it. Proof of this is found in Nicaragua's history during the twenty-five years that preceded the defeat of the dictatorship, a history that included attempted coups such as the civil-military rebellion of 1954, acts of individual heroism such as the execution of the dictator in 1956 by a citizen, guerrilla activities that preceded the Cuban revolution, ascent of the popular movement in the episodes of 1962–1963 and 1966–1967, resistance on the part of various political and social sectors (including the Catholic church), press attacks, conspiracies of exiles, and a permanent guerrilla movement that was beheaded only to reappear again and again. All these happenings were overcome by the dictatorship to the degree that none of them found propitious conditions for the success of a generalized insurrection. It could be said that what was especially lacking was social forces with mobilizing ability and an objective interest in the substitution of Somocism.

The three essential elements on which the absolute power of Somocism was based can be seen as according with the basic functions that supported the Nicaraguan state: unity in the dominant bloc of power, efficient military control, and international support by the world's most powerful power. It is no accident that for as long as Anastasio Somoza Debayle held these three elements, no effort of the opposition to overthrow him had the expected success. However, things changed when these three stability factors were in crisis. The first internal manifestations of the crisis showed in the breakup of the dominant bloc of power. This was followed by a decline and—later—withdrawal of the support the U.S. government traditionally had given Somoza through its embassy in Managua and finally by the collapse of the National Guard.

Naturally, there are other factors that affected the popular rebellion. Some of them in time came to play a more important role than those that have been pointed out, as did international solidarity, the internal class alliances to overthrow the dictatorship, and the undisputable existence of a politico-military avant-garde. However, it is believed that none of these factors would have sufficed to overthrow the dictator if the three legs on which the dictatorship was established had remained solid.

Breakup of the Dominant Power Bloc

Until 1975–1977 in Nicaragua, the dominant power bloc was constituted by the bourgeoisie of the agricultural-export sector, the financial sector, and the developing industrial sector. The ascent and enrichment of the different groups it consisted of was carried out in the shadow of a paternalistic state represented by, and under the hegemony of, Somoza. It was not, therefore, an autonomous social class with a coherent social projection and ideology, as it would appear during and after the fall of Somoza. Neither could it offer anything that the dictator himself was not offering to the process of capitalist accumulation.

Studies carried out on the structure of economic power in Nicaragua showed the existence of three groups: one group formed around the Nicaraguan Bank, the second around the Bank of America, and the third around Somoza. All three were closely linked to foreign capital and had oligopolistic dominion in all the branches and activities of the country's economy. As long as the agricultural diversification and the model of economic integration imparted an unusual impulse to economic growth, there was harmony based on a gentlemen's agreement among the three groups, which had their areas of influence clearly defined by sectors and territories.

But the terms of the problem changed radically when that pattern of development started to give signs of exhaustion and above all when the crisis, beginning in 1967, became more acute during the first half of the seventies. It was at that time that the economic group of Somoza decided to clamp down on the non-Somocist bourgeoisie. By means of the state apparatus that was at its personal and exclusive service, it started what the bourgeoisie would term "unloyal competition." In collusion with the transnational enterprises and especially with the U.S. multimillionaire Howard Hughes, the Somocist group started to invade areas of economic activity reserved to and traditionally exploited by the other financial and entrepreneurial groups. On the other hand, the other groups intruded into areas of Somocist dominion, with the predictable result, considering their disadvantage. This explains the sharpening contradictions inside the dominant bloc after 1972, which for the first time reached the level of evident antagonism and showed that Somoza Debayle was no longer the motor of development of the productive forces in Nicaragua. It also explains the radicalization of a considerable part of the bourgeoisie and the middle sectors, leading them to look for an alliance with the revolutionary movement, which at that time already had an unquestionable presence in national political life.

Other events accelerated the crisis of Somocism. The most important one was the earthquake that devastated the Nicaraguan capital. Another was the limitless voracity of the dictator, who—not satisfied with the embezzlement of the international aid to the earthquake victims—wanted to strike new blows at the bourgeoisie by creating a complete juridical and economic infrastructure that made him the main beneficiary of Managua's reconstruction.

This breakup of the dominant bloc of power, in which the non-Somocist bourgeoisie expounded the overthrow of the dictatorship, may have been of fundamental relevance to the end of the dictatorship, along with the economic power of the bourgeoisie to support the insurrection and the general strikes that preceded Somoza's fall. Probably the bourgeoisie's main contribution consisted in projecting an image of national unity both at home and abroad. It generated confidence with different international sectors. Some of these, by giving indirect help, contributed substantially to the success of the revolution; some others at least did not offer resistance.

Does this breakup of the dominant bloc of power also exist in El Salvador, Guatemala, and the other countries of the region? This can be denied without fear of being mistaken—the experience of Nicaragua is unrepeatable.

But the stagnation of the development pattern was not the cause of economic decline for the bourgeoisie only. Other social sectors were also dragged down by their worsening living conditions, the population sector with little resources being the one that suffered most from the effects of the crisis. There are eloquent facts about unemployment, misery, unsanitary conditions, crowding in marginal slums, the loss of all hope of improvement of living conditions, hunger, delinquency, and social decomposition; on top of it all, there was systematic repression and ubiquitous official corruption. This was indeed a true social powder keg ready to blow up at any moment.

Popular Basis of the Rebellion

Such was the prevailing situation on January 10, 1978, when the regime murdered the newspaper man Pedro Joaquín Chamorro, whose death undoubtedly furnished the emotional explosive that started the popular rebellion. Did Chamorro really represent an alternative to the Nicaraguan social order? The several interpretations of this point are not relevant here. Altogether unquestionable is the fact that Chamorro was the last charismatic leader of an epoch in which his peronal boldness and his incorruptibility, accompanied by an unfaltering antidictatorial stance, rightfully gained him the most prominent place in the opposition until the day of his assassination.

No less important were the church's persistent critique of daily outrages committed by the regime and the attacks of the students and the labor-union movement. There existed, therefore, an explosive situation such as had never before existed either in the history of that country or in other countries of the region.

A similar situation with regard to the popular sectors reigns in El Salvador, even though with less intensity than in Nicaragua, where the figure of Anastasio Somoza Debayle was the unifying factor to the struggle of all groups, classes, and sectors of the Nicaraguan society. Thus, a second relevant element to understanding the success of the popular rebellion in Nicaragua is the circumstance that all sectors of the population, without exception, did not limit themselves to a simultaneous rejection of the dictatorship (although on different flanks), but instead turned such rejection into a rebellion of surprising magnitude and multiplying effect.

Here it is worthwhile to underline that the most radical groups of the revolutionary movement had the surprising ability of accepting the need to form alliances and adequately using social sectors and personalities that shared the urge to overthrow the dictatorship. Was this a situation in which the radicals of the orthodox left wing, because they constituted a simple minority, did not have any other alternative than to share with the majorities the constant and versatile attacks at Somocism? Or on the contrary, did this attitude correspond to a line of policy scrupulously defined with, or at least maintained on, direct and efficient international advice?

On more than one occasion the popular rebellion went beyond the leadership abilities of the various political movements. Sometimes managing the course of events became a true "relay race," whenever the situation changed more rapidly than the political and revolutionary organizations were able to respond. The whole of the population had rushed to join the struggle, calling for guidance and new options. In that instructive process the ability of the different national sectors was put to the test, and many succumbed before a responsibility that was beyond their material, organizational, and ideological powers. That context is precisely where the role of a political vanguard becomes relevant, not so much in generating a situation that—as can be easily proved—originates in various different circumstances, but in overcoming its own internal contradictions and wisely conducting a patently irreversible process.

Evolution of the Sandinist Front

The Sandinist Front of National Liberation, as is well known, evolved in little time from a clandestine organization into a politically hegemonic force. What factors enabled this metamorphosis? First, it must be recognized that this organization was the most experienced in the struggle against the dictatorship. It was the best organized and most disciplined, and its ideological conceptions were more coherent than those of the rest of the opposition to Somocism. Besides, it had something that turns out to be fundamental in these processes: the power of "mysticism" in a double sense. For one thing, the Sandinists were seen by the people of Nicaragua as the unquestionable heirs of Augusto César Sandino, the highest symbol of Nicaraguan nationality. For another, the revolutionaries had provided ample evidence that the invincibility of the National Guard was a myth to be broken (for instance, by some most spectacular military actions mainly carried out by the Terceristas, the faction of the FSLN headed, among others, by the legendary Commander Zero).

Second, it must be considered that the Sandinists (especially their orthodox left wing), fighting under new historic conditions, were capable of incorporating into the antiimperialism of Sandino the essentially empiric elements of the Leninist strategy of revolution. For this reason, present Sandinism links two principles of the contemporary class struggle: the intransigent antiimperialism and the Leninist experience in gaining political power, including the "blows below the belt" of its "route companions," and the constant internal purges.

There is an aspect of singular importance in the experience of the Nicaraguan rebellion: the role of the FSLN as vanguard. Its politico-military structure, its organization, its mystique, its class content, its experience, and some other elements of its political-revolutionary task are indispensable to gaining power in antidemocratic societies. This exemplary political practicality and discipline aimed at a strategical objective is precisely what led the Sandinists to form a block with the bourgeoisie, among other things. Many movements and democratic parties in Latin America have lacked that, notwithstanding their more than good intentions to transform society.

Third, the implementation of a democratic and multiclass cover, at first with the so-called Group of Twelve and afterwards with other sectors of the bourgeoisie and the church, was crucial. It was a prerequisite to Sandinist expressions of their positions from platforms of great influence on national and international public opinion.

The National Guard

This analysis would lack thoroughness if it did not link the dimensions of the popular rebellion and of Sandinism to the characteristic of the National Guard. This military institution, formed to substitute for the occupation army of the United States, was identified by its organizational and ideological structures as a military body at the exclusive service of a family. This did not mean that as policemen of the Central American area National Guard members were not assigned to other tasks related to the functioning of the socioeconomic system and to the protection of the interests of the United States in the region. After all, among these two functions there was no incompatibility whatsoever. The underlying fact is that the principal function of the Guard was the defense of the will and the particular interests of the Somoza family.

Its lack of institutionality and its involvement with crime and corruption tied the National Guard to the destinies of a family in peace and in war. For that reason the National Guard crumbled when Anastasio Somoza Debayle abandoned the country. This also explains why they could not play the role of mediator in times when even the Sandinists promoted a negotiation with the supposedly honest army officers. The

National Guard's true nature as a praetorian army was shown by its demoralization and stampede; its lack of institutionality was demonstrated by its collapse in the face of the advancing insurrection.

The aforesaid is not meant to underestimate the victories of the Sandinist army. On the contrary, without the military capacity of the revolutionaries, the rebellion could not have been successful. The crucial point was that many success factors in the military field were crowned by these particularities of the National Guard, which probably are not present in any other Central American army, insofar as their institutions correspond to structures and ideologies of a different nature.

International Factors

Since the Vietnam War probably no incident has attracted the sympathies of international public opinion as much as the liberation war of Nicaragua. Independent of the extraordinary impulse of international solidarity promoted by Nicaraguans and foreigners—the effects of which were decisive in the final triumph—were elements and circumstances that today do not prevail, to the same degree, in the experiences of the other Central American countries. Among them, those having to do with the official policies of governments and international organizations are of special importance. Carter's policy on human rights, as well as the position of the international press (not to mention the activity of some Latin American countries and European political organizations), guaranteed an efficient solution to the conflict, especially with regard to the specter of a possible foreign military intervention during catalepsy of the dictatorship.

The influence of Carter's policy on human rights in the case of Nicaragua has to all practical purposes been generally recognized. Undoubtedly it was a stimulant for the anti-Somocist bourgeois groups to charge against Somoza. For the first time the dictatorship saw itself heavily attacked by the press and by the Congress of the United States. The opposition bourgeoisie took considerable advantage of this break and turned their backs on the government of Nicaragua, a stance they had never taken before. That situation worsened throughout Washington's successive directives with regard to the economic, political, and military blockade of Somoza and the National Guard. Never before had there been a similar situation in the history of the relations between Nicaragua and the United States, and probably neither will it happen in the other countries of the region. In those countries the United States' influence is becoming more adverse the more the present administration's position departs from that of Carter.

Public opinion in the United States was particularly sensitized by the genocide in Nicaragua. Analyzing press articles, those published in the United States as well as those by reporters in Managua, one immediately feels the sympathy for the revolution with which they were written. Probably the revolution of Nicaragua owes more than is usually acknowledged to the international press and to the reporters who, out of opportunism or in good faith, showed the world the atrocities of the dictatorship. There is the case of newspaper reporter Bill Stewart, whose murder shook the conscience of North Americans more than any other of the daily news items about the genocide. The world press has not shown any bias vis-à-vis the genocide in El Salvador either, but seems to handle this item with much more caution than in the case of Nicaragua.

Another factor in this context is the space that the insurrection of Nicaragua occupied in the newspapers, magazines, and television screens all over the world. During the most crucial moments of the Nicaraguan war, Nicaragua was exclusive news. There seems to have been no other event of greater international transcendence, allowing Nicaragua to monopolize the world's attention. The Salvadoran situation is different, as it has had to share newspaper space with other events of great international relevance, such as the Soviet invasion in Afghanistan, the U.S. hostages in Iran and the war between Iran and Iraq, the successes and failures of the Polish labor-union movement, and Ronald Reagan's triumph in the U.S. elections and his subsequent reactionary policy.

With respect to the international organizations, the Nicaraguan process was also very lucky. The Organization of American States (OAS), which traditionally had been controlled by the United States, for the first time changed its balance of power when it opposed the creation of an inter-American military force to intervene at the moment when the Sandinist army was controlling the situation. Other countries, such as those of the Andean Pact, played an extraordinary role by supporting the revolutionary forces. More significant even was the support received from Central American countries like Panama and Costa Rica, especially the latter, because it confirmed a historical experience that for a military triumph it was essential to have an open border and the support of a neighboring country. The role played by countries considered as regional middle powers was a determinant for the triumph of the popular rebellion. Venezuela, Cuba, and Mexico played different roles at different times, but all of them were crucial in guaranteeing the people's victory.

Some help of incalculable value was given by the Socialist International and its more well-known leaders. In more than one international meeting they expressed their political and material support to the struggle of the Nicaraguans, notwithstanding the lack of strong ideological commitment and the use that would be made of its support by the more radical left-wing followers of official Sandinism.

Evaluating the present Salvadoran situation inevitably leads one to the sad conclusion that many social and political forces that internationally supported the Nicaraguan revolution today maintain a distant, neutral, or even hostile position regarding El Salvador. Some others, like Mexico, Venezuela, and the Socialist International, continue giving their support and demanding neutrality and nonintervention in the conflict. But times are changing, and the policies carried out by the National Directorate of the Sandinists have been the main obstacle for the Central American revolutionary projects to get the validity and credibility they need so much.

Conclusions

The separation between the national and international factors determining the success of the popular rebellion in Nicaragua is more didactic than real. Essentially, the Nicaraguan experience shows that the external and internal factors jointly produced a linkup of effects in the political process in this Central American country.

A global evaluation concludes that the following were the factors of success in Nicaragua.

1. The breakup of Somocism's traditional bases of support: the dominant bloc of power, the support by the government of the United States, and the National Guard.

2. The crisis of the economic development model implemented by the dictatorship, whose negative consequences—such as economic concentration, regression, and exclusive allotment of the benefits of modernization—created conditions of discontent among the broad masses that had arrived at the threshold of the most absolute misery.

3. The appearance of new social classes and sectors, which—shut out from the process of decision making and from any other substantial participation in the social administration—decided to take up arms against the dictatorship.

4. The opportunity to form a common front of struggle against the Somocist dictatorship, between the opposing bourgeoisie and the popular and revolutionary sectors within the framework of a projection originally conceived as democratic, pluralist, and nationalist.

5. The general support offered not only by the not so well-to-do sectors of the Nicaraguan population but also by all associations and organizations, such as the Catholic church, newspaper reporters, managers, merchants, women, workers, students, and others, in the course of the insurrection.

6. The existence of a revolutionary organization with the experience, discipline, and organization as well as ideological structures to make it the vanguard of a political process, at a time when the right wing's attempts at leadership had failed.

7. The Nicaraguan National Guard's specific character of praetorian army with ties to a family whose leadership was based on corruption and on openly violating the institutional rules of military organization. This was an important cause for the Guard's noisy breakdown when faced with the flight of the dictator and the advance of the popular insurrection.

8. The human rights policy of Carter and the outlook that such policy gave to public opinion, the press, and the Congress of the United States.

9. The international solidarity promoted by nationals and foreigners, who established contacts, required help, and made all the details of the process well known, denouncing the violations of human rights on the part of the dictatorship and of its National Guard.

10. The solidarity shown by a bloc of Latin American governments committed in favor of Nicaragua, such as the Andean Pact countries, Venezuela, Mexico, Cuba, Panama, and Costa Rica.

11. The existence of an open frontier with Costa Rica, which became a source of supply and foreign help to the guerrilla forces.

12. The support of international political organizations, like the Socialist International, which served as interlocutor to the world public opinion and to certain foreign governments, besides helping the revolution politically and materially.

13. The certainty that Nicaragua, once freed from Somocism, would become a democratic alternative, a hybrid model providing exemplary and adequate answers to the process of growing polarization and alignment; that in this alternative the content and significance of political pluralism would open new perspectives to the other democratic processes of Latin America; and, finally, that the experience of the Nicaraguan upheaval would be a valuable contribution to the theoretical and practical shaping of a new blueprint for autonomous, plural, democratic, and nationalistic development.

14. The fundamental cause of the popular rebellion's triumph in Nicaragua: the spirit of struggle and sacrifice of the Nicaraguan people, without which it would have been impossible to achieve this great success of putting the revoutionary movement in power.

4
Sandinist Democracy: Problems of Institutionalization

Heinrich-W. Krumwiede

This chapter poses a basic question. What are the possibilities, and probabilities, that a form of government will be found in Sandinist Nicaragua that fills the following criteria: It should be tolerable to Western industrialized states, including the United States, and it should, in principle, deserve support because it conforms sufficiently to liberal democratic norms or respectively differs satisfactorily from the communist state-party model. In terms of this question, the analysis of political developments in Nicaragua since the overthrow of Anastasio Somoza Debayle is of interest only to the extent that it permits a better assessment of future developments.

Before making any attempt to formulate criteria and present information that would permit a realistic answer to the basic question, it is necessary to outline the international importance of the problem of choosing the appropriate form of government for Nicaragua[1] and to discuss the suitability of current Western democratic expectations vis-à-vis Sandinist Nicaragua. It would make no sense to discuss this theme if I believed either that Nicaragua was already "lost to communism" or that political developments were underway that almost automatically would lead—in some form—to communism. It is probably unlikely that Sandinist Nicaragua will adopt a parliamentary democracy like that in Costa Rica, as the governments of the United States and Western Europe would prefer. But there are some convincing arguments and indications that a more or less democratic system could be found for Nicaragua that Western industrialized states, after sober consideration of the circumstances and a realistic evaluation of the problems inherent in other alternatives, could view as worthy of support.

On the International Significance of the Question of the Nicaraguan Form of Government

It is common knowledge that the Reagan administration considers Nicaragua "lost to communism." It has discontinued economic aid to the country, is pursuing plans to isolate and destabilize the Sandinist regime, and refuses to rule out military intervention. In contrast, most West European governments and certain Latin American countries (Mexico deserves special mention) still are counting on the possibility that the FSLN (Frente Sandinista de Liberación Nacional) will in the end decide in favor of a political regime and a socioeconomic order that to a sufficient extent takes into account Western political expectations and Western concern about a communist takeover. They have thus continued to cooperate with Sandinist Nicaragua. In particular those social-democratic and socialist parties that belong to the Socialist International (SI) advance the thesis that cooperation with Sandinist Nicaragua could moderate radical tendencies within the FSLN and could prevent a shift toward a communist state-party system.

From the viewpoint of Western Europe, and in particular of the SI—which, through its support for the FSLN, has made a considerable political "high-risk investment," the behavior of the FSLN on the question of choosing the definitive form of government has taken on an almost paradigmatic importance that transcends Nicaragua itself. The answer to this question could have consequences for the future political posture of West European governments and parties toward social-revolutionary movements not only in Central America, but also throughout the whole Third World.[2]

Nicaragua is seen as a kind of test case for the willingness of social-revolutionary, Marxist-oriented movements to try to arrive at some kind of arrangement with the basic principles of Western pluralist democracy and to avoid alliance with international communism. It is assumed that it would be impossible to place much confidence in the democratic promises of such movements in the Third World if the FSLN were to adopt a regime with a communist orientation. Nicaragua is such a test case for two reasons. First, the FSLN is judged by the extent to which it is willing to turn its promises into reality: respect for social and political pluralism, establishment of a mixed economic order, pursuance of a credible nonalignment policy. Second, and perhaps even more important, because of the "objective" circumstances that exist, it would make sense for the FSLN to establish a more or less pluralist-democratic form of government.[3]

1. The Somoza regime was overthrown by a very broad political and social coalition including social-revolutionary and bourgeois forces. The Somoza-family regime, finally both socially and politically totally isolated, was overthrown by a veritable people's insurrection under the guidance of the FSLN. In spite of all contradictions, the historical hostility toward Somozism is common to the Sandinists and the internal political opposition. Thus, in this respect there exists a quite favorable climate for compromise between the FSLN and the internal opposition, which favors a parliamentary democracy.

2. The huge property holdings of the Somoza clan made it possible for the Sandinists to redistribute national wealth in grand style without doing grave injury to the proprietary rights of the bourgeoisie. This took the bite out of the problem of redistribution of wealth, normally one of the primary sources of conflict following a takeover by social-revolutionary movements. Compromise over the question of redistribution of wealth between social revolutionaries and bourgeois forces came easier in Nicaragua than would be the case following a possibly successful revolution in, for example, El Salvador or Guatemala.

3. The Sandinist revolution enjoyed international support, particularly in the West. That the United States, under Reagan, has discontinued economic aid to Nicaragua need not necessarily force Nicaragua to turn toward the Eastern Bloc. Because Nicaragua is a small, underpopulated, economically underdeveloped country, it is not as economically dependent on the United States as, for example, Mexico is. From this viewpoint it is therefore more independent ("independent" in the sense of a diversification of dependencies). Western Europe could, if it were willing, act as an economic substitute for the United States of America vis-à-vis Nicaragua.

On the Rationality of Western Expectations of Democracy in Sandinist Nicaragua

The expectations voiced by Western governments that the Nicaraguans should establish an Anglo-American–or West European–style pluralist democracy—and this in the shortest possible time—can be seen as rather unrealistic from a Latin American perspective.

1. One must realize that democracies in Latin America are more the exception than the rule. In addition, political regimes in Latin America that are classified as democratic rarely have corresponded, during their often very brief existence, entirely to the norms of Anglo-American or West European democracy.

2. Nicaragua has never gone through a phase of political development that could have earned the name democracy. It is a country totally

without any true democratic tradition. Today's Nicaraguans have experienced pluralist democracy only in the perverted form of the Somozist facade-democracy. In contrast to Nicaragua, certain other Latin American countries—for example Chile, with its present authoritarian government—can look back on a longer, genuinely democratic tradition.

3. A pluralist democracy like that practiced in the United States and recommended to the Sandinists holds little attraction for Nicaragua. That country has experienced the United States as *the* imperial power, which treated Nicaragua like a satellite state, occupied it from 1912 to 1932, supported the Somoza regime for more than four decades, and today questions the revolution and the revolutionary regime.

4. In general, Latin America has quite a different understanding of the term *democracy* than does the United States or Western Europe. The definition of democracy widely accepted in Latin America is based not only on a liberal democratic tradition with Anglo-American–West European origins, but also on a powerful Hispanic political tradition with strong organicist, patrimonial, and corporatist elements. Latin Americans seem to place less importance on criteria that are constitutive for the Anglo-American understanding of democracy. Howard Wiarda, who attempted to define and to operationalize the most important criteria in the Latin American understanding of democracy, stated: "Nowhere in this listing of characteristics for measuring democracy in Latin America is the notion of a formalized, constitutional 'separation of powers' or 'checks and balances' given central focus, nor do elections, political parties and the like constitute the chief criteria."[4] And he points out that for Latin America, not only political but also—and to the same extent—social and economic criteria (economic development and social justice) are constitutive for its understanding of democracy. It should be mentioned that Wiarda, in his list of nineteen Latin American countries, ranked Cuba tenth on his scale of democracy, based on an operationalized definition of the Latin American understanding of democracy.[5] Normally Cuba comes out last in the usual measurements of democracy, which are oriented toward the Anglo-American understanding of democracy.

5. In the Sandinist understanding of democracy—and here Sandinists are representative not only of the social revolutionaries but also of the social-reformist left in Latin America—socioeconomic criteria are given clear priority over political criteria. Where the choice must be made, social justice takes precedence over free elections. The concept popular in the United States that equates the "democratic creed" and the "capitalist creed" is foreign to Sandinists' understanding of democracy. They tend rather to espouse the European democratic-socialist tradition that does not consider democracy and socialism to be mutually exclusive, but rather—in principle—complementary and mutually supportive forms of

social organization. The National Directorate of the FSLN, in a statement in which it justified postponement of the election date until 1985, gave the following explanation:

> For the Frente Sandinista, democracy is not measured solely in the political sphere, and cannot be reduced only to the participation of the people in elections. Democracy is not simply elections. It is something more, much more. For a revolutionary, for a Sandinista, it means *participation* by the people in political, economic, social and cultural affairs. The more the people participate in such matters, the more democratic they will be. And it must be said once and for all: democracy neither begins nor ends with elections. It is a myth to want to reduce democracy to that status. Democracy begins in the economic order, when social inequalities begin to diminish, when the workers and peasants improve their standard of living. That is when true democracy begins, not before. Once these aims are achieved, democracy is immediately extended to other fields: the field of government is broadened; when the people influence their government, when people determine their government, whether this pleases some people or not. In a more advanced phase, democracy means the participation of the workers in the running of factories, farms, cooperatives and cultural centers. To sum up, democracy is the intervention of the mases in all aspects of social life. We point out all this to establish on a principled basis what the FSLN understands by democracy.[6]

In order to fit the Sandinist regime into the historical context of Nicaragua, it may be interesting to quote the opinion of one of the leaders of the Nicaraguan Conservative party (Partido Conservador Demócrata—PCD), as expressed in a confidential conversation. According to this member of the political opposition, the Sandinists, by having come to power through armed force and now trying to establish a kind of *partido único* (single party) system, are merely following the classical political tradition of Nicaragua. He believed that the Conservative party could accept a Sandinist dictatorship if the Sandinists would stick to a reformist course. He said that the FSLN without any doubt enjoys considerable popular support and that Nicaraguans for the most part are uninterested in elections. After all, there have never been any true elections in Nicaragua. Only during the U.S. occupation were more or less clean elections held. It would be pure hypocrisy for these same North Americans who for decades supported the pseudoelections of the Somoza regime now to demand open, competitive elections from the Sandinists. In short, he felt the Sandinist regime would certainly be acceptable as a social-reformist variant of dictatorship continuing the political tradition of Nicaragua. What in the case of the Sandinists could be considered new, disruptive, and conflict-breeding is their national and international "romanticism," their domestic radicalism, and their missionary ambition to export the revolution. This conservative leader recommended that the Sandinists learn from the "realism," or "cynicism," of the Mexican PRI (Partido Revolucionario Institucional) elite.

To summarize: If the FSLN does not want to lose the continued support of other important Western states, it will have to refute the suspicion that Nicaragua is turning to communism by soon making a basic decision on the form of government it is going to adopt. That the same Western industrialized states that in the case of the rightist authoritarian regime in Brazil have been satisfied by almost two decades of announcements of liberalization and democratization and have shown every understanding for the problems the Brazilian military had and still is having with its withdrawal from direct politics—that these states should now confront the Sandinists with the demand that they decide as soon as possible on a democratic form of government naturally severely irritates the Sandinists. One can, however, explain this double standard by pointing out that, from a certain Western viewpoint, rightist authoritarian regimes can be seen as "potentially democratic," whereas communist regimes are viewed as lost forever to democracy and the West. No normative attempt is made here to reflect on the desirability of either a more pluralist or a more socialist democracy for Nicaragua. Still, if one assumes a Latin American perspective and considers Nicaragua's political tradition, it is possible from both an analytic and descriptive viewpoint to determine that a hegemonic party system like that in Mexico, which simultaneously guarantees a limited political pluralism, could be accepted as a sufficiently democratic or sufficiently noncommunist form of government for Nicaragua.

Development and Structures of the Present Sandinist Provisional Regime[7]

The FSLN has postponed until 1985 any definitive answer to the question of which form of government will be established in Nicaragua. Only then will elections be held to choose a constituent assembly. Until now, no party or election law has been passed that would permit any conclusions about what kind of elections will be held and about the extent to which opposition parties at least formally will be given an equal competitive chance.

An analysis of the political development of Nicaragua after the overthrow of Somoza Debayle would make it seem unlikely, if one extends the trend lines, that the final decision would favor a parliamentary democracy like that found in Costa Rica. In 1979, the FSLN, in several documents of principle (government program, fundamental statute, declaration of basic rights) did at first commit itself to a clearly pluralist, rather parliamentary form of democracy. This was followed by recognition of the famous triad of basic principles (political pluralism, mixed economic order, nonalignment). For the transition period until elections would be held, the FSLN originally consented to a system of power sharing between itself and its allied organizations and the bourgeois forces in the form of a coalition government. From this, however, a provisional regime developed in which the FSLN exercises functions and competences that are typical of a hegemonic party. The present Sandinist regime certainly cannot be described as totalitarian, but neither as genuinely pluralist. It is stamped with the contradiction between the pluralist promises and hegemonic ambitions of the FSLN.

The FSLN Political Hegemony

An important foundation of the hegemonic position of the FSLN is the monopolistic control of certain key areas of political life. The *comandantes* (FSLN leaders), who consider themselves a politico-military elite, gave particular attention to the buildup and forced expansion of the armed forces, security forces, and the militia, which are controlled exclusively by the FSLN. Even in the nomenclature (Sandinist People's Army, Sandinist People's Military, Sandinist People's Police), the impression is made that no politically neutral armed forces and security forces and militia were to be created, but rather that they are instruments loyal to the FSLN and the revolution. The nucleus of the military-police apparatus is the former Sandinist guerrilla and militia organizations. The most important commando positions are securely in the hands of Sandinist commanders. Special emphasis is placed on revolutionary-ideological education.[8]

The most important means of mass communication—television—is firmly in the hands of the Sandinists. Elsewhere in the media sector there is a kind of limited pluralism. Several radio stations and the newspaper with the largest circulation in the country, *La Prensa,* which considers itself the voice of the opposition, are still privately owned. However, in 1982 a state of emergency was declared and rigid censorship of the press imposed. This severely limits the information and criticism functions of those media not under direct control of the FSLN. *La Prensa,* the most important organ of the opposition, has several times briefly been refused permission to continue publication.

The FSLN and its allied people's organizations dominate all state organs with the exception of the supreme court (see the discussion of checks and balances). There can be no doubt that the National Directorate, established by the nine *comandantes de la revolución,* in the true sense of the word is not a state organ but rather a party organ that establishes the poltical guidelines and coordinates the work of the government. Its members hold the most important national leadership positions. The coordinator of the Governing Junta of National Reconstruction, the chairman of the State Council, and the ministers of interior, defense, agriculture, and planning are *comandantes de la revolución.* The majority of the *comandantes guerrilleros* (over thirty leading Sandinists were awarded this title in recognition of their services during the civil war) hold central national and political leadership positions. The ratio of the Sandinists to the "bourgeoisie" representatives in the governing junta was at first three to two; during the reorganization of the junta in spring 1981 it became two to one. The ratio is similar in the cabinet, where the Sandinist elites, in particular the *comandantes de la revolución,* occupy key ministries. And in the State Council, a corporative body in which all important political and social groups in Nicaragua, including parties, interest groups, and the church, are represented, the FSLN and its allied people's organizations enjoy a clear majority. The State Council is a kind of substitute parliament—serving, however, only in an advisory capacity—for the period until the constituent assembly has been convened.

The Sandinist regime is one of organized mass mobilization in which the FSLN, as a kind of cadre and avant-garde party, has surrounded itself with a tight ring of people's organizations. In the area of lower-class and in part also middle-class organization, the FSLN has achieved a hegemonic position by founding its own organizations while absorbing and supplanting existing organizations. The Sandinist Workers' Central (Central Sandinista de Trabajadores) now has by far the greatest number of union-organized workers. Membership and influence of non-Sandinist union organizations such as the Christian democratic union federation CTN (Confederación de Trabajadores Nicaragüenses) seem to be steadily decreasing. The Sandinist ATC (Asociación de Trabajadores del Campo) has a de facto organizational monopoly over the country's agricultural workers. The Sandinist UNAG (Unión Nacional de Agricultores y Ganaderos) broke the monopoly of the rather conservative UPANIC (Unión de Productores Agrícolas de Nicaragua) and successfully drew into its ranks a large number of small- and medium-scale land holders.

The party organizations of the FSLN include, besides the Sandinist Youth and Women's Organization, the Sandinist Defense Committees (CDS—Comités de Defensa Sandinista), supposedly with approximately 300,000 members. The CDS serve a variety of functions, including the parapolice function of maintaining order (protecting the barrios from criminal and "counterrevolutionary" elements), distributing rationed foodstuffs, recruiting for the militia, and participating in social-reform activities (for example vaccination and literacy programs) and community-development projects. In a functional sense, one can also include the militia in this list of Sandinist people's organizations.

FSLN Economic Policies

The extent to which the state is involved in the economy is not particularly great. It is estimated that approximately 55 percent of the gross national product (GNP) is generated by the private sector. The state share of the GNP grew from 15.3 percent in 1978 to 40.8 percent in 1980, primarily as a result of the nationalization of the Somozist economic empire. But since the Sandinists nationalized not only the Somoza holdings, but also foreign trade and the whole financial sector, one can say that the Sandinist state occupies the strategically important economic "commando heights."

Until now the Sandinists have exercised restraint not only in their nationalization policy but also in their policy of redistribution of wealth. A model example of this is the agrarian reform, which in terms of past experience and announced intentions can by no means be called radical. The Sandinists waited until 1981 to pass an agrarian reform law that foresees expropriation of unused or underused farmlands covering more than 350 hectares. The expropriated land should not be used to create state-run operations but rather to establish small-scale and cooperative units. The Salvadoran agricultural reform law of 1980, for example, foresees far more extensive changes in the distribution of land. The Sandinists have attempted, primarily by means of social reform, to raise the standard of living of the lower classes and to satisfy their basic need for food, health care, education, and work. Their efforts have included literacy campaigns that lowered the illiteracy rate from 50 percent to 13 percent, drastic increases in budget expenditures in the social sphere, programs of preventive medicine and introduction of free health care, and price supports for basic foodstuffs. In order not to endanger economic cooperation with Western industrialized states and to remain "credit-worthy," the revolutionary regime has assumed the huge debt burden of the Somoza regime ($1.6 billion). In general, it is thus possible to say that the Sandinists have restricted themselves to the task of building up and expanding a mixed economic order and have by no means pursued a radical socialist economic policy.

Checks on the FSLN

It is undeniable that the FSLN enjoys certain privileges usually reserved for a hegemonic party. The right to and possibilities for expansion of the other parties (the FSLN does not yet define itself as a party and demands special status as *the* revolutionary movement) are severely limited. The strict censorship of the press since the declaration of a state of emergency and the ban until 1984 on all party propaganda and mass meetings certainly puts those parties that form an opposition to the FSLN at a severe disadvantage. Those bourgeois forces in Nicaragua that contributed to the overthrow of Somoza Debayle have seen their hopes dashed that the FSLN would grant them a proportional share of power in the relevant state organs of the provisional regime and that it would quickly hold new elections that would give them an equal competitive chance. The FSLN itself feels that its willingness to grant minority political rights of participation to the bourgeois forces and its guarantee of most existing property rights are convincing evidence of its willingness to compromise. It points out that it held "total power" in the period immediately following Somoza's overthrow but then willingly set self-imposed limits on this power. In addition, it points out that it was not the bourgeois forces, which up until the very end were willing to negotiate with Somoza that were the deciding factor in the revolution, but rather it was the Sandinists who used armed force to overthrow him.

An opposition camp has been formed from a coalition of entrepreneurial organizations, rightist and centrist parties, and their allied union organizations, with *La Prensa* acting as its voice. The majority of Catholic bishops also identify with the demands of this opposition (early elections, establishment of a pluralist-parliamentary political system, no sweeping economic socialist "experiments"). Generally, the opposition suspects that the FSLN, after accepting a transition phase marked by tactical considerations, will actually attempt to establish a state and social system based on Marxist principles. A part of this opposition has become radicalized and has, after leaving the country, called for the overthrow of the revolutionary regime by force. A perfect example of the radicalizing process is the bourgeois party MDN (Movimento Democrático Nicaragüense); the chairman of the party, Alfonso Robelo Callejas, was a member of the first governing junta. The only *comandante* who has joined this opposition is Edén Pastora Gómez.

But even though this opposition in Nicaragua today is at a disadvantage, there are still other elements of a system of checks and balances that put limits on any FSLN concentration of power. Only one member of the supreme court belongs to the FSLN. This institution is a kind of bastion of power of the conservative party PCD, to which the majority of its members belong. Since there still is no constitution, the supreme court does not function as a constitutional court. However, in the role of a kind of supreme administrative court it has demonstrated certain independence. For example, it rescinded some acts of expropriation by the institute for agrarian reform because they did not conform to the law.

The smaller parties that have entered into a governing coalition with the FSLN also perform a limited control and criticizing function. Here the leftist Catholic PPSC (Partido Popular Social Cristiano) and the Independent Liberal party (Partido Liberal Independiente) deserve special mention. Their criticism and legal initiatives contributed, in the course of consultations in the State Council, to the liberalization and democratizaton of an FSLN draft of a law on the function of parties.

The private sector enjoys a certain veto power in the mixed economy of Sandinist Nicaragua since its investment behavior determines to a considerable degree the course of the whole economy. One also must not forget that the organizational-political hegemonic ambitions of the FSLN are limited to the lower and lower-middle classes and that the established upper-class interest groups continue to exist.

The very powerful Nicaraguan Catholic church places limits on the power aspirations of the FSLN and has adopted a critical stance toward its activities. The bishops have energetically resisted attempts by leftist priests and Catholic groups to identify the church with Sandinism. Rather, they lean toward the political positions of the internal opposition.

It is also possible to uncover elements of pluralism, rather more potential than real, within the Sandinist camp itself. The Sandinist people's organizations are relatively independent from the state. They receive only small state subsidies and are financed for the most part by membership fees and contributions from foreign nongovernmental institutions. They employ only a few poorly paid full-time and part-time functionaries. For the most part, they exist on the volunteer services of their mostly young members, who cannot just be ordered, but must constantly be motivated to perform their work. One wonders if the Sandinist people's organizations could not in certain circumstances play a more autonomous role vis-à-vis the Sandinist state and the FSLN. They could perhaps function as elements of limited pluralism within the Sandinist camp. This camp is not the least held together by the feeling that all are threatened by the danger of foreign intervention. If, for example, after the next presidential elections in the United States the Sandinist camp no longer needs to feel like a defense community struggling for survival, then the differences and divergences within the Sandinist movement will probably become more obvious.

Finally, it should be pointed out that Sandinist Nicaragua, as confirmed by the Human Rights Commission of the Organization of American States, can boast a positive balance in its liberal human-rights policy. In this respect it differs very favorably from "democratic" El Salvador or "predemocratic" Guatemala, both of which are considered by the Reagan administration to be allies against "communist" Nicaragua.

Toward What Form of Government Are the Sandinists Heading?

In the end it is difficult to answer the question of what kind of state and socioeconomic order the Sandinists would like to see in Nicaragua. Any attempt to do so must of necessity be of a speculative nature.[9]

According to their own statements, the leading Sandinists had prepared no "blueprint" for the period following their takeover. Rather, they had concentrated almost totally on the problem of deciding which strategy and tactics, under the leadership of the FSLN, would succeed in toppling the Somoza regime. Most of the basic decisions in post-Somoza Nicaragua were made without the benefit of a firm plan, under tremendous time pressure, and without long discussion.

The leading Sandinists are Marxist-oriented socialists who have adopted certain of Lenin's views on power politics as their own. Neither the Sandinists nor their Tercerista wing can be characterized as social democrats, since they do not have the social-democratic penchant for a parliamentarian-pluralist system. In my opinion, however, it would be false to impute to the majority of them an orthodox Marxism-Leninism that aims single-mindedly, although through a tactical transition phase and via certain detours, at the establishment of a communist state-party model. Rather, it would seem that the majority of Nicaragua's revolutionary elite cultivates a quite open and undogmatic Marxism. The Sandinist elite, although several of its members lived for some years in Cuba, cannot be labeled as Marxist scribes.

Whoever in the guerrilla camp had read not only Lenin's "What Is To Be Done?" and "The State and Revolution" but also other works had already earned the reputation of being a true Marxist intellectual. Since 1975, many faithful Christians (priests and lay people) have found their way to the FSLN. These are often people who accept Marxism less as a doctrine than as an analytic method. (At least one-fourth of the members of the *asamblea sandinista,* the second-most-important organ of the FSLN after the National Directorate, have such a Christian, in part directly theological, background.) There has been little systematic schooling in orthodox Marxism within the FSLN. Texts by Sandinist *comandantes* like Carlos Fonseca Amador, Jaime Wheelock Román, Humberto Ortega Saavedra, and Carlos Núñez Téllez form the backbone of the political education of the FSLN cadre. And these texts cannot be labeled orthodox Marxist. The fact that the leadership of the FSLN is composed of a politico-*military* elite to which ideological zeal is not of primary importance lends the Marxism of the FSLN a certain pragmatism and flexibility. In judging questions of power and in estimating domestic-

and foreign-policy maneuverability, the *comandantes* until now have demonstrated considerable sobriety.

I have the impression that when the *comandantes* confess—at times even publicly—to being "Marxist-Leninist," they mean more or less the following.

1. The FSLN should remain in power because during the civil war it demonstrated the validity of its claim to leadership and because it alone possesses the ability, the intelligence, and the "maturity" (*madurez,* a term the young revolutionary elite of Nicaragua delights in using) to make the "revolutionary national project" a reality, thereby freeing Nicaragua from social misery, social injustice, and imperialistic domination. The *comandantes,* however, do not seem quite certain in what form the FSLN should remain in power. Nor are they sure how much power and autonomy of other, chiefly opposition groups, would be compatible with the claim of the FSLN to be the country's avant-garde.

2. The "bourgeoisie" should be given no opportunity to return to power.[10] A return of the bourgeoisie is unacceptable because it could imply the threat that Nicaragua would once again become dependent on the United States—the result could be a "Somozism without Somoza." The bourgeoisie is seen as a class that has lost forever any right to political leadership and that should be satisfied with the right to economic profit conceded to it by the revolutionary state. It would seem that the *comandantes* are not yet quite sure which social groups are to be considered bourgeois and how they are to be kept from political power or allowed a certain participation.

3. "Socialism" for the time being is translated with the term "social justice." An experiment is underway to test which economic system will distinguish itself in the given circumstances through efficiency, productivity, and social justice. If, given these criteria, the present mixed economy proves successful, it will probably be maintained. Should it fail, then given the international circumstances, it will sooner or later probably be replaced by a socialist planned economy.

The basic attitude of the FSLN toward the question of elections further exemplifies and concretizes its position. The FSLN still does not know which kind of electoral system should be adopted nor to what extent opposition parties should be given a chance to compete. It is certain that an electoral mode will be sought that will guarantee the FSLN a majority. In the viewpoint of the FSLN, elections in revolutionary Nicaragua should not be a "lottery" in which the bourgeoisie and the opposition parties would have any chance to win. On the other hand, the elections certainly should not lack a certain element of competition and choice. In general, as discussed earlier, elections are not considered the most important characteristic of democracy, and the Sandinists consider the holding of elections more an international obligation to which they have agreed and which they must now carry out than an urgent national commitment.

In summary: The FSLN certainly will not consent to a parliamentary democracy that offers the opposition parties and the allied bourgeoisie any chance to come into power. The fact that the entrepreneurs and the government of the United States so vehemently demand the establishment of a parliamentary democracy is taken as proof by the FSLN that this form of democracy must be understood as the political order designed to assure the dominance of the class opposition. One cannot assume, however offhand, that there is a dominant tendency within Nicaragua's revolutionary elite inclined to form a monopoly party. Past affiliation with any of the three historical tendencies within the FSLN reveals little about the present political attitude and long-range goals of the individual actors. Thus any attempt to classify *comandantes* or ministers as moderate or radical leftists must be approached with considerable skepticism.

Chances for the Establishment of a Hegemonic Party System with a Limited but Secure Pluralism

The only political order that would normally be acceptable to the various conflicting groups is most probably one that does not gravely injure the basic interests of any important group. With this in mind, the problem in Nicaragua is to find a system of government that would satisfy the demand of the various political actors for a greater degree of expectation security or at least to fulfill their wish for a reduction of existing expectation insecurity.[11]

In all probability, the FSLN will not accept a parliamentary competitive democracy. Being a system of institutionalized insecurity, such a system contains the risk for the FSLN of losing power to the opposition, with all the thereby feared consequences. Of all the parties or movements, the FSLN probably enjoys the greatest popular support. That the FSLN, however, could possibly lose against a united bloc of opposition parties in the 1985 elections cannot be completely ruled out. Contrary to what had been assumed in the first economic plan and the first economic projections, in 1985 Nicaragua will probably be in a situation of severe economic depression. For various reasons the hoped-for growth rates did not occur, and the country has headed into an economic crisis. The factors in this crisis are unfavorable terms of trade for important export goods, an investment restraint on the part of the private sector, failures in planning and evidence of inefficiencies in the nationalized economic sector, natural catastrophes, reduction of favorable credit from Western industrialized countries, high state expenditures for the development of the social and education sectors as well as for the armed forces, high debt-repayment obligations, and general problems with the reshaping of the Somozist economic order.

Only in the 1990s will per capita income again return to its 1975 level, and individual incomes of the lower and middle classes will probably not grow during the next years. The FSLN could not and cannot fulfill, within the foreseeable future, the unrealistic—but at the same time very real—expectation of the lower classes that the revolution would bring immediate and lasting improvement to its social situation. Following the declaration of a state of economic emergency in 1981, the workers had to be forced to exercise restraint in their wage demands by the imposition of a strike prohibition.

If one adheres to the theorem of the diminishing political returns of "public goods," then it is doubtful whether the FSLN will be successful in maintaining the political loyalty of the lower classes merely by referring to its public social-reform measures (reducing illiteracy and expanding the educational system, free medical care, state-guaranteed low prices for basic foodstuffs, and so on). In addition, the FSLN, with its structural reform policy (nationalization, agricultural reform, tax reform) that until now has been restrained and moderate (not the least out of respect for the Western fear of communism), has been unable to satisfy its followers' expectations of radical reform. Given this constellation, if the private sector continues to restrain investment and if the Western countries do not offer higher credit, the FSLN could find itself forced to pursue a more radical political course.

Both the Western foreign countries and Nicaragua's entrepreneurs are interested in reducing expectation insecurity. Western industrialized states will probably grant more new credits and greater amounts of development aid only if the FSLN, through compromise, clearly and convincingly demonstrates that it will not establish in Nicaragua a more or less communist state and social order. Similarly, the entrepreneurs also justify their disinclination to heavy investment with the fear that the FSLN is striving for a communist order. In a conversation with me a representative of the COSEP (Consejo Superior de la Empresa Privada), the umbrella organization of the Nicaraguan entrepreneur associations, expressed the viewpoint that agricultural reform could be more radical if only there were some assurances that the FSLN would definitively adhere to a mixed economic order.

The Reagan administration's persistent demand for the introduction of a parliamentary democracy in Nicaragua while at the same time pursuing plans for the destabilization and possible overthrow of the Sandinist regime gives the opposition in Nicaragua the feeling that there could be a realistic alternative to the hegemonic claim of the FSLN in the foreseeable future. If the United States would drop its insistence on this specific form of democracy, which most probably is unacceptable to the FSLN, and be satisfied with a "Sandinist-dominated form of democracy," then the opposition camp might show a greater willingness to compromise with the FSLN in choosing a form of government, and the entrepreneurs might be willing to risk long-term investments.

A compromise over the form of government that could be acceptable to the opposition might, for example, contain the following elements designed to guarantee the existence of pluralism of independent parties: access to the media (right to freedom of opinion and criticism), public engagement in party activities (right to at least limited party-political mobilization), and the right to electoral participation and the right to reasonable representation on public bodies like the State Council or parliament. It would *not*, however, include the right to a takeover of government power following a possible victory in elections.

Various institutional practices are conceivable that would make it possible for the FSLN to remain in power and at the same time guarantee a limited political pluralism. For example, a parliament could be selected not only through elections but also according to corporatist principles, in such a way that the FSLN would retain governmental control with less than 50 percent but more than 40 percent of the votes. A consociational democratic transition arrangement—similar to the Colombian Frente Nacional—is conceivable. Prior to elections, it would set the number of parliamentary seats and under certain circumstances the number of cabinet seats to be allocated to the Sandinist camp (FSLN and its allied parties) and to the opposition camp. Under such a consociational democratic solution, elections would only decide the strength of the individual parties within each camp and not which camp would exercise exclusive political power.

My impression is that the majority of the FSLN elite is willing to find a system of government that guarantees not only the hegemony of the FSLN but also the continued existence of a limited but secure pluralism. Besides this subjective factor, which is always difficult to assess, there are also certain objective factors that further the willingness of the FSLN to come to some kind of arrangement with basic principles of Western democracy and to reach a compromise with the internal opposition over a system of government acceptable to both sides. The Eastern Bloc, in particular the USSR, does not seem willing to finance a "second Cuba" in Nicaragua. Therefore, if the FSLN does not wish to practice a "hunger socialism," it is dependent on Western credit, which will flow freely only under certain conditions. In the viewpoint of the FSLN the truly dangerous opposition that would support an overthrow of the Sandinists has already left the country. By continually vowing to retain a certain degree of pluralism, the FSLN is now committed to accepting a formula for political legitimacy against which it will be measured both domestically and internationally and which it cannot easily afford to violate.

The hostile policies of the Reagan administration vis-à-vis Nicaragua have on the one hand had a radicalizing effect on the FSLN by nourishing the fears that all internal opposition groups tend to agree with the anti-Sandinist plans of the United States government. On the other hand, this foreign threat could also induce the FSLN to seek a broad-based coalition, if possible even including bourgeois forces, that would be willing to defend the revolution against foreign intervention.

Notes

1. See Part 2 of this book.

2. For details, see Heinrich-W. Krumwiede, "Centroamérica vista desde Europa Occidental," in Donald Castillo Rivas (ed.), *Centroamérica: Más allá de la crisis* (Mexico, D.F.: Sociedad Interamericana de Planificación [SIAP], 1983), pp. 407–423.

3. See Chapters 2 and 3.

4. Howard J. Wiarda, "The Struggle for Democracy and Human Rights in Latin America: Toward a New Conceptualization," in Howard J. Wiarda (ed.), *The Continuing Struggle for Democracy in Latin America* (Boulder: Westview Press, 1980), p. 247.

5. Howard J. Wiarda, "Latin American Democracy: The Historic Model and the New Openings," in Wiarda, *The Continuing Struggle for Democracy in Latin America*, p. 288.

6. Quoted in George Black, *Triumph of the People. The Sandinist Revolution in Nicaragua* (London: Zed Press, 1981), pp. 255–256.

7. For details, see my article on Nicaragua in Peter Waldmann and Ulrich Zelinsky (eds.), *Politisches Lexikon Lateinamerika* (München: C. H. Beck, 1982), pp. 224–238. For descriptive analyses of the Sandinist regime, see George Black, *Triumph of the People;* Thomas W. Walker, *Nicaragua: The Land of Sandino* (Boulder: Westview Press, 1981); Thomas W. Walker (ed.), *Nicaragua in Revolution* (New York: Praeger, 1981); and Manfred Wöhlcke, *Gegenwärtige Tendenzen des sozioökonomischen und politischen Wandels in Nicaragua: Sozialistisch nach innen, blockfrei nach aussen?* (Ebenhausen: Stiftung Wissenschaft und Politik, 1982).

8. The Sandinists reject the accusation that they encourage the militarization of Nicaragua. Certainly the number of military and paramilitary forces in Sandinist Nicaragua is substantial when compared to the rest of Central America (according to estimates—there are no official figures—the armed forces number 25,000, and according to plan the militia should finally number 200,000 men and women). However, given the plans for destabilization and possible intervention by the United States and by Nicaragua's neighbors Guatemala, El

Salvador, and—in particular—Honduras in conjunction with anti-Sandinist Nicaraguan paramilitary groups (ex-Somozistas, etc.), the accelerated buildup of military and paramilitary organizations, which are trained primarily for defense, would seem quite understandable.

9. My analysis is based upon reading of the official newspaper *La Barricada,* various statements and speeches of the *comandantes* as published by Secretaría Nacional de Propaganda y Educación Política del FSLN, and a series of interviews with leading members of the Sandinist government conducted in fall 1982.

10. See, for example, Sergio Ramírez Mercado, "Los sobrevivientes del naufragio," in Asociación Nicaragüense de Científicos Sociales (eds.), *Estado y clases sociales en Nicaragua* (Managua: Centro de Investigaciones y Estudios de la Reforma Agraria, 1982), pp. 65–87.

11. Most stimulating in this context is the theoretical article by Adam Przeworski, "Some Problems in the Study of the Transition to Democracy," paper presented at the conference on "Prospects for Democracy: Transitions from Authoritarian Rule," Woodrow Wilson Center, Washington, D.C., September 25–26, 1979.

5
The Civil War in El Salvador

Harald Jung

Negotiations Offer the Only Way for a Solution

Since the January offensive in 1981, the guerrilla force in El Salvador has gained such a military strength that only massive support from the United States could save the Salvadorean army from defeat. However, in spite of this support, as of October 1982 the army has not been able to crush armed resistance. For about the last year, the military situation can be described as being in a state of "strategic equilibrium."

In September 1981, France and Mexico declared their recognition of the Salvadorean guerrillas as being at war with the regime and began a diplomatic offensive to solve the conflict on the basis of negotiations. The possibility of such a solution was proposed by the Frente Democrático Revolucionario/Frente Farabundo Martí de Liberación Nacional (FDR/FMLN). Thanks to French and Mexican diplomacy, this solution was also subsequently supported by the governments of Sweden, Holland, Denmark, Ireland, Greece, Yugoslavia, and Algeria; by the Socialist International; and by numerous Democratic and Republican members of Congress and senators in the United States.

The Reagan administration and the Salvadorean junta, at that time composed of the Christian Democrats and the military, saw the first step toward a solution of the conflict in holding an election for a National Assembly. Due to the actual state of war and anticipated corruption concerning the election, the left opposition boycotted the election carried out in March 1982, in which only the middle-right, right-wing, and fascist parties took part. Voter participation was high. But in May and June 1982, the Catholic University in San Salvador, Universidad Centroamericana (UCA), published a detailed study that indicated that approximately half the ballots counted had been given up after the polling stations had closed and that massive manipulation and intimidation had taken place during the election.[1] Even the chairman of the election committee, Jorge Bustamante, admitted that the election had been manipulated.[2]

The election resulted in a defeat for José Napoleón Duarte, president at the time, and for the Christian Democrats, who only managed to win twenty-four of the sixty seats in the National Assembly. Thirty-six seats were gained by the five extreme right-wing parties that had formed around the Partido de Conciliación Nacional (PCN), the former military party, and the fascist Alianza Republica Nacionalista (ARENA), led by ex-major Roberto D'Aubuisson, who had been expelled from the army for attempting to overthrow the government several times. In April, the right-wing majority elected D'Aubuisson as president of the assembly. Giving way to pressure exerted by the United States, which was worried about the international reputation of a possibly right-wing government, Alvaro Magaña, an independent conservative, was elected by the National Assembly as provisional president of the republic. However, all significant positions of public office were given to members of the extreme right, so that D'Aubuisson is in fact still the dominating figure in the background.[3]

Despite the fact that the government was taken over by the extreme right, the FDR/FMLN still stuck to its proposal of finding a solution to the conflict through negotiations. It has been attempting to make contacts with government representatives since June 1982 in order to discuss this possibility. At the same time, the guerrillas declared that they had taken on the reform program of the first civil-military junta of October 1979 (see section on the 1979 and 1980 juntas) as their program and thought that they thus had found a platform on which all political fractions and the Salvadorean army, with the exception of the extreme right, could meet.

After the leader of the FDR, Social Democrat Guillermo Ungo, in Mexico in October 1982 made an official offer to negotiate, only the extreme right and its representatives in the government categorically rejected this offer. José Napoleón Duarte's Christian Democrats and the Reagan administration were prepared to discuss the proposal made by the FDR, although only under certain conditions and with restrictions.

A solution based on negotiations, which additionally would become part of an extensive effort toward peace negotiations in the Central American region (being undertaken at present by Cuba, Nicaragua, Mexico, and Venezuela[4]), seems to be within the realm of possibility. In order to determine the limitations, conditions, and practicability of such negotiations, a knowledge of the political and social background surrounding the conflict and of the dynamics of inner political developments in El Salvador is necessary. I shall attempt to convey these briefly in the following account.

Stability and Dynamics of the Traditional Military Regime

From the time the military took over power in 1931 until approximately 1972, the strength of the regime was based mainly on two things:

- the alliance between the military and the coffee plantation landowners, who also gained control of industry and trade in the 1960s[5]
- a policy of selective social reform and repression serving to divide the middle and lower social sectors

While the military maintained control over the position of president and all politically relevant ministerial positions, the coffee landowners took control of the economically relevant positions and even withdrew some of these completely from state control. This applied especially to all state measures concerning coffee cultivation and trade; these were subsequently put under control of the coffee landowners' organizations and no longer under that of the ministry for agriculture. The same was true for the Central Reserve Bank and the Banco Hipotecario, which controlled agricultural credits. The distribution of these competences remained the same through all changes of government until the 1970s. Political differences between those prepared to discuss reform and the repressive forces ranged in all directions throughout both groups of this military-landowner alliance.

The combination of these two forces resulted in a policy that led to privileges for a few groups in the middle and lower sectors of the population and reforms carried out in their interests, but at the same time to ruthless suppression of other sectors. In this way, the regime was able to prevent the development of a united opposition front and to win the support of large parts of the population, especially among the poor and exploited.

This policy arose out of the socioeconomic development during the 1940s, 1950s, and 1960s. The expansion of the cash crops of coffee and cotton and the increasing concentration of capital in these two areas, both at the expense of the traditional hacienda and land-leasing systems, had varied results. On one hand, the small tenants were expelled from their land and the small farmers were forced to live in poverty. On the other hand, the agricultural population gradually became proletarian. Finally this resulted in a replacement of permanent employees by seasonal and migrant workers.[6]

Only a small number of the unemployed agricultural workers streaming into the cities could find employment in the capital-intensive industrialization process of the 1960s, which was largely export oriented due to the opening up of the Central American market. This meant that a continuously growing part of the urban population was forced to work in marginal jobs and thus to live in poverty. At the same time, a new urban middle social sector that arose, composed of independent workers and those employed in public-service branches, soon became the advocate of democratic political demands.[7]

As a result of this socioeconomic development, new social groups arose: peasants and landless farmers, permanent plantation workers, seasonal workers, migrant workers, farm workers, street tradespeople and small business people, industrial workers and urban marginal workers, a new urban middle social sector, and so on. The different interests of these newly arisen groups were cleverly used to prevent the development of a united opposition front by following the policy of selective social reform and repression.

Selective Social Reform and Repression

In the 1950s, the industrial workers were allowed to form trade-union organizations on a relatively free basis for the purpose of representing their reform and wage demands. A minimum wage legislation and the beginnings of a social-welfare system for industrial workers were introduced; however, trade unionists who were working toward an overthrow of the regime were persecuted, imprisoned, and assassinated. In this way, the military government party was able to keep the biggest trade unions among the urban workers on friendly terms with the government. In the country, on the other hand, all forms of trade-union organization were illegal. However, while the masses of *colones* (those doing forced farm labor in exchange for private land use), farm workers, and farmers had no protection and consequently suffered from the expansion and capitalization of the large agricultural export crops, the government was able to create a small middle social sector living in the country by introducing state credits and a price-control system for basic foods.

This policy was extended in the 1960s to include three additional points. First, in the country, where all forms of trade-union organization remained illegal, the permanently employed farm workers became more privileged than the seasonal and migrant workers through the introduction of social and minimal-wage legislation. Second, as a result of the industrialization process, a new middle social sector arose in the cities. The regime granted this sector the right to found its own parties. The urban workers were only allowed to form organizations for the purpose of trade-union demands. Revolutionary, militant workers were still persecuted and murdered. The left gained a certain amount of freedom of speech in the universities. Third, although autonomous forms of organization remained illegal for those living in the country, the military began to build up the paramilitary organization ORDEN (Organisación Democrática Nacionalista) among the country people. Members of ORDEN were given special privileges: (1) small farmers belonging to ORDEN were offered loans under favorable conditions, (2) seasonal workers were often given permanent employment, and (3) ORDEN members were employed to carry out the work on government-initiated projects. The socioeconomic fractioning of the population in the country was thus strengthened by a political fractioning. In return for their privileges, ORDEN members kept an eye on the villages and reported every attempt at organizing made by the farmers and farm workers to the regime.

In the beginning of the 1970s, one-tenth to one-fifth of the agrarian population was in some way connected with ORDEN. Discord between members and nonmembers of ORDEN arose in every village. Thus, the generals had found a way to derive a political advantage out of the poverty of the agrarian population.

The success attributed to this policy is characterized by Salvadorean social scientists as follows: "The society has been transformed into a conglomerate of people fighting against each other for survival, without reflecting who their real enemies are and without taking these into consideration. . . . The society has disintegrated and is organized according to a battle-array."[8]

Political Organization in the Traditional Regime[9]

The policy of selective reform and repression determined the development and organization of the various political forces, both those that supported and those that opposed the regime. Among the armed forces, two poles developed—one more reformist, the other more repressive. The National Guard, the National Police, and the Customs Police, whose officers were tightly connected to the large landowners through various forms of corruption, always belonged to the repressive fraction. Within the army itself, both poles were represented, alternately controlling the power by overthrowing each other—in 1944, 1948, 1960, 1961 and 1972—although neither fraction was able to completely exterminate the other while it was in power. Among the fourteen largest bourgeois families in the country, the De Solas became the advocates of a democratic turning during the industrialization process of the 1960s.

The opportunity allowed by the regime to demand reforms was made use of by the parties that were mainly supported by the urban middle social sectors and that fought for their aims within the constitutional framework. The Partido Demócrata Cristiana (PDC), founded in 1960, not only demanded democratization of the regime but also replacement of capital-intensive industrialization with worker-intensive industrialization and the right to organize for the country population. The party was also able to gain significant support among the urban workers. And it was the Christian Democrats and priests who built up the first illegal farmer and farm-worker organizations out of which the revolutionary mass organizations grew in the mid-1970s.

Social Democrat and socialist positions were advocated by the Partido Acción Renovadora (PAR), which gained strong support among the urban workers in the election of 1967 and was declared illegal for this reason. With this step, the attempt at democratization and institutional reorganization aimed at by the landowner-military bloc in the Constitution of 1962 was nipped in the bud. Thereafter, the Social Democratic forces in the PAR joined together in Movimiento Nacional Renovadora (MNR) founded in 1964-1965; the left-wing socialists in the PAR together with the communists founded the Unión Democrática Nacionalista (UDN) in 1968-1969.

Radicalization of the Political Conflict

The traditional regime was relatively stable because it ruthlessly suppressed part of the population on one hand and on the other hand allowed another part—the workers and the middle social sectors in the cities—a limited amount of freedom for reform and political activity. The extent of this freedom has been continuously reduced since the beginning of the 1970s, leading to a radicalization of parts of the reform-oriented forces and to the development and expansion of revolutionary forces. There were several reasons for restricting this margin for reform:

- In the first half of the 1970s, a quantitative growth of the industrial working force was accompanied by a continuously decreasing real wage. Restricting the politics of the trade unions to dealing solely with wages, which had been successful in the 1960s, had reached its limits.[10]
- Honduras closed its borders after the war between Honduras and El Salvador in 1969. The social situation of the Salvadorean agrarian population thus worsened as the emigration of landless farmers to the relatively thinly settled Honduras was no longer possible. The struggle for land was intensified since the outlet through emigration was now closed.
- Diversion of the agrarian migration into the cities caused a sudden rise in the marginal population and consequently an increase in potential social conflict.[11]

- The reform parties PDC, MNR, and UDN united to form an oppositional front, the Unión Nacional de Oposición (UNO), for the presidential election in 1972. They won a majority of the votes and could only be prevented from taking office through massive manipulation of the election and through an overthrow of power by the military. The reform forces had grown to be a factor threatening to the system for the landowner-military bloc and thus could no longer be tolerated.

The result of all these events was an increasing radicalization of part of the opposition force. Although the UNO took part in eleven "elections" (up to 1977), parts of the UNO, especially parts of the trade-union movement, had given up hope of bringing about change through elections. The Catholic Farmers' Federation (Federación Católica de Campesinos Salvadoreños—FECCAS), together with other trade unions, founded the mass organization Frente de Acción Popular Unificada (FAPU) in 1974. FAPU wanted to work together with the reformist forces, combining parliamentary with nonparliamentary struggles, to fight for minimal improvements in living conditions and for democratic rights. In 1975, FECCAS separated from FAPU because the farmers' federation no longer saw any hope of succeeding by going through parliamentary channels and working together with reformist forces; they joined together with the farm workers' trade union, Unión de Trabajadores del Campo (UTC), and several other urban trade unions to form the largest existing mass organization, the Bloque Popular Revolucionario (BPR). BPR concentrated its activities in mobilizing and organizing workers, farmers, and students.

Parallel to the mass organizations, three small but well-organized guerrilla groups had developed: in 1970, the Fuerzas Populares de Liberación (FPL); in 1972, the Ejército Revolucionario del Pueblo (ERP); and in 1975, the Fuerzas Armadas de Resistencia Nacional (FARN). These groups strove to establish a basis among the people, especially in the cities. They succeeded in doing so by recruiting students and union-organized workers forced to go underground due to persecution of even solely reformist trade unions. The masses joining these forces, which no longer only demanded reforms within the regime but strove toward destroying the regime, gained steadily from the mid-1970s onward. This constantly increasing popularity can be attributed to three things.

1. The regime continually diminished the possibility of carrying out reform and persecuted even the most moderate oppositional forces with increasing rigorousness. The continuing economic crisis intensified the struggle between labor and capital, forced an ever-growing portion of the population to live a marginal existence in poverty, and led to a radicalization of even the traditional trade unions.

2. The regime lost its ability to act uniformly and began to disintegrate into blocs operating uncoordinately. This made it impossible to carry out the traditional policy of selective social reform and repression (already made difficult because of the economic crisis). The extreme right wing of the regime not only turned against the opposition and the constitutional forces of the old landowner-military bloc but also prevented every attempt at reform proposed by the military regime, which was already extremely repressive. Thus, a very moderate agrarian reform, which was to ease the social tensions in the eastern cotton regions, was rejected in 1975–1976 because of the determined resistance of the agrarian oligarchy, the employer federations, and the extreme right wing of the military and security forces. At the same time, the extreme right began to build up its own terror squads, which raged and rioted, above all among the country people.

3. The extreme right was able to get Gen. Carlos Humberto Romero elected as president in the "elections" of 1977, in which the UNO also took part, by means of fraud and by having the military occupy the polling stations. A mass movement under the leadership of the UNO in support of the constitution and honest elections was violently destroyed by the military and the security forces; on February 28, 1977, demonstrators were massacred in the center of San Salvador. Thereafter it was certain that the political and constitutional way to democratization had failed.

Under the protection provided by the declared state of emergency, extreme right terror squads, almost all the security forces, the right wing of the army, and the hard-liners of the organization ORDEN (which had developed more and more from a reactionary-conservative mass organization toward a right-wing radical killer squad) began to systematically liquidate opposition persons and groups—not even hesitating to carry out mass massacres. Even members of the church and the great bourgeois family De Sola were not exempt from the persecutions. The mass organizations and the left guerrilla forces, both of which experienced an immense increase in growth rate after the failure of the constitutional way proved certain, mobilized against this terror from the right that was supported by the state and the majority of the bourgeoisie. The development of a civil war in El Salvador had begun.

The Carter administration put pressure on Romero to lift the declared state of emergency, which was done in May 1979, and to open up toward the moderate Christian and Social Democratic opposition in order to build a stabilizing middle bloc, thus preventing further polarization. The attempt to build a Foro Nacional failed because Romero refused to fulfil the conditions demanded by the PDC and the MNR, namely the disbandment of ORDEN and the right-wing terror squads.

Alternatively, the opposition parties, the trade unions in the cities, parts of FAPU, and the Liga Popular 28-F (which was formed after the massacre on February 28, 1977) joined together to form the Foro Popular and worked out a common platform. The first signs of cooperation between the moderate oppositional parties and the radical mass organizations had begun to appear.[12]

For the mass organizations, the victory of the Sandinists in Nicaragua was proof of the fact that a determined people are able to subvert a military dictatorship. In September 1979, the rioting increased to such an extent that civil war seemed to be unavoidable.

The Juntas of October 1979 and January 1980

In May 1979, Col. Ernesto Claramount, a Christian Democrat leader living in exile in Costa Rica, had already appealed to the constitutional sectors of the army to overthrow the regime. Preparations for an overthrow of the regime were carried out after June 1979 independently by three military groups: (1) the young constitutional officers organized by Col. Adolfo Arnoldo Majano Ramos, who intended to carry out extensive reforms; (2) a pro-U.S. fraction of the army, which wanted to introduce moderate reforms that could be utilized to defeat the mass organizations at the same time; and (3) an extremely reactionary fraction organized by Gen. Carlos Humberto Romero, Major D'Aubuisson, and the police force, which—in collaboration with the oligarchy—intended to suppress all forms of reform.

After the young constitutionalist officers led by Colonel Majano Ramos succeeded in taking over power in October, the United States put them under pressure to include Col. Jaime Abdul Gutiérrez and Col. José Guillermo García, as representatives of the pro-U.S. fraction, in the governing regime or in the cabinet. The new government also included representatives of the UNO parties, Christian humanist intellectuals, and representatives of the bourgeoisie. The mass organizations remained excluded from the new government. The junta's program was aimed at the establishment of a parliamentary democracy based on a market economy with larger social components. An agrarian reform and a reform of the financial system were planned; it was stressed, however, that private property was to be guaranteed.[13]

Aside from the junta, a second power bloc existed; it consisted of a network of the extreme right in the army and the security forces. This organization, Agencia Nacional de Servicios Especiales de El Salvador (ANSESAL), which had been built up by Romero since January 1979 and had survived Romero's overthrow, controlled the secret services and the security forces, ORDEN, and the right-wing terror organizations. The members of ANSESAL held the most important positions in the army, obeying orders given by a hierarchy independent of the official chain of authority and operating behind the backs of the official authorities.[14] This extreme right cooperated with the oligarchy and influenced the junta.

The power bloc of the extreme right intensified the persecution of the mass organizations. As a rule this was against the junta's orders, but it had the support of Colonel Gutiérrez (as a member of the junta) and Colonel García (as minister of defense). In collaboration with the employers' federations and with the conservative representatives of the bourgeoisie in the cabinet, the two colonels were able to prevent or undermine even the most moderate reform proposals. The reform-minded members of the junta and the cabinet were powerless against the alliance of the Gutiérrez-García fraction of the junta with the extreme right and the oligarchy. On January 3, 1980, these members resigned. The Christian Democratic PDC remained in the junta in the hope of being able to push through the planned reform program. However, blockage of the reforms and continuing intensified repression carried out against the population by the right-wing bloc and the Gutiérrez fraction led to growing criticism from PDC party members of the party's taking part in the government.

After the right had taken to assassinating even prominent leading members of the PDC (for example, Mario Zamora Rivas, leader of the Christian Democratic youth organization) and after the U.S. chargé d'affaires, James E. Cheek, put pressure on the Christian Democrats in January and February 1980 to utilize the agrarian reform for a "clean anti-subversive war,"[15] Christian Democrat Héctor Dada and PDC junta representative José Antonio Morales Erlich left the junta. José Napoleón Duarte from the party's right wing replaced Dada. From the tenth of March onward reform-minded Christian Democrats resigned from the government and the PDC. Some of them had to flee to other countries; some of them founded a new Christian Democratic party, the Movimiento Social Cristiano (MSC). Among them were—aside from Héctor Dada—Rubén Zamora Rivas (executive committee member of the PDC and ministro de la presidencia of the junta after October 15, 1979), García Billas (executive committee member of the PDC), Oscar Menjívar (Christian Democrat minister of economics), Eduardo Colindres (Christian Democrat minister of education), and Jorge Villacorte (Christian Democrat vice-minister of agriculture).

Loss of Power of the Right-Wing Christian Democrats

With the failure of the junta in October 1979 and January 1980, which also meant failure of the last attempt at reform, the reform-minded moderates joined the revolutionary left. In April and May 1980 the Social Democrats, the communists, the Christian Democrats of the MSC, the mass organizations, and the Christian-humanist representatives of the church, economic, and cultural circles joined together to form the Frente Democrático Revolucionario (FDR) under the leadership of Social Democrat Guillermo Ungo. The armed section of this opposition front is the Frente Farabundo Martí de Liberación Nacional (FMLN), which was formed in October 1980 by a union of the guerrilla groups that previously had operated independently from one another.

The right wing of the Christian Democrats remained in the junta under the leadership of José Napoleón Duarte. However, he never had decisive influence over the politics there; he served to give the junta a moderate touch in the international public eye but was powerless against the right-wing bloc both in and outside the government. This became obvious in February 1980, as junta member García planned a coup d'etat against the reform forces in the junta and the government (Majano Ramos and the PDC). The coup was prevented, but all officers who took part in the coup remained unpunished and continued to hold their positions.

In May 1980, a group of officers attempted to overthrow the government under the leadership of the extreme right-wing ex-major, D'Aubuisson,[16] who had been expelled from the army. The Christian Democrats threatened to resign from the junta if D'Aubuisson was not sentenced, and junta member Majano Ramos, at that time commander-in-chief of the army, ordered D'Aubuisson's arrest. However, the right radical minister of defense, García, let all those who took part in the coup, including D'Aubuisson, go free. The officers who were active in the coup were moved to other commanding positions. The Christian Democrats did not leave the government. Commander-in-chief Majano Ramos was removed from his position and replaced by junta member Gutiérrez. In September 1980, all Majano Ramos's followers in the army were removed from their positions; in December 1980, Majano Ramos was expelled from the army, and a warrant was issued for his arrest. As a result of these events, after the guerrilla forces began an offensive in 1981, many soldiers and officers of the Majano Ramos fraction joined the guerrillas.

After eliminating the Majano fraction in the army, the extreme right directed its offense against junta president Duarte's Christian Democratic PDC. The former agrarian reform program deteriorated to an instrument used to justify repression against the agricultural population and to a counterinsurgency program.[17] And then when the government actually gave a lot of land to the Christian Democrat–oriented farmers' cooperatives and members of the government's own Instituto Salvadoreño de Transformación Agraria, cooperatives were destroyed by the right-wing terror squads and the uniformed security forces, and leading members were assassinated (this was confirmed by the Christian Democrat vice-minister for agriculture after his resignation).[18] The economic oligarchy began a slander campaign against the PDC's and Duarte's *comunitarismo* (Christian Democratic ideology) as being the stepping-stone to communism;[19] D'Aubuisson openly mobilized his followers against "communism" in the PDC. The fact that even conservative Christian Democrat mayors were murdered after the elections in March 1982[20] was thus neither accident nor the work of misled followers, but part of a plan deliberately carried out by these right-wing forces. It was the logical result of an extermination campaign consequently carried out by the extreme right, which also formally holds the state power today.

Parallel to the actual loss of power of the right-wing Christian Democrats, the opposition front has gained in political importance as a result of its growing military strength; this has forced the government since September 1982 to be more open for negotiations. Although the army launched forty-six large-scale offensives against the guerrillas in 1981, it has been unable to wipe them out. Since December 1981 the military initiative has gone over to the guerrilla groups of the FMLN, which succeeded in increasingly demoralizing the army during the first three months of 1982. This transformed the FMLN army bit by bit into a regular army. Since June 1982 the FMLN army has been capable of defeating the regime's elitist brigades, which have been trained in and by the United States. Since their October offensive in 1982, the FMLN army has begun to attack and occupy strongholds of the regular army. A year before the FMLN had not even been in a position capable of defeating larger army troops in maneuver.[21]

Evaluation and Future Perspectives

The development since the failure of the October reform attempts in 1979 can be summarized as follows: (1) The extreme right has managed to seize the state power bit by bit at the expense of the Christian Democrats and Majano Ramos's fraction; (2) the revolutionary and reformist left united to form a common opposition front and thus gained a political and military strength that has made them as of yet undefeatable;[22] and (3) the Christian Democrat reformist wing joined the opposition front; the conservative fraction is politically isolated and also exposed to persecution carried out by the extreme right; part of the Majano fraction of the army joined the guerrilla forces.

The situation is therefore extremely polarized, with the left and the reform-minded middle (mass organizations, urban reform-oriented opposition parties and trade unions, the reform fraction of the former PDC, and part of the deserted military) being on one side and the extreme right (the oligarchy, the security forces, and the majority of the military) being on the other.

If both sides show the first signs of being prepared to negotiate,[23] then this is largely a result of the military situation, which as yet has not made the victory of one side over the other possible. A compromise between both sides concerning the actual questions at hand does, however, seem to be difficult to imagine. Even if it were possible to call an armistice and to bring the conflict onto a purely political level, free of violence, the question remains as to how the main problem behind this conflict can be solved. This central problem, as I have explained, is the socioeconomic development in El Salvador. The regime's traditional stabilizing method, the policy of selective reform and repression, has failed, and the basis for such a policy no longer exists. The reforms that were necessary for the economic system have always been violently suppressed by the oligarchy. Even today, the oligarchy does not appear to be prepared to allow even the most moderate reforms concerning the economy. For this reason, the opposition and the poverty-stricken sectors of the society that support the opposition had to resort to armed struggle. These sectors of the population, which are becoming increasingly poorer and at the same time more politicized, cannot do without these economic reforms, since they would then abandon the possibility of establishing a tolerably sufficient economic basis for their existence. An armistice, to be more or less acceptable, must therefore be accompanied by economic reforms. The basis for such a reform concept could be the program originally intended by the first military junta of October 1979: wide-ranging agricultural reform and nationalization of the banks and export trade.

This reform program of the first junta would meet with approval from the opposition front and the guerrillas as well as parts of the army. It is not possible, however, as an outside observer to estimate how large and influential the fraction of the army is that is prepared to discuss reforms after the expulsion and laming of the Majano fraction. Whether the parts of the army that were formerly more or less unpolitical have become politicized toward the right under the influence of the guerrilla war or whether they have become worn out, tired of war, or even aware of the problems of the country will play an important role with respect to their views concerning such a reform program. The guerrillas maintain that the reform program intended by the junta of October 1979 still has a significant basis in the army.[24]

The oligarchy and the extreme right would try to sabotage and prevent this program at all costs, as they have done in the past, and would have to be forced to accept this program by means of outside pressure. The Reagan administration, which has, up to now, definitely contributed to preventing these reforms through its policies and military assistance, will still play an important role. If it withdraws its support from the extreme right and forces the oligarchy to accept the necessary economic reforms, then a solution by means of negotiation is perhaps possible. If the Reagan administration continues to give the extreme right massive support, an end to the war in the near future cannot be expected.

Notes

1. UCA-Centro Universitario de Documentación e Información, "Elecciones: organización y votación," *Proceso,* nos. 66, 67, 68, 1982, San Salvador.

2. Cited from: Jesus Ceberio, "La mitad de los votos de las elecciones salvadoreñas fueron despositados fraudulentamente tras el cierre de los colegios," *El Pais,* June 10, 1982, Madrid.

3. UCA-Centro Universitario de Documentación e Información, "Alta tension politica, Batallas parlamentarias," *Proceso,* no. 61, 1982, San Salvador.

4. Hugh O'Shaugnessy, "Mexico and Venezuela Call for Peace Plan," *Financial Times,* September 17, 1982, Frankfurt and London.

5. George Black, "Central America, Crisis in the Backyard," *New Left Review,* no. 135, Sept./Oct. 1982, London, pp. 5–34, here p. 12.

6. More detailed in Harald Jung, "Class Struggles in El Salvador," *New Left Review,* no. 122, July/Aug. 1980, London, pp. 3–25, here p. 4ff.

7. Ibid., p. 8ff. More detailed in: Hugo Molina, "Las bases económicas del desarrollo industrial y la absorción de fuerza de trabajo en El Salvador," *El fracaso social de la integración centroamericana* (San José: EDUCA, 1979), pp. 218–275.

8. Estudios Centroamericanos–Editorial, "Apertura democratica, una salida a la crisis nacional," *Estudios Centroamericanos,* no. 359, September 1978, San Salvador, p. 683.

9. More detailed in Harald Jung, "Class Struggles in El Salvador," p. 10ff.

10. In the mid-1970s, 27 percent of those employed in urban areas were industrial workers. Jung, "Class Struggles in El Salvador," p. 9. In 1975, the real wage was at the same level as that of 1965. J. W. Wilkie and P. Reich, *Statistical Abstract of Latin America,* vol. 18 (Los Angeles: University of California, Latin American Center, 1977), p. 222.

11. Jung, "Class Struggles in El Salvador," p. 8ff.

12. See ibid., pp. 14–20.

13. Ibid., p. 20ff.

14. FAPU, *Polémica Internacional,* April/May 1980, San Salvador, p. 44ff.

15. Philip Wheaton, "La reforma agraria en El Salvador; Un programa de pacificación rural," *Nueva Sociedad,* no. 54, May/June 1981, San José and Caracas, pp. 192–220, here p. 204ff.

16. D'Aubuisson is presently leader of the right radical party ARENA and president of the National Assembly. His participation in assassinations and massacres was so obvious that he was even forbidden entrance to the United States until he won the "elections" in March 1982.

17. Wheaton, "La reforma agraria en El Salvador," p. 211ff.

18. Ibid., p. 210.

19. "Hinton warns off private sector," *Latin America Regional Reports, Mexico and Central America,* August 14, 1981, London, p. 4.

20. Beth Nissen, "El Salvador: At Last, Signs of Progress," *Newsweek,* October 18, 1982, p. 27.

21. This military evaluation is based on statements made in an interview by the leading FMLN commander Cayetano Carpio. (Cayetano Carpio, "El FMLN es ya un ejército regular," *El Pais,* October 23, 1982, Madrid.

22. The other side, however, continually maintains that the FMLN is on the verge of defeat and that it is only a matter of time before victory is won over the FMLN.

23. Nissen, "El Salvador."

24. Carpio, "El FMLN es ya un ejército regular."

6
The Salvadoran Military and Regime Transformation

Cynthia J. Arnson

On October 15, 1979, junior officers of the Salvadoran Army overturned the regime of Gen. Carlos Humberto Romero in a bloodless coup. The young officers—captains, majors, and lieutenants of the Young Military Movement (Movimiento de la Juventud Militar)—elected Cols. Adolfo Arnoldo Majano Ramos and Jaime Abdul Gutiérrez as representatives to a new governing junta. They turned to El Salvador's universities and opposition parties to select civilian participants in the government. On the day of the coup, the officers announced their program for a democratic and antioligarchic government in the Proclamation of the Armed Forces. They outlined profound economic and social changes and promised an end to the corruption and human-rights violations that had characterized the previous Romero regime.

Almost immediately, however, hard-line officers committed to maintaining the status quo maneuvered into key positions in the military High Command. Their opposition to the scope of the proposed reforms and their military commitment to eradicating the left led to the progressive alienation of reformist civilians in the junta. The first civilian-military junta collapsed on January 3, 1980, after scarcely 2½ months in office. Subsequently, power in the Salvadoran armed forces became increasingly concentrated in the hands of rightist officers, and civilian authority was largely symbolic. The policy of the United States—the primary objective of which was to support the Salvadoran military in its effort to wipe out guerrilla insurgency and subsequently co-opt "moderate" sectors of the left into an expanded "center"—served to reinforce the consolidation of power within the army at the expense of civilian members of the government and to stiffen the resistance of high-ranking officers to accepting a negotiated or mediated resolution of the conflict. Ultimately, the attempt of the Reagan administration to put a "democratic face" on a government dominated by the military opened the way for an extreme rightist takeover of politics.

Preliminary Observations

Before the coup of October 1979 the military had ruled El Salvador virtually without interruption since 1931.[1] The economic crisis of the 1930s, which precipitated a fall in coffee prices and widespread labor unrest in El Salvador, served as the backdrop for direct military intervention in politics. Before that time, the Salvadoran oligarchy, with an economic base in coffee, cotton, and sugar, held both economic and political power.

In crushing the Salvadoran peasant uprising of 1932 (resulting in the deaths of twenty to thirty thousand peasants), the new head of state, Gen. Maximiliano Hernández Martínez, spelled out in blood what would be a principal mission of the armed forces—defense against an "internal enemy," or "communist subversion," of the existing socioeconomic order. Arbitrary violence, repression, and wholesale corruption by the military have been steady features of Salvadoran politics ever since.

To maintain the socioeconomic order, special branches of the armed forces, all under the command of the minister of defense and public security, served as political and rural police.[2] The security forces—the National Guard, the Treasury Police, and the National Police—along with a wing of the army, consistently identified with the most reactionary sectors of the oligarchy and opposed all political and economic reform. To extend its control over El Salvador's predominantly rural population, the leadership of the security forces created and sustained paramilitary spy networks in rural areas (ORDEN). The defense ministry, through local military commanders, also oversaw the activities of civil-defense patrols whose membership overlapped with that of ORDEN and of the Army Reserves. In addition, members of the security forces doubled as assassins for right-wing death squads such as the Unión Guerrera Blanca (UGB), Anti-Communist Armed Forces of Liberation (FALANGE), the Organization for the Liberation from Communism (OLC), and the Maximiliano Hernández Martínez Brigades.[3]

The military monopolized formal political power for close to fifty years by dominating the official parties: the Partido Revolucionario de Unificación Nacional (PRUD), founded in 1948, and the Partido de Conciliación Nacional (PCN), founded in 1961. Even though the military allowed civilian parties to participate in local elections and control municipal administrations (which the Christian Democratic party did during the 1960s with great success), they maintained control at a national level, doing so through massive electoral fraud, most notably in 1972 and 1977.

Within the military itself, power relationships and patronage were rooted in an informal system of overlapping alliances and loyalty based on *tandas* (one's graduating class at El Salvador's military academy). A look at the composition of the High Command following the coup of October 1979 illustrates the force of these relationships. Although the coup was promoted by junior officers, positions of power were assumed by representatives of four graduating classes: José Guillermo García (minister of defense), class of 1956; Nicolás Carranza (vice-minister of defense), Carlos Eugenio Vides Casanova (head of the National Guard), and Jaime Abdul Gutiérrez (junta member), class of 1957; Rafael Flores Lima (army chief of staff) and Adolfo Arnoldo Majano Ramos (junta member), class of 1958; Carlos Reynaldo López Nuila (head of the National Police), class of 1959.

Although the political and economic order imposed by the military served the interests of a tiny elite, the armed forces' relationship with it has not been fixed. In the 1940s, a sector within the army emerged with limited conceptions of military professionalism and modernization; it was somewhat influenced by the United States, but also coincided with the development of a Salvadoran industrial and export sector. Coups led by Andrés Ignacio Menéndez (1944), Rafael Córdova Rivas (1948—the time of the Oscar Osorio government), and junior officers (1961) represented this more progressive and developmentalist outlook, but constitutionalist sectors of the military never succeeded in introducing reforms that structurally challenged the power of the landed oligarchy (hence the failure of a modest land reform proposed by Col. Arturo Armando Molina in 1975). The seizure of power by Gen. Carlos Humberto Romero in 1977 placed the most conservative sectors of the military back in control, at a time when the system needed to open, not shut down further. The electoral frauds, the activities of grass-roots Catholic clergy, and the growing militancy of mass-based popular organizations had severely eroded the legitimacy of the regime.

The Coup of October 15, 1979

The Nicaraguan revolution—and its success—provided the backdrop for a shifting consensus within the Salvadoran Army over how to prevent a similar kind of revolutionary upheaval in El Salvador. Three distinct, and to a certain extent contradictory, notions of "how to save the system" emerged within the military.[4]

Three Groups Within the Military

One wing—identified with General Romero, Maj. Roberto D'Aubuisson (former National Guard chief of intelligence), and the leadership of the security forces—opposed all reform, rejected any opening of the political system, and preferred to eliminate the left through sheer repression. It was this group that temporarily "lost out" on October 15. Approximately sixty officers of this group were subsequently purged from the armed forces (only to link up more formally with ultrarightist organizations such as the Frente Amplio Nacional and later the ARENA party and eventually return to political power).

A second group, which Colonel Majano Ramos symbolized, located the roots of instability in El Salvador in the country's unjust socioeconomic structure. The core of younger officers, which numbered around sixty, recognized that the institutional survival of the armed forces rested on carrying out basic changes in the country. The ideas set forth in the October 15 Proclamation of the Armed Forces—structural economic reform, the end of human-rights violations, and democratization based on political compromise with the left—reflected the reformist vision of the Juventud Militar. While promoting political "openings" and economic reforms, however, the younger officers also endorsed selective military campaigns to eliminate guerrillas who persisted in their efforts to overthrow the system as reforms were being carried out.

Junior officers responsible for the October coup formed the Consejo Permanente de las Fuerzas Armadas (COPEFA) as a political body within the army to ensure that the principles of the proclamation were carried out. Because COPEFA was composed of junior officers, however, it never succeeded in establishing its authority over senior commanders, who actively worked to prevent COPEFA from assuming the political function it was designed to serve.

The third group within the military—modernizing "hard-liners"—ultimately emerged as the most powerful and dominant. Associated with Col. José Guillermo García and junta member Col. Jaime Abdul Gutiérrez, these officers, although formally endorsing the Proclamation of the Armed Forces, did not subscribe to the scope of the proposed reforms. (Those they reluctantly endorsed, such as the agrarian reform, were seen only as elements of a counterinsurgency strategy and further opportunities to involve the army in corruption.) They viewed as the first priority a series of military actions against the left, in order to liquidate the guerrilla movement and destroy or neutralize the mass organizations. In this effort, they overlapped most clearly with the goals of the security forces, with whom they became increasingly identified.

Internal Power Struggles

The period of the first civilian-military junta (October 15, 1979–January 3, 1980) was consumed by an internal power struggle in the armed forces. Civilian members of the junta and the cabinet acted primarily as a "pressure group," articulating demands but lacking the power to carry them out. Civilians were not consulted when Colonel Gutiérrez selected Colonel García, former director of the telecommunications network Asociación Nacional de Telecomunicaciones (ANTEL), as minister of defense. García subsequently appointed all the heads of the security forces; in addition, he appointed his former subordinate at ANTEL, Colonel Carranza, to be his vice-minister of defense. García and Carranza found their most natural ally in the junta in private-sector representative Mario Andino, who as head of El Salvador's Phelps Dodge subsidiary had been the sole provider of copper cable to ANTEL.[5]

Several events during the tenure of the first junta help to illustrate the pattern of civilian-military relations, as well as the struggle within the military.

1. Repression at the hands of the security forces soared in the first weeks of the junta, with the rate of civilian deaths exceeding that of the last nine months under General Romero. Said junta member Guillermo Ungo, "our principal grievance . . . is that the Army continues to view as the enemy not the rural oligarchy, but the organizations of the left."[6] Some, including El Salvador's Archbishop Oscar Arnulfo Romero y Galdamez, suggested that the increase in repression reflected a conscious strategy of the security forces to undermine confidence in the junta's ability to govern. Whether this is true or not, it is clear that civilians in the junta, along with Colonel Majano Ramos, were adamant that the security forces be brought under control, but were incapable of halting the violence.

2. Conservatives in the military set out consciously to erode the power of COPEFA, spreading rumors that it had not been elected democratically and forcing a second vote that resulted in the election of numerous members of the security forces. By December, García was claiming that "we have succeeded in controlling [COPEFA] and converting it into a body of administrative consultation."[7] García also often refused to consult with Majano Ramos in matters relating to the ministry of defense.

3. The younger officers, distrusting the left (which stepped up its attacks immediately after the October coup), did not side with civilians in the government to purge hardline commanders in the military and push through with reforms. Out of a sense of insecurity, institutional loyalty, and—some say—disorganization, they refused to take any action

that would threaten the unity of the armed forces. Rightist elements within the army capitalized on the fears of the junior officers by staging acts of sabotage and blaming it on the left. In one incident, members of the security forces killed two soldiers in the San Carlos barracks, leaving behind guerrilla propaganda in an attempt to demonstrate to enlisted men "who the real enemy was." Officers protested to Colonel García, who threatened them to keep the matter quiet.[8]

On December 28, 1979, twenty-one cabinet ministers and vice-ministers issued an ultimatum to COPEFA citing the "displacement of power which has signified a rightward swing in the political process"[9] and demanding that the junior officers assert their leadership within the armed forces and reaffirm their adherence to the principles of the coup proclamation. COPEFA responded on January 2, 1980, saying that

> COPEFA is not a political body, but rather a special one representing the Armed Forces, constituted to MAINTAIN THE UNITY OF ALL THE ELEMENTS THAT MAKE IT UP. . . . [Capitalization in original] The body for political communication between [the junta]/and the Armed Forces is the Ministry of Defense. . . . It is the obligation of the people and their Armed Forces to defend their achievements and avoid the destruction of the Republic, and hence of its Armed Institution. . . . The proposals of the document in reference are not our responsibility, and an attitude of intransigence could generate unpredictable results, putting in danger the process of change initiated . . . and creating a situation of unfortunate consequences for the Republic.[10]

By the next day, civilians in the junta and all but one in the cabinet—Colonel García—had resigned.

From January 1980 on, the idea that progressives in the military dominated the armed forces and were committed to a process of structural reform was largely a myth. Subsequent events, most of them taking place during the period of Christian Democratic participation in the junta, further illustrate the pattern of isolation of the Juventud Militar:

- Officers, including members of the High Command who were implicated in a right-wing coup in February 1980, went unpunished and retained their command posts.

- Majano ordered the arrest of rightists, including retired Major D'Aubuisson, for plotting another coup in May 1980. The Christian Democrats threatened to withdraw from the government if D'Aubuisson was not "tried and sentenced." García then released D'Aubuisson, and the active duty officers arrested with him were transferred to other posts without prosecution. The Christian Democrats remained in the government.

- The armed forces voted in May to replace Colonel Majano Ramos with Colonel Gutiérrez as head of the army.
- Colonels García and Gutiérrez issued in September an "order of battle" removing virtually all the supporters of Majano from their command posts. Majano was not consulted in the order.
- Majano was expelled from the junta in December and then ordered arrested for not complying with an order to accept the post of military attaché in Spain.

Subsequently, in January 1982, García, Gutiérrez, and National Guard chief Carlos Eugenio Vides Casanova were self-promoted to the rank of general. Gutiérrez effectively disappeared from the political scene in mid-1982, following national elections that resulted in the naming of three vice-presidents (a position held by Gutiérrez when José Napoleón Duarte was appointed president). It was rumored that Gutiérrez had become too identified with the Christian Democrats and clashed with the leadership of the new Constituent Assembly.

The Role of the United States

The United States turned its attention to Central America while the Nicaraguan war was underway. Two currents—both conditioned by the desire to prevent further revolutionary upheaval in the region—emerged that shaped policy toward El Salvador. On one side were the Pentagon, CIA, and the National Security Council, which urged a reinstatement of military aid to General Romero in June 1979 as trouble for the regime was deepening.[11] (Aid had been suspended in 1976, after Salvadoran Army Chief of Staff Manuel Rodríguez Ramos was convicted in New York of trying to sell millions of dollars worth of armaments to undercover agents he thought were members of the U.S. Mafia.[12] On the other side was the State Department, uring limited political reforms (the advancement of elections and a political amnesty) to defuse the rising tensions. Ultimately, the two strains merged into pressures within the context of military aid to "professionalize" the armed forces and upgrade their equipment. The coup in October 1979 was met with great optimism, for it promised to initiate a process of controlled reform while keeping the armed forces institutionally intact.

After the coup, however, U.S. emphasis on law and order (as articulated by then Ambassador Robert Devine and Assistant Secretary of State for Inter-American Affairs William G. Bowdler) and the postponement of economic aid were significant factors contributing to the rightward swing in the military.[13] Levels of U.S. military assistance to El Salvador before the coup had been extremely modest ($16.7 million from 1950 to 1979) and remained limited during the first junta. Symbolically, however, they took on great importance: The first U.S. material response to the change in government was a shipment in November 1979 of riot-control gear and a four-member Mobile Training Team to train troops in riot control.[14] (Later, a U.S. Defense Survey Team visited El Salvador without the knowledge of civilian members of the junta.)

The logic of providing such aid complemented the interests of the Salvadoran military, even if riot-control equipment did not have the desired effect. In the U.S. view, excessive brutality on the part of government troops had to be controlled, for it served to further alienate the population from the regime (as Nicaragua had forcefully demonstrated). For the Salvadoran military, however, the incentive to control violence was nowhere near as great as the recognition that the United States "needed" them if the left was to be controlled. U.S. aid provided during the Carter administration never succeeded in having an impact on the actual behavior of government troops, even though, in the face of charges of excessive brutality on the part of the regime, the Carter administration declined for over a year to provide overtly lethal weapons.

The insistence of U.S. officials on a more refined version of counterinsurgency also served to alienate civilian members of the Salvadoran government. The proposal made by U.S. chargé d'affaires James E. Cheek to the Christian Democrats in February 1980 for a "clean anti-subversive war" and the sending of U.S. military advisers were principle factors in the decision of Héctor Dada to resign from the junta in March, as well as in the decisions of other leading Christian Democrats to leave the government and the party shortly thereafter.[15]

Military assistance, even though not achieving the desired reduction in official violence, did have a certain impact on the perceptions of the armed forces as to the kind of war they were waging. In February 1980, U.S. opposition to a coup from the right was based on the assessment that a right-wing coup enhanced, internally and internationally, the long-term prospects of the left in El Salvador. The political participation of civilians in the government and the existence of a reform program, if only on paper, was essential to maintaining the regime's legitimacy—and to obtaining approval in the United States for further military assistance. Although the formal coup ultimately did not take place, in many respects it was unnecessary—those involved retained their command positions. (It is important to note here that the United States did not single-handedly stop the February coup. Officers in the central San Carlos barracks reportedly threatened to revolt if the coup took place. The High Command decided not to risk splitting the armed forces.)

The introduction of the agrarian reform in early March 1980 represented a shift on the part of the High Command to support of the reform project only insofar as reforms were part of a counterinsurgency strategy with political as well as military components.[16] That the armed forces would use the agrarian reform for purely military ends, moreover, became clear in the actual behavior of government troops in the first days of the effort. Lands were seized as military units spread throughout the countryside after the declaration of a state of seige and assassinated peasant leaders, suspected members of peasant unions, and newly elected representatives of state-organized peasant cooperatives.[17] In the name of supporting the reform, the United States was willing to provide critical transport, communications, and night-vision gear.

Aside from the ostensible "leverage" that military assistance provided the United States, it filled concrete logistical needs. This was especially true in the areas of mobility and communications infrastructure. Low levels of training began to be remedied by a crash program for Salvadoran officers at the U.S. Army School of the Americas in Panama. As the war intensified, the United States provided virtually all of the weapons needs of the Salvadoran Army, including a new air force following a guerrilla raid on Ilopango Air Force Base in January 1982. A massive training effort to create one-thousand-member rapid reaction airmobile battalions began in March 1982.

The period of "non-lethal" assistance to the Salvadoran military ended during the last days of the Carter presidency, after the left had begun its major military offensive against the regime. In the space of four days, the United States leased to El Salvador several helicopters, released five million dollars in aid that had been suspended after the December murder of four U.S. churchwomen, and provided another five million dollars in emergency funds to purchase lethal weapons—rifles, ammunition, grenade launchers, hand grenades, and so on.[18]

The supplies were publicly justified by the Carter administration on the grounds that the guerrillas were receiving substantial quantities of sophisticated arms from Cuba and the Soviet Union through Nicaragua, a theme that would be taken up with vigor by the incoming Reagan administration. The shipments contributed significantly to troop morale (even though U.S. officials later claimed that the equipment was not used in putting down the January offensive) and sent a strong signal to the Salvadoran military that the United States would give them what they needed to "do the job."

The decision of the Reagan administration in March 1981 to send additional quantities of lethal materiel and fifty-six noncombat advisers confirmed the earlier Carter message, while adding a new twist: It posed El Salvador as a test case of U.S. determination to counter Soviet and

Cuban aggression worldwide, thus demonstrating U.S. resolve to defend its global interests. But both the political and military strategy pursued by the Reagan administration contributed to the continued polarization of Salvadoran politics in 1981 and 1982 and held no prospect for ending what became a generalized situation of war.

The Conduct of the War

The failure of the guerrillas of the Farabundo Martí National Liberation Front (FMLN) to achieve their stated objectives during the January 1981 offensive led to a premature "triumphalism" on the part of the Salvadoran Army and U.S. policymakers. The failure to spark a popular insurrection and topple the government led U.S. policymakers to conclude that the guerrillas lacked popular support and that defeating them was essentially a question of drying up foreign supply lines. But by late 1981, predictions of early success had dissolved into statements of concern over a military "stalemate."[19] Indeed, according to a report in the *Washington Post*, "the Salvadoran Army appears to have lost control of approximately one-fourth of its territory to guerrilla forces. . . . The 'stalemate' was broken some time ago and the guerrillas of the Farabundo Martí National Liberation Front are now gaining ground faster than government troops can hold it."[20]

From late 1981 onward, U.S. military strategists appeared to have adopted a "guardedly optimistic"[21] medium- and long-term view of the war, one relying on continuous and intensive training of Salvadoran recruits and officers, a change in army war-fighting tactics, and a steady upgrading of the equipment (and especially air power) of the Salvadoran Army. The aim, in the words of Assistant Secretary of State for Inter-American Affairs Thomas O. Enders, was to reduce the guerrillas to the level of "banditry" while solidifying El Salvador's nascent "democracy" and moving toward the presidential elections of 1984.[22]

Perhaps the greatest source of conflict, however, between the United States and the leadership of the Salvadoran Army was over the kind of tactics to use in fighting guerrilla warfare. Minister of Defense José Guillermo García sided with most local brigade commanders in refusing to adopt the "small unit tactics" or saturation patrols advocated by the Pentagon—a way of confronting the guerrilla army using its own methods. Instead, García continued to throw large concentrations of troops into battle against rebel strongholds, a strategy that invariably led to heavy army—and civilian—casualties. In rejecting U.S. advice, García reminded U.S. military officials that they had lost in Vietnam and therefore had no business telling the Salvadorans how to fight.[23] (Ironically, Lt. Col. Sigfredo Ochoa—the one officer promoted by the

U.S. Embassy as an example of someone who had effectively used small unit patrols in Cabanas province—was a political ally and former classmate of Roberto D'Aubuisson.) Ultimately, the massive U.S. training efforts may result in a politically significant cleavage within the army, a cleavage between young officer cadets and troops versed in Pentagon counterinsurgency doctrine and their senior counterparts who adhere to traditional theories of conventional warfare.

U.S. optimism over the course of the war resurged in March 1982 following the disorganization of guerrilla efforts to respond to the national elections. But major guerrilla drives in June, October, and November succeeded in throwing the army on the defensive; during the October campaign the FMLN extended the number of towns under its control in the northern provinces of the country, disrupted transportation on El Salvador's two major highways, blacked out half the country in sabotage operations designed to pin down and disperse the armed forces, and inflicted what General García admitted were "heavy casualties" on the army.[24] In response, the army in November unleashed six thousand troops in Chalatenango province in the largest—and for the most part unsuccessful—counteroffensive in the history of the war. And for the second time in fewer than five months, Honduran troops participated massively in the assault by sealing their common border with El Salvador and allegedly entering Salvadoran territory itself.

The Political Crisis and Implications for the Army

The elections of March 1982 deepened the political crisis of the regime by providing the vehicle for a return of the ultraright to political power. The elections had originally been conceived as a way of legitimizing and strengthening the rule of the Christian Democrats and especially that of José Napoleón Duarte. In fact, the Christian Democrats, although winning the largest share of votes, were consistently outweighed and overruled by a coalition of right-wing parties in the National Assembly, led by Assembly President Roberto D'Aubuisson.

As a consequence of rightist domination of the political apparatus, the army was forced to resume direct participation in the political process. Generals García and Gutiérrez, under pressure from the U.S. Embassy, were instrumental in preventing the assembly from naming D'Aubuisson as provisional president of the country, a post that ultimately went to one of three army candidates, banker and lawyer Alvaro Magaña.[25] After the assembly suspended key portions of the agrarian reform (provoking a storm of protest in the U.S. Congress and threats of an aid cutoff), key military commanders, including García, made highly visible appearances in which they gave land titles to peasant beneficiaries and restated their commitment to the reforms.

What emerged, then, as a personalized conflict between the leadership of the army (García) and the rightist leadership of the assembly (D'Aubuisson) was in essence a conflict of two alternative concepts of organizing the Salvadoran state. One was reformist, recognizing that a military victory over the guerrillas could be achieved only with a measure of popular support due to a process of reforms; the other was oligarchic, pursuing a military victory while turning economic and political power back to those who had held it prior to 1979.

The role of the United States in Salvadoran politics was also a matter of great controversy. The fraction of the army represented by García recognized that continued U.S. military and economic aid (proposed by the administration but approved by a skeptical and contentious U.S. Congress) was contingent on upholding the reforms—at least in name—and preventing the more unpalatable political figures from assuming positions of national preeminence. Deference to political realities in the United States was thus little more than "enlightened" self-interest. The political and military sectors represented by D'Aubuisson, however, were anti-American to the point of autarky, believing that El Salvador could "go it alone" in its war against communism and deeply resenting U.S. pressures, which were decried as interventionist, proconsular, and imperial.[26] Underlying the D'Aubuisson rhetoric, however, was a calculation—perhaps not overdrawn—that the Reagan administration would support the Salvadoran government no matter what coalition ruled, rather than see the country overrun by Marxists.

As 1982 came to a close, sectors of the right-wing business community, emboldened by the new predominance of their representatives in the assembly, sought actively to promote a coup with the aim of returning El Salvador to the pre-1979 period of oligarchic domination. In a July communiqué condemning the murder of Salvadoran industrialist Nicolás Estebán Nasser, seven of the most powerful private-sector organizations "demanded of the High Command of the Armed Forces the carrying out of the Constitution and the Laws," and the demonstration of "utmost determination to end the anarchy which is drowning us in a sea of blood."[27] The accusation that "certain leaders of the Armed Forces" were not fulfilling their duties to maintain order and defend the constitution was, in effect, a call for their ouster. Later, in October, an anonymous document presumably authored by D'Aubuisson supporters circulated widely within the army and business community. It vigorously attacked all aspects of the reform program and especially the inability of the High Command to bring the war under control. García was singled out as an "accomplice of subversion."

Perspectives for the Future

Although predictions are always difficult—especially when existing information is incomplete—it is possible to identify several factors that may influence the political outcome in El Salvador.

First, should the right-wing regain—in fact and in name—formal control of the government and the armed forces, the war is likely to intensify. D'Aubuisson pledged during his electoral campaign to "exterminate the subversives within three months"[28] (including by use of napalm), and his direction of military strategy would undoubtedly include heavy—and indiscriminate—bombing.

Whatever military advantage might be gained, however, it would almost certainly be temporary and undercut by political factors. Even though civilian casualties would undoubtedly soar during a heavy counterattack, it is likely that the guerrillas, given current strength, could survive the onslaught. The political isolation of the regime would certainly accelerate, both inside the country and abroad, and the economic and military lifeline to the United States would likely be cut or restricted significantly. Finally, the group of officers loyal to Majano—as of late 1982 disarticulated and without leadership—could once again find in its opposition to the existing regime sufficient coherence to become a significant political actor.

Second, for a mediated solution to the conflict to succeed, at least two conditions would have to exist: The Salvadoran Army would have to think that it could not win, and the major international supporters of the regime would have to put their full force behind the negotiations. Given the attitude of the Reagan administration and Salvadoran right, neither condition seemed obtainable in late 1982. The Reagan administration, by opposing FDR/FMLN initiatives toward a negotiated settlement of the war, reduced its options for the future. The Reagan administration rejected the notion of a mediated settlement as proposed by the left (based on a restructuring of power relationships in the political, economic, and military spheres) as "refusing to give the guerrillas at the bargaining table what they could not win on the battlefield."[29] Instead, it urged the opposition to lay down its arms and participate in the existing electoral process. The lack of a viable political proposal thus led the administration to embrace an essentially military solution to the war, one the Salvadoran Army, because of its own internal contradictions, could never hope to achieve.[30]

The Reagan administration's policy rested on several flawed assumptions: that the elections of 1982 laid the groundwork for participatory democracy in El Salvador; that outside political, military, and ideological support for the guerrillas was more important to their effort than internal factors; that the army—with steady U.S. assistance—could win the war; and that the economy could revive without a comprehensive political settlement. This left room for essentially three alternatives. One was a continuation of the war over the next several years, with its resulting toll in human lives, economic destruction, and spiritual embitterment. A second, and related, alternative was the greater regionalization of the war as Honduran troops continued to come to the aid of their Salvadoran counterparts, prompting possibly a further response from revolutionary movements in Honduras and El Salvador.[31] The third alternative was a more decisive form of U.S. intervention in the event that a military victory by the left appeared imminent. (The possibilities of such an intervention—as well as its nature—would ultimately depend on a constellation of political factors within the United States, not the least of which would be the perceived congressional and public opposition, the predominance of domestic economic concerns over those of foreign policy, and the proximity to 1984 presidential elections.) A fourth outcome, the military defeat of the FMLN, may once have appeared a possibility, but no longer seems to be an option.

Notes

1. For background on this period, see Thomas Anderson, *Matanza: El Salvador's Communist Revolt of 1932* (Lincoln: University of Nebraska Press, 1971); Rafael Guidos Vejar, *El Ascenso del Militarismo en El Salvador* (San Salvador: UCA/ EDITORES, 1980); Stephen Webre, *José Napoleón Duarte and the Christian Democratic Party in Salvadoran Politics 1960–1972* (Baton Rouge: Louisiana State University Press, 1979); David Browning, *El Salvador, Landscape and Society* (London: Oxford University Press, 1971); and Amnesty International, *Assigning Responsibility for Human Rights Abuses: El Salvador's Military and Security Units* (London: Amnesty International, September 1982).

2. The National Guard was formed in 1912 out of the rural police that had been created in the late nineteenth century, in order to evict peasants from their land as communal properties were abolished by the new coffee-growing elite. (Browning, *El Salvador,* p. 357.)

3. According to Salvadoran Army captain Ricardo Alejandro Fiallos,

> it is a grievous error to believe that the forces of the extreme right, or the so-called "Death Squads," operate independent of the security forces. The simple truth of the matter is that *Los Escuadrones de la Muerte* are made up of members of the security forces and acts of terrorism credited to these squads such as political assassinations, kidnappings, and indiscriminate murder are, in fact, planned by high-ranking military officers and carried out by members of the security forces

(See Fiallos testimony in U.S. Congress, House Appropriations Subcommittee on Foreign Operations, Hearings, *Foreign Assistance and Related Programs Ap-*

propriations for 1982, 97th Cong., 1st sess., U.S. Government Printing Office, Washington, D.C., 1981.)

4. See Marcel Salamín, *El Salvador: Sin Piso y Sin Techo* (Panama: N.p., 1980), pp. 23–26; and Frente Acción Popular Unida (FAPU), *Polémica Internacional,* San Salvador, April–May 1980.

5. See Cynthia Arnson, *El Salvador: A Revolution Confronts the United States* (Washington, D.C.: Institute for Policy Studies, 1982); Carolyn Forché, "The Road to Reaction in El Salvador," *The Nation,* June 14, 1980; and Tommie Sue Montgomery, *Revolution in El Salvador* (Boulder, Colo.: Westview Press, 1982).

6. Quoted in Salamín, *El Salvador,* p. 31.

7. Ibid., p. 36.

8. Interview, Salvadoran Army officer in exile, Washington, D.C., April 1981.

9. "A la Fuerza Armada de la Republica de El Salvador, a Traves de su Organismo Representativo: El Consejo Permanente de las Fuerzas Armadas (COPEFA)," San Salvador, December 28, 1979.

10. "Al Pueblo Salvadoreño y a los Señores Ministros, Sub-secretarios, y Demas Funcionarios que Suscribieron el Documento Dirigido a la Fuerza Armada a Traves del Consejo Permanente," San Salvador, January 2, 1980.

11. *Washington Post,* August 2, 1979.

12. See *Union Leader,* Manchester, N.H., April 22, 1982; and Carolyn Forché and Leonel Gómez, "The Military's Web of Corruption," *The Nation,* October 23, 1982.

13. See, for example, Montgomery, *Revolution in El Salvador.*

14. Documents received by the author under the Freedom of Information Act.

15. Press conference by Rubén Zamora Rivas, Héctor Dada, and Alberto Arene, Washington, D.C., March 17, 1980, and subsequent interviews. It is interesting to note that Robert White, upon arriving in El Salvador as U.S. ambassador in March 1980, declared one of his principal objectives to be the removal of Colonel García as minister of defense. By late in the year, White was claiming that one could not "name names" as the basis for moving toward a negotiated settlement. White also pressured, unsuccessfully, for the removal of Treasury Police chief Col. Francisco Morán.

16. According to the logic, agrarian reform would erode the guerrillas' peasant base by addressing a basic grievance in rural areas—access to land. See also Alberto Arene, "La Reforma Agraria como Estrategia Politico-Militar de la Contrarevolucion en El Salvador," *Estudios Centroamericanos* (UCA, San Salvador), December 1980; and Amnesty International, "Press Release," London, March 16, 1980.

17. According to the proreform peasant federation—the Salvadoran Communal Union (UCS)—in December 1981, "at least 90 officials [of UCS]" and a "large number of beneficiaries" of the reform "have died during 1981 at the hands of the ex-landlords and their allies, who are often members of the local security forces," and more than twenty-five thousand sharecroppers or tenants had been forcibly evicted from their farms "in the majority of cases with the assistance of members of the military forces." (Memorandum from the Unión Comunal Salvadoreña—UCS—to President José Napoleón Duarte, December 10, 1981.)

18. For specifics on U.S. military assistance to El Salvador and Central America, see Cynthia Arnson, *Resource,* updates 1–7 (Washington, D.C.: Institute for Policy Studies, 1980–1982).

19. According to Lt. Gen. Wallace Nutting, head of the U.S. Southern Command, "I think we are now observing a stalemate. And in that kind of war, if you are not winning, you are losing." (*Time,* September 7, 1981.)

20. *Washington Post,* November 10, 1981.

21. Statement by Col. Mark Richards, spokesman for the U.S. Southern Command (Mexico City Daily Bulletin, August 22, 1982).

22. Testimony of Assistant Secretary of State for Inter-American Affairs Thomas O. Enders to the Senate Appropriations Subcommittee on Foreign Operations (question and answer period), July 15, 1982.

23. See, for example, interview with General García in *Diario Las Americas,* August 31, 1982, and testimony of former U.S. senator Dick Clark, House Foreign Affairs Subcommittee on Inter-American Affairs, August 10, 1982.

24. In an August 31, 1982, report to the Constituent Assembly, General García stated that army casualties had totaled 3,800 in Fiscal Year 1981/1982 (July 1, 1981 to August 30, 1982), including 1,073 dead, 2,583 wounded, and 144 captured. He added that the armed forces had been expanded by 80 percent during the fiscal year. Thus, the casualty rate was between 12 percent and 21 percent, an extremely high figure. (Centro Universitario de Documentación e Información, *Proceso,* No. 79, August 30–September 5, 1982; and *El Diario de Hoy,* September 1, 1982.)

25. On April 20, 1982, special U.S. envoy Gen. Vernon Walters (retired) arrived in San Salvador for meetings with the High Command and leaders of all the political parties. He carried a letter from then Secretary of State Alexander M. Haig stating that U.S. aid would be jeopardized unless politicians came to some agreement on an acceptable presidential candidate. See *Washington Post,* April 7, 17, 23, and 27, 1982; and *New York Times,* April 10 and 27, 1982.

26. The private sector issued a scathing attack on U.S. Ambassador Deane Hinton in early November 1982 following a speech in which Hinton blamed "the gorillas of the [right-wing] Mafia, every bit as much as the guerrillas" for "destroying El Salvador." (Quoted in *Washington Post,* October 30, 1982.) Prompting Hinton's comments was a Salvadoran judge's decision to release a Salvadoran lieutenant (who was also a former D'Aubuisson aide) arrested for the assassination of two U.S. land-reform workers from the American Institute for Free Labor Development and the head of the Salvadoran land-reform agency José Rodolfo Viera in January 1981. According to the testimony of two Salvadoran corporals, Lt. Isidro López Sibrian of the National Guard ordered the murders and army captain Eduardo Avila provided a gun to one of the assassins. After López Sibrian was released for lack of evidence, D'Aubuisson called him and Avila "good officers" and his friends. General García appeared to be under intense U.S. pressure to carry out the prosecutions, even though García is alleged to have been involved in the original ordering of the murders. (See *Washington Post,* October 8 and 10, 1982; and *New York Times,* October 6, 1982.)

27. *El Mundo,* July 14, 1982.

28. Quoted in *Washington Post,* April 3, 1982.

29. See Arnson, *El Salvador: A Revolution Confronts the United States,* p. 87.

30. An additional element that is likely to have a significant impact on the army's morale and will to fight is the FMLN's decision to turn captured prisoners over to the Red Cross, a procedure that began in mid-1982.

31. U.S. and Honduran officials claimed that individuals linked with the FMLN had been responsible for acts of terrorism within Honduras and that FMLN guerrillas used Honduran territory as a base of operations. They thus claimed that Honduran participation on the borders was in legitimate defense of national sovereignty. This, however, did not obviate the fact that U.S. officials actively pressed for greater Salvadoran-Honduran cooperation in the border zone and that Honduran officers were primarily motivated by the fear that a revolutionary triumph in El Salvador would jeopardize Honduran security.

7
Problems of Democracy and Counterrevolution in Guatemala

Edelberto Torres-Rivas

The Impossible Return

The popular struggles in Guatemala in recent years and the political crisis that has accompanied them present democracy as a program strictly linked to two orders of facts that are like two sides of a coin: the conquest of power, on the one hand, and the reorganization of the fundamental bases of society, on the other. The issue of democracy in Guatemala, therefore, concerns itself with finding out what are the prerequisites for the existence of democracy in backward societies where a democratic state of law has never existed and in which sustained policies of popular welfare have never been implemented.

Popular forces in Central America pose the question of democracy in a special and "distinct" way, not as a merely electoral issue, but as a social one. And I say distinct because in this region we are *not* currently witnessing the *first* symptoms of the deterioration of an authoritarian structure nor the first rays of a democratic dawn casting light into the dark dictatorial night. On the contrary, we are witnessing what in effect are the *last* manifestations of an authoritarian vigor that, having run its historical course, resorts solely to terror in order to survive.

The democratic reconstitution of bourgeois power was a concern of popular movements during the intense social activities of the postwar era. The struggle against the dictatorship of Jorge Ubico, which united all social forces of the nation, took as its banner respect for political liberties, for democracy, and for a constitutional state order. Not only the popular classes, but Guatemalan society itself, learned from the daily experience of these struggles that bourgeois democracy is not the only political form that the capitalist state assumes, and that the not inconsiderable economic growth that had occurred since 1950 and the corresponding effects of social differentiation and the multiplication of social interests had not in and of themselves created the conditions for representative democracy and a state of law. Thus the democratic demands of today's popular movements obey a different historical logic, and the programs for implanting democracy are, from the point of view of the established order, probably the most subversive of watchwords. But such democratic demands also constitute the heart and nucleus of the popular movement's program for social progress.

In Guatemala, democracy has never existed except in a scant and transient manner; it is difficult to reconstitute something that never was well structured to begin with. It would be a journey to no end and, moreover, useless. The question of democracy should rather be looked at in terms of the future. The actualization of that future will depend, among many other factors, on the coalition of social forces capable of implanting democracy and on the essentially popular nature of this coalition. The struggle for democracy forms part of the larger struggle for the construction of a new society, not in terms of the immediate development of socialism, which is a long-term task, but rather for the establishment of democracy as the fundamental feature of the new social order. The quest is for democracy and socialism in full articulation, without the sacrifice of either.

Politics and Power in a Situation of Crisis (1954–1963)

The nature of the Guatemalan state changed significantly as the result of a historic act that warped its bourgeois development: the defeat of the national-popular movement in 1954 at the hands of a military conspiracy representing an extremely conservative movement of landowners, inspired and directed by people from the United States. The 1954 overthrow of the Arbenz regime was less a strategic victory for the emergent local bourgeoisie than a tardy reprisal of traditional agrarian elites. What is certain is that the "victory" opened a large period of crisis and instability, which can be considered as a manifestation of the weakness of the dominant class. The turmoil following 1954 constituted a ratification of the difficulties of establishing democratic forms of power with the attributes that normally are inherent in bourgeois dominion: stability, legitimacy, participation.

That which was defeated in June 1954 began as a bourgeois program that sought to base itself on orthodox social forces and political styles. It was a momentary alliance of bourgeois classes of landowning origin, peasants barely beginning to organize, petite bourgeoisie who lacked political development—a group that could not remain united for a long period of time, but one that had the intention of assuring that capitalist development would have a national character and a popular base. Through the eyes of those who were convinced of the inevitability of the so-called bourgeois-democratic revolution in Guatemala, the 1954 debacle signified the end of an ideological illusion, along with the failure of a political strategy that relied upon the bourgeoisie to democratize society.

The period that began in June 1954 has been classified by forces of the left as a counterrevolutionary phase, a special form of bourgeois counterrevolution in which the bourgeoisie liquidated what was initially their own project. In this light, leftist forces interpret the preceding regimes of Juan José Arévalo and Jacobo Arbenz Guzmán (1944–1954) as democratic years, referring to the nationalistic and revolutionary character of the Arbenz Guzmán program and to the economic policies and political styles that favored the oppressed classes. But in Guatemala, just as in other underdeveloped societies where power is concentrated in the hands of rural landlords, the first political expression of class rapidly fuses with antioligarchic and antibourgeois sentiments and takes on the character of popular nationalism. It is not a merit of social backwardness, but its natural result, that the emergence of oppressed classes into politics occurs on behalf of nonpopulist causes. That is to say that even without having a clear class profile the organization of the 1954 popular movement was independent, resisted bourgeois pretensions of directing it, and in addition demanded a profound shift in political power rather than only an improvement in living standards. Citizen activists, as a result of the turmoil of mass politics, turned a reformist program into revolutionary conduct. And it was this that most frightened the dominant class, forcing the bourgeoisie to retreat.

The alliance of forces, united by the counterrevolution, could not manufacture a return to the past; that is to say, they could not promote the political restoration of a traditional dictatorship like that of Ubico. In the tradition of Central American political culture, this return would signify the reconstitution of the old-style personal dictatorship of one ambitious or influential *caudillo* (charismatic personal leader) or another, whose repressive actions would be backed by a landowning faction. The dilemma of reconstituting power was evident from the very first moment. I have already mentioned that it was not possible to reconstruct either the old landowning-commercial alliance, which had already forfeited its historical opportunity, or the popular-bourgeois pact that in 1954 had been defeated by the bourgeoisie themselves. The political crisis began as a struggle within the bourgeoisie that initially was disguised by the furor of the bourgeoisie's anti-*campesino* violence. Expropriated landowners took advantage of their property rights to punish those peons who, as beneficiaries of land reform, dared to be property owners, if only for a short period of time. The antipopular violence of the counterrevolution has marked the Guatemalan regime ever since, making it clear there is no victory more bloody than that achieved by a reactionary class.

Since 1954, Guatemala has lived in a situation of unresolved crisis. This instability, inherent in the protobourgeoisie's incapacity to fully assimilate the fruits of their political victory, has dangerously prolonged itself, with various effects. An *estado de excepción* has arisen, that is, a state confronting a situation of crisis, combating it by whatever means appear necessary and taking on whatever shape political tradition or circumstance permits it. The *estado de excepción* is a variation of a military dictatorship, emerging in response to a particular kind of political and economic crisis and characterized by its continuous difficulty in maintaining order by legal means. In general, the implantation of this state of exception presupposes an exacerbation of class struggle. In this case it is the growth of a disproportionate fear in the dominant class that, whether fact or fiction, will serve as the pretext for the assumption of an antidemocratic posture. The bourgeois counterrevolution constructs its own enemy.

The *estado de excepción* may "stabilize" the regime politically, but does not necessarily imply a solution to the crisis. Between 1954 and 1966, factions of the ruling class utilized the entire repertoire of resources and strategies to defeat their similarly bourgeois competitors. It is well known that Col. Carlos Castillo Armas became president through an uncontested election in which he received 485,531 votes (in comparison with only 369 against him). Before three years were up, however, he was assassinated in July 1957 by one of his closest collaborators. The assassination was followed by elections (October 1957) that were declared fraudulent and then by another election that ushered in the pseudo-democratic interregnum of Miguel Ydígoras Fuentes. That was interrupted by a coup d'etat in March 1963, after which a permanent state of siege was established until the March 1966 presidential elections. The recognition of the victory of lawyer Julio César Méndez Montenegro constituted the final episode. In a secret pact between the time of the election and the examination of election returns, the civilian government humiliatingly capitulated before military power. Méndez Montenegro did assume power, but from this moment on no doubt remained as to where the real power lay: the army.

The Epoch of Anticommunist Democracy

There are many reasons why in all of Central America and particularly in Guatemala the permanent organization of democratic politics has been difficult. Many aspects of the inegalitarian culture of the Spanish colony—forced labor, racial and ethnic superiority—prevailed until 1944 and continue even today to permeate Guatemalan social and ideological attitudes. Property requirements for voting formally ended with the liberal constitution of 1856, but the majority of Guatemalans who were unable to read (65 percent, according to the 1950 census) did not nor could vote for Arévalo's election in 1944. Thus, the dimensions of political participation were sharply limited.

The right to vote is only one indication of the existence of liberal democracy. The existence of competitive political parties and an independent press are also necessary. It is this democratic political culture that never had the opportunity to flourish in Guatemala nor to construct a tradition in which the constitutional division of powers, the equilibrium of their functions, and the legality of their jurisdictions were facts of daily life. What emerged instead was a strong and personalistic power and a legislature of ritual, almost symbolic, function. The arbitrary concentration of decision-making power in an executive appeared to be legitimized by the existence of a formal, albeit powerless, legislature. Thus, the authoritarian tradition grew with vigor. The constants were law with a merely ornamental function on the one hand and on the other the disorderly and arbitrary abuse of personal power. The dictator, whether civilian or military, was the human figure whose function was to negate democracy in this manner. Manuel Estrada Cabrera (1899–1920) and Jorge Ubico (1930–1944) were the embodiments of this model.

It is upon this antidemocratic base that the counterrevolution, since 1954, has established the rules governing the political game and the administrative process. The defeat of the popular forces in itself had antidemocratic consequences, and the new state power that arose in the wake of popular defeat constantly reaffirms its antidemocratic character. There is horror not only at the idea of the effective and independent participation of the masses, but at any kind of mass participation at all, even at the manipulation of the masses by bourgeois populists.

It is useful to mention a few factors that have been forced to conform to the limits of "anticommunist democracy." In the first place, a system of ideological domination has been brutally restored, in countervention of the liberal and secular tradition that had been established earlier in the centruy. The political resurgence of the conservative bourgeoisie was paralleled by a return of the Catholic church to power. It is difficult to tell whether it was the church itself or the bourgeoisie that brought this about. But both of them, aligned in the antipopular offensive, have converted themselves into obstacles to the genuine functioning of democracy. The constitutions of 1956 and 1965 gave the church legal standing with its accompanying rights and privileges and returned to it properties that the liberal revolution had given to the state eighty years earlier.

Properties, privileges, and the establishment of Catholicism as the official religion in the public schools were the benefits the church received for its support of the counterrevolution. In sum, the Guatemalan counterrevolution received extensive aid from the power and influence of the Catholic church; the state showed its gratitude by bestowing upon the church old privileges and new rights. And religious elements, politically motivated, nourish the anticommunist ideology.

The ideology of the anticommunist democracy is the second factor. Anticommunist ideology? The fact is that no conservative intellectual—no leader of the parties of the right—has been able to elaborate a coherent doctrine justifying the counterrevolution and its violent methods, much less a theory of power and society, and not even a partial assimilation of Spanish Falangist (Francoist) thought, which in its emotionalism and lack of inner logic more closely approximates Guatemalan anticommunism than does German National Socialism. The counterrevolutionary movement has no doctrine other than anticommunism, which in itself reflects the profound ideological poverty of the established order. But with the implantation, in the aftermath of 1954, of a profoundly antidemocratic system, the fight against communism has turned into a fight against democracy.

A third important factor of the nondemocratic system of domination is a readjustment of the position of bourgeois groups both in civil society and in the state apparatus. In Guatemala, class-party-state relations were never organic. In fact, the Guatemalan right had lacked a good and coherent party organization before 1954. Between 1954 and 1980 only two parties survived on the national level: the Movement of National Liberation (Movimiento de Liberación Nacional—MLN) of the extreme right and the Christian Democrats, whose political opportunism led them to articulate a moderation that was unable to convert itself into an alternative political model. After 1958 the Revolutionary party emerged. Linked to the left in its early days, it later shifted to the center where it lost all political credibility, and finally moved to the right, in order to gain a share in the government. It is evident that no genuine party of the left could have functioned legally in the country.

Notwithstanding the importance of a party like the MLN, which is tenaciously supported by traditional landlords and is implacable in its definition of political enemies, the relationship of the Guatemalan bourgeoisie to the state is of a different nature. It occurs through the mechanism of producers' associations and chambers of commerce. In the Arbenz Guzmán epoch, the right-wing opposition utilized the Guatemalan Association of Agriculture, then the Chambers of Commerce

Table 7.1 Presidential Elections

Year	President	Total Votes In Favor	% of Victor	% Participation of Eligible Voters
1944	Juan José Arévalo	255,660	85	62
1950	Jacobo Arbenz Guzman	263,234	63	48
1958	Miguel Ydigoras Fuentes	190,972	38	Not known
1966	Julio César Méndez Montenegro	201,077	44	19
1970	Carlos Manuel Araña Osorio	251,155	39	26

and Industry, and since 1977, the Coordination Committee of Chambers and Associations of Commercial Agriculture. That is to say, it is a relation of class-association-state that has an inevitably corporatist flavor.

These circumstances permitted the introduction of semicorporatist forms in the relations between business organizations and the state. The organic network of the so-called interest groups consolidated itself very rapidly, despite its lack of previous history in Guatemala. Since 1954 the business associations have become something more than vulgar pressure groups; in effect they are the single most powerful channel for mediating between state and business power. The most important function of these business groups is control of production and commercialization in their corresponding areas of activity, which collectively gives them an inordinate degree of control over the nation's economy. Their economic and political power has created a form of articulation between state and class that has had profoundly antidemocratic consequences: The political vigor of these business interests and their monopolization of the nation's wealth is not counterbalanced by any force on the left. Moreover, political decisions no longer pass through the legislature or the political parties but instead through these corporatist channels.

This combination of factors makes the democratic game both difficult and unnecessary. Difficult because the means to incorporate the popular classes have not been established, unnecessary because the bourgeoisie's relationship with the state is a direct one, by means of the semicorporatist associations. These two factors, in turn, account for the lack of electoral participation (see Table 7.1, which was compiled from various newspaper reports) and the general limits to anticommunist democracy. There is no information on the 1974 and 1978 elections because they were so fraudulent that it has never been possible for the public to obtain the results.

In any case, from the statistics in Table 7.1 a few logical, even commonsense, deductions can be made. No president has been elected in Guatemala with more votes than Arbenz obtained; in the anticommunist democracy, in which only parties of the right participate, the growing tendency toward abstention underscores not so much the disinterest of the citizenry, but rather the devaluing of formal electoral proceedings in the minds of the people. The anticommunist presidents have been elected by what are actually minorities in both absolute and relative terms.

The Guatemalan *Estado de Excepción*

The coup of March 31, 1963, was important in the course of the national political history that has been sketched summarily, because for the first time the army *as an institution* assumed control of the government, suspended political party activity, annulled the 1956 constitution, and planted a power strategy of a new kind. The 1963 takeover is known as the Coup of the Thirteen Colonels because the decision to replace the constitutional president Ydígoras Fuentes was jointly taken by thirteen of the nation's military zone commanders. Col. Enrique Peralta Azurdia, the minister of defense, was named chief of state by the army.

Thus, the first *institutional* intervention of the army in Latin American history took place with the intention of bringing law and order to a society supposedly gravely threatened by left-wing subversion. The army's intention to restore order momentarily took on a Bonapartist face, if only in its explicitly stated objective of protecting the entire nation from "political selfishness and social corruption." This action by the army had numerous and significant implications for Guatemala's future historical development.

- The internal divisions within the armed forces ended, and with them a long tradition of personalistic coups.
- From that time on (1963), the army became the pivot of state power; military intervention was no longer a response to circumstance but a conscious strategy, with the aim of unifying the bourgeoisie and providing new resources for its continued class domination.

- The army began a counterinsurgency terror. The counterrevolution had utilized violence as its primary resource in confronting social problems since 1954, but after 1963 terror was applied in a systematic fashion.

The guerrilla movement began to take shape during 1961–1963. It took root in rural zones in the country's northeast between 1965 and 1966 and was temporarily crushed between 1966 and 1970. The guerrilla struggle provided the opportunity for the state to rationalize its defense of the system and to apply a new kind of violence, the violence of the counterinsurgency.

The new authoritarian stage permitted a relative advance in the stability of the *estado de excepción,* which this time was confronting a crisis of a different nature. In the face of this more serious crisis, the organization of the state assumed an ever more dictatorial form. From 1963 on, the military presence has been decisive and growing. It constitutes the dominant force within the state apparatus, even though the electoral ritual continues. Since 1966 there have been elections for president every four years and for members of congress and local officials every two years. The 1965 constitution, which strengthened the anticommunist tendencies of the regime, also created an institutional structure that lent it an apparent legality. But if one sees where the real, rather than formal power, was located, it becomes obvious that the constitution actually set up a military dictatorship in which military drill was the special apparatus of control. In turn, the military has joined with diverse bourgeois interests, so that the appearance of a civilian and political-party structure is maintained. In practice, the top hierarchy of the military operates in direct coordination with the highest representatives of the bourgeoisie. It unites with some and displaces others to form what in fact is the only real political party of the dominant class.

The *estado de excepción* in Guatemala is a counterrevolutionary state that utilizes all the material and ideological instruments of counterinsurgency. The ideology of counterinsurgency is distinctive in that it looks not for the defeat of the adversary but rather for total physical annihilation. The confusion between war and politics inherent in anticommunist ideology supports the resort to violence. This counterrevolutionary state is the most successful attempt since 1954 at constructing a system of domination that corresponds to a stage in which the popular movement has been defeated but in which the formation of the local bourgeoisie is incomplete. Yet the result has not been the one hoped for. Counterinsurgency violence has been prolonged beyond its function of exterminating guerrillas and instead has produced a resurgence of the left, to the point that today armed struggle has become generalized.

Although state terrorism may be able to neutralize the popular struggles, it can never succeed in securely establishing counterrevolutionary power.

The counterrevolutionary state is not the same thing as a fascist state, although it adopts some of the same methods. It is the bourgeoisie's form for the defense of the system in an extreme situation. Terror is seen as the only mechanism available in the face of the impossiblity of the bourgeoisie's achieving a hegemonic domination that will be accepted by consensus.

The Possibility of Democratic Change?

The crisis represented by the *estado de excepción* is not temporary and refers more accurately to long-term structural defects that permit us to speak of a "permanent exceptionality." As a result of the crisis it confronts and its lack of the social bases of support, it is not a strong state. The support of the army gives it only armed force. But this notwithstanding, it ought to be added that since the end of the seventies, a historical articulation of interests between the armed forces and the bourgeoisie has existed in Guatemala, by means of (or with the opportunity for) state control. It is necessary to specify that it is this unstable alliance of high-ranking military officers and certain segments of the bourgeoisie that, with the aid of a middle-class bureaucracy, can act to realize mutual political-strategic and socioeconomic interests.

It is a symbiosis of interests that does not have to be transient. For the military hierarchy, the direct link to large amounts of capital affords the opportunity for enhanced social prestige and an unheard-of personal enrichment. For the bourgeoisie, the link to the military and their influence in the government enables a new type of urgent and reckless capital accumulation, a capitalism that is savage but necessarily shortlived because all other values are sacrificed in the pursuit of profit. The alliance with foreign capital and the geopolitical situation of the country reinforce this symbiosis, hardening its defense of the status quo, which has become rigid in the face of change. But it would be wrong to draw the conclusion that this combination of interests forms a military bourgeoisie, which is a contradiction in terms. Nor is the composition of these business groups, with their Mafia-like conduct in the realms of production and competition, bourgeois in the traditional class sense. Rather, these are entrepreneur-adventurers whose pressing need is to reap fast and easy profits that they can ship abroad.

The question here is whether or not this power structure is durable. In principle, no authoritarian structure is capable of reforming itself unless outside forces propel the change. European fascism, for example, was destroyed only by World War II, and Latin American dictatorships since 1944 have been destroyed only by broad-based popular movements in which various social classes participated.

Is it possible for the counterrevolutionary Guatemalan state to internally evolve into some form of bourgeois democracy? This transition is not possible in Guatemala if one conceives of it as an internal movement, a self-dismantling of the state apparatus to make room for a participatory structure incorporating popular classes and their organizations and representatives.

But history always enriches theory. The Spanish experience is a good example of the political democratization of an authoritarian regime, but it occurred only after two or three generations and the death of Francisco Franco. The South American experience demonstrates in 1982 and 1983 that to aim at democratization of an authoritarian regime requires the fulfillment of at least three basic conditions: the exhaustion of the possibilities for the military to serve as a political force, a slowdown or halt in economic growth that creates pressure for a regime change, and the disappearance of the leftist "threat" from the political horizon. It is difficult to believe that democracy arises as the result of a formal electoral exercise, even more if that formality is the result of external pressure supporting "human rights."

Notwithstanding the nature of the politico-military alliance that in Guatemala explicitly began in 1966 (or perhaps after 1954), the fall of the government of Gen. Fernando Romeo Lucas García in March 1982 was without doubt an expression of crisis. It is a crisis in the interior of the reactionary pact, which exhibits all the weaknesses of the authoritarian model: international isolation and disrepute, administrative corruption, malfeasance in the conduct of public business. The abuses of the government of the Lucas García group raised the level of the contradictions of the Guatemalan political crisis to the point that in March 1982 the fraudulent election results, which always accord victory to a military officer, were not even respected by the military themselves. It should be emphasized that were it not for the strength of the popular armed struggle, neither the electoral fraud nor the coup would have been necessary.

Consequently, it is popular struggle that explains Efraín Ríos Montt's ascension to power. Perhaps a new period has begun in Guatemalan history. Until now, the chiefs of the counterinsurgency, prisoners of their own inflexibility, have been incapable of distinguishing between the democratic character of certain struggles and the revolutionary nature of others. For the fault of this Manichaean vision of society, the military men and bourgeoisie in Lucas's group completed the destruction of the political center, forcing a greater polarization in the social, political, and ideological life of the country.

The task facing Ríos Montt is to reconstitute—in the face of opposition from those within the state who continue to hold counterinsurgency positions—those political forces that will enable him to practice reformism of the right as an alternative way of limiting popular armed struggle. Several elements appear to be working in his favor: He is a general without troops under his command, a former Christian Democratic candidate for the presidency from whom the right fraudulently stole the 1974 elections, and a born-again Christian of the sect of The Word (which is linked to the North American group called Gospel Outreach).

Utilizing a hypocrisy-ridden rhetoric in the fight against corruption (not a single military officer has yet been charged or detained), Rios Montt has employed the formula that state terrorism uses as a justification until the very end: that to eradicate the guerrilla movement it is also necessary to destroy its social bases. Between June and September 1982, the Guatemalan army, with Israeli and U.S. military aid, began a "scorched earth" offensive against densely populated Indian zones where guerrilla groups had once been based. The offensive resulted in more than eight thousand deaths, including those of women, children, and elderly people. It is difficult to see how democratic processes benefited from such a genocide. Here we are witnessing something even more brutal than the violation of human rights; we are witnessing the systematic desecration of the most sacred values and customs of Indian culture.

The Ríos Montt government, which appears to be trying to express both the necessity and urgency of change, undoubtedly finds itself confronted by those obstacles intrinsic to the Guatemalan power structure that have been discussed at length in this chapter. And there appears to be no hurry to disarm this structure. Instead, there seems to be an intention to repeat what the Salvadoran experience has already proved: that reforms accompanied by repression do not favor change, in the same way that elections do not democratize political life.

The political crisis, which today includes both the internal structural factors and the particular international dimensions of the economic crisis, will continue into the foreseeable future. So will the struggle of popular forces that began long ago with the goal of creating a more just society. It is difficult to foretell what form democratic socialism will take in an underdeveloped agrarian society, which has, up to this moment, been ravaged by counterrevolutionary violence and the guerrilla response. But it is not difficult to maintain the conviction that neither socialism nor democracy can be sacrificed. That the obstacles inhibiting Central

America's ability to make an original contribution in the construction of a new society do not have only internal roots is part of the crisis. Until now, U.S. foreign policy, in its complicity with the Guatemalan right, has been unwilling to coexist with the processes of change in Central America.

8
Perspectives of a Regime Transformation in Guatemala

Piero Gleijeses

In June 1954 the government of the United States scored a signal victory by achieving, at very little cost, the overthrow of Guatemala's president Jacobo Arbenz Guzmán. Today, over a quarter century later, the Guatemalan people are still paying the heavy price of Washington's victory. Meanwhile, in the United States the Reagan administration appears eager to help maintain in the land of the quetzal what some irresponsibly term a "moderate repressive" regime.

The first part of this chapter examines the key characteristics of the Guatemalan state from June 1954 through the first year of the Reagan administration.[1] Within this period, particular attention is paid to two consecutive phenomena that appear to be in sharp contradiction to one another, yet unfold in logical sequence given the nature of the Guatemalan system: the timid "modernizing" attempt of 1974–1977 and the reign of terror of the Lucas presidency. I will then consider the U.S. response under four years of Carter, as well as at the outset of the Reagan administration, to the emergence of an armed opposition that not only threatens the "social tranquillity" of Guatemala (as had the guerrillas in the 1960s), but also, for the first time since 1954, endangers the very survival of the post-Arbenz regime.

The Legacy of the U.S. Victory over Arbenz

In 1953–1954, while clamoring for a U.S.-sponsored overthrow of Arbenz, many U.S. liberals urged that the Red President be replaced by a moderate leader, a Guatemalan Figueres. Such were the views of men like Adolf Berle and, in Costa Rica, José Figueres Ferrer himself. They argued that a Third Force (the magic "center" that liberals would later seek again in Guatemala and other countries of the Western Hemisphere) would be more satisfactory morally than a highly repressive regime; above all, it would far better guarantee, in the long term, the indispensable pro-U.S. stability.

As on later occasions, the liberals' argument, if sincere, showed a deep misunderstanding of the reality of Guatemala. There was no center in that country to serve Washington's interests. The middle class was too weak to play anything but an ancillary role. The only forces that could replace the Arbenz regime—and that had been desperately seeking its overthrow—belonged to those powerful landed groups who bitterly opposed any change that might affect, however slightly, their entrenched privileges. There was no realistic choice between a "liberal" and a "reactionary" coup against Arbenz Guzmán: The only choice was the one, of marginal significance, between Carlos Castillo Armas and Miguel Ydígoras Fuentes.[2]

For their part, despite their formal lamentations, the liberals preferred the overthrow of Arbenz, whatever the nature of the coup, to a continuation of his regime. In the same vein, nine years later, John F. Kennedy preferred a military coup in Guatemala to the "threat" of Arévalo's return to the presidency, and in 1980 the Carter administration, despite its criticism of the Lucas government, preferred that regime to the only realistic alternative, an eventual victory of the forces of the guerrilla focus and their civilian allies.

The Major Characteristics of the Guatemalan Political System from 1954 to 1982

The same logic that dictated the character of the coup against Arbenz has marked the nature of the Guatemalan political system ever since. The most important change within this system has not been emergence of different sectors of the bourgeoisie (agro-exporting, industrial, and commercial), but the shift in the relative importance of the military.

In the wake of Arbenz's overthrow, the army was the junior partner of the triumphant landowning class. Discredited and divided into a series of cliques, the army was stained, in the eyes of Castillo Armas's Liberacionistas and of its U.S. mentor as well, by its earlier toleration of Arbenz—a stain that its last-moment betrayal could not erase.

The alliance between the military and the bourgeoisie has continued to the present day. But the military has progressively become the senior partner in the alliance, acquiring in the process, particularly in the 1970s, its own independent economic base.[3] Having developed a relative degree of unity, the Guatemalan armed forces are now the country's strongest political "party," ruled by a "central committee" of a few senior officers. Throughout the 1970s, this "party" has determined the selection of Guatemala's presidents. As a result the other parties of the right (which now definitely include also the Partido Revolucionario—PR) have been reduced to a secondary role, and the presidential elections, already meaningless for a large majority of Guatemalans, are becoming increasingly meaningless for the "civilian" parties of the right as well. With this proviso, the key characteristics of the Guatemalan political system throughout the period can be summarized as follows:

1. Guatemala has lived under a *reactionary class dictatorship.*[4] The bourgeoisie have ruled the country, minor quarrels notwithstanding, in peaceful coexistence with the armed forces. The middle class, whose elements have been co-opted, cowed, or destroyed, has played no independent political role.

2. This reactionary class dictatorship has inflicted on the Guatemalan people waves of extreme violence (as in 1966–1968, 1970–1973, and since 1978) and periods of "moderate" repression (as in 1974–1977). The crucial factor affecting the swing of the pendulum has been the degree of challenge from below felt by the dominant class.

3. The political center has been emasculated or eliminated through physical violence. Whereas the Lucas government chose the latter approach, emasculation was the fate of Pres. Julio César Méndez Montenegro and his PR government in the 1966–1970 period—a period that marked the demise of the PR as a centrist force.

4. Guatemala's economy has experienced on average an adequate growth rate over the period. This growth has not been accompanied, however, by even modest social reforms.[5] This pattern of economic growth without social reform has resulted in a structurally weak economy with a limited internal market for domestic industry and, more importantly, has further exacerbated social tensions within the country.

In its first three years, the government of Kjell E. Laugerud García (1974–1978) took the unusual step of implementing some modest reforms: Notably, it provided financial assistance for cooperatives in the Altiplano. Moreover, beginning in the last months of the presidency of Gen. Carlos Araña Osorio (1970–1974), the repression acquired a more "moderate" character, and on repeated occasions Laugerud refrained from "settling" strikes through violence. The combination of these developments—so modest in another setting, yet so uncharacteristic of post-1954 Guatemala—afforded hope to elements of the political center and moderate left of an incipient opening in the ruling system that might lead, by the 1982 elections, to a degree of democratization without the need for a hard and bloody fight.

By 1978, however, it was evident that these had been naive hopes. The government's "modernizing" effort had assumed that a limited amount of circumscribed reforms, accompanied by a decrease in repression, would succeed in co-opting strategic sectors within the laboring force. But the reforms were too modest to allow such co-optation to take place to any significant degree. On the other hand, the slackening of the repression, the number of successful strikes, the hopes awakened by the government's timid steps—and the frustration that resulted from their shallow character—all contributed to increased radicalization of large sectors of the population. In the countryside, instead of a tame and government-controlled cooperative movement, the militant and politically conscious Comité de Unidad Campesina (CUC) rapidly gained strength. In the cities, by early 1978 the trade unions, although still weak, had reached their highest peak in numbers and militancy since 1954.

Thus, the Guatemalan ruling class faced a stark pair of alternatives. It could, in order to pursue a more realistic attempt at co-optation, embark on a process of more significant, and painful, socioeconomic reforms. Or it could abandon its timid reformistic attempts and unleash a wave of terror. Given the nature of the regime, the latter was the most consistent answer. The last months of Laugerud's administration saw the beginning of yet another wave of fierce repression, a further demonstration that the alternating cycles of extreme and "moderate" violence owed little to the personal attitudes of the men in power.[6]

During the Lucas García government (1978–1982), Laugerud's timid "modernizing effort" was replaced by a few cosmetic reforms engulfed in a wave of repression that reached a level of indiscriminate violence unprecedented even by Guatemalan standards.[7] The feeble political center has been ruthlessly crushed. Within the logic of the Guatemalan system, this policy is quite rational, since it eliminates the only potential alternative that the United States might tolerate or favor (depending on which administration is in power).

The assassination of well-known centrist leaders like Alberto Fuentes Mohr and Manuel Colom Argüeta was only a modest beginning. In this regard, the fate of the very moderate Democracia Cristiana (DC)—the tamest of the country's centrist parties—is worthy of note. The DC was the only nonrightist party to participate in the April 1980 municipal elections, thus lending some credibility abroad to a meaningless exercise in which only 12.5 percent of the electorate bothered to vote. The DC scored relatively well in the ballots. Since then, several of the elected DC mayors have been murdered, while increasing repression is decimating the rank and file of the party. The comment of a Guatemalan right-winger—"de los lideres de la democracia cristiana los que no han muerto estan aterrorizados" ("the Christian Democratic leaders who are not dead are terrorized")[8]—is a fitting description of the country's political life. The DC is cowed, in complete disarray; its leaders are in hiding; and the party headquarters have been closed—a most effective object lesson for those centrist elements who held to the delusion of a peaceful coexistence with the ruling class. But if the ineffectual centrist "threat" has been fully extirpated, leaving the Guatemalan state nothing to fear from that quarter, this is certainly not the case with the real challenge, the one from the left.

Official U.S. Attitudes Toward Guatemala

The Carter Administration's Search For a Center

In very broad terms, the Carter administration's policy toward Central America had two major phases, separated by the period between the summer of 1978 (when the Sandinistas occupied the Congressional Palace in Managua) and the summer of 1979 (when Anastasio Somoza Debayle was overthrown).

In the first phase the administration felt little threat from the left in Central America. Hence it appeared possible to have a "human rights" policy without endangering U.S. interests. After the shock of the Sandinista victory, the administration saw the pro-U.S. stability in the area threatened by sudden winds of revolution. It reacted to this unexpected nightmare with an effort to co-opt the Sandinistas in Nicaragua. In somewhat contradictory fashion, it sought to strengthen the military in Honduras while simultaneously pushing for an opening of the political system; in El Salvador it pushed forward a "third force" experiment with mounting disregard for reality.[9]

In Guatemala, after the fall of Somoza, the Carter administration continued, as before, to press for "democratization." It was argued that a centrist solution, however difficult in the short term, would in the long term prove the most effective way of preventing a popular explosion and a victory of the radical left. In the meantime, any slackening of repression and implementation of even modest reforms were seen as positive steps to help decrease tensions.

The Carter policy toward Guatemala failed miserably. The Guatemalan ruling class—never known for its political sophistication—became increasingly convinced that the State Department was dominated by Marxists (including men like William G. Bowdler and James E. Cheek, who in its view cunningly persecuted and finally removed from his post the staunchly anticommunist ambassador Frank Ortiz). Continuing pressure and public chastening from Washington led only to a break in communications between the two governments, while within Guatemala repression wreaked havoc upon those centrist groups that enjoyed Washington's support.

By 1980, a debate began in earnest within the Carter administration. The Defense Department, the National Security Council, and "hard-liners" in the State Department argued that the policy of the "stick" toward the Lucas government had failed. They therefore advocated an improvement in relations and the resumption of military assistance. By proffering the "carrot"—and thus resuming the dialogue—the Carter administration, they argued, would be able to regain the confidence of the Guatemalan regime and could eventually persuade it to adopt some reforms. Although this proposed policy shift was rejected, it is important to understand the rationale of those State Department "liberals" who opposed it. They, too, strongly preferred a Lucas government (however unredeemed) to a Sandinista-type victory in Guatemala. They would have advocated military assistance for the regime, had they believed that it was necessary for its survival. But in their eyes the Guatemalan government was not yet seriously threatened, hence the United States could afford to wait (while military assistance was provided by Argentina, Israel, and other countries). In this fashion, the Carter administration would avoid "dirtying its hands" as long as possible, thus preserving the facade of its "human rights" policy. Meanwhile, the frustrating effort to moderate the Lucas government continued in an atmosphere that was increasingly divorced from reality.

The Reagan Administration's Response

The Reagan administration came to power promising to return the United States to its former grandeur and to redress Carter's policy of "blunders" based on humiliating concessions to communist and radical states and on the betrayal of loyal allies like Anastasio Somoza Debayle and the shah of Iran.

For the architects of Reagan's "New Orthodoxy," the U.S. decline had subjective rather than objective roots. As Norman Podhoretz poignantly asked, "Do we lack power? Certainly not if power is measured in brute terms of economic, technological and military capacity. . . . The issue boils down, in the end, to a matter of will."[10] A strong economic base and military buildup were indispensable conditions for the reassertion of an imperial America, but the will to act, at once, as a great power abroad was of critical importance.

Geography and history made it inevitable that Central America would occupy a critical place within a vision that stressed the need to reassert America's will, for how could the world respect the United States if it failed to maintain the Pax Americana in its own backyard? But Central America was not merely a troubled area requiring the attention of the Reagan administration: It also presented an opportunity to demonstrate

America's new resolve.[11] In order to project the image of an effective, resurgent United States, an immediate foreign-policy victory would be most advantageous. Neither Afghanistan nor the [Persian/Arabian] Gulf were appropriate places for a swift and easy success—but Central America's geographic proximity to the United States, the small size of the nations threatened by "Communist aggression," and the ease with which the United States had traditionally imposed its will on the region seemed to hold out this promise. The Reaganites' intense desire to make Castro pay for his past actions was an added incentive to reassert U.S. will in the area. Hence Central America was thrust into the forefront of Reagan's foreign policy.

Within this imperial logic, the "test case" selected to demonstrate the United States' new-found will was El Salvador—in fact, since January 1981, U.S. policy towards Nicaragua has been largely a function of developments in El Salvador. As had been the case under Carter, Guatemala was seen by the incoming Reagan administration as a less urgent problem.

Within the administration, a majority of high-ranking officials (in particular new Reagan appointees) saw the Lucas government as a "moderate repressive" regime whose excesses had to be understood within the violent context of Guatemala's history and of what they saw as aggression by terrorists backed by Cuba and the Soviet Union. The United States had to provide assistance to a beleaguered and loyal ally, rather than indulge in intemperate and naive criticism of a deeply rooted social reality. Reforms were welcome, but only at the pace and within the scope accepted by the Guatemalan ruling class.

Another group—which included perhaps a majority of career officials working on the region, especially within the lower and middle-ranking echelons—acknowledged that Guatemala desperately needed social reforms. For them, the Guatemalan regime was repressive to a degree that could not be justified either by the country's history or by aggression from the left and that in the end might well prove self-defeating. They argued, however, that Carter's intolerance had failed to persuade the Lucas government to temper its own policies. By resuming the "dialogue," Washington might eventually succeed in convincing the Guatemalan ruling class that it was in its own interests to accept some reforms. In any case, they concluded, the United States had no other alternative.

Thus, both approaches stressed the need to provide military assistance and maintain a close relationship with the Guatemalan government. The "hard-liners" overlooked the need for reforms; those with a more pragmatic bent acknowledged the importance of reforms, yet emphasized that the Guatemalan government should not be pressured, but convinced, and had to be supported in any event. Their case rested on the hope that the Guatemalan ruling class would at last reveal instincts for self-preservation. Both approaches also agreed on the administration's need to make support for the Guatemalan regime more palatable to Congress by uplifting the sordid image of the Lucas government.

Guatemala's Possible Evolution: Reactionary Class Dictatorship or Challenge from Below?

Ronald Reagan's victory over Jimmy Carter improved the international situation of the Lucas government. Theoretically, this could have driven the attitudes of the Guatemalan ruling class in either of two directions: It might have brought a softening of the "siege mentality" and thus led to some socioeconomic reforms or it might have stiffened the regime's intolerance and hardened its policy even further.

Several U.S. analysts (and a few Guatemalans) argued that the "modernizing option" was a likely outcome of the improvement in the regime's international position. Briefly summarized, their argument was the following: They claimed that a few senior Guatemalan officers (as well as numerous junior officials and "enlightened" members of the bourgeoisie) acknowledged that the Guatemalan crisis required more than a purely military solution. Signs of this more flexible attitude were seen in personal statements of several officers, in the government's civic-action policy, and in official documents, such as the Plan de Acción Social. While rejecting any real agrarian reform, the regime would be willing to tolerate minor social reforms, such as cooperatives, improved working conditions, and higher salaries. This "reformist" policy would be accompanied by continued repression that would seek not only to eliminate the guerrillas and their supporters but also to clamp down on illegal strikes and prevent the development of an independent leadership in trade unions and peasant cooperatives (resorting to selective assassinations, whenever necessary). Political democratization—even in a limited form—would not be a component of this "modernizing" formula, which would instead rely on a combination of severe (but not indiscriminate) repression and limited economic concessions. The remnants of the political center would be allowed to play, at best, a totally dependent role; the middle class's function would be to staff an expanded bureaucracy.

Those U.S. analysts who, with varied misgivings, argued that a "modernizing" solution was possible in Guatemala, also added that it would be possible only if several conditions were met:

- pressure by the Reagan administration in favor of a policy of reforms, requiring, to quote from one of these analysts, "a more rational approach on the part of the hardliners"
- U.S. economic assistance, since the Guatemalan ruling class would not be willing to shoulder the cost of these reforms alone
- a significant improvement in the quality of the Guatemalan bureaucracy, which would have to administer the reforms
- an end to indiscriminate repression, since the government's blind violence has been radicalizing large sectors of the population

One could argue that a "modernizing" formula including only limited social reforms would, in any case, fail to stem the rising tide of radicalization among the Guatemalan masses. It is, moreover, extremely unlikely that the Guatemalan ruling class will implement even such a modest "reformist" solution. Although they apparently do exist, the "modernizing" elements of the armed forces and the bourgeoisie are only a small minority. The assassinations by rightist squads of men like Jorge Torres Ocampo and Julio Segura Trujillo do not augur well for the physical security of members of the bourgeoisie who are too "enlightened."

The Guatemalan ruling class, for its part, shows very little willingness to shoulder even a part of the cost of reforms, while the bureaucracy—never highly efficient, even by Central American standards—has been further weakened by the recent waves of repression. Finally, the Guatemalan armed forces do not have the political sophistication, even if they had the will, to respond to a strong threat from below (such as exists at present) through a policy of selective rather than indiscriminate repression.

It is also unlikely that the Reagan administration will be willing to apply any "undue" pressure on the Guatemalan ruling class. In fact, its first steps indicated a great deal of "restraint" and warm understanding for the "plight" of the Guatemalan regime. Highly tentative suggestions for moderation were accompanied by scathing denunciations of the "terrorist" aggressions against the Lucas regime and by fierce statements that the Reagan administration would never tolerate a "Communist" takeover ("Communists" and "terrorists" being, in the administration's semantics, synonymous with the Guatemalan guerrillas and their supporters).

As his critics have argued, Carter's "stick policy" had indeed little chance to reform the Guatemalan regime. But Reagan's "carrot approach" is even more naive and will ultimately strengthen the hand of those within Guatemala who argue that the "Communist" threat must be met with old, trusted methods. For the great majority of the ruling class, the answer will not lie in "painful and dangerous" concessions (which produced "ill results" in the 1974–1977 period). They will instead resort, with customary blindness, to the one response that they know so well and to which they have so freely resorted in the past: violence.

But will these long-trusted methods prove equally reliable in the future? Fundamental changes have intervened in Guatemala, and the ruling system faces a far more formidable foe than it did in the 1960s and early 1970s.[12] In assessing the strength of the left-wing challenge, the following points deserve particular emphasis:

- The Guatemalan left is clearly in the process of overcoming its past divisions.
- The present guerrilla groups have learned from the mistakes of the past. Rather than concentrating exclusively on military actions, they have paid increasing attention to the creation of a peasant base, which is spreading through several departments.
- The urban labor movement is showing a degree of organization and a combativeness that the recent wave of repression has failed to curb and that a few cosmetic reforms will not assuage.
- In recent years, an increasing number of peasants have become politicized (which in Guatemalan terms means radicalized). The growing militancy of CUC need not be emphasized.
- Although Cardinal Mario Casariego remains a pillar of the reactionary class dictatorship, more and more of the clergy are turning against the government and even adopting the message of the theology of liberation. At the same time, elements of the middle class and remnants of the old centrist parties are turning toward the left-wing groups.
- It is, above all, important to stress that ever-larger groups of the Indian population are reaching out to support or join the guerrillas and left-wing mass organizations (such as CUC). Thus, for the first time in the history of Guatemala, the caste division is being overshadowed through the realization of a common class interest. This evolution represents a potentially devastating blow to the ruling class, which has traditionally profited from the contradiction between caste prejudices and class interests.

Conclusion

The main conclusions of this chapter, as they bear on the future of Guatemala, can be summarized as follows:

- there is no possibility of a centrist solution
- the likelihood of a "modernizing right" ruling the country is extremely slim at best
- the only two realistic alternatives are a continuation of the reactionary class dictatorship or a takeover by the forces of the guerrillas and their sympathizers (but in the short term, the guerrillas have no chance of seizing power)

Even "moderate conservative" U.S. analysts acknowledge that in the longer term—that is, over the next five years—the old order may well crumble in Guatemala. The combination of cosmetic reforms and willful repression that the Lucas government had been offering to the populace is likely to have an effect opposite to the one sought by the ruling class, since the popular struggle—in all its different forms—has reached an unprecedented level in Guatemala.

The day will probably come, by the mid-1980s, when the United States will be confronted with the highly unpleasant alternative of intervening militarily or accepting the victory of the left. That day has not yet come, yet it must be remembered that the longer the United States stubbornly supports a Guatemalan ruling class that is unable to "modernize," the more it will force the radicalization of the Guatemalan left and complicate an eventual *modus vivendi* between a new Guatemala and a less conservative administration in Washington, D.C.

Notes

1. In addition to written sources, this article is based on a series of interviews with U.S. government officials, Guatemalans of different political views, and other observers.

2. Much to Gen. Miguel Ydígoras Fuentes's indignation, the CIA finally selected Colonel Castillo Armas to head the plot to overthrow Arbenz (for Ydígoras's self-serving explanation of why the CIA passed him over, see his highly entertaining if misleading account in *My War with Communism*, Englewood Cliffs, N.J.: Prentice-Hall, 1963, pp. 49–51). Ydígoras's turn finally came in 1958, when he became president of Guatemala following Castillo Armas's assassination.

3. This represents an important difference from the situation of their Salvadorean counterparts throughout most of the 1970s. It is only through the October 1979 coup and the 1980 "reforms" that the Salvadorean army has acquired a formidable potential economic base at the expense of the civilian ruling class.

4. I borrow Edelberto Torres-Rivas's apt formulation, far more exact than the often used but misleading characterization of *burguesia restringida*. See Torres-Rivas's excellent essay, "Guatemala: Crisis and Political Violence," *NACLA: Report on the Americas* 14, no. 1 (Jan./Feb. 1980), pp. 16–27.

5. Nonpartisan documents such as the 1978 and 1980 World Bank reports on Guatemala have eloquently stressed this failure.

6. It is interesting to note that serious observers, by focusing on formal symbols that are hardly relevant for Guatemala, had at the outset characterized the Lucas administration as center-right—misled by the fact that it had "won" the elections with the support of the PR and included Francisco Villagrán Kramer as vice-president of the republic.

7. The February 1981 report by Amnesty International conclusively documents the fact that "tortures and murders are part of a deliberate and long-standing program of the Guatemalan government" and lays to rest the wornout tale of death squads of the extreme right acting against the government's wishes (*Guatemala: A Government Program of Political Murder,* London: Amnesty International, 1981, quote p. 3).

8. Personal interview.

9. See Piero Gleijeses, "The United States and Turmoil in Central America," in *The 1980s: Decade of Confrontation?* (Washington, D.C.: National Defense University Press, 1981), pp. 123–142.

10. "Making the World Safe for Communism," *Commentary,* April 1976, p. 11.

11. For a more detailed assessment by the author of Reagan's policy in Central America, see Piero Gleijeses, *Tilting at Windmills: Reagan in Central America* (Washington, D.C.: The Johns Hopkins Foreign Policy Institute, April 1982).

12. For reasons of space, this chapter does not discuss the role of Cuba and Mexico or the possible impact of increased Guatemalan oil production. But Mexico and Cuba have been playing a minor role in recent developments in Guatemala and no major change is foreseen in the near future. In addition, the extent of Guatemala's oil reserves is debatable, but it is unlikely that they will be very large; in any case, the "modernization" of the Guatemalan political system is not a problem of lack of resources, but fundamentally of lack of will. Finally, the guerrillas have already demonstrated their ability to sabotage the highly vulnerable pipelines that bring the oil to the coast.

9
The Central American Church and Regime Transformation: Attitudes and Options

Margaret E. Crahan

Much of what is written about the Catholic church in contemporary Latin America presumes that it was monolithically conservative before Vatican II (1962–1965) and Medellín (1968).[1] This is as questionable as the notion that the church in Central America today is uniformly progressive. Prior to the 1960s there was a relatively broad spectrum of opinion and behavior within the church, although that spectrum has expanded considerably since then, particularly on the left. The institutional weight of the church favors gradualistic political, economic, and social reform that does not interfere with the church's stated mission to see to the salvation of all sectors of society.

Official calls for identification with the poor coexist with preoccupation with institutional preservation. The attitudes and actions of clerical and lay leaders continue to be influenced by traditional alliances with national elites, fear of radicalism, and historical patterns of behavior that emphasize hierarchy and the maintenance of privilege. These factors have been somewhat obscured in the present crisis in Central America by the attention paid to those church people identified with the revolutionary left. The latter, although a vocal minority, are not necessarily the principal influence on policy, in part because they have turned their attention away from internal church politics toward secular issues.

This chapter is an attempt to assess the respective weight of the conservative, moderate, and progressive tendencies within the Catholic church in Central America in order to suggest some directions for the future political behavior of that institution. Given the predominance of the Catholic church in Central America, I will not include any discussion of other denominations. Furthermore, the term *church* is used to refer to the institution rather than a community of believers. This does not obviate the fact that there are a good number of church people, especially progressives, who define the church in noninstitutional terms. Nor does it deny the contribution of the grass-roots church to the politicization of the institution and its involvement in the present crisis in Central America. Nevertheless, it is the church as an institution that has had the most measurable influence on the debate over regime transformation.

Since discussion of the political options of the church has developed principally as a result of circumstances in Nicaragua, El Salvador, and Guatemala, this chapter will focus primarily on the Catholic church in those countries. In order to establish the probability of political alliances between the church and secular groups and institutions, I will examine specific actions of the Catholic church in contemporary Central America, the attitudes that underlie them, and the options to which they give rise.

The Catholic Church in Contemporary Central America

Politicization of the Church

It is a mistake to identify opposition by church people to a dictator and state terrorism with a commitment to a specific political option or to revolutionary change. The Catholic church in Nicaragua, which by June 1979 officially took an anti-Somoza stance, is not pro-Sandinista. Current criticism of the civilian-military junta in El Salvador and the government of Efraín Ríos Montt in Guatemala does not constitute support for the forces attempting to overthrow those regimes. What it does reflect is the politicization of the Catholic church and its clergy since the 1960s, as a result of the impact of escalation of pressures for socioeconomic and political change in areas such as Latin America. These pressures were reinforced and, to a degree, legitimated by the church's commitment at Vatican II and Medellín to social justice and the elimination of oppression. In addition, the conclusions of both these meetings with respect to decreasing the hierarchical exercise of power within the church and increasing the participation of clergy and laity in decision making fell upon particularly fertile ground in Latin America. New theological formulations, especially liberation theology[2] and pastoral practices, served to facilitate the spread of reforms, particularly via the Comunidades Eclesiales de Base (CEBs), lay evangelizers, and progressive Christian student and workers' groups, as well as organizations of the clergy.

The CEBs provided for many of the rural and urban poor in Central America an institutional base and resources to work for the satisfaction of their needs. The utilization of the CEBs to express socioeconomic discontent resulted in their transformation into vehicles of protest that attracted the ire of secular authorities. At the same time the concerns voiced via the CEBs helped arouse the consciences of the clergy to a far greater degree than previously. While the impact, at least initially, was primarily horizontal, the politicization of priests, nuns, and other religious eventually affected the upper echelons of the clergy both positively and negatively. The extent of socioeconomic injustice in Central America was brought home strongly to the hierarchy, as well as the need to address its causes. What was not as clear was the proper means to eliminate those causes and the debate over this has served to stimulate divisions within the church.

A good number of social-welfare groups organized by the church among the poor became vehicles for political demand making. The clergy involved were prompted to ally themselves with individuals and organizations with like concerns, whether they were church related or not. These efforts tended to proliferate somewhat independently of the church and to accept progressive, including socialist, political analysis. When the hierarchy attempted to curb them, as happened throughout Central America in the mid-1970s, the level of resistance demonstrated that the base was operating somewhat autonomously of the institutional church. It also resulted in the departure of a number of clerical and lay leaders from the church, some of whom joined revolutionary movements.

Such divisions within the Catholic church have been transcended somewhat by the closing of ranks in the face of increasingly generalized repression and the kidnapping, torturing, and killing of church people, including clerics. In Somoza's Nicaragua, in El Salvador since 1977, and more recently in Guatemala and Honduras the response of the institutional church to attacks on its personnel has been sharp. This, together with its grass-roots and humanitarian activities, has tended to make the Catholic church a focal point of popular resistance, a situation that has made some bishops uncomfortable. Official church response has tended to consist largely of denunciations of state terror and a distancing of the church from governing elites. Throughout there have been notable exceptions of both individuals (e.g., Archbishop Oscar Arnulfo Romero y Galdámez) and groups (e.g., Maryknollers). On the grass-roots level, the church frequently has served to provide refuge and resources for the opposition, as was the case in Nicaragua during the insurrection and as is presently occurring in El Salvador and Guatemala. Strong support for revolutionary change continues, however, to be a minority position among both the clergy and the laity.

Divisions Within the Nicaraguan Church

The unity within the church forged by repression and broad-based violations of rights tends to diminish once there is some improvement. This is the case in Nicaragua, where since the overthrow of Anastasio Somoza Debayle in July 1979 there has been increasing articulation of disagreements within the church over its proper role in a revolutionary situation. Even though pastoral letters on July 30, 1979, and November 17, 1979, supported the new government, the episcopacy has been careful not to support socialism as a political and economic option. By mid-1980 the Nicaraguan bishops were increasingly expressing reservations about the direction the country was taking.[3] Of note is the insistence on the church having a special role as a critic of the process. The episcopacy justified this on the grounds that the church has the welfare of the populace as a whole as its overriding concern and is above ideology and partisan politics. This position is similar to that of a good number of Cuban church leaders in the late 1960s. Their efforts to carve out such a role foundered on the Castro government's insistence that criticism was only valid if it flowed from those who participated in the process of revolutionary change. Even though a number of clerics and lay leaders have been integrated into the Nicaraguan revolution, the church as an institution has maintained its distance.

As ideological and political debate has sharpened within Nicaragua, so have divisions within the Catholic church. In addition, there have been increased attempts by all sides to utilize church personnel and institutions to legitimate particular stances. Given the varieties of opinion within the church, it has been possible for both pro- and antigovernment forces to adduce support. The "battle of the quotation" from church leaders and papal documents in the pages of *La Prensa* and *El Nuevo Diario* testifies to this. Increasingly the episcopacy, however, has been identified with antigovernment elements. For its part the government has generally tried not to alienate the prelates, although it is very preoccupied by the increasingly critical statements of the hierarchy and their identification with antigovernment elements. The rapid reversal of the expulsion of two priests and three nuns from the Atlantic Coast area in early 1982 for allegedly counterrevolutionary activities strongly indicates the level of government concern. Subsequent detentions of religious workers, particularly from Protestant fundamentalist denominations, have occurred.

Among liberal and progressive sectors in the Catholic church there is increasing tension with the episcopacy and particularly with Archbishop Miguel Obando y Bravo. The prelate's distaste for Somoza and public support for the insurrection in June 1979 garnered him considerable popularity in Nicaragua, a fact not lost on the Sandinistas, who sought initially to use him to legitimate the Government of National Reconstruction. The presence of clerics in very visible positions in the government reinforced the efforts toward legitimation and was accepted originally by the episcopacy as a means of influencing the course of the new government. However, as antigovernment attitudes among the bishops hardened, the prelates have increasingly lent their support to opposition forces. The frequency with which the episcopacy's and especially Obando y Bravo's activities and statements appear on the front page of *La Prensa* testifies to this.

Allegations that Obando y Bravo, or his assistants, instigated the removal of some progressive priests or religious from working-class parishes or base communities resulted in sit-ins in a number of churches in 1982. Although the archbishop has on a number of occasions denied involvement, there is conflicting evidence from some of the religious superiors involved. Obando agreed to enter into discussions with representatives of the protesters, but this did not defuse the situation. In fact, by July 1982 dissension had reached such a point that when the auxiliary bishop of Managua, Monsignor Bosco Vivas Robelo, went to the church of Santa Rosa to retrieve the blessed sacrament during a sit-in to protest the removal of a priest of the parish, Monsignor José Arias Caldera, a scuffle ensued. Obando y Bravo responded by placing the parish under interdict and excommunicating those who were alleged to have roughed up the bishop. This incident marks a low point in relations between the hierarchy and progressive grass-roots elements within the church. It also occurred at a time when tensions between the government and the bishops were high and Obando y Bravo's credibility as a neutral critic of the revolutionary process was in question.

In July 1982 the Nicaragua government decided to no longer allow U.S. foreign aid in support of private business, educational, and church groups into the country. Of the several million dollars involved, $115,000 went to the archbishop of Managua for overhead for existing programs, the creation of small ecclesial communities, and leadership training. The latter two were regarded as means to compete with progressive grass-roots communities and lay leaders. In testimony before Congress, Assistant Secretary of State for Inter-American Affairs Thomas O. Enders and Agency for International Development (AID) official Otto Reich affirmed that the funds were intended to support groups in opposition to the present government of Nicaragua.

In addition, there has been increasing insistence from the popular sectors within the church that attempts to reassert episcopal authority and impose doctrinal and political orthodoxy are the principal sources of dissension within the church. They also argue that there are no grounds for charges that the grass-roots church is intent on establishing a parallel institution and progressive clergy and religious, a parallel magisterium. The national conference of religious (Confederación Nacional de Religiosos de Nicaragua—CONFER), student and youth groups, the Instituto Histórico, and Centro Antonio Valdivieso have all been intent on combating such charges, arguing that they believe in one church, led by the episcopacy, but with greater dialogue to resolve differences and misunderstanding. Progressive elements within the church have repeatedly asserted their respect for the hierarchy and rejected charges that they were intent on flouting established church authorities. Such efforts do not, however, appear to have had much impact on diminishing the growing distance between progressives and the hierarchy.

The most serious breach between the government and the episcopacy was precipitated by the removal of several Indian communities to the interior of Zelaya Province in early 1982. This action was the result of incursions by anti-Sandinista elements and was highly controversial within and without Nicaragua and strongly criticized by the Catholic hierarchy as resulting in grave violations of human rights. The bishops alleged that there had not been sufficient consideration of the weak, elderly, women, and children and that there had been unjust destruction of homes, goods, and livestock and some deaths. The latter was not substantiated. They called for an investigation of the removal and for the government to bend every effort to establish peace, tranquillity, and justice in the area. They also called upon the inhabitants of the area to conserve, cultivate, and defend their Christian faith. For their part, the bishops promised to intensify efforts to evangelize the region and called upon the government to assist them in relief efforts.[4] The government reacted strongly to what it regarded as unjust accusations and lack of appreciation of the military situation in an area where there had been increased fighting with anti-Sandinista elements based in Honduras. Beyond this the government criticized the bishops for not having accepted its invitation to inspect the new settlements and for failure to use the means of communication established to maintain dialogue between the leadership of church and state. The government categorized the episcopal document as political rather than pastoral and as a calculated effort to undermine national unity in line with U.S. objectives. The government asserted that the bishops' failure to condemn the climate of terror created in the region by the actions of counterrevolutionaries, including some former National Guard members from the Somoza period, raised questions about the bishops' motives. Finally the government pointed out that the bishops had said nothing about the fact that some Moravian pastors and Catholic deacons had been providing support for the counterrevolutionaries. The gulf between the government and the bishops was confirmed by the former's call for a Vatican mission to discuss Nicaraguan church-state relations.[5] The Vatican did not accept this suggestion.

Although overall there continues to be a conviction among the majority of church people that the present Nicaraguan government is committed to meeting the basic needs of the people, there is disquiet over the possibility that the profound polarization of society will result in broad-based armed conflict, thereby exacerbating internal divisions within the churches. There is considerable preoccupation, especially among the bishops, over the possibility of a Marxist-Leninist government that would be inimical to the church's continuing to occupy an influential role in society and functioning as moral arbiter, but concern over alienating progressive church people if too strong a stand with respect to the government is taken has tempered reactions. The bulk of the faithful are perturbed by the current divisions within the Catholic church and hence some of them are being attracted to those denominations and secular groups that offer more psychological reassurance in the midst of the ferment of revolutionary Nicaragua.

The image of the Catholic church as a unified institution, hierarchically organized, and speaking with one voice is no longer supported by reality. Instead the church is a pluralistic organization, attempting to fulfill its stated goals through a blending of traditional patterns of behavior with strategies that allow it to adapt to new circumstances and thereby survive as an institution. That tends to involve the church in societal conflict to a greater extent than in the past. As a consequence, concern over the survival of the institutional church has increased among the episcopacy and in Rome. The strategy promoted by John Paul II and followed by the Nicaraguan bishops is to reassert their authority, as well as doctrinal and political orthodoxy, only to the degree circumstances permit. Pragmatic recognition of the strength of progressive sectors within the church, as well as the preferential option for the poor, led the Nicaraguan bishops to initially tacitly support the Government of National Reconstruction, while working to establish the church as a neutral critic of the government. Political polarization within Nicaragua, however, hindered such a strategy. As political struggle within Nicaragua increased, the church was increasingly divided. Under similar circumstances the church historically has most often opted for institutional survival, suggesting that it will gradually attempt to distance itself from current debates. To date this has not occurred, and the dynamic of the Nicaraguan situation in the future may not permit it.

Attitudes

Even though the Catholic church has become eminently more progressive in Latin America in recent years, a review of church documents since Medellín, including the pastoral letters of the Central American bishops, confirms the traditional preference for gradualistic change and fear of Marxism.[6] There is more openness at the base to Marxist-Christian dialogue, yet the majority of clerical and lay leaders attempt to avoid identification with partisan politics and specific political and economic options. The calls for a more just socioeconomic order and greater popular participation entail very little specification of how to achieve these goals. When faced with a revolutionary situation as in Nicaragua, the tendency of the church has been initially to adapt to the reality of the situation by offering cautious and qualified support. Church people who have provided unqualified support are a minority. If the government veers increasingly left, the traditional fear of Marxism within the episcopacy tends to reassert itself—giving rise to mutual distrust between church and state.

What is paramount is the desire of the church to maintain the loyalty of all sectors of society. In situations of class struggle, such a position is somewhat at odds with the stated preferential option for the poor. The inclination of the base toward the latter results in greater involvement in and support for programs and strategies for restructuring the existing order. Although grass-roots Catholics have participated in substantial numbers in reconstruction in Nicaragua, the institutional church does not want to coexist with a Marxist government. There is fear of the government as a competitor for the loyalty of the people, of governmental interference in religious activities and schools, and of the spread of atheistic materialism. There is also a preoccupation that when and if the revolution is consolidated, the government will no longer need to cultivate the church and will relegate it to a marginal role in society. As a consequence, the episcopacy has increasingly been critical of the government, while at the same time attempting to maintain open options within a rapidly changing situation.

In El Salvador, Guatemala, and Honduras the episcopacy has been even more cautious in identifying itself with a specific political option. The involvement of a strong minority of the diocesan priests in San Salvador[7] and elements of the Jesuits, Maryknollers, and Capuchins in support of the Frente in the face of a conservative hierarchy reflects the strong divisions within the Salvadorean church. The bulk of the clerical supporters of the Frente are aligned with the more moderate groups, including dissident elements of the Christian Democrats and the Social Democrats. Although the international networks of various religious groups, most notably the Jesuits and Maryknollers, have been brought into play to generate opposition to the junta, they have not been used as extensively to promote support for the Frente. Furthermore, Rome has been increasingly critical of political activism by church people in El Salvador, as well as elsewhere in Central America.

In Guatemala and Honduras the official statements of the church have been largely limited to denunciations of gross violations of human rights and government involvement in them. Emphasis has been on humanitarian responses to crisis situations. In both these countries there has not been the same development of extensive networks of CEBs, lay evangelizers, and Christian self-help organizations as in Nicaragua and El Salvador. As a consequence, there is not the same degree of politicization at the grass-roots level, although continued repression, particularly in Guatemala, is stimulating it.

Underlying church behavior throughout Central America has been the ideological conservatism of the episcopacy, rooted in their class backgrounds, training, and a pragmatic realization of the weaknesses of their institutional bases that have traditionally led to cultivation of the political and economic elites. In the past the paucity of vocations and inferior quality of the clergy served to limit the influence and activism of the church. The influx of missionaries in the post–World War II period, as well as generalized socioeconomic change, challenged ill-prepared national churches to make difficult decisions concerning widely differing political options. The most frequent response was to avoid making them.

More recently, as a result of generalized societal pressures, together with the increase of progressive tendencies within the church, there has been some cautious support for radical change as the only means of dealing effectively with wide-scale poverty and oppression. The preference is, however, for such changes to be introduced via reform rather than revolution. When faced with the latter, initial receptivity can change to fear or hostility if the episcopacy becomes convinced that the institutional church would no longer occupy a preeminent position within society.

The political options implicit in the behavior and attitudes of the Central American episcopacy and clergy cluster around reform of the status quo and limited structural changes, with the majority content with gradualism. Denunciations of the excesses of capitalism have been accompanied by comparable denunciations of communism. Involvement of the institutional church, in contrast to individual church people, in organizations and programs committed to socialism has generally been motivated by shared objectives and a desire to mold and channel them in a moderate direction. The Catholic church as an institution does not have a theological, ideological, or practical base for supporting a socialist option. This is in spite of the fact that the theology of liberation has had considerable impact in the area. Even though this has facilitated Marxist-Christian dialogue and cooperation, it has not resulted in translation of the preferential option for the poor into support for socialism by the institutional church. This is particularly clear in Nicaragua.

This results from the fact that the major current within liberation theology in Central America has emphasized popular pastoral activities rather than the strategic analysis of specific political and economic options. Epitomized by Archbishop Oscar Arnulfo Romero y Galdámez, this trend encouraged identification with the poor and oppressed and denunciation of their exploitation. Although there is openness to the construction of a better society, it is defined as neither capitalist nor Marxist. Despite the substantial difference of this theology from historical formulations that emphasize traditional religious values, the sacral aspects of the church, and hierarchical authority, it is neither sufficiently developed nor sufficiently widespread to result in the church's supporting the socialist option.

Furthermore, involvement of clerics in the process of building socialism in Nicaragua has not received official support either from the local episcopacy or Rome.[8] Acceptance of such participation reflects the pragmatism of the hierarchy and the adaptability of the church to its existential situation. Support for literacy campaigns and social-welfare projects stems from humanitarian motives and a desire to identify with and influence these activities. Efforts such as those of the Instituto Histórico of the Universidad Católica and the Centro Antonio Valdivieso to reevaluate the past role of the church in Nicaragua and to promote ecclesiastical participation in the revolutionary process have been strongly criticized by some clerical and lay leaders. Such activities can challenge the hierarchy by questioning the legitimacy of their past actions and present views.

Cooperation between the CEBs and the Sandinistas during the insurrection has already given way in some areas, such as Estelí, to competition. Where the CEBs were weak, they have increasingly been supplanted by Sandinista organizations.[9] This has preoccupied the institutional church and caused it to place increased emphasis on generating loyalty through evangelization and the promotion of popular religiosity, as a means of limiting the inroads of secular ideology.

Beginning with its pastoral letter of June 2, 1979, the Nicaraguan episcopacy has repeatedly emphasized its belief in the necessity of political and ideological pluralism and a competitive party system. It has also expressed its desire to identify with the Nicaraguan people as a whole, rather than a specific political group. Fear of what is termed "state ideologies" and "massification" has been a constant. Freedom of expression and criticism are recommended as the only way of ensuring that the revolutionary process does not err substantially. Furthermore, it is asserted that no historical movement can have the same breadth as the church's efforts to promote justice and human dignity. The church would prefer that the Sandinistas encourage greater participation by already existing political parties, as well as new ones. The argument that an escalation of political competition in the traditional vein at this juncture would hamper the task of reconstruction is not widely accepted among the bishops.

In its November 17, 1979, pastoral letter and throughout 1980 and 1981 the Nicaraguan Episcopal Conference has repeatedly stated that it could not accept a socialism that attacked individual rights and religious motivation. In addition, the bishops insist there can be no interference with parents' rights to educate their children according to their convictions. By 1982 the Nicaraguan episcopacy and some of the clergy and laity had become disenchanted with the government and fearful of the increasing influence of Marxists. When faced with the possibility of a sharper swing to the left, the institutional church has increasingly allied itself with the counterrevolutionaries. This furthers the distance between the church leadership and progressive elements that are most numerous at the base and raises the possibility of serious splits.

Although a minority of the clergy in Guatemala and Honduras are involved in revolutionary activities, the bulk are moderate to conservative. If repression increases, however, there may be a swing to the left. This is what has been occurring in El Salvador. In all three countries there has been a tendency not to link criticism of the existing governments with explicit support for their opponents. The majority of clerical and lay leaders still prefer mediation and negotiation to revolutionary warfare. Emphasis is on denouncing rights violations rather than offering political and economic options for a more just society.

Possibility of Political Alliances

In general, the likelihood of the institutional church in Central America forging concrete political alliances is very slim. The official position of the church has historically been that it is apolitical, and this continues to be the case. Even though the intensification of political and socioeconomic crisis in Central America in recent years has prompted the church to define its political preferences more clearly, there continues to be strong resistance to particularizing them. Where circumstances require the taking of a position—as during the Nicaraguan insurrection or the present crisis in El Salvador—the tendency is to support change in government without necessarily supporting the programs of any of the groups spearheading the opposition.

Increasing support by church people for change stems largely from the diminution of political options in the present crisis and a pragmatic decision to attempt to influence those groups that may come to power. This was the case in Nicaragua. However, worsening economic conditions in that country, increased political polarization, growing opposition from moderate lay leaders, government radicalism, and the disaffection of increasing numbers of clerical and lay leaders could cause a total breach between church and state. This would tend to increase the gulf between the episcopacy and the base and threaten hierarchical authority.

In El Salvador the institutional church clearly prefers to avoid alliance in favor of a role as critic of current abuses of state power and as a potential mediator of the contending factions. In Guatemala and Honduras those that support radical change are relatively few in number, although they are increasing in the face of escalating repression. The majority support greater respect for human rights on humanitarian grounds and oppose violence as a means of effecting change. Where alliances have been made with progressive forces, they have generally been at the local level or around specific issues—they do not reflect an official predisposition. Throughout the recent period of increased conflict the Catholic church as an institution has continued to define itself as apolitical and above ideology, as well as partisan politics. As a consequence, it has continued to reject formal political alliances. Cooperation with and cautious support of change-oriented groups or governments flows more from greater identification with the poor than from structural analyses of political and economic options. Such analyses, although they do exist, are not the prime motivating factor. Rather humanitarianism and pragmatic adaptation to current circumstances in Central America have resulted in a more flexible church. This has not been sufficient, however, to cause it to abandon its historical desire to appeal to all individuals within society, even with the recent emphasis on the preferential option for the poor. Nor has it been sufficient to overcome the fear of Marxist-Leninist states. Hence support for revolutionary movements ultimately is quite circumscribed.

Furthermore, in its desire to maintain its universal appeal, the church has attempted to curb those elements within it that would insist on support for socialism. The policy of the episcopacy has been to tolerate a broadened political debate within the church without permitting it to lock the church into a specific commitment. This is likely to continue to be the case, although internal divisions within the church may sharpen. This could prompt even more caution on the part of the institutional church and cause it to attempt to define its mission in even less particular terms. This would be supported by Rome, which is opposed to the further politicization of the clergy and favors a reinvigoration of a more evangelical orientation for the church. Substantial worsening of conditions in the area could challenge this strategy as counterrevolutionary and might increase divisions within the church. This could greatly diminish its capacity to play a critical role in the resolution of the crisis.

Notes

1. Vatican II was the meeting of the Catholic hierarchy convoked by Pope John XXIII in 1962. It stimulated wide-ranging doctrinal, liturgical, and administrative reforms. In particular, the church as community rather than as institution was emphasized, and there was a decentralization of authority to provide local bishops, priests, and religious and lay leaders with greater input into decision making. In addition, there was strong assertion of the role of the church in promoting peace and social justice. The 1968 meeting of the Latin American bishops in Medellín, Colombia, was heavily influenced by Vatican II, particularly in promoting social action on behalf of the poor and oppressed. This preferential option for the poor was reaffirmed at the Latin American bishops conference in Puebla, Mexico, in early 1979. For the conclusions of Vatican II, see W. Abbott, *The Documents of Vatican II* (New York: America Press, 1966); on Medellín, see Conferencia del Episcopado Latinoamericano (hereafter referred to as CELAM), *The Church in the Present Day Transformation of Latin America in the Light of the Council* (Bogotá: CELAM, 1970); on Puebla, see CELAM, *III Conferencia General del Episcopado Latinoamericano, Puebla: La Evangelización en el Presente y en el Futuro de América Latina* (Bogotá: CELAM, 1979).

2. The theology of liberation is based on a redefinition of the salvific mission of the church that emphasizes the realization of the Kingdom of God on earth, as well as individual salvation in the hereafter. As a consequence, the responsibility of the Christian to struggle for social justice and human dignity in this world is highlighted. While some liberation theologians use Marxist socioeconomic analysis in evaluating the causes of chronic poverty and oppression, most support a type of humanistic socialism. It is held by a minority of clerics, although it has served overall to legitimate the increasing progressivism of the church. Liberation theology had considerable impact on the grass-roots Christian communities known as the Comunidades Eclesiales de Base (CEBs), which proliferated in the 1960s and 1970s. Emphasizing communal theological reflection and a deepening of individual spirituality and social consciousness, these groups tended to encourage greater social activism by participants.

3. Conferencia Episcopal de Nicaragua, *Presencia Cristiana en la Revolución: Dos Mensajes—Momento Insurrecional 2 de junio 1979; Iniciando la Reconstrucción, 30 de julio 1979* (Managua: Comisión Justicia y Paz, 1979); Conferencia Episcopal de Nicaragua, "Carta Pastoral," November 17, 1979, Managua; and "La Iglesia en Nicaragua," *CELAM* 19, 158 (January 1981), pp. 11–21.

4. Conferencia Episcopal de Nicaragua, "Documentos de la Conferencia Episcopal, 17 de febrero de 1982," *Informes CAV,* no. 11–12 (March 1982), p. 2.

5. Secretaría General de la Junta de Gobierno de Reconstrucción Nacional, "Respuesta a la Conferencia Episcopal: Miskitos tienen el derecho a la vida, al progreso y la paz," Casa de Gobierno, Managua, Nicaragua, February 22, 1982, *Informes CAV,* no. 11–12 (March 1982), p. 3.

6. For example, Conferencia Episcopal de El Salvador, "Carta Pastoral," May 17, 1977, San Salvador; Conferencia Episcopal de Guatemala, "Carta Pastoral," June 13, 1980, Guatemala City; Conferencia Episcopal de Nicaragua, "Cartas Pastorales," July 30, 1979, and November 17, 1979, Managua; and Conferencia Episcopal de Panamá, "Carta Pastoral," June 29, 1978, Panamá.

7. Tommie Sue Montgomery, "The Church in El Salvador," MS. (1980), pp. 7–8.

8. In June 1981 priests holding political office in Nicaragua were urged by most of the episcopacy to resign from their posts. After the officeholders made clear their unwillingness to do so, an agreement was reached whereby the priests could retain their offices, but would not use their clerical status to support the government. Christopher Dickey, "Nicaraguan Priests to Stay in Office Under Compromise," *Washington Post,* July 17, 1981, p. A24.

9. Michael Dodson and Tommie Sue Montgomery, "The Churches in the Nicaraguan Revolution," paper presented at the Latin American Studies Association National Meeting, Bloomington, Indiana, October 16–19, 1980, pp. 29–32. Published in Thomas W. Walker, ed., *Nicaragua in Revolution* (New York: Praeger, 1982), pp. 161–180.

Part 2

External Interests and Strategies

10
The Internationalization of the Central American Crisis

Wolf Grabendorff

In the period following World War II, Central America made few headlines in the world press: in 1954, when a reformist policy was attempted in Guatemala and quickly foundered on U.S. resistance; in 1969, when the conflict between El Salvador and Honduras, played down as the "Soccer War," broke out; and finally in 1979, when revolution flared in Nicaragua. The latter was by no means, as frequently held today, the decisive factor in the region's crisis-prone development.

Unlike the international reaction to the Cuban revolution twenty years earlier, when the United States was still the undisputed hegemonic power in the region the events in Nicaragua and the civil-war situation in El Salvador and Guatemala have now led to the involvement of numerous national and transnational actors. Because the superimposition of the North-South conflict by the East-West conflict in the Third World has rarely become so evident, it is imperative to examine more meticulously the different interests and alliances in the crisis region of Central America. It must be pointed out that the violent conflicts in this region originate in the underdevelopment and exploitation of the individual countries by their own elite and cannot be attributed to the presence or interests of international actors.[1]

The Decay of Political Structures

The rapid decay of political structures in the so-called banana republics (Guatemala, Honduras, El Salvador, Nicaragua) in the past two decades was ignored by nearly all international actors for a long time. It was based on a socioeconomic development, in which frequently precapitalistic conditions were replaced by a capital-intensive, export-oriented economy through regional integration and national modernization. This contributed to a rapid change in the social structures of these nations. When the international economic crisis at the end of the 1970s severely struck those nations that were dependent on the export of farm products (coffee, bananas, cotton), the long-smoldering conflict among the different political groups in those countries erupted. The traditional alliance among the property-owning oligarchies, the export-oriented merchant elite, and the military experienced a crisis almost everywhere. Instead of an extension of greater political and economic participation to the new social groups—especially in the middle class—that had established themselves in the meantime, governmental and semigovernmental repression was increased.[2] In the "facade democracies" typical of these nations, characterized by the direct or indirect participation of the military and by regular election fraud, groups aspiring to political participation in state affairs saw less and less chance for a democratic takeover. The simultaneous oppression campaign against all political opposition, including the reformist Social and Christian Democratic parties, caused considerable domestic radicalization in nearly all Central American nations.

The special historical circumstances of the Nicaraguan revolution cannot be traced solely to these structural developments. They are also linked to the brutal rule of over forty years of Somoza dynasty. The aforementioned circumstances suddenly changed the situation for both the ruling elite in Central America and the legal or illegal counterelites of that region. The Nicaraguan revolution seemed to have proved that traditional power structures can be changed, partly with foreign support.[3]

Although the common preconditions for developments such as those in Nicaragua were overestimated and the national characteristics were underestimated, the revolution of 1979 led the different political groups, particularly in El Salvador and Guatemala, to the conviction that the power struggle had also begun in their countries. The ruling military governments in El Salvador, Honduras, and Guatemala moved closer together,[4] but intensified communication and coordination also began between the guerrilla groups and the political opposition in various countries. When, in this critical situation, Ronald Reagan was elected president of the United States in 1980 and a change in U.S. foreign policy began to take shape, a further hardening of the positions in Central America was unavoidable.[5]

From Carter to Reagan: Changes in U.S. Foreign Policy

In the first years of the Carter administration, Central America did not play an important role, aside from the negotiations with Panama concerning a new canal treaty. But it was precisely this treaty that signaled that the United States, under Carter, was quite prepared to deal with a small republic of the Third World in a respectable manner and to do away with old quasi-colonial relations. For the elite in the other Central American countries, this was the first sign of a fundamental change in their relations with the United States. This development became much more distinct in the human-rights policy accentuated by Carter. For Central America, this was to be a touchstone of the new pattern of relationship with the hegemonic power. All the republics of the region, with the exception of democratic Costa Rica, considered this policy an affront against their sovereignty. Already in 1977 Guatemala and El Salvador had rejected the traditional U.S. military assistance because it was tied to conditions relating to their human-rights policy. Considering that the United States viewed the Central American republics as relatively unimportant strategically and economically, the Carter administration saw in this region an opportunity to assert, in an exemplary way, its conception of human rights as an instrument for social change and democratization. The purpose of the Carter administration's "controlled evolution" idea was to reform the political system in Guatemala, Honduras, El Salvador, and Nicaragua through pressure on the military establishment and simultaneous advancement of democratic parties, especially the Christian and Social Democrats.[6]

Support of the status quo was refused by the Carter administration on the grounds that it could not be sustained in the long run. It was felt that immediate instabilities had to be accepted in order to help a pro-U.S., but domestically legitimized, elite to power. It soon turned out, however, that the leaders in these republics resisted pressure from Washington. On the contrary, they recognized the destabilizing influence on their interests and made an open attempt to obtain their military equipment in other countries, such as Israel.[7]

Precipitated by the murder of the democratic, unofficial opposition leader Pedro Joaquín Chamorro on January 10, 1978, events in Nicaragua began to follow in rapid succession, and Carter's policy was confronted with very difficult decisions. Since the summer of 1978, there had been civil war—not a dispute between Marxist guerrillas and a bourgeois regime, but a revolt of the people, with industrialists and Marxist guerrillas on one side and dictator Anastasio Somoza Debayle with his National Guard on the other. At the end of 1978, the Carter administration's only possibility was to support Somoza militarily or adjust to a victory of the Sandinist Front of National Liberation.[8]

Despite its desperate efforts to prevent seizure of power by the FSLN, the Carter administration, in accordance with its general Third World policy, nevertheless declared its willingness to come to terms with the new rulers after their seizure of power in Managua on July 19, 1979. Hoping to promote a pluralistic development within Nicaragua and to prevent the export of revolution from Nicaragua to the rest of Central America, the United States, as well as other industrial nations, attempted to help the war-torn country back upon its feet.[9] Behind this was also the fear that isolation of the FSLN, which obviously enjoyed wide popularity, would only provide the conditions for the creation of a "second Cuba." On the other hand, it was hoped that social reforms and extensive foreign aid could, perhaps, make a "second Costa Rica" out of Nicaragua in the medium term. However, only a year after the revolution, the United States discovered that it had completely underestimated the natural dynamic of revolutionary developments in Central America.[10]

In El Salvador, events seemed to reflect U.S. expectations at first. When on October 15, 1979, only three months after the revolution in Nicaragua, a civilian-military junta seized power in El Salvador, the Carter administration saw a chance to demonstrate in that country the controlled social change that had been its aim. Primarily the financial assistance of the initial reform measures (nationalization of banks, agrarian reforms, nationalization of foreign trade)[11] was supposed to deprive the radical guerrilla groups and mass organizations in El Salvador of their social basis and help stabilize the prerevolutionary situation. However, the progressive civilians in the junta could not prevail against the "hard line" of the military toward the mass organizations, and such a policy proved unsuccessful. The Carter administration, toward the end of its tenure, was therefore again actually willing to supply military aid to El Salvador and—by sending military advisers—to stabilize by military means what no longer could be stabilized politically.

For the Reagan administration the controversy in Central America, and especially in El Salvador, has an entirely different significance. For this government, the dispute is part of the global East-West conflict.[12] The starting point is the conviction of the Reagan administration that this conflict is an action inspired by the Soviet Union and initiated by Cuba, both of whom attempted to exploit the weakness of the United States during the Carter presidency in order to prove that the superpower is not in a position, even in its own geopolitical backyard, to keep friendly governments in power. Thus, in order to make clear in the East-West dispute that the United States will not tolerate such subversion, the Reagan administration found it necessary first to decide the military aspect of this conflict unequivocally in favor of the U.S.-supported governments, particularly in El Salvador. Parallel to this, at the very beginning of the Reagan presidency, a diplomatic-propagandist counteroffensive in the form of a White Paper[13] portrayed Cuba and the Soviet Union as the real sources of the civil war in El Salvador.

The diplomatic offensive used by the Reagan administration in the spring of 1981 to motivate its European allies and friendly Latin American governments to concerted action in El Salvador contributed to still further internationalization of the Central American conflict and simultaneously made the Reagan administration, in some respects, a "hostage" of developments in El Salvador. The United States can lose this conflict on three different fronts:

- in the military conflict in El Salvador, if the guerrillas cannot be defeated despite increasing U.S. support for government troops
- in the domestic political differences within the United States, in case the longer-term support of such a repressive government meets with resistance from the public and above all from members of Congress
- in the diplomatic disagreement with friendly Latin American countries and European allies, should these nations be unprepared to support a long-range policy of "reassertionism"

The position of the Reagan administration toward the developments in Central America very clearly reflects its global foreign-policy principles. Even during the election campaign Reagan left no doubt that his main task would be to reestablish the power position of the United States through a policy of strength, including military might. The focal point of this policy is to limit the influence of the Soviet Union and radical nations of the Third World in regions of strategic and/or economic importance for the United States.[14] The Reagan administration no longer views the shifting of the East-West conflict toward the Third World as a danger, but rather as a necessity. The lesson drawn by the Reagan government from this is that security and stability must take priority over development and social change in the Third World nations. Consequently, military aid was increased over economic aid. As a result of the "loss" of Nicaragua, a new domino theory has been advocated by the Reagan administration. It is based on the thesis that the communist strategy is to spread its influence through Central America, from Nicaragua to El Salvador and Guatemala and on to the oil fields of Mexico so as to gain a deployment zone against the United States.[15]

In contrast to the Carter administration, the Reagan government considers flexibility toward the new political groups in Central America more of a weakness than a strength on the part of the United States. Its attitude toward the revolution in Nicaragua does not differ substantially from the reaction of the United States toward the revolution in Cuba twenty years earlier. The attempt to destabilize or isolate revolutionary developments that might result in similar political changes in Latin

America has been a constant in U.S. policy during the past two decades.[16] The Reagan administration is endeavoring to combat, on three fronts at the same time, the problems created for it by the crisis center of Central America.

- It has supported the government in El Salvador with massive military and economic aid and has simultaneously pressured it to give the impression of legitimacy, at least outwardly, by voting in the midst of civil war.
- It has attempted to stop Nicaragua's and Cuba's propagandistic and material support for the guerrillas in El Salvador and, at the same time, to isolate or destabilize the Sandinista government in the region through direct or indirect pressure.
- It has attempted, at times, to exert pressure on Cuba in order to prevent both the support of the guerrillas in El Salvador and the consolidation of the Cuban-Nicaraguan alliance.

With these measures the Reagan administration wanted to demonstrate in El Salvador a typical example of renewed American forcefulness, as well as Cuban-Soviet incapacity in this region. This was supposed to invalidate fears in Honduras and Guatemala of a political conflagration in Central America and to degrade Nicaragua as an "exceptional case." In addition to these intensive bilateral sanction mechanisms, the Reagan administration had also prepared a plan to combat the socioeconomic causes of the political disputes in the region. The proposed Caribbean Basis Initiative[17] development program was supposed to offer all the small Central American and Caribbean republics the opportunity to improve their economic and social conditions in the coming years with U.S. help. From the beginning, the Reagan government has tried to interest several regional powers of the Western Hemisphere in this project, through the so-called Nassau Group.[18] Canada, Mexico, Venezuela, and subsequently Colombia were to participate with different financial means in this initiative. But a common basis could not be found with Mexico and Canada, because they were not willing to exclude unequivocally from this development program the region's revolutionary models: Cuba and Nicaragua.

The Reagan administration's geopolitical policy toward Central America, which is wholly oriented to the national-security interests of the United States, represents essentially a return to traditional U.S. Central American policy. However, it encounters a change in U.S. freedom of action, not only because of the internal developments in the individual nations of the region but also because of the new significance of regional powers within and on the rim of the Caribbean Basin. The greater international status of these nations has complicated the enforcement of the national-security interest of the United States. In the future, their attitudes will probably be of greater importance than the other international actors in the region.

Interests of Regional Powers

The region's four middle powers—Mexico, Cuba, Venezuela, and Colombia—demonstrate different influence and have shown this at different opportunities in the region. Thus Cuba's interest in the guerrilla groups and political developments in Central America is almost as old as the Cuban revolution. As a result of its historical links to the Central American nations, Mexico's interest is considerably older; it was, however, not manifested until the administration of Luis Echeverría Alvarez in the 1970s. Venezuela's interest in the region is closely connected with the ideological, Christian and Social Democratic links between several parties in Central America and its own two large political parties. Colombia's interest in Central America was formerly concentrated almost exclusively on Panama, but it has gained clearer contours since the revolution in Nicaragua.

The common interests of these regional powers are obvious. Although different motives are involved, all four of them are interested in replacing U.S. hegemony with a new political subsystem, the structure of which thus far is as controversial as the path offering the best prospects for the realization of such a goal. Distrust of the United States as an order factor is especially pronounced in Mexico, Venezuela, and Cuba. All three nations are attempting to influence the political and economic models in Central America in order to increase their own regional weight.

This results in a tendency toward "intervention," the antithesis of the "doctrine of nonintervention" repeatedly advocated by all Latin American nations. None of the regional powers wants to pass up the chance of utilizing the rapid deterioration of authority and rule in Central America for gains in international status. At times, Venezuela and Colombia recognized the possibility of increasing their influence through coordination or solidarity with U.S. policies. All four regional powers consider their possibilities of exerting influence in Central America as a measure of the maneuverability of their foreign policy as a whole. Despite some general agreement, however, all four nations are also pursuing very different interests. Nevertheless, three of them (Mexico, Venezuela, Colombia), together with Panama, formed the Contadora Group on January 9, 1983, as a common effort to solve the regional crises.

Mexico

On account of its own revolutionary past and its long experience in dealing with revolutionary regimes, Mexico generally has a positive attitude toward political change in Central America. Mexico's confidence in its own "revolutionary political system" is so strong that the revolutionary disputes in neighboring nations are regarded not only with calmness but even with a certain satisfaction. A spread of such developments in Mexico, often anticipated in the United States,[19] is largely ruled out in Mexico. In view of the parallels to its own historical development, Mexico considers every interference by the United States in Central America's process of change to be of graver consequences than the instabilities connected with this process of change. Mexico also appears to be willing to accept one or several socialist nations in Central America. Its long-term interests are most likely aimed at integrating, rather than isolating, such nations in a regional subsystem of the future.[20]

Currently, Mexico is pursuing a clear-cut double strategy in the Central American conflict.[21] On the one hand, it stresses its own revolutionary tradition and provides the guerrilla groups with at least verbal, and probably also financial, support. Through its diplomatic actions, it paves their way to international respectability in a way that should not be underestimated. In 1979, for example, Mexico, together with Costa Rica, severed relations with the Somoza regime and recognized the struggling Sandinistas as a war-waging party. In 1981, a parallel occurred when a Mexican-French declaration recognized the opposition in El Salvador as a representative political group, which in turn led to increased international support for the FDR (Democratic Revolutionary Front).[22] In 1982, Pres. José López Portillo proposed a comprehensive peace plan for the region with the inclusion of the United States and Cuba, in view of the potential armed clashes on the Central American land bridge.[23] Mexico's close relationship with Cuba is especially decisive in its attitude toward Central America. Indeed, the almost friendly relations permit Mexico to exercise a certain degree of influence over Cuba's attitude toward Central America.

On the other hand, Mexico's strategy in distributing funds for development aid has been rather more unemotional. The oil facility established through the San José Protocol of August 3, 1980, which is jointly financed and subsidized by Mexico and Venezuela, not only favors the transfer of development aid to the "revolutionary models" in the Caribbean and Central America but also benefits Guatemala, El Salvador, and Honduras. At the same time, Mexico perceives the necessity of taking U.S. interests into consideration as a restraining factor for its own policy toward the region. With the aid of its dual strategy, Mexico is evidently attempting a long-term consolidation of its status as a dominant power vis-à-vis the new and old elites in the region, beyond the current conflict constellations.

Cuba

Cuba's role as a regional power is by no means uncontested. Critics point out that Cuba, as a small island, owes its oversized foreign policy solely to the support of the Soviet Union. This tends to jeopardize the credibility of Cuba's policy in the region among several political groups, but increases it among others. Cuba's contacts to various guerrilla groups in Central America reach back to the 1960s. However, they essentially consist of training opportunities in Cuba and only to a small extent of material aid. Recently, Cuba has striven both to bring about revolutionary unity as a prerequisite for the takeover and to stress the necessity of an "own way," following a successful change of power. Only when the motto "the revolution must be made in one's own country"[24] has been complied with does there seem to be a willingness, as in the case of Nicaragua, to support the revolutionary regime in the stabilization or in resisting destabilization.

In view of the present situation in Central America, Cuba is confronted with an obvious dilemma regarding its national interests. On the one hand, it must be interested in securing the evolvement of more socialist-oriented nations in addition to Nicaragua in order to gain a stronger position in the region. On the other hand, it fears that the Reagan administration holds Cuba responsible for all revolutionary developments in Central America, thus creating acute threats to its national security. In view of the development of Soviet-Cuban relations during the past twenty years, it cannot be assumed that Cuba and the Soviet Union share identical interests with regard to Central America. Both are interested in diminishing the hegemonic influence of the United States, but Cuba's risks here are considerably higher than those of the Soviet Union. This explains why Cuba recommended to the Sandinistas in Nicaragua moderation in achieving their domestic goals and in their relationship with the United States. It had also advised the guerrilla groups in El Salvador in October 1979 to support the reformist junta. One principle of Cuba's foreign policy is to operate cautiously in spite of all the propagandistic support for guerrilla groups and to withhold massive support until the power question has been decided. Of course, this policy does not rule out the fact that guerrilla leaders are still being trained in Cuba and that Cuba has certainly procured weapons for the guerrilla groups in Central America.

Because of Cuba's continuing extensive military and developmental engagement in Africa, it is doubtful if it can take up a similar commitment in El Salvador or, later, in Guatemala, considering current commitments in Nicaragua. It seems more likely that Cuba has reached the limit of its resources available for overseas engagement.

Venezuela

Of all the four actors in the region, Venezuela probably practiced in recent years the most active Central American policy. This dates back to an initiative of former Pres. Carlos Andrés Pérez, who provided the Central American nations with extensive credit lines in 1974.[25] In 1978–1979, Venezuela probably played a most significant part in organizing financial and arms aid for the Sandinistas in Nicaragua. The initiative within the Andean Pact of helping the FSLN to gain diplomatic recognition also originated from Venezuela. After the change in government and the takeover by the Christian Democrats in 1979, the Central American policy changed not in intensity but in its ideological orientation. Although continuing to support the government of Nicaragua initially, Venezuela focused its involvement on the junta in El Salvador, led by the Christian Democrats. The reasons for this were personal as well as ideological: Junta chief Duarte had spent many years in exile in Caracas. Since Reagan's inauguration, Venezuela has shown increasing willingness to support U.S. policy, especially with regard to El Salvador.

The formerly very close cooperation between Venezuela and Mexico, especially in support of the revolution in Nicaragua, could for a time be viewed as a rather rival situation between both regional powers for influence in Central America. For example, Venezuela, together with Colombia, authored the counterdeclaration to the French-Mexican initiative favoring El Salvador's opposition, which was signed by a number of Latin American nations. The Falklands/Malvinas conflict prompted in 1982 a renewed change in the political direction of the Venezuelan government under Pres. Luis Herrera Campins; this led to a new rapprochement with the Sandinista regime in Nicaragua and with Mexico's position. However, this reorientation must also be viewed in connection with Duarte's loss of influence following the 1982 elections in El Salvador.

Colombia

For a long time, Colombia's position in its policy toward Central America seemed indifferent. Along with Venezuela, it had initially supported the Sandinistas; later—also with Venezuela—it sided with the junta in El Salvador and—jointly with Venezuela—became the guarantor for the Comunidad Democrática Centroamericana (CDC), which included Costa Rica, Honduras, Guatemala, and El Salvador. Actually, as an especially reliable ally of the United States, Colombia had always followed the U.S. foreign-policy initiatives on all these issues.

As Carter cautiously prepared to pursue an opening to the Central American opposition, Colombia also applauded this move. Since Reagan's election, Colombia has been among those who frequently drew attention to Cuban and Soviet influence in Central America. This, however, was predominantly for domestic reasons, since Colombia is one of the few South American nations facing intense internal oppositions from guerrilla groups and suspecting Cuban influence behind these actions. The virulent controversies with Nicaragua are of a less ideological nature, however. These are prompted by a territorial dispute over the Colombian islands in the Caribbean (San Andrés and Providencia), over which Nicaragua has renewed claims since the takeover of the Sandinistas.[26] Since Belisario Betancur became president in 1982, Colombia has taken a more critical view of U.S. policies in the region and begun not only to cooperate with Mexico and Venezuela on regional peace initiatives but also to take at times a leading role in the Contadora Group.

Argentina

Besides the middle powers, Argentina has played a special role in Central America. Its willingness to support the regimes in Guatemala, El Salvador, and Honduras with the provision of arms and military advisers was partly attributable to ideological affinities and partly to a close cooperation with the United States in the area of defense policy.[27] This "proxy" role ended during the Falklands/Malvinas conflict, however, whereas the relations with Nicaragua and Cuba improved.

Extraregional Actors

That such a great number of actors has contributed in recent years to the internationalization of the conflict in Central America results from three central factors.

1. In view of the traditional cooperation between the ruling elite and the United States, the opposition groups in Central American nations have sought support abroad. Here, of course, ideologically related party groups such as Social or Christian Democrats, Communists (in the case of Cuba), and the socialist countries of Eastern Europe presented themselves as partners. This transnational component is a distinct expression of the process of modernization and internationalization that has taken place in the political systems of Central America in recent years, at least on the side of the opposition.

2. The traditional elite felt isolated during the Carter administration and sought diplomatic and military support from other authoritarian regimes.

3. The conflict in Central America is a prime example of the controversy between the national and transnational actors who favor the status quo in the Third World and those who consider radical change the only possibility of improving the living conditions of the majority of the population. This is the basis of all ideological contrasts between East and West, North and South, capitalism and socialism, Christian Democrats and Social Democrats, military and guerrillas in the region.

Thus Central America, for example, also offers a variant of the Middle East conflict, where the Palestine Liberation Organization (PLO) and Israel stand on opposite sides of the political spectrum. Israel provides training and military assistance, whereas Libya, Algeria, and Iraq support the guerrilla groups, that is, the Sandinista regime in Nicaragua, with financial aid or credit. The PLO provided the Sandinistas with military experts both before the revolution and after.[28]

The socialist nations, particularly the Soviet Union[29] and the German Democratic Republic (GDR), have very clearly revealed their political preferences in the region. Apart from the great accompanying propaganda effort, they have backed Nicaragua economically and provided advisers since the FSLN's assumption of power.[30] The extent to which arms supplies from the socialist countries reach other countries of the region has not yet been proven. Undoubtedly, the socialist countries regard Central America as a useful side theater, suitable for diverting the attention of the Third World, in particular, from the events in Poland and Afghanistan. Except for its confirmation of support for Cuba against every threat and its conspicuously extensive arms shipments to Cuba in 1981,[31] however, the Soviet Union has exercised surprising moderation with regard to developments in Central America. Since the nations of this region have little to offer the Soviet Union economically and lie in the geopolitical sphere of influence of the United States, it is, in fact, mainly the propaganda effect that the Soviet Union deems important. Both the geographical distance and the apparent ideological divergencies with several important opposition movements make closer ties between the socialist camp and Central America rather unlikely. Although granting more credit to Nicaragua in 1982, the Soviet Union would hardly consider closer ties with that nation for economic, ideological, and especially defense-policy reasons. Under present international conditions, the Soviet Union would hardly be capable of providing a security guarantee for this country.

Western Europe's role in this conflict region is extremely ambiguous. One side is represented by the firm stand of François Mitterand's French government together with Mexican policy; on the other side, Christian and Social Democrats are heavily involved in the conflict through their international organizations. Both groups advocate social change as a basis for the stabilization of the region. The difference lies in their views of how social change should come about. The Christian Democrats tend to lean in the direction of U.S. policy, thus overemphasizing, at least temporarily, the East-West dimension of the controversy in Central America.[32] The Social Democrats, on the other hand, are more concerned with working—through the Socialist International—toward integration of the revolutionary groups into the political systems in Central America. Therefore, the Social Democrats do not reject a priori political models such as the one in Nicaragua, even if they find it increasingly difficult to support the Sandinistas because of their growing radicalization and militarization.[33] In contrast to the United States, the Socialist International advocates a negotiated political settlement in El Salvador. In concurrence with France and Mexico, it wants to prevent a situation in which the opposing forces are left with the sole option of seeking close ties with the socialist camp if they disagree with the present conditions.

Three Competing International Tendencies

The polarization in Central America intensified the internationalization of the conflict, and this internationalization, in turn, hastened the polarization. At the same time, the necessity of a radical structural change grew, but the possibilities for political compromise declined. The variety of actors not only reduced the possibilities of controlling developments in the region but also raised the question of a political alliance among the different international actors. Three groups are distinguishable:

- the status quo alliance: the United States, the Christian Democratic World Union, Israel, and the governments of Guatemala, El Salvador, Costa Rica, and Honduras
- the social-change alliance: Mexico, the Socialist International, France, Panama, Colombia, and Venezuela (since the Falklands/Malvinas conflict)
- the revolutionary-change alliance: Cuba, the socialist nations, Libya, the PLO, Algeria, Nicaragua, and the guerrilla movements

The leadership of the respective groups has crystallized formally or informally during recent years. The United States, Mexico, and Cuba are, in that order, the decisive external actors in the crisis region. Affiliation with the respective groups is, of course, by no means fixed, especially as it concerns the Latin American members; rather, it has changed considerably since immediately after the revolution in Nicaragua. Such changes of positions have to do with whoever happens to be defining national interests at the time and, furthermore, with the strength of U.S. influence on the respective elites. The domestic legitimacy of a government also shapes its attitude toward the conflict. Latin American regimes who themselves have to contend with guerrilla movements or face a guerrilla revival are not interested in supporting the "demonstration effect" in Central America as well.

To enforce their interests, the international actors in the region have five different categories of instruments at their disposal: (1) use of force, or threat of force; (2) bilateral economic or military aid, or denial thereof; (3) logistic and training assistance, or denial thereof; (4) diplomatic legitimation, or denial thereof; and (5) multilateral credit and trade advantages, or denial thereof. In past controversies, almost all these instruments have been used against Nicaragua, El Salvador, and Guatemala, mostly by the United States. Each of the leading powers within the three rival international tendencies endeavors to arrange and coordinate as many as possible of these measures within its own group. This naturally causes alliance problems, with negative effects that are reflected in quite different areas. In the presence of the aggravated East-West differences, the options of the various groups begin to diminish. The outbreak of hostilities within a regional context becomes ever more probable with the dangerous increase of border conflicts between the individual Central American countries under ideological premises and the inclusion of obvious superpower interests. On the other hand, the question of the settlement of these conflicts in Central America simultaneously raises—especially for the nations of the Western alliance—the question of their ability and willingness not only to tolerate but support social change in the Third World.

Should the East-West conflict indeed be decided in the Third World in the long run, the settlement of structural conflicts in Central America will require a scrupulous differentiation between the prestige demands of a superpower and the developmental necessities of small nations in their geopolitical environs. The more the controversies as to El Salvador's form of government and Nicaragua's economy are turned into a test case for international relations among different nations, the more imminent the danger that the development in Central America will assume the form of a "self-fulfilling prophecy."

Notes

1. José Napoleón Duarte himself emphasized this repeatedly: "The root of the evil in El Salvador lies not in the Soviet Union or in Cuba, but in the social injustice prevailing here." See interview in *Die Zeit*, February 12, 1982.

2. See the work of the former vice-president of Guatemala, Francisco Villagrán Kramer, "The Background to the Current Political Crisis in Central America," in *Central America: International Dimensions of the Crisis*, Richard E. Feinberg (ed.), (New York: Holmes and Meier, 1982), pp. 15–35.

3. Thus, for instance, Joaquin Cristobal, a guerrilla leader from Guatemala, thought that the successful revolution in Nicaragua proved "that a people can overthrow dictatorships like Somoza's in Nicaragua, and . . . conquer the armies . . . through the revolutionary process. . . . We believe that the progress of the revolution of the Central American people cannot be halted." Cited in *Monitor-Dienst, Latin America*, June 16, 1980, p. 5.

4. See Marlise Simons, "3 Armies Collaborate in Central America," *Washington Post*, October 27, 1981, in which the goal of the military governments of El Salvador, Guatemala, and Honduras—to fight collectively against guerrilla activities—is described.

5. The influence of the reorientation of the U.S. Latin American policy to the complex regional network of relationships is described by Richy Singh and M. S. Wallace, "The Caribbean Circle of Crisis," in *South* (January 1981), pp. 21–25; and Antonio Cavalla Rojas, "U.S. Military Strategy in Central America: From Carter to Reagan," *Contemporary Marxism*, no. 3 (Summer 1981), pp. 114–130. On the other hand, the guerrilla units in El Salvador had attempted to bring about a military decision in their favor before the inauguration of Ronald Reagan, but failed in this in January 1981.

6. "The advocates of controlled evolutionism believed, or hoped, that the rulers of Guatemala, El Salvador, and Nicaragua could be prevailed upon to begin a process of political transition." Richard E. Feinberg, "The Recent Rapid Redefinitions of U.S. Interests and Diplomacy in Central America," in *Central America: International Dimensions of the Crisis*, Richard E. Feinberg (ed.), (New York: Holmes and Meier, 1982), pp. 58–84 (quote on p. 62).

7. Klaus Ellrodt, "Israeli Arms for Nicaragua," *Frankfurter Allgemeine Zeitung*, May 9, 1978; and "Israel Steps Into the Breach," *Latin America Weekly Report*, December 18, 1981.

8. Interview with Luigi Einaudi, "U.S. Seeks To Keep Contact as Central American Nations Change," *United States Wireless Bulletin*, no. 189 (October 7, 1980), pp. 27–33.

9. "The net impact of the assistance we are giving is to keep in the game not only the United States, but precisely the Nicaraguan entrepreneurial and business elite who joined the struggle against Somoza," ibid., p. 30.

10. For a summary of Carter's policy see Jorg Lawton Casals, "Crisis de la hegemonia. La politica de Carter hacia Nicaragua: 1977–1979," *Cuadernos Semestrales*, no. 6 (1979), pp. 59–113. The criticism of this policy was most sharply formulated by Jeane Kirkpatrick, "U.S. Security and Latin America," *Commentary* 71, no. 1 (January 1981), pp. 29–40.

11. For a discussion of the effectiveness of these reform attempts, see Philip Wheaton, *Agrarian Reform in El Salvador: A Program of Rural Pacification* (Washington, D.C.: Epica Task Force, 1980); and Roy L. Prosterman, Jeffrey M. Riedinger, and Mary N. Temple, "Land Reform and the El Salvador Crisis," *International Security* 6, no. 1 (Summer 1981), pp. 53–74.

12. Richard Allen, then national security adviser, promised "quick action against Fidel Castro's Soviet directed, armed and financed marauders in Central America, specifically Nicaragua, El Salvador and Guatemala." Cited in *Latin America Weekly Report*, November 14, 1980.

13. "El Salvador: Communist Interference and a Brief Background," *Department of State Bulletin* 81, no. 204 (March 1981), pp. 1–11.

14. Interview with Alexander Haig, *U.S. News and World Report*, (December 21, 1981), pp. 22–23.

15. "I think we are seeing the application of the domino theory . . . and I think it's time the people of the United States realize . . . that we are the last domino," Ronald Reagan, *International Herald Tribune*, October 13, 1980. See also Carlos Rangel, "Mexico and Other Dominos," *Commentary* 71, no. 6 (June 1981), pp. 27–33; and Jiri Valenta, "The USSR, Cuba, and the Crisis in Central America," *Orbis* 25, no. 3 (Fall 1981), pp. 715–746.

16. As was the case at the beginning of the 1960s, after the Cuban revolution, the cooperation of the United States with Latin America's military elite is now increasing. See "Comentario de Antonio Cavalla Rojas a la Ponencia presentada por Margaret Daly Hayes," *Cuadernos Semestrales*, no. 10 (1981), pp. 80–92 (quote on p. 92).

17. Bernhard Gwertzman, "Latin Policy: A New Plan, U.S. Outlines Program for Central America," *New York Times*, December 6, 1981; and Barbara Crossette, "Caribbean Aid Plan Advances but Faces Hurdles," *New York Times*, January 15, 1982.

18. *Estados Unidos: Perspectiva Latinoamericana* 6, no. 11 (November 1981), pp. 123–125.

19. Constantine C. Menges, "Current Mexican Foreign Policy and United States Interest" (Hudson Institute, Washington, D.C., June 1980, Mimeographed).

20. For Mexico's long-term goals in the Caribbean and Central America, see John F. McShane, "Emerging Regional Power: Mexico's Role in the Caribbean Basin," in *Latin American Foreign Policies*, Elizabeth G. Ferris and Jennie K. Lincoln (eds.), (Boulder, Colo.: Westview Press, 1981), pp. 191–209.

21. Edward J. Williams, *Mexico's Central American Policy: Apologies, Motivations, and Principles* (Carlisle, Pa.: Strategic Studies Institute, U.S. Army War College, 1982).

22. Declaración Conjunta Mexicano-Francesa sobre El Salvador, *Revista Internacional y Diplomatica* 31, no. 370 (September 1981), p. 8.

23. López Portillo emphasized in his speech in Managua on February 21, 1982: "Los mexicanos queremos ser útiles, queremos conducto, enlace, comunicacíon entre quienes han dejado de hablarse o quienes nunca lo han hecho." *El Día*, February 22, 1982.

24. Statements of the Cuban vice-president Carlos Rafael Rodriguez in his interview in *Der Spiegel*, no. 40 (1981), pp. 187–194.

25. At the meeting of Central America's presidents in Puerto Ordaz on December 13, 1974, Venezuela offered credit to stabilize revenues from coffee exports. *La Politica Internacional de Carlos Andrés Perés*, vol. 1 (Caracas: Ed. Centauro, 1980), pp. 173–176 (specific details on p. 175).

26. See Gerhard Drekonja Kornat, "El Diferendo entre Colombia y Nicaragua," *Colombia: Politica Exterior* (Bogotá: La Editora, 1982), pp. 105–129. For Colombia's position see Diego Uribe Vargas, *Libro Blanco de la República de Colombia 1980* (Bogotá: Ministerio de Relaciones Exteriores, 1980); for Nicaragua's position, Ministerio del Exterior, *Libro Blanco sobre el caso de San Andrés y Providencia* (Managua: Ministerio del Exterior, 1980).

27. Statements concerning Argentine aid, especially to the junta in El Salvador, are found in "U.S. in Central America: Helper or Hegemonist," *South,* no. 16 (February 1982), pp. 19–21 (specific details on p. 20); "Argentina ofrece ayuda militar al gobierno salvadoreño," *El Pais,* March 20, 1981; and "Argentina Hovers on the Brink of Central American Adventure," *Latin America Weekly Report,* February 12, 1982.

28. See León Hadar, "Strange Alliance," *Jerusalem Post,* International Edition, August 16–22, 1981, describing PLO activities in Latin America. Libya granted Nicaragua US$100 million in credit; see *New York Times,* April 26, 1981. For Israel's activities, see "Israel Steps Into the Breach," *Latin America Weekly Report,* December 18, 1981.

29. See "Central America: The Perspective from Moscow," *International Herald Tribune,* July 3, 1981; the Latin American view, in *Estados Unidos, perspectiva Latinoamericana* 7, no. 1 (January 1982), pp. 1–5 and *Latin America Weekly Report,* January 15, 1982; and the comprehensive analysis of Robert S. Leiken, *Soviet Strategy in Latin America,* The Washington Papers, no. 93 (New York: Praeger, 1982).

30. See *Washington Post,* December 2, 1981, referring to a US$28 million credit from the Soviet Union, and *Neue Zürcher Zeitung,* February 2, 1982, where it is said that GDR development aid amounted to over US$100 million.

31. Thomas O. Enders, assistant secretary of state for inter-American affairs, commented: "Cuba is systematically expanding its capacity to project military power beyond its own shores. The arrival this year of a second squadron of Mig-23/Floggers and the 63,000 tons of war supplies imported from the Soviet Union come on top of what is already by several times the largest air, land and sea inventory of the region." *United States Wireless Bulletin,* no. 23, February 3, 1982.

32. See "Ratifican Apóyo a la Junta salvadoreña 17 partidos democristianos de América," *El Día,* July 15, 1980; and Josef Thesing, "Krisenherd Mittelamerika: Nicaragua und die revolutionären Folgen," *Die politische Meinung* 24, no. 187 (November 1979), pp. 64–72.

33. For the significance of democratic and revolutionary groups in Central America, see Klaus Lindenberg, "Streitkräfte und politische Parteien," *Lateinamerika, Herrschaft, Gewalt und internationale Abhängigkeit,* Klaus Lindenberg (ed.), (Bonn: Neue Gesellschaft, 1982), pp. 87–102. For the general policy of the Socialist International toward Central America, see Pierre Schori, "Central American Dilemma," *Socialist Affairs,* no. 1 (1981), pp. 33–39.

11
Central America: Options for U.S. Policy in the 1980s

Richard E. Feinberg

Informed American opinion is deeply divided over the role the United States should play in today's world. This absence of consensus is generally discussed in terms of instruments of policy. In fact, there are profound differences over objectives, which, in turn, reflect differing conceptions of U.S. interests.

The hard underlying question, that of defining the national interest, is not often explicitly addressed. Political leaders naturally want to leave the impression that they are instruments of a unified national will, so it ill befits them to even suggest that alternative visions of the national interest might exist. Rather they prefer to maintain that they are most capable of defending "the national interest."[1] Even for lay analysts, the issue of "national interest" is difficult to engage dispassionately, since the fundamental values and image of the nation and—by implication—of oneself are at stake.

In some areas of the world, U.S. national interests are relatively clear. In the Middle East, for example, the free flow of oil and the physical security of Israel are "obvious" interests (although they may be in conflict!). In Western Europe, the containment of Soviet power is a clear U.S. interest. In Central America, however, the U.S. national interest is especially illusive. There are no crucial raw materials at stake, no important allies to protect. Economically backward and politically fragmented—an area in isolation—Central America clearly is not of major significance. Central America becomes important only in terms of its impact on a broader global, or at least hemispheric, definition of U.S. interests.

The heated debate over policy toward Central America is explicitly or implicitly invoking a series of elements that would contribute to a definition of the U.S. national interest. Some of these elements are in conflict; others can be grouped to form a more or less coherent conceptualization of the national interest. The first part of this chapter will discuss the various elements of the national interest. The second will selectively group these elements into three alternative perspectives of the national interest and proceed to detail their implications for U.S. policy toward Central America.

Elements of the National Interest

Ideology

Many Americans have long believed that the U.S. national interest is best defended by having the world, and especially the hemisphere, populated by states ruled by ideologies compatible with those of the United States. Systems of state socialism have traditionally been excluded from the circle of acceptable ideologies, partly but not wholly because of the tendency of such states to be allied with the Soviet Union. Ideas themselves are a driving force in history, and a United States on the ideological defensive would increasingly find itself in a hostile world. Within the United States, however, a fierce debate rages over which political systems are compatible with U.S. values. The Carter administration's human-rights policy denied the older cold-war assumption that right-wing authoritarian states—including the Central American variety—fell within the sphere of acceptability.[2] Only open political systems were held to be truly compatible with U.S. values, even if alliances of convenience with repressive regimes might still be honored. The Reagan administration has returned to the earlier, more inclusive perspective.

Security

A consensus exists that the Soviet Union ought to be denied military bases in Central America. Wide disagreement arises, however, over the dangers of a lesser degree of Soviet influence. Some argue that even if Central America itself is not of great importance, spreading Soviet influence there could eventually drive north and south, toward the oil fields of Mexico[3] and the locks of the Panama Canal. Indeed, a destabilized Mexico could even directly threaten the internal security of the United States, since unrest in Mexico could be transmitted into the United States through its large and growing Latino population.

Geopolitics

Once again Cuba has become the central focus of concern for many Americans watching the Caribbean. This view holds that the United States is engaged in a serious conflict for regional influence with Cuba.[4] The Caribbean Basin, including Central America, is seen as the relevant geopolitical arena, and the outcome of events in each Central American state affects the power balance and the momentum in the U.S.-Cuban competition. To varying degrees, Cuba is seen in this competition as a "pawn" or at least as a client state of the Soviet Union, but Cuba itself has sufficient strength to be considered a dangerous opponent.

Global Power

In the last few years the idea has gained rather wide currency in the United States that American power has declined in the world because of the "Vietnam syndrome,"[5] that is, an unwillingness to forcefully impose sanctions against enemies (states and political movements) and to stand firmly beside friends. The perception around the world that the United States is unwilling to act on such principles has led to a snowballing decline in the U.S. influence over events, according to this view. The failure of the United States to act forcefully in Central America—a region seen by many foreigners as the natural sphere of influence of the United States—would be another, dramatic demonstration of U.S. weakness.

Economic Interests

Even though there would be wide agreement that U.S. economic interests are too limited in Central America to be the driving factor in policy, they can be relevant. U.S. direct investment, while small in any single country, totals about one billion dollars, and U.S. bank exposure is considerably more. There is a general concern in U.S. business circles that Central America remain integrated into the global financial and trading system. A decision by Central American states to opt out of the Western economic system, while annoying in itself, would also be considered a dangerous precedent for other Third World states. The fragile and worried international banking community would be especially upset at the potential demonstration effects of national defaults.

In addition to these general, systemic concerns, firms or individuals doing business in Central America may have access to influential officials and thus have disproportionate influence. The support Anastasio Somoza Debayle enjoyed in the U.S. Congress almost certainly reflected such particular financial interests.

THREE CONCEPTIONS OF THE U.S. NATIONAL INTEREST

The elements outlined above may be selectively grouped to formulate three conceptions of the U.S. national interest. Each of the three visions has a reasonable degree of internal consistency. "Reassertionism," "regionalism," and "neo-realism" describe the informal theoretical tendencies of their advocates, rather than actual self-identifications. Elements of the first, reassertionist view are expressed today by many supporters of the Reagan administration. The Carter administration combined elements of all three perspectives, but particularly the second and third. The discussion of each conception includes a sample offering of logical policy deductions.

Reassertionism

Reassertionists combine strong concerns for a perceived global ideological conflict, a maximalist worry over the security threat emanating from Central America northward and southward, and a dominant desire to reassert U.S. power. They sometimes emphasize "balance of power" politics, while sometimes their concerns are expressed in more ideological terms.[6] Although reassertionists are anxious about an expansionist Cuba, the geopolitical contest in the Caribbean Basin (their geopolitical unit of analysis) is viewed primarily in the broader East-West framework. Soviet power, they argue, has already penetrated the Caribbean Basin through its client state in Cuba.[7] This penetration of the American "Mediterranean" must be sealed off and contained.

Reassertionists give little explicit attention to economic interests, although individual advocates may have personal interests at stake in Central America. Rather, the reassertionists view the turmoil in Central America as largely the product of U.S. government errors, which the Cubans have been quick to exploit. The decline of U.S. influence in Central America is seen as just one example of a weakened U.S. global posture. The "loss" of Nicaragua was an otherwise avoidable result of a "weak" U.S. foreign policy.

The Vietnam syndrome, which inhibited the projection of U.S. force abroad, has combined with President Carter's human-rights campaign to destabilize U.S. allies and give a free hand to U.S. enemies. The reassertionists would seek to reverse this trend by standing loyally by friendly governments, while offering no quarter to forces hostile to U.S. interests. Power is seen as being heavily dependent upon perceptions, and the reassertionists believe that the successful projection of U.S. influence requires that both our allies and our enemies perceive U.S. coercive threats to be credible.

Central America has assumed considerable importance for the reassertionists, for several reasons. First, if the United States cannot control events in its own "backyard," then where can it? Second, Central America seems to present favorable terrain for a visible demonstration of a renewed U.S. will and strength.[8] Third, reassertionists typically accept that great powers both enjoy and require a safe sphere of influence—and Central America falls within the U.S. sphere. Fourth, securing the southern flank of the United States is a prerequisite for keeping U.S. forces free for engagement elsewhere, in potential trouble spots of greater inherent strategic or economic importance.

As the reassertionist school surveys the current circumstances in Central America, it can choose among several tactical approaches to achieve its basic objectives. These approaches might be grouped under two broad headings: a very hard-line "unilateral militarism" and a somewhat more complex "modernization" approach.

Unilateral Militarism

One wing of the reassertionist school believes that the United States can and should go it alone in pursuing its interests in many areas of the globe, especially in the Western Hemisphere. This radical nationalist strain of thinking is highly skeptical of the reliability and stamina of Western Europe.[9] Secondary or regional powers (such as Mexico and Venezuela) can be useful if they are prepared to follow the U.S. lead, but can be bypassed when they are not. Indeed, in an increasingly neutral or hostile world, the "solidarity" of the Western Hemisphere has assumed a renewed importance. This security-oriented framework sees military power as the key element in protecting U.S. hemispheric interests. The United States should reestablish its frayed ties with Latin security forces and provide them with the moral and material support they need to counter subversion. Should that fail, the United States should seriously consider the direct application of U.S. forces.

The unilateral militarists favor the extension of sufficient security assistance to the Salvadorean security forces to enable them to win a military victory against the guerrillas. Complementary assistance would be extended to the Guatemalan and Honduran security forces to attempt to dry up arms flows to the Salvadorean left. If the Salvadorean Christian Democrats are perceived to be inhibiting the effectiveness of the security forces, their ouster from the government might be desirable. Certainly the agrarian reform, the bank nationalizations, and the government's control over agricultural exports would each be reexamined. More important than seeking to gain peasant support through such political reforms would be the rebuilding of a solid alliance between the security forces and the business sector, the effective pursuit of the antiguerrilla war, and the restructuring of the Salvadorean economy along "efficiency" criteria. The costs, in terms of international opinion and diplomacy, of reversing some of the reforms would be given a relatively low weight.

The Sandinista government in Nicaragua represents an intolerable penetration of the Central American isthmus by pro-Cuban forces. The objective must be the removal of the FSLN from power.[10] Although a combination of measures might be employed to accomplish this end, the unilateral militarists would not rule out assisting friendly troops attempting to physically oust the FSLN. Should the Cubans or Soviets dare to send substantial military aid to the FSLN, the planes or boats being used for transport would be seen as fair game for U.S. interceptors, and even Cuba itself might be considered a target for retaliation.

The security of Guatemala would be another major objective. Guatemala is important because of its potential oil reserves and its proximity to the Mexican oil fields. If leftist forces are permitted to gain ground in Guatemala, Mexico itself—and even the United States—might be destabilized. If secured, Guatemala could become an important asset in assisting El Salvador and Honduras to resist subversion, and Guatemala could even help reverse the current situation in Nicaragua. The Guatemalan military, then, would become a linchpin in reestablishing control over the region, fulfilling the role once played by the Somozas.

Honduras would be seen primarily in terms of the need to secure neighboring states. If the harder-line elements in the Honduran military were best disposed to play this role, and they preferred to exercise political power, the United States would drop its support for the political liberalization process.

Modernization

The modernization strain recognizes that internal dynamics have played at least some role in generating instability. The recommended response—counterinsurgency—contains a major military component, but is also concerned with winning the "hearts and minds" of the people.[11] Thus, whereas the unilateral militarism approach might settle for the "Haitianization" of El Salvador, counterinsurgency advocates would seek to "dry up the ponds" in which guerrillas swim by fostering a more balanced economic modernization. A substantial U.S. aid effort would seek to involve the peasantry and urban poor in projects identified with the Salvadorean government. Those who were persistently hostile would be denied such benefits, and, if necessary, neutralized.

This approach might press for gradual land-reform programs in Guatemala and Honduras. Peasants would be resettled on new lands, and some inefficiently run haciendas would be purchased and divided into smaller, family-sized farms. The intention would be to simultaneously alleviate some of the discontent among the peasantry while creating a new, conservative group of landowners.

The modernization strain of reassertionism would attempt to persuade NATO (North Atlantic Treaty Organization) allies, as well as regional powers, to follow U.S. policies, in part to share the costs of the "civic action" programs.

Regionalism

A regionalist perspective emphasizes regional geopolitics and contains an ideological strain tilting toward centrism and evolutionary change.[12] Reform-minded governments are preferable to highly exclusionary, repressive ones because they are more ideologically compatible with U.S. values and because they offer greater prospects for nonsocialist stability. In the regionalist's mind, the United States is involved in a competitive struggle with Cuba for influence in the Caribbean Basin, but U.S. global prestige is only marginally at stake. If conditions for centrist democracy are not as favorable in Central America as they might be in the more developed South American nations, an activist U.S. policy can give sufficient strength to a struggling "middle." In practice, the regionalist's desire to preclude an opening for ideologically incompatible and Cuban-tied socialist forces results in a cautious preference for gradual change. In order not to risk the unity of the army forces, a right-center coalition is favored, thereby creating a government that it is hoped is more legitimate than a purely rightist one without allowing an opening to the armed left. When conditions permit, elections are seen as ideologically desirable and as an instrument generally likely to prove unfavorable for the left, while conferring enhanced legitimacy on the elected moderates.

Regionalists generally would have supported the Duarte government in El Salvador and viewed the election of March 1982 with favor until it became clear that the extreme right turned out to be the winner. Regionalists also would support the process of democratization in Honduras and would try to pressure the Guatemalan government toward reform. The sudden appearance of Rios Montt, with his promise of moral renewal and modest change, would have been seen as a positive step. Regionalists would not, however, use force to save a disintegrating regime, except perhaps with the prior support of other important regional powers. In Nicaragua, they would maintain normal relations only so long as an acceptable degree of pluralism and private enterprise was tolerated.

The regionalists feel more comfortable with Christian Democracy. Christian Democrats are equally opposed to Marxism and favor certain modernizing reforms, in order both to make an economy more efficient and to decrease political tensions. They have proved willing, at times, to create tactical alliances with the security forces to accomplish these objectives. (Although the reassertionists sometimes consider Christian Democrats to be useful, often they see them as weak, irresponsible, and dangerous "Kerenskys.") Thus, the regionalists would have advocated sustained support for José Napoleón Duarte in El Salvador. Had Duarte consolidated the reforms already begun, the left's appeal would have withered. As the business sector came to understand that the Christian Democratic strategy of reformism was the wisest political response to insurgency, the social base of the Duarte regime would have become stronger. The remaining task would have been to deprive the guerrillas of weaponry. The regionalists would have used the relative legitimacy of the Duarte government to try to persuade neighboring states to impede the flow of weapons into El Salvador.

Regionalists place considerable emphasis on working with other countries in the region, especially with the local "influentials." Working with such powers increases the legitimacy of U.S. actions, spreads any financial burdens, and provides Latin sources of influence to counter Cuban designs. Thus, the regionalists would encourage Mexico, and especially Venezuela, to play an active role in post-Somoza Nicaragua. But the differences in the basic approaches of Mexico and Venezuela mirror the confusion in the regionalist's approach to the current Nicaraguan dynamic. In the advocacy of a nonaligned foreign policy and pluralistic politics for Nicaragua, the regionalist is uncertain as to whether the end result can be closer to the Mexican or the Venezuelan model. A Mexican definition of pluralism would still allow for the FSLN to monopolize control over the executive branch, with pluralism characterizing the economy and culture. The Venezuelan model would imply a gradual evolution to a competitive political system that would allow for non-Sandinista political parties to gain control of the government through elections. Most regionalists would prefer the Venezuelan model, but consider that pressuring the FSLN too hard would only result in the rapid construction of a national-security state "to defend the revolution." Thus, the regionalist probably would adopt a swerving and ambiguous course, trying to nudge the FSLN to yield ground, but not pushing so hard as to provoke a radicalization of the Nicaraguan process.

The regionalists are supportive of the process of democratization in Honduras and encourage the civilian political parties in their efforts to strengthen the legitimate and moderately reformist government. Guatemala, however, presents a more formidable challenge. While the still-united Guatemalan elites represent the strongest conservative force in the region, regionalists worry that, in the long run, Guatemala is dangerously explosive. The country possesses the natural endowments to undertake the types of socioeconomic reforms that could diffuse the gathering political storm—but the Guatemalan military and business sectors believe that simple repression is a more reliable guarantor of stability. Some regionalists believe that a more forthcoming U.S. policy would place the United States in a better position to nudge Guatemala in the desired direction. The emergence of the Rios Montt government strengthened this tendency, at least temporarily. Other regionalists would favor a diplomacy of "disassociation," in order to encourage more reformist elements to surface and to proceed either to pressure those in power to undertake the necessary reforms or else to seize power themselves.[13]

Regionalists are concerned that the wide diversity of political models existing in the region today is itself a source of major and chronic instability. The mutual distrusts, as well as the differing economic models, have made a casualty of regional economic integration. Thus, the regionalists would like to see a greater convergence of political systems, with both Guatemala and Nicaragua moving in the direction of the moderate reformism now in power in Honduras or Costa Rica.

Neo-Realism

Neo-realists rather fatalistically accept the declining ability of the United States to control the domestic politics of the Third World states.[14] Instead, they argue that the diffusion of power among numerous competing poles and the relative decline in U.S. strength have forever placed many international events beyond the reach of the United States—as well as beyond that of the Soviet Union.[15] Furthermore, since U.S. economic interests are now compatible with a wide variety of political models, the U.S. can accommodate to a range of regimes in the developing world. In this sense, the neo-realists take a more relaxed view toward domestic ideologies, emotionally preferring centrist democracies, but believing that regimes of both the right and left can be compatible with a range of important U.S. interests. They feel strongly that the Soviets ought to be denied military bases and that U.S. diplomacy should seek to prevent the Soviets from gaining political control over Central American states, but neo-realists reject a "domino" theory that Mexico or Panama is necessarily vulnerable because of events in Central America.

Economic forces are primarily relied upon to maintain U.S. influence in the Third World, and it is believed that any rational regime will want access to U.S. and Western technology and capital. Such trade and financial ties will generate the minimal sense of shared interests to allow for acceptable bilateral relations. The maintenance of a smoothly functioning international economic system is seen as the key to U.S. strength and the West's ability to continue to integrate the developing countries into that system.

Neo-realists might be more willing to accept some Cuban influence in Central America. Cuban influence can best be limited, if not denied, by supporting political reforms that will reduce Cuba's opportunities. Should a leftist regime come to power, economic necessity and inherent nationalism should be relied upon to draw the regime toward the West's economy and into a genuinely nonaligned foreign policy.

Far from a defeat, the Nicaraguan revolution offered the promise of a revolutionary state that has, at least so far, avoided becoming a client state of the Soviets and has assiduously sought to maintain its trading and financial links to the United States and the West. From the neo-realist perspective, the danger in revolution is either anarchy—which disrupts economic interchange—or the development of a security relationship with the Soviet Union. Thus, a policy of economic aid and diplomatic openness, combined with multilateral effects to dampen disputes between Central American nations, makes sense as the best method for helping to reconstruct the Nicaraguan polity and economy and for shortcircuiting the dynamic of mutual distrust and hostility that could drive the FSLN toward the Soviets. The reduction of U.S. political influence in Managua is less important than the continued integration of Nicaragua in the global economy and the development of a nationalist regime independent of either Cuba or the Soviet Union.

Because the neo-realists are especially concerned about the current instabilities in the international financial system, a priority is placed on maintaining the solvency of debtor countries. The neo-realist would therefore voice strong opposition to any attempts to economically strangulate Nicaragua, for fear that a desperate FSLN might repudiate its substantial debt due the international financial community.

The neo-realists would be concerned that the conflict in El Salvador could simultaneously sour U.S.-Nicaraguan relations, undermine political and economic stability throughout the region, and draw the United States into a costly and protracted intervention. Therefore, more important than the restoration of U.S. control or the denial of any increase in Cuban influence is a peaceful and sustainable resolution of the Salvadorean crisis. The exact terms of the solution are less important than its durability, provided that the emergent regime adopts economically rational policies, avoids either a virulent anti-U.S. or slavishly pro-Soviet diplomacy, and, of course, permits no foreign bases on its soil.

Whereas regionalists look to Venezuela as the more reliable and compatible ally in Central America, neo-realists would place greater weight on a Mexican role. Neo-realists would not be as concerned about Mexico's tolerance for less controlled social processes and would be attracted to Mexico because of its financial and diplomatic potential. Rather than viewing Mexico as flirting dangerously with Havana, Mexico would be seen as building considerable economic and diplomatic leverage over the Cuban government. Mexico might thus displace Cuba as the emerging external force in Central America. For this to occur, however, Mexico would have to move rapidly to overcome its traditional "non-interventionist" scruples.

Neo-realists would be concerned that a political explosion in Guatemala could endanger regional stability. Like reassertionists, the neo-realists would worry about possible repercussion into Mexico, where the economic and security stakes are high, but would be more prepared to rely on Mexico to defend its own interests. In Guatemala as elsewhere, the neo-realists would be supportive of any serious Mexican effort to mediate or otherwise resolve political conflict.

Conclusion

Each of these three conceptualizations of the U.S. national interest has elements with mass appeal to the American electorate. Reassertionism responds to the popular sense of frustration at the decline in American power. Regionalism appeals to democratic idealism and the anti-Cuban feeling widespread in the United States. Neo-realism adheres to values central to American culture: pragmatism, materialism, benign internationalism. For the moment, the reassertionist view is on the political offensive, and influential members and supporters of the Reagan administration adhere to important elements of it.

Whichever perspective or combination of perspectives dominates policymaking in the coming years, translating general U.S. interests and objectives into operational policies capable of successfully influencing events in Central America will be a difficult challenge.

Notes

1. For a discussion of the importance for policymaking of clearly defining the national interest, see Donald Nuechterlein, *National Interest and Presidential Leadership: The Setting of Priorities* (Boulder, Colo.: Westview Press, 1980).

2. An analysis of the objectives and implementation of the Carter administration's human-rights policies can be found in Richard E. Feinberg, *U.S. Human Rights Policy: Latin America*, Monograph, vol. 6, no. 1 (Washington, D.C.: Center for International Policy, 1980).

3. See Constantine Menges, "Mexico: The Iran Next Door?" *San Diego Union* (August 1979); and "Central America/Mexico: A forecast of strategic trends, 1980–83," *International Strategic Issues* (April 1980). For a view that the Mexican state will be able to withstand turmoil in Central America, see René Herrera Zúñiga and Mario Ojeda, "Mexican Foreign Policy and Central America," in Richard E. Feinberg (ed.), *Central America: International Dimensions of the Crisis* (New York: Holmes and Meier, 1982), pp. 160–186.

4. In its first months, the Reagan administration clearly adopted this view. See Tad Szulc, "Confronting the Cuban Nemesis," *New York Times Magazine,* April 5, 1981.

5. For a critique of the "Vietnam syndrome," see Robert Tucker, "America in Decline: The Foreign Policy of Maturity," *Foreign Affairs* 58 (Spring 1980), pp. 449–484.

6. A discussion emphasizing the role of ideology in U.S. policy can be found in Norman Podhoretz, "The Present Danger," *Commentary* (March 1980). Another more politico-military argument for a reassertion of global containment is Paul H. Nitze, "Strategy in the Decade of the 1980s," *Foreign Affairs* 59 (Fall 1980), pp. 82–101.

7. For a discussion of Cuban activities in the Caribbean Basin, see Jeane Kirkpatrick, "U.S. Security in Latin America," *Commentary* (January 1981), pp. 29–40. See also James D. Theberge, "Rediscovering the Caribbean: Toward a U.S. Policy for the 1980s," *Common Sense* (March 1980), pp. 1–20.

8. For an interpretation of the Reagan administration's emphatic support for the government in El Salvador as being such a demonstration, see "Psychodrama in El Salvador," *New York Times,* February 27, 1981, p. 26.

9. Concern over the "Finlandization" of Western Europe is expressed in Walter LaQueur, *A Continent Astray* (New York: Oxford University Press, 1979), pp. 222–245.

10. See Cleto di Giovanni, Jr., and Alexander Krüger, "Reports: Central America," *The Washington Quarterly* (Summer 1980), pp. 175–186.

11. For an argument that certain lessons from the Vietnam counterinsurgency experience are applicable to El Salvador, see William Colby, "El Salvador: Which Vietnam?" *Washington Post,* April 20, 1981, editorial page.

12. A speech delivered by a Carter administration official contained important aspects of this perspective. See Viron P. Vaky, "Central America at the Crossroads," *Hearings,* U.S. Congress, House, Subcommittee on Inter-American Affairs, Committee on Foreign Affairs, 96th Cong., 1st. sess., September 11, 1979, pp. 9–12.

13. These issues were hotly debated during the tenure of the Carter administration. See "Controversy Looms Over Bid to Aid Guatemala," *Washington Post,* March 11, 1979.

14. For an early discussion of the term *neo-realism,* see Tom J. Farer, "Searching for Defeat," *Foreign Policy,* no. 40 (Fall 1980), pp. 155–174. A full exposition can be found in Richard E. Feinberg, *The Intemperate Zone: The Third World Challenge to U.S. Foreign Policy* (New York: W. W. Norton, 1983), especially the introduction and chap. 5.

15. These ideas were developed, to varying degrees, in such works as George Ball, *Diplomacy for a Crowded World: An American Foreign Policy* (Boston: Little, Brown, 1976); and Robert Keohane and Joseph Nye, *Power and Interdependence: World Politics in Transition* (Boston: Little, Brown, 1977).

12
A Question of U.S. National Interests in Central America

Robert A. Pastor

When a new administration takes office in the United States, one of its first steps in international affairs is to consult with its Western European allies and to reassert the importance it attaches to the NATO alliance. It was therefore not surprising that the Reagan administration would send a high-level diplomatic mission to Bonn, Paris, Brussels, and London in early February 1981. What was surprising, however, was that the top item on the U.S. agenda, the first test of alliance solidarity, was Central America. Europeans have always been sensitive to U.S. concerns with its border area, but they questioned whether El Salvador was the place to draw the line against Soviet expansionism.[1] By what stretch of the imagination could one consider the United States strategically threatened by the local insurgencies in Central America? What U.S. interests were really at stake?

The questions raised by the Europeans have also been raised by Americans; they are addressed in this chapter. But before examining those questions, let me briefly discuss the origins of the crisis in Central America, since perceptions and prescriptions for policy necessarily follow from the picture one has of the origins and the nature of the problem.

Origins

The Presidents' Explanations

There are two rather simple and direct explanations of the origins of the Central American crisis. In his speech at the Organization of American States (OAS) on February 24, 1982, when he announced his Caribbean Basin Initiative, Pres. Ronald Reagan attributed the crisis to "imported terrorism," a "new kind of colonialism" that "stalks the world today and threatens our independence. It is brutal and totalitarian. It is not of our hemisphere but it threatens our hemisphere";[2] it is communism, and it is exploiting the economic crisis caused by the increase in the price of petroleum and the fall in the prices of the principal exports of the region—coffee, bananas, sugar, and cotton.

Mexico's Pres. José López Portillo had offered an alternative explanation in a speech in Managua on February 21: "The Central American and Caribbean revolutions currently taking place are most of all struggles by poor and oppressed people to live better and with more freedom."[3] Although most of Reagan's explanation aimed at Cuba as the source of the problem, López Portillo's speech did not mention Cuba, except to suggest that it is one of the countries of the region "struggling to change domestic and foreign structures which very much resemble the colonial order." López Portillo did, however, mention the United States frequently, both by insinuation and by direct reference:

> I can assure my good friends in the United States that what is taking place here in Nicaragua, what is taking place in El Salvador, and what is blowing throughout the whole region does not constitute an intolerable danger to the basic interests and the national security of the United States. What does constitute a danger for the U.S. is the risk of history's condemnation as a result of suppressing by force the rights of other nations.[4]

One is reassured to learn from the White House press spokesman that the two presidents hit it off so well together. After reading the two speeches given three days apart on the same subject and finding absolutely no conceptual overlap, one is left wondering whether their excellent relationship was brought about by conversing in different languages without the aid of an interpreter.

Which is it? Poverty and injustice as the Mexican president suggests or oil prices and Cuban terrorism as the U.S. president maintains? A neat irony hides in their arguments.

If López Portillo is correct, then one might wonder why Mexico is not in flames. It has one of the most inequitable income distributions in Latin America—worse than it had before its "revolution" in 1910 and worse than El Salvador's today. Indeed, in a report in 1979 the World Bank found an improvement in the distribution of income in El Salvador from 1965 to 1977—the lower 40 percent had increased their share of the economic pie while the top 20 percent had a reduced share. The distribution was still grossly inequitable, but the trend was positive, which was not true in Mexico during the same period.[5]

But the theory that poverty is the cause of the turbulence in Central America is refuted more generally, by both time—the revolutions did not begin twenty years ago when all the nations were poorer—and by space—the region falls comfortably in the middle class of the developing world; forty-six developing countries are poorer than the poorest, Honduras, in Central America.

If Reagan is correct, and all the trouble in Central America is caused by Cubans and Russians, why is similar mischief not being made in the United States? The Cubans and the Soviets have the greatest incentive to export their terrorism to the center of the empire. Why bother stepping on the emperor's toes, when you can plunge a dagger into his heart?

An Alternative Explanation

There is an alternative explanation: The instability in Central America stems from the region's socioeconomic progress and politicomilitary stagnation. (Access for all groups to participate in the political process is one important reason Panama, Costa Rica, and Mexico have been able to escape the instability.) It is, of course, true that most of the people of Central America are poor, not just by U.S. standards but by world standards. The United Nation's Economic Commission on Latin America estimates that 42 percent of the population in the six countries of Central America live in a state of "extreme poverty."[6] The level of economic development ranges from Honduras (per capita income of $530, adult literacy rate of 60 percent, and life expectancy of fifty-eight years) to Costa Rica (per capita income of $1,820, adult literacy rate of 90 percent, and life expectancy of seventy years).[7]

But what is most remarkable is not the poverty in the region, which has been its burden since the dawn of man, but the recent extraordinary rate of economic growth. Between 1950 and 1978, the six nations averaged an annual real rate of growth of 5.3 percent, doubling the real per capita income during this period. This occurred despite the population's having nearly tripled from 8.6 million to 23 million; without population growth, the per capita income would have quintupled.[8]

Primarily banana or coffee exporters in 1950, the six nations have multiplied their trade by a factor of eighteen, and trade has been the stimulus for expanding and diversifying the entire economies. Exports now include a wide range of agricultural products, manufactures, and services. Physical infrastructure—roads, telephones, electrical energy, port facilities, mass communications—expanded severalfold. Just from 1960 to 1976, the adult literacy rate increased from 44 percent to 72 percent.

The changes in the societies wrought by this burst of progress were genuinely revolutionary—as distinguished from changes of governments—and except for Costa Rica and Panama, the other countries simply could not adjust. An enterprising middle and professional class emerged. There was an expansion of medium-sized, efficient agricultural units. A working class also emerged and organized in both the urban and rural areas. The church, which had legitimized the status quo for centuries, likewise underwent a profound transformation in this period, and many priests began to help and identify with the poor.

Utilizing a well-known formula of political alchemy, the new groups sought to change their new economic muscle into political power; they found their path blocked by the old order. In 1972, rejecting the advice of his friends as well as his political enemies, Anastasio Somoza Debayle changed the Nicaraguan constitution and secured a second presidential term for himself. In the same year, the Salvadoran oligarchy colluded with the military and overturned an election won by a coalition led by José Napoleón Duarte of the Christian Democratic party and including the Social Democratic and the Communist parties. Two years later, the same scenario was repeated in Guatemala. In each case, the U.S. government winked as the democratic process was discredited. Human rights had not yet arrived; the United States confused the status quo with stability and is paying the price for that confusion today.

Guerrilla groups roamed the political landscape of Central America throughout the 1960s and 1970s. Cuban support varied, but was never extensive. Only in Guatemala in the late 1960s did the guerrillas represent a threat, and although some saw "another Vietnam," the movement was pushed back into relative isolation and obscurity.[9]

Three related developments in the 1970s gave the guerrillas a chance to emerge from obscurity. First, the population explosion and increased educational opportunities provided the guerrillas with a new and educated leadership, more recruits, and also a politically awakened population. The demographic profile is a critical starting point for understanding the current struggle in Central America. It pits not only old sources of power against new social forces, but what is even more important, it pits an older generation against a younger, better-educated one, representing larger numbers.[10]

Second, the clogging of the political arteries in Nicaragua, El Salvador, and to a lesser extent Guatemala made the guerrillas the only opposition game in town. When the middle class was denied access to power, the guerrillas stole their reformist programs and by doing so enhanced their legitimacy and widened their base. The children of the middle class joined the revolution and persuaded their parents either to stay neutral politically or to front for the guerrillas.

Repression, which long had been the military's way to maintain order, became a counterproductive instrument; a younger population is not intimidated when the security forces slaughter a father or sister—it is politicized. The military thought they were killing the left, but in fact they have been recruiting for them. The famed *muchachos* (very young boys and girls who joined the guerrillas) that made up the bulk of the Sandinistas in Nicaragua and have expanded the guerrilla movements in El Salvador and Guatemala are the result of a collision between a population that is younger overall and a discredited militaristic approach to politics.

Third, the rise in oil prices in 1979 followed by the collapse of the prices of sugar, coffee, bananas, and cotton halted the economic growth and exacerbated unemployment in economies that already could not cope with an annual increase of the labor force of about 3 percent. The war between the military and the guerrillas spooked any further investment and prompted a larger transfer of capital from Central America to the United States. It is currently estimated at more than one-half billion dollars annually, which is more than the U.S. aid program to the region. During the war, GNP fell by 25 percent in 1979 in Nicaragua and by 9 percent in 1980 in El Salvador.[11]

Population pressures, political obstructionism and military repression, and a severe economic depression—these are the medium- and long-term causes of instability; the tinder awaited the spark. The immediate cause—the veritable spark—for the current instability in Central America was the Nicaraguan revolution, which traumatized the region. The left became bolder; the right more intransigent; the middle more precarious. Polarization—the process by which the middle is forced to choose sides, flee, or die—gained momentum. Both the extreme left and right are committed to making the political reality conform to their perceptions and propaganda: that there is no middle. The left claims the choice is between the oligarchy and the people; the right, that it is between communism and Christian values.[12]

Interests

Few Americans—except the unvarnished Cold Warrior of the early 1950s and the Fidelista of the late 1960s—could feel comfortable with such choices. When Nicaragua's dictator Anastasio Somoza Debayle said, in effect, it's either the communists or me, at the same time that everyone was demanding his resignation—the Nicaraguan church, the Chamber of Commerce, and virtually every political group in Nicaragua and most democratic governments outside—the dominant feeling in the United States was either disbelief or revulsion. U.S. sympathies naturally side with the democratic process, the middle class, the underdog; as the polarization process grinds up these groups and values, it is quite natural for Americans to be drawn to original questions: What are U.S. interests in Central America, and do they justify our deep involvement?

Americans cannot help but ask whether El Salvador might not be better off if we were a little less possessive. If we are better off today by letting the Panamanians run the Canal, why would we not be better off tomorrow if we "Let El Salvador Be El Salvador" today? Or Guatemala, Nicaragua, or Honduras? In short, why bother?

It would be unusual for an administration to ponder such original questions, especially when taxed by international crises and endless bureaucratic debates. When an administration does address original questions, as it formally does in testimony before Congress or in speeches, it has no time to devise original answers, and so bureaucrats dust off traditional answers. The explanations that President Reagan and former Secretary of State Haig offered for their policies in Central America certainly have the ring of history. "Make no mistake," Reagan said in his Caribbean Basin speech, "the well-being and security of our neighbors in this region are in our vital interests." Why? "The Caribbean region is a vital strategic and commercial artery for the United States. Nearly half of U.S. trade, two-thirds of our imported oil, and over half of our imported strategic minerals pass through the Panama Canal or the Gulf of Mexico."[13] U.S. ambassador to the OAS J. William Middendorf has said that the region is on our strategic doorstep and that rather than referring to it as our backyard, we should realize that the Caribbean is our strategic front yard. In addition, the United States has economic and ideological interests, defined positively as a concern for freedom and democracy or negatively as anticommunism. These answers have sustained U.S. engagement in the region since the turn of the century, but they are no longer convincing.

Merely to list these interests is to understand why the Reagan administration has been having so much difficulty persuading the American people that a decisive battle is being fought in Central America. A "vital interest" is presumably one for which the United States is willing to fight. In 1914, the United States occupied the port of Veracruz, Mexico, to gain respect for the U.S. flag. In 1916, the United States fought to ensure that customs taxes would be collected in the Dominican Republic. In 1927, U.S. troops died to ensure a free election in Nicaragua. Not only would few Americans consider any of these interests vital today, but it would be hard to identify a consensus in the United States around any interest that would justify unilateral U.S. military intervention in Central America; in a poll published by the *Washington Post* on March 24, 1982, 80 percent of those interviewed said they would oppose any fighting by the United States in El Salvador.[14]

Our interests are not immutable; they have changed as the world and our capabilities have changed. Moreover, new administrations often attach very different weights to each interest; to see this, one need only compare the importance that the past three administrations have given to U.S. national interests in human rights abroad.

There is no better example of the changing character of U.S. interests and the implications of the change for U.S. strategy than the Panama Canal, which has been the center and the symbol of U.S. interests in Central America since the turn of the century. Even today, there are many who believe that the principal reason for preventing instability in the rest of Central America is that the canal must be protected, lest a hostile neighbor interfere with its traffic. Through World Wars I and II, the canal was an invaluable strategic asset. With the advent of aircraft carriers, which were too large to pass through the canal, U.S. interests in it changed—from strategic to primarily economic, from facilitating the movement of the U.S. fleet to providing a marginal economic advantage in the shipment of supplies. U.S. interests in an open and efficient canal remained important, but they could hardly be considered either vital or strategic. At the same time, the canal became vital for countries such as Panama, Ecuador, Colombia, Nicaragua, and Costa Rica, which shipped much larger percentages of their trade through it. Closure would only marginally affect the United States; it would be catastrophic for these countries. The new canal treaties between the United States and Panama ratified in 1978 reflected these changing interests and the necessity of a new approach to protect these interests.

Economic Interests

Let us look at the interests offered by the administration to justify U.S. involvement in Central America. First, U.S. *economic interests* in the region are currently marginal—less than 2 percent of U.S. investments abroad are in Central America and less than 2 percent of our trade is with the region. Moreover, the long-standing fear that the establishment of communist regimes would close the "open door" of Western trade and investment has been questioned by none other than David Rockefeller, who recently returned from a trip to Africa and declared that he could do business with the communist regimes if the U.S. government would let him. The same holds for Cuba, which has invited foreign investors to participate in joint ventures.[15]

U.S. interests in *strategic minerals* also have changed. For years, access to such minerals meant guaranteeing access for U.S. companies, but in the 1960s and 1970s developing countries asserted control over their natural resources. The refusal to recognize this central principle led to both diplomatic and investment disputes, jeopardizing access to strategic minerals. Provided that we accept the principle of sovereignty over natural resources, it is hard to conceive of a country that would not want to sell its resources to the United States. The only thing preventing

Cuba from selling its nickel to the United States is our embargo. Our strategic stockpile insulates the United States from temporary interruptions of supply of strategic minerals, but this is an academic point since Central America has none of these minerals anyway.

Although an impressive quantity of U.S. trade flows through the region, what country would seriously consider either trying to sink U.S. vessels or closing one of the *strategic sea lanes?* Certainly, the Cuban leadership understands that to do so would provide the U.S. government with the kind of pretext many nationalist Americans have been seeking for the past twenty years to punish Cuba militarily. As long as we support the principle of freedom of the seas, the Soviet navy will be able to carry out regular naval maneuvers in the Caribbean as they have done since 1969. One Cuba is more than adequate to service the needs of the Soviet fleet. Soviet interference with our shipping is unlikely short of a nuclear exchange, which makes any further discussion irrelevant. Even if there were a conventional war with the Soviets, it is unlikely that Cuba or other Soviet allies in the Caribbean would risk interfering with U.S. shipping because of their extraordinary vulnerability to U.S. retaliation. Anyway, there is not much that we are not already doing that will make the sea lanes less vulnerable. Undoubtedly, the Pentagon will insist on building up its capabilities in the Caribbean and argue that an increased Cuban military buildup requires still larger budgets, but the threat is not directly against the United States. Rather it is against other sovereign nations in the region that have the option of turning to the OAS or the United States for defense if they feel the need.

Security Interests

That is not to suggest that we have no security interests in the region, only that traditional exhortations about strategic arteries, or even for that matter Soviet bases or expanded military capabilities in "surrogate Cubas," do not strike the same chord in Americans that they once did. This is because the administration's case against the Soviet threat to this hemisphere is a caricature based on three exaggerated assertions.

First, the administration argues that the guerrillas fighting in Central America are merely tools of the Soviet Union and Cuba. As Reagan told the *Wall Street Journal* during the presidential campaign, the Soviet Union is the source of all instability in the Third World.[16] In warning Cuba to stop fomenting insurrection throughout Central America, former Secretary of State Alexander M. Haig said "it is our view that this is an externally-managed and orchestrated interventionism, and we are going to deal with it at the source."[17]

Haig's assertion met with incredulity in the United States and Western Europe, and he sought repeatedly to substantiate the charge. On March 2, 1982, he announced that he had "overwhelming and irrefutable proof" that Salvador's guerrillas were operating under instructions sent to them from a "Command and Control Center" outside the country.[18] Since he did not share that proof, except for the nineteen-year-old Nicaraguan guerrilla who denied everything, it is difficult to judge except to say that it is apparently refuted by the uncoordinated operations of the five guerrilla groups, even with respect to the elections—with some groups trying to sabotage them violently, others encouraging a boycott, and still other groups doing nothing. Moreover, if the United States has located a Command and Control Center, presumably the Salvadoran government would have beaten the guerrillas in every confrontation since then, as they would have had access to the guerrillas' strategic plans and instructions. Or to put it another way, if the guerrillas intercepted cable traffic between the State Department and the U.S. Embassy in San Salvador, they might also conclude that the Salvadoran government gets its instructions from "a Command and Control Center" outside the country. They would be as wrong in reaching that conclusion as former secretary Haig was in thinking that the guerrillas would fade away if only we could cut off their flow of arms and instructions.

This caricature of the guerrillas as tools only invites people to leap to a mirror-image caricature of the guerrillas as representing a wholly indigenous and autonomous response to decades of oppression and repression. The second caricature obscures the political, military, and ideological links between Central American revolutionaries and the Soviet Union and Cuba and the extent to which the guerrilla leaders look to Castro's Cuba as a politico-military, if not an economic, model and to the United States as the source of all their nation's problems. (It is true that the left is quite heterogeneous, including disaffected Social and Christian Democrats in El Salvador, for example, but the guerrilla leaders with the guns openly profess their adherence to Marxism-Leninism in interviews with the Mexican and Cuban press, although they do sound more like Social Democrats when interviewed by American reporters.[19]) Surely a more realistic appraisal of the guerrilla movements in Central America should recognize their indigenous roots and their ideological branches, their idealistic motives and their hunger for power by force of arms, their professed interest in "democracy" and their own authoritarian organizations, their concern about social injustice and their belief in the class struggle, their admiration for Cuba and their obsessive hatred for "U.S. imperialism."

Second, the administration suggests that the emergence of "new Cubas" in Central America constitutes a security threat to the United

States, and in Haig's words, "a profound challenge to the security of the hemisphere, to the whole character of the southern hemisphere, its political orientation and its compatibility with traditional hemispheric values."[20] Leaving aside the question of what values unite Augusto Pinochet Ugarte, Castro, and Pres. Luis Herrera Campins of Venezuela, the problem with this assertion is that people in the United States find it easier to visualize Central America as composed of six relatively poor and weak countries with a justifiable preference of being viewed in their own terms rather than as kings or pawns in a global chess game.

On March 9, 1982, the administration deliberately noted that the person who would brief on the Nicaraguan military buildup was the same person who briefed on the Cuban missile crisis.[21] The implication—that the military buildup constituted a security threat to the United States, perhaps equivalent to the installation of Soviet missiles in Cuba—is absurd. A Nicaraguan army of seventy thousand just does not represent a threat to the United States comparable to the installation of Soviet missiles—either from a strategic perspective or even from that of the possible effect on global perceptions of U.S. power. With slide shows depicting the threat in such unrealistic and melodramatic terms, the administration repeats the same mistake as with its first assertion. The result is that people are driven again to a mirror-image caricature that suggests that *no* security interests are at stake—an equivalent mistake.

Nicaragua's neighbors do have grounds for fearing the military buildup, but not because Nicaragua will invade, which would probably provoke an OAS response. When combined with Nicaragua's support for insurgencies in neighboring countries, the increased military capability acts to deter any neighbor from "hot pursuit" or "going to the source." The United States is not the appropriate country and the State Department is not the appropriate forum, however, to make this case; the evidence should have been presented by Central American governments, with U.S. assistance, before the OAS, where a multilateral response could be requested.

The establishment of a Soviet base that could be used to threaten other countries or even the United States is a legitimate security concern, and a nation in the region that was on a collision course with the United States would certainly have an incentive to issue an invitation to the USSR, much as Cuba did in 1962. From a U.S. perspective, the issue is how to minimize the chance of this happening. There are two ways: reduce the probability of Marxist-Leninists coming to power in the region who would look to the USSR and Cuba for security support, or try to reduce the level of hostility with such groups if they do come to power. Although some have referred to this concern with the possible emergence of hostile regimes as a presumption of U.S. hegemony or imperialism, in fact the concern is shared by all governments, whether of the right, left, or center. However, this concern must be kept in perspective. The emergence of a hostile regime is primarily a regional problem affecting *important* U.S. interests, but it is not one that alters the global strategic balance and threatens *vital* interests.

The administration's third assertion is that the choice for Central America, according to President Reagan in his Caribbean Basin speech, is between "two different futures"—a positive, democratic one and a negative, communist one. Would that it were so. Though the phrases are reminiscent of the Truman Doctrine of thirty-five years ago—and unfortunately of equal subtlety—the American people are not so trusting as they were then nor as ignorant of the real choices we face in Central America. As the United States retreats from its defense of human rights, the black-and-white choices begin to blur into one another. The Marxist future in Central America—at least as it is evolving in Nicaragua—is simply not as dark as the administration would have us believe, and the democratic future for El Salvador and Guatemala can hardly be considered virginal.

It is precisely because the alternatives are so unattractive that some Americans are driven again to the mirror-image caricature, that there is *no* choice—a plague on both your repressive houses. Others feel that the dissolution of the old oligarchical structure can present an opening for greater freedom and justice, and that it is a mistake to believe that if the left comes to power, it cannot be co-opted. These arguments are more persuasive in refuting the administration's single formula for resisting all revolutionary movements than they are for replacing it with an alternative formula that suggests we should support or can co-opt all revolutionary movements. Of course, U.S. policies can make revolutionaries either a little more or a little less hostile, but the probabilities argue against converting those Marxist-Leninist guerrillas, who have been fighting U.S. imperialism for a decade or so, into either democrats or friends of the United States.

In the search for a new and relevant answer to the old strategic question, we have ricocheted between two caricatures—one suggests that our most vital security interests are at stake and the other that there are no objective security interests, only errant perceptions based on what Abraham Lowenthal described as our "hegemonic presumption."[22] The irony is that the logic of both caricatures leads the United States to ignore our other humanitarian interests and undermine our security concerns.

In assuming that the insurgents are not members of nationalist movements but rather tools of the Soviets and therefore fixed in their hostility to the United States, in assuming that the cause of the instability is external, and in assuming that the only struggle in Central America is against the left the Reagan administration distorts the struggle into a confrontation with the USSR and invests the full prestige of the United States in the outcome, over which we have considerably less than full control. Moreover, the strategy of bringing the full weight of the United States against the insurgents is counterproductive in that it provides the right with a blank check to be intransigent and repressive in their war against communism and the left with a target they can use to establish their nationalist credentials.

Those who would withdraw from Central America because they do not perceive any security interest either do not see or do not care about the covert extension of Cuban influence on behalf of Marxist-Leninist revolutionaries, do not want to do anything about rightist terrorism, or do not think we can do anything. But they should be clear that the consequences of withdrawal would be the intensification of the struggle; the right would be unshackled, and the communist supporters of the left would be less inhibited in transferring weapons.

There is another security-related interest that needs to be explored more fully—the realm of political psychology. To what extent does the emergence of a radical regime in Central America affect other nations' perceptions of U.S. power? It is probably true that the development of a more independent regime like Panama's improves the U.S. image in the developing world and translates into an enhanced ability by the United States to influence developments. But this is unlikely to hold for a genuinely hostile regime.

Ideological Interests

The question of national-security interests returns at one point or another to the question of U.S. ideological interests—human rights, democratic government, a pluralistic and open international system. When former Secretary of State Haig stated in early 1981 that international terrorism would take the place of human rights in U.S. concern, this deliberate act of unilateral disarmament by the Reagan administration not only deprived the United States of the most powerful weapons in its ideological arsenal but also betrayed U.S. history and values and placed the administration in opposition to a vigorous transnational human-rights movement. It is a mistake to view our security and human-rights interests as contradictory; they are mutually reinforcing. Let me illustrate this point with two sets of examples. In the early 1970s, U.S. preoccupation with stability led us to wink at the discrediting of the democratic process in Nicaragua, El Salvador, and Guatemala, and the entire region is paying the cost of closing those political avenues. In 1978, the United States placed its full weight behind democracy in the

Dominican Republic, Honduras, and Panama, and that weight contributed to restraining the military in all three countries, which are now relative paragons of stability.

Jeane Kirkpatrick argues that the United States should have supported Somoza because the Sandinistas are worst.[23] That same logic would lead us to resist all changes and to embrace all dictators, since the alternatives are almost always more uncertain. The Nicaraguan people had a lot more to say about whether Anastasio Somoza Debayle would remain in power than the United States, but even if the United States had had the choice and backed Somoza, we would not only have backed a loser, but would have tainted our nation's values—perhaps irrevocably—in the area. Nothing would have weakened the U.S. security position more than to have gone down with Somoza.

What kind of neighbors do we want? What kind of system of government do we want our friends to live under? Certainly, the United States cannot be silent on these questions, and the answers must be some form of democracy where human rights are respected. We cannot ensure that democracy will take root everywhere, but we should never uproot it where it does exist, and we should use whatever influence we have to increase its chances by trying to assist those who would correct social injustice, restrain rightist repression, and offer an alternative to Marxist-Leninist revolutionaries. We can neither walk away from such a struggle nor take sides with the right against the left.

If the Carter administration's problem with human rights was its apparent inconsistency, the Reagan administration's flaw is far more serious—it simply lacks credibility. In the pursuit of anticommunism, the Reagan administration has given military dictators a green light.

Systemic Interests

The United States also has systemic interests in contributing to a world economic and political system that is open, more balanced, and pluralistic. In Central America, this means that it is in the long-term interests of the United States to encourage greater independence and autonomy, since this would permit more balanced and respectful governmental relationships. Of course, this particular interest is generally eclipsed during a political crisis when it is more important for the United States to try to influence internal political developments, but it is a mistake to totally ignore it. U.S. strength is derived from its respect for political diversity abroad and at home. We have an interest in influencing developments in Central America but not in dominating those countries as the Soviet Union does in Eastern Europe. The United States would not be served by a Reagan corollary to the Brezhnev Doctrine.

When President Reagan says that the problem in El Salvador is "imported terrorism" and that attempts by guerrillas armed and supported by and through Cuba to impose a Marxist-Leninist dictatorship on El Salvador are part of a larger imperialistic plan, he is not only missing the point but also the American people. And he compounds the skepticism when he suggests that the reason people do not agree with him is that a propaganda campaign has misled many people in Europe and in the United States as to the true nature of the conflict in El Salvador.

If the debate in the United States on the war in Vietnam became a dialogue between the deaf and the dumb, that on El Salvador increasingly sounds like a shouting match between those who are committed to stopping communism and those who are committed to ending U.S. intervention. To really begin to understand why the struggle in Central America matters to the United States, one has to go beyond the traditional questions and answers on U.S. interests and explore the psychological relationship between the United States and Central America. One finds that the United States is so much a presence in Central America that to debate nonintervention is to elicit utter bewilderment from Central American leaders. And in the evolving debate in the United States, which is growing more intense and polarized, one finds for the first time that the region is beginning to exert a profound impact on the United States.

Mutual Intervention

Franklin D. Roosevelt became a hero to Latin Americans just for taking seriously the principle of nonintervention that Latin jurists and diplomats had been preaching to the United States for generations. The second U.S. president to take that principle seriously was Jimmy Carter, but Latin Americans reserved judgment on him since they had heard other presidents make the pledge and then break it. Only in Central America did they take Carter seriously; there, however, they feared he might be true to his word.

In March 1977, before a congressional committee, an exiled Salvadoran Christian Democrat by the name of José Napoleón Duarte explained why the Carter pledge was not just irrelevant, but immoral.

> . . . the U.S. cannot assume that it does not intervene, because even at this moment if the U.S. decides not to intervene at all, it will mean that it sustains the structure presently existing in Latin America; it will mean the continuing existence of all the dictators imposed on the people. Therefore, there is a continuing historical intervention. . . . The U.S., at

> this moment, has a historical duty . . . in support of those basic principles which form the basis of the American way of life. . . . If the U.S. starts presenting its international policy based on moral principles, on the concepts and values of the American way of life, then there is hope that the world will find a new destiny, better than the one we are living in today.[24]

The U.S. presence pervades Central America's politics and contorts the psychology of its leaders so much as to make it difficult at times for outsiders to understand what is happening. During the Nicaraguan insurrection, the Sandinistas repeatedly claimed that the United States was aiding Somoza, hoping by making such claims that the independence of Somoza would be further compromised and also that the United States would perhaps be embarrassed enough so that it would consider supporting them. At the same time, Somoza used the U.S. news media to claim that the United States was destabilizing him, hoping by such statements to both reestablish his independence and to press the United States to come to his support.

The only ones in Central America who resolutely oppose U.S. involvement are those who are certain that the United States will not support them. Virtually everyone else tries to maneuver the United States into supporting them, and if they fail, they blame the United States for their problems. Even those who cannot decide what political path to follow blame Washington for failing to send a clear signal. The psychology of dependence is much more captivating than the reality.

Central Americans preach nonintervention, but practice mutual interference. Ever since the Central American federation fragmented in the early nineteenth century, a strong leader—a *caudillo*—would consolidate power in one country and then try to establish friends or overthrow enemies in neighboring countries. The United States was always invited by one side or the other or both. (A new element is that Central Americans now solicit the USSR and Cuba for military assistance and the governments and political parties of Western Europe for political support.) Even though U.S. troops have not fought in Central America since they were withdrawn from Nicaragua in 1933, the memory lingers. And even leaders like Torrijos or Somoza, who often appeared the most dependent on the United States, but were actually the most independent and manipulative—even these leaders always felt that their destinies were determined in Washington. And indeed, the greatest source of U.S. influence in the region remains the myth of control, the perception that the United States shapes all events.

U.S. influence in Central America is neither new nor news; what is both is Central America's influence on the United States. After a century of trying to shape developments in the region, the United States for the first time is on the receiving end and subject to a more subtle and pervasive process of change than the blunt instrument of U.S. diplomacy.

Like the Americans who went to Panama in the first decade of this century to dig a canal but brought back malaria, we have gone to El Salvador to save it from communism, but have found ourselves instead infected by the dreaded Central American disease—political polarization. Of course, in Central America, the people in the middle are attacked with guns instead of placards, but the same principle—that the middle becomes more precarious as the struggle becomes more intense—governs the struggle in El Salvador and the debate in the United States. And increasingly, the two struggles parallel each other and are drawn to each other.

Why are we so psychologically involved in El Salvador today? The geographical proximity and the administration's own highly charged rhetoric partly explain the intensity of the debate. The administration has defined the issues in black-and-white terms, and this promotes polarization in the United States and contributes to it in the region. But there are two other more important reasons why the conflict in El Salvador is polarizing the United States: the psychological proximity of the Vietnam trauma and the "Caribbeanization" of the United States.

Vietnam Redux

All wars leave deep prints on a nation's consciousness, affecting its self-perception and the way it looks at the world for at least a generation. Certainly, World War II deeply affected an entire generation of Americans; as U.S. involvement reflected so many of our nation's most-valued myths—the United States as underdog, democracy versus dictatorship, total war, unconditional victory—our nation emerged with a positive feeling of unanimity, assured of its rightness in fighting and its moral and physical strength in winning. After the war, it was relatively easy to transfer this perspective to a new enemy—the Soviet Union and communism.

The Korean War partly breached this consensual view. President Dwight D. Eisenhower sensed this and avoided involvement in Vietnam in 1954 because he realized that the American people were not yet prepared for "another Korea." The total breakdown of the World War II consensus occurred in Vietnam, an episode that divided the nation then and continues to divide it today. There is agreement that it was a mistake, but that is where the consensus ends. Particularly relevant to El Salvador are two views of the Vietnam conflict: one, that U.S. leaders lacked the will to win; the other, that U.S. involvement was a mistake that should not be repeated.

The first view was articulated by President Ronald Reagan in February 1981 in a ceremony to present the Medal of Honor to a Vietnam war hero. Reagan said that the U.S. military were withdrawn "because they'd been denied permission to win."

No consensus is evident within the administration on the implications of Vietnam for Central America. The Defense Department appears to be reluctant to get involved militarily in the absence of broad national support, whereas former Secretary of State Alexander M. Haig believed that if the United States is to play its proper role in the world, it must get over the Vietnam Syndrome and demonstrate its resolve for both friends and adversaries. This explains why Haig was so eager to make El Salvador the key test for U.S. foreign policy: It was close to home and presumably an easy win. Of course, it did not develop as he intended, but there is no indication that he was diverted from a belief that unless the United States demonstrates a willingness to apply force, as the Soviet Union has done either directly or by proxy in at least six instances since the United States withdrew from Vietnam, U.S. diplomacy will become less credible. According to this view, there is no reason to rearm the United States if the rest of the world does not believe that the nation has the will to use its arms.

Before Congress, in March 1982, Secretary of State Haig said that the problem in Vietnam was that the government had failed to decide whether or not our vital interests were involved. "If they had concluded negatively, then we would never have become involved in the first instance," he said. If they had decided our vital interests were at stake, "I believe they would have taken actions commensurate with that judgment. . . . Now, let me tell you," he said, "I come down on the side of, in such an assessment in Central America, that the outcome of the situation there is in the vital interest of the American people and must be so dealt with. . . . I know the American people will support what is prudent and necessary providing they think we mean what we mean and that we are going to succeed and not flounder as we did in Vietnam."[25] In short, Haig was saying that the survival of the United States is at stake in Central America.

The White House reads the polls and knows how divisive is the conflict in El Salvador, and so the military option has not received any support. What the White House has apparently not recognized is that Reagan's use of the term "vital interest," as further developed by his former secretary of state, commits the administration to stopping the left in Central America; the cost is irrelevant when the survival of the country is at stake.

Secretary of State Haig may have been over the Vietnam Syndrome because he never had it. But the second view of Vietnam—that it was a mistake to have been involved there—is held by a majority of Americans, according to the polls.[26] The formative political experience of an entire generation—that of the baby boom of the late 1940s and early 1950s—was marching against the war and turning the U.S. government around. In some ways, this was as heady an experience for that generation as winning World War II was for their parents. And just as the older generation enjoys recapturing the memory of its experience in movies or by marching in veterans' parades, the younger generation is ready to recapture its lost youth by marching against another war alongside a new generation ready to develop its own antiwar experience. This explains why the insertion of U.S. troops in Central America would divide America again as it did in Vietnam.

For those whose views of the Vietnam War were shaped by watching it on television, the conflict in Central America promises to be much more riveting. Central America is much more accessible, not just geographically but also because the language and culture are more easily understandable than Vietnam's. Moreover, there are many more Central Americans living in the United States today, helping people focus on the human consequences of the conflict.

Though individual journalists may be divided between the two views described above, there is a "Vietnam generation" of journalists ready to replicate the biggest story of the last decade, and a new generation ready to cut its teeth on a new war. This partly explains why the coverage of the conflict has been much more extensive than in Vietnam; more journalists covered the National Assembly elections in El Salvador on March 28, 1982, than were in Vietnam at the height of the war. Over 500,000 U.S. combat troops fought in Vietnam, whereas there are fewer than 50 military advisers in El Salvador; either the media are anticipating, or they are trying to recapture the war of the past on a new battlefield. Their presence, however, serves the useful function of a self-denying prophecy; the more Americans focus on El Salvador, the more certain people are that they do not want to repeat Vietnam.

Thus, the divided legacy of Vietnam continues to divide the United States.

Caribbeanization: The Process

There is another, more profound reason why the consciences of more and more Americans are aroused by the political violence in Central America and why U.S. interests in the region are permanent, not transitory: Simply, the United States is becoming a Caribbean nation. The character of U.S. society is being subtly reshaped by the most massive influx of migrants from a single region since nearly nine million people arrived from southern and eastern Europe at the turn of the century.

Since the 1965 amendment to the Immigration and Naturalization Act liberalized entry to the United States from the developing world, the composition of the immigrant population has changed rather dramatically. From 1900 to 1965, 75 percent of all immigrants were of European extraction, whereas since 1968, when the new law took effect, 62 percent of the immigrants have been from Asia and Latin America. By 1980, about 85 percent of all immigrants and refugees were from these two regions, while less than 6 percent came from Europe.[27]

Although the new immigrants came from more countries than at any previous time in U.S. history, the largest source of immigrants was the Caribbean Basin—Central America, the Caribbean, and Mexico. Before 1960, roughly 4 percent of U.S. immigrants came from that area. Since then, nearly one-third of all immigrants to the United States, two-thirds of all political refugees, and nine-tenths of all undocumented workers have come from the region. The total number of people who have come to the United States from the Caribbean Basin since 1960 is approximately 8.5 million—more than half of the people who have come to live in the United States since 1960.[28] As the numbers from Southeast Asia decline, the percentage from the Caribbean Basin can be expected to increase even further.

In large part because of immigration, the Hispanic community has become one of the fastest-growing ethnic groups in the United States, increasing from 9 million or 4.5 percent of the population in 1970 to 14.6 million or 6.4 percent of the population in 1980.[29]

An examination of the social, demographic, economic, and political dynamics of the Caribbean Basin leads to the inescapable conclusion that absent any new immigration law by the United States, the flow will increase as dramatically over the next two decades as it did over the past two. The population of the region will double by the end of the century. The economy of the region has progressed sufficiently to expose even poor Salvadorans to the material attractions of the United States and to put entry into the country within reach of a one-thousand-dollar payment to a smuggler. But the economies have not been successful enough to provide jobs for a labor force expanding at 3 percent annually. Nor are the political institutions in the region flexible enough to channel the energies of a youthful and demanding population where more than half of the population is under fifteen.

Until a few years ago, the majority of basin immigrants came from Mexico and the islands in the Caribbean, but the recent political and economic turmoil in Central America has changed the composition so dramatically that most estimates now show an increasing proportion of political refugees and undocumented workers coming from Central America. El Salvador, with the highest population density in the region, was destined to become a major source of migrants even if there had not been a civil war; indeed, the so-called Soccer War of 1969 between Honduras and El Salvador was essentially the result of the overflow of El Salvador's population problem. Current estimates suggest that as many as 500,000 Salvadorans—more than 10 percent of the population—have come to the United States in the past two years. As many as 3,500 people every month leave the violence of El Salvador, where at least 6,116 were killed in 1981, for the peaceful and pastoral environment of New York City, where only 1,826 were murdered the same year. And some estimates hold that 10 percent of the population of Nicaragua—about 250,000 people—has come to the United States in the past few years.[30]

An increasing number of people had considered migrating for economic reasons but were finally motivated to depart by political violence. These people not only have an additional reason to come, but also an additional excuse to stay—to claim asylum. Large numbers of such people can be expected from El Salvador, Guatemala, and Nicaragua in the years to come, particularly because the first enterprising wave has already settled and adjusted to the United States. Families and almost entire villages have been transplanted from San Salvador to Washington, D.C., and Chicago, from Managua to Miami, from Guatemala to New Orleans; these communities serve as transnational bridges for bringing friends and relatives to the United States, for finding them jobs and documents, and for easing their cultural adjustment.

The strongest nation in the world has been powerless to manage the flow of people across its southern border. Some of the weakest nations have found in this spontaneous and largely illegal flow a source of real power—an instrument for exporting unemployment (and in the case of Cuba, its "undesirables"), an independent source of foreign exchange and welfare payments (through remittances), a means to relax social pressures, and a means for their most pervasive impact on the United States.

Attorney General William French Smith has warned that we have lost control of our borders. It is not the entire phenomenon of Caribbean Basin migration that troubles Smith and most of the country, but one dimension of it—illegal migration. In 1979 and again in 1980, about one million Mexicans were apprehended while trying to cross the border illegally. Each year, at least 500,000 people elude the border patrols or enter the United States legally and overstay their visas, and it is estimated that 90 percent of them come from the Caribbean Basin. Although

Mexicans account for the largest single group, an increasing percentage comes from other nations in the region.

The U.S. government has been wrestling with this issue since the Ford administration. When faced with a bill sent by President Carter, Congress dodged it and established a Select Commission on Immigration and Refugee Policy to do a comprehensive and learned study. The distinguished commission, chaired first by Reubin O. Askew and then by the Reverend Theodore M. Hesburgh of Notre Dame, submitted its report with detailed recommendations and a suggested law to President Reagan. After another study, the Reagan administration submitted legislation to Congress. Then in February 1982, Republic senator Alan Simpson of Wyoming and Democratic representative Romano Mazzoli of Kentucky, after exhaustive hearings on all of the issues related to immigration and refugee policy, submitted another bill. It was almost a synthesis of the numerous proposals that had been offered but in many ways the best of all of them and also the most likely to pass. The bill (since passed) penalizes employers who hire illegal aliens; establishes a worker-identification system; legalizes immigration of 425,000 people per year, excluding refugees; and doubles admissions from Canada and Mexico to a combined total of 40,000.

Like most issues before Congress, that of illegal migration is subject to lobbying by groups on both sides. Unique to this issue, however, is the fact that many people find themselves on both sides of it. Liberals are sympathetic to the plight of illegal migrants but also oppose their entry because it undermines organized labor. Conservatives favor the silent invasion either because they believe in a single labor market or because they sympathize with those businessmen who cannot find Americans to do the work, and they oppose illegal migration for fear that the United States is losing control of its borders and losing its Anglo culture. Conflicting emotions as well as conflicting interests have paralyzed the policy process.

Caribbeanization: The Result

The full impact and implications of this new wave of migration have not been fully grasped, and indeed its effects will only become apparent over the next two decades. The new migration occurs at a time when the U.S. fertility rate is at a historical low. In a recent study projecting the impact of this new migration on the composition of the overall population, Leon Bouvier of the Population Reference Bureau estimated that if the current rate of fertility and immigration is maintained, 40 percent of the U.S. population one hundred years from now "will consist of post-1980 immigrants and their descendants."[31] During the next two decades, the concept of an "American" is likely to be changed as much as at any previous time in U.S. history. Those looking for a snapshot of the entire Caribbean Basin region might well find it by looking at the changing face of the United States. One will find that Miami or Newark airports look more like those in San Juan or Mexico City than Columbus or Nashville. Or a Connecticut Yankee might be shown around Boston's newly restored Faneuil Hall by a newly arrived Guatemalan taxi driver.

Many U.S. cities increasingly resemble the small nations of the Caribbean Basin not only in ethnic composition but also in economic structure. These cities suffer from a weak or declining industrial base and a top-heavy, inefficient public sector oriented more toward social services than toward productive investment. If we can share problems with the region, can we share solutions? The new ties among the people of the region may soon lead us to such questions if not to their answers.

While some may debate whether the United States is the cause of the problems in Central America, it is a fact that the United States has come to share in the social consequences of political and economic instability in the region. The conflict in El Salvador is no longer a vague and abstract foreign-policy issue to be debated only at the State Department and in universities; it is a real and practical concern for the Department of Health and Human Services and for cities like Miami, Los Angeles, Boston, and Chicago that have to adjust their local services in a time of budgetary austerity to meet the growing needs of their Central American and Caribbean populations. U.S. interests in the region have grown at least as quickly as the region's impact on the United States. U.S. policy on bilingual education or on legal services has as much impact on our foreign relations in the region as U.S. policy on negotiations in El Salvador has on whether Los Angeles ought to build a new elementary school. Our peoples and our problems are increasingly intertwined.

The new economic dynamism of the southern part of the United States attracts migrants from the Northeast as well as from the Caribbean Basin. This Caribbean border area mixes the people, values, and culture of all our nations into a new melange that facilitates the flow of goods, investments, and people. It is to be hoped that it will increase the capacities of all the nations to understand each other.

As in all previous large migrations, the new wave from Central America and the Caribbean has stimulated some nativist fears and calls in Congress to limit the migration lest it lead to cultural and linguistic division comparable to the problem Canada has with Quebec. Although it is true that the foreign-born population has increased in the past decade to 6.2 percent after a steady decline since 1920 and that Spanish has become the second-most-used language in American homes, still both figures are too small to merit any anxiety. Ninety percent of the people polled by the Census Bureau in 1980 spoke English in their homes; another 5 percent spoke Spanish; another 5 percent spoke other languages.[32] Unlike the French in Quebec, Hispanics are geographically dispersed throughout the United States, and although they may have a language in common, their nationalities and cultures reflect wide differences. Studies on acculturation and assimilation, although still quite preliminary, suggest that the new migrants are assimilating as rapidly as the old migrants and that they recognize that their ticket to social and economic advancement in the United States is education and the English language. Moreover, like past migrants, new immigrants—as contrasted with refugees—utilize about the same number of social services as the average U.S. citizen and contribute as much to the economy. Perhaps even more than private initiative, the immigrant mentality may have been the engine of U.S. economic and social dynamism in the past and is likely to continue to be in the future; the immigrants will just have come from a different direction. The illegal flow of immigrants serves some U.S. economic interests, and we are of two minds what to do about it. The "push" forces from the region explain why it continues. However, although illegal migration may serve everyone's short-term interest, it serves no one's long-term interest. The illegal flow is a problem for migrants, who are subject to exploitation, first by the smuggler who brings them and then by the employer, who often keeps migrants' illegality secret for a price. It is a problem for the United States because it weakens respect for the law, undermines labor unions, and, by allowing the development of an underclass of people without rights, is contrary to U.S. values. And it is a problem for the sending country because a nation that exports its economic difficulties—whether rapid population growth or unemployment—has little incentive to solve them and a nation seeking to develop a sense of nationhood is humiliated when its citizens volunteer for exploitation.

At the present time, civil-rights and Hispanic groups have blocked attempts by the U.S. government to deport illegal aliens, euphemistically called "undocumented workers," and there is no federal law prohibiting employers from hiring illegal aliens. If the Simpson-Mazzoli bill discussed earlier sharply reduces illegal migration, as it is likely to do, the pressures due to increased unemployment and returning workers would generate social and political tensions in Central America where they do not exist and exacerbate them where they do. The United States would find itself exchanging one end of the problem—illegal migration—for another end—more political instability. The consequences would probably be more costly for the United States; they would certainly be more costly for the other nations. The Reagan administration's Caribbean Basin

Initiative could help address the broader problems of unemployment and economic development, but only if it were more comprehensive and related more directly to the immigration issue than is presently the case.[33]

Like the black community, Hispanics are mostly preoccupied by bread-and-butter, domestic issues. The leaders of the Hispanic community who care about foreign policy generally are Cubans and Nicaraguans who are virulent anticommunists or Chicanos and Puerto Ricans who are more sympathetic to the insurgents in Central America. The community in the United States therefore increasingly reflects the political polarization in Central America. The influence and existence of the Hispanic community have heightened U.S. interest and interests in the region, but to the extent that the community's political views cluster around one ideological pole or the other, they have made a clear policy response more difficult to achieve.

Human-rights groups and the Catholic church are playing increasingly important sociopolitical roles in Central America by helping the poor, the dispossessed, and the brutalized and giving them a voice and a haven in the United States. Even if Americans were inclined to ignore the suffering in the region, the church would not let them any more, and that is to the nation's benefit.

Politically, the church is as divided as the United States and almost as much as Central America, and growing more polarized, but those who are sympathetic to the left appear more vigorous and motivated. The White House in both the Carter and the Reagan administrations was repeatedly surprised by the large numbers of letters and telegrams that were received from church groups urging the United States not to intervene in Nicaragua or to stop military aid to the Salvadoran government. The church has become a political force to reckon with in Central America and in the United States and in connecting the United States to Central America.

The new migration is slowly changing the way the United States looks at itself and at Central America and the entire Caribbean Basin. Just as the problems of Poland are felt more intensely by the American people because of the Polish-American community, those of Cyprus because of the Greek-Americans, those of the Middle East because of the Jewish community, or as earthquakes in Italy resonate through Italian neighborhoods in the United States—so too will the new immigrants from Central America force the United States to watch the region with more sensitivity and concern.

The United States will continue to have a major presence and impact on Central America, but the nature of that impact will change as Central America's presence begins to be felt more directly in the United States.

Some of the most important U.S. interests in the world derive from the interest and concern of our multiethnic population. It is this "Caribbeanization" of the United States that may very well be one of the most compelling and enduring interests in Central America.

Changing Interests Should Determine Strategy

U.S. interests in Central America have changed. Economic and strategic interests, as they traditionally have been defined, are of declining importance, whereas ethnic and humanitarian interests have increased. These new interests, broadly defined, encourage the United States to assist those who would respect human rights and construct democracy and resist those who would enforce an inequitable or repressive status quo or impose a "popular" Marxist-Leninist dictatorship. As the United States itself has changed, new ties—human bonds—have sensitized the United States to the region, and political change is having a more direct and immediate impact on its own politics.

Although the new, *important* interests of the United States appear to bring it to similar objectives—to resist the establishment of a hostile Marxist-Leninist regime, to support democracy—as those of its old, *vital* interests, there is a key difference. In the past, the United States was seeking to defend in a foreign environment what it considered its own—whether the Panama Canal or U.S. investment; force was sometimes effective in pursuing these interests. Today, with the increasing importance of nationalism in Central America and elsewhere in the developing world and with the changing composition of U.S. interests, the United States is seeking to influence what it never can control—the political struggle in sovereign nations. The threat or use of force is usually counterproductive. It is both a distortion of reality and a serious strategic error to trivialize the struggle among Nicaraguans or Salvadorans by calling it a battle between the United States and the Soviet Union because it only engages the United States in a way that makes it "our war" rather than "theirs."

The short answer to the strategic question is that the United States has the best grounds of all for trying to influence the course of the struggle in El Salvador and elsewhere in Central America—it will have a potent direct and indirect effect on the United States if one extreme or the other wins a violent struggle for power.

For all the reasons described above, and particularly because of the gradual conversion of the United States to a Caribbean nation, it is no more possible for the United States to ignore the struggle in Central America in the 1980s than it was to ignore the racial crisis of the 1960s. So the question is what to do about it?

The debate in the United States over whether to overcome or avoid Vietnam in El Salvador suffers from a major defect: it has nothing to do with El Salvador. In their study of the U.S. policy toward Vietnam, *The Irony of Vietnam,* Leslie Gelb and Richard Betts found that U.S. policymakers were so preoccupied with containing world communism that they failed to understand the complexities of the local political struggle, and they did not follow the logic of their calculations on the probable failure of their strategy. The ironic parallel is that while the United States continues to refight the Vietnam War on a different battlefield, both sides are repeating the Vietnam mistake.

The formulation of U.S. policy does not follow automatically from a definition of U.S. interests. U.S. policy toward Central America is not made in a vacuum; it must take into account the constraints and capabilities of the United States and what is feasible and effective in Central America. If the president, for example, decided that vital interests were at stake in El Salvador, it does not necessarily follow that he should contemplate any or all means at his disposal to defend those interests. Part of the problem in using the term "vital" rather than "important" interests is that it encourages Americans to think that their own survival is at stake. In the wake of Vietnam, however, Americans are skeptical when their government mentions "vital interests." Therefore, in the interest of rebuilding the trust between government and the U.S. citizen, the administration should rethink U.S. interests and develop policies more appropriate to the United States and also to the region.

An essential point of departure is to recognize that the United States cannot control developments in the region, but that if its policy is well designed and takes into account the balance of internal forces within each country, U.S. influence can be reasonably important. The questions for U.S. policy, therefore, are where to place U.S. weight and for what purpose. U.S. long-term interests are best served by placing the full weight of U.S. influence clearly and consistently in support of those leaders and groups intent on meeting the four central challenges facing Central America: to develop a national identity, to widen the socioeconomic base, to develop democracy, and to depoliticize the military.

1. *U.S. strength is demonstrated in the region not by military maneuvers but by a willingness to negotiate legitimate concerns.* Negotiations with Panama on new canal treaties did not represent a retreat of U.S. power but rather the preservation of U.S. interests in the canal and an enhancement of U.S. legitimacy and influence in the area. In El Salvador, the left is not a unified, coherent Marxist-Leninist movement like that of the Viet Cong, but rather a heterogeneous umbrella over five guerrilla groups, hundreds of political organizations, and disaffected Social and Christian Democrats. Sincere negotiations aimed at forging a democratic

alternative would naturally separate those who are interested in democracy but want genuine guarantees if they are to participate in elections from those who are interested in imposing a Marxist-Leninist dictatorship.[34]

2. *Just as the way to protect the Panama Canal was for the United States to relax, not tighten, its control, so too the way to win the struggle in Central America is for the United States not to fight it.* Though some may believe that the United States obtains useful leverage by keeping all its options open, the unilateral use of U.S. troops is one option that should be ruled out, as it would be so internally divisive as to make the Vietnam demonstrations of the 1960s appear only a minor historical prelude to the antiwar riots of the 1980s. Moreover, U.S. troops would not be landing in the Central America of the 1930s but in the politically awakened region of the 1980s, provoking such a hostile nationalistic reaction that it would be the best gift the United States could ever give to the left. In short, the United States would lose at home and abroad.

3. *The best way to defeat the Marxist-Leninist left in Central America is not to go to the source but rather to concentrate on the target and break the hammerlock of the traditional power centers of the right.* Central America is writhing in its struggle to free itself from a feudalistic past that is no longer acceptable to its expanding and demanding youthful population. The left feeds off the intransigence of the right and the repression of the military; the best way to reduce the support for violent revolution is to open the political channels for peaceful change. Shutting off the flow of arms to a combat force of 500,000 would be meaningful; not so to a group of 3,000–4,000 guerrillas, who can obtain smaller quantities of arms from many sources.

4. *The best way to help the government in El Salvador is to be equivocal in our commitment.* Total support for the government in El Salvador is inappropriate since some of our enemies are potential allies and some of our so-called friends are really our enemies. By "drawing lines," the Reagan administration discarded the leverage necessary to influence the military to end the repression. In establishing its credibility against the communists, the Reagan administration lost its credibility against the right. As a supporter of Roberto D'Aubuisson's rightest National Republican party told the *Washington Post* in April 1982, when the United States was pressing it to accept the reforms and the Christian Democrats or risk losing U.S. support: "Reagan will never let the Communists win here. It's just a complete bluff." The only way to restore credibility is to reduce support and aid.[35]

5. *The best way to strengthen your enemy in the region is to initiate a confrontation that infringes on the enemy's sovereignty.* Despite all the potent socioeconomic forces unleashed in the twentieth century, the

most awesome tool for mobilizing a population is still the old nineteenth-century idea of nationalism. A key concept that apparently has eluded some Americans is that the so-called retreat of U.S. power is the result not of the diminution of U.S. will or capabilities, but rather of the advancement of nationalism in the developing world. The days when the marines could take over a Central American country or the CIA could overthrow one are long gone; their involvement now is more likely to produce the opposite of U.S. objectives by providing adversaries with the great energizer of nationalism.

The Reagan administration's strategy of confronting the Nicaraguan government has given the hard-liners the pretext to stifle internal dissent; it has given the government an excuse for its own failures to fulfill its promises and the nationalistic edge it needed to mobilize the population. In the spring of 1982, Edén Pastora Gomez (Commander Zero), the Nicaraguan revolutionary who led the fight against Anastasio Somoza Debayle only to find the revolution stolen from him and other nationalists by Marxist-Leninists with Cuban advisers, announced his decision to take up guns again to rid his country of Cuban and Soviet military advisers and to fulfill the original promises of the revolution. In his announcement he showed his understanding of the importance of taking the nationalistic argument away from the Sandinista leadership by condemning both U.S. threats to Nicaraguan sovereignty and the presence of Soviet advisers. Unfortunately the Reagan strategy of confrontation is making it more, not less, difficult for Pastora to try to steer the Nicaraguan revolution in a more democratic direction.

6. *One way to elicit support in the region is for the United States to demonstrate respect and understanding for the almost desperate need in the region for reciprocity.* One of the arguments against the canal treaties was that if the United States gave in to Panamanian demands for the zone, the demands would escalate, and soon Panama would try to throw out the U.S. military. The opposite happened. Military cooperation became so close that in August 1980 Omar Torrijos accepted a parachute-jump exercise seventy miles west of the canal by the 82nd Airborne. He set only one condition: reciprocity. And so the same day, a Panamanian airborne company parachuted into Fort Bragg. The United States can go a long way in the region by recognizing the need of unequals for equality.

Torrijos also had a lesson for Central America's leaders about how to deal with the United States, by appealing to the U.S. sense of justice and by not hesitating to influence the U.S. political process directly, just as the United States tries to influence Central American politics. His major disciple in the region today is none other than Edén Pastora Gomez. In announcing his new revolution, Pastora said that Torrijos had taught him that the secret of having good relations with the United States while maintaining an independent, non-aligned foreign policy was to play with the chain but not with the monkey.

The parting irony of the Panama Canal treaties is that Ronald Reagan now probably wishes that he had one to negotiate with each of the other Central American nations to bring to them the stability that the treaties brought Panama. But alas, the political instability in Nicaragua, Guatemala, and El Salvador, the uncertainty in Honduras and Panama, and the economic crisis in Costa Rica cannot be solved by a treaty that only looks simple in retrospect. The crisis of Central America goes back at least a decade, but the solution that might have worked then—opening the political process to new groups and forces—is unlikely to be adequate today. Still, that is the first step.

The strategic challenge the United States faces in Central America is difficult precisely because it has less to do with traditional concepts of national security than previous challenges did and much more to do with trying to influence the process of political change in a sensitive Third World environment. The time when the United States could bring political stability to the region is long past; all we can do now is contribute to the problem or to the solution. The United States can contribute to the problem by demonstrating an unwillingness to negotiate, an eagerness for unproductive threats and military confrontation, a penchant for military responses to political problems, and a preference for unilateralism instead of regional cooperation. Or the United States can seek social and economic justice even as it resists communism, condemn human-rights violations even as it denounces Cuban-supported terrorism, promote democracy, and seek to depoliticize the military. The United States may also find that a little more distance may mean a lot more influence.

Notes

1. Elizabeth Pond, "U.S. Tries Hard Sell in Europe of Hard Line on El Salvador: Support is Not Immediately Forthcoming as Some Nations Save Up for More Pressing European Defense Issues," *Christian Science Monitor,* February 19, 1981, p. 7; and Richard M. Weintraub, "U.S. Allies Cool To El Salvador Drive," *New York Times,* February 27, 1981, p. 1. For an excellent description of the divergent perceptions between the Reagan administration and the Europeans, see Wolf Grabendorff, *The Central Amerian Crisis and Western Europe: Perceptions and Reactions* (Bonn: Research Institute of the Friedrich-Ebert-Stiftung, 1982).

2. *New York Times,* February 25, 1982.

3. *New York Times,* February 22, 1982.

4. Ibid.

5. World Bank, *Economic Memorandum on El Salvador,* Report no. 2287-ES, May 7, 1979, Table 5, p. 19. World Bank, *Income Distribution and Poverty in Mexico,* Staff Working Paper no. 395, June 1980.

6. United Nations, Economic Commission for Latin America (hereafter cited as UN ECLA), *Central America: Nature of the Present Economic Crisis, The Challenges It Raises and The International Co-operation For Which It Calls,* August 26, 1981, p. 2.

7. The statistics are taken from the World Bank's 1981 World Development Indicators, the Statistical Appendix to *World Development Report, 1981,* Table 1.

8. These statistics and those that follow are from the sources in Notes 3 and 4.

9. See, for example, Thomas and Marjorie Melville, *Guatemala—Another Vietnam?* (Middlesex, England: Penguin Books, 1971).

10. See Inter-American Development Bank, General Studies Division, *Report on Demographic Trends and Projections for Central America* (Washington, D.C.: Inter-American Development Bank, July 1977).

11. The estimate on capital flight is a conservative estimate. The UN ECLA study noted that it made "a decisive contribution to the loss of international monetary reserves of almost $900 million in 1980" (p. 21). The statistics on the decline in GNP are in the same study, Table 1, p. 19.

12. For a description of these divergent perspectives and prescriptions, see Robert Pastor, "Three Perspectives on El Salvador," *SAIS Review* 2 (Summer 1981), pp. 35–48.

13. *New York Times,* February 25, 1982.

14. Barry Sussman, "Majority in Poll Oppose Reagan on El Salvador," *Washington Post,* March 24, 1982. 70 percent said they opposed any plan to send more military equipment or weapons to El Salvador. By a ratio of 2 to 1, those interviewed said they expected the United States to send troops to El Salvador eventually if the government could not defeat the rebels, but 80 percent said they would oppose such action. Indeed, 50 percent said they would support young Americans who resisted the draft.

15. "David Rockefeller Cites 'Advantage' to U.S. of Normal Ties With Angola," *Washington Post,* March 3, 1982, p. A1.

16. "Let's not delude ourselves," Ronald Reagan told Karen Elliott House of the *Wall Street Journal* in June 1980, "the Soviet Union underlies all the unrest that is going on. If they weren't engaged in this game of dominoes, there wouldn't be any hot spots in the world."

17. Prefacing this statement, Haig made a rather incautious slip: "I think the situation . . . in which Cuban activity has reached a peak is no longer acceptable in this hemisphere whether it be in El Salvador, Honduras, Guatemala, or any other of our [*sic*] sovereign republics." Quoted in John M. Goshko and Don Oberdorfer, "Haig Calls Arms Smuggling to El Salvador 'No Longer Acceptable,'" *Washington Post,* February 28, 1981, p. A12.

18. Haig made these statements before a hearing of the House Foreign Affairs Committee. Bernard Gwertzman, "Haig Claims Proof Outsiders Direct Salvador Rebels," *New York Times,* March 3, 1982, p. 1.

19. See, for example, the interview with Cayetano Carpio, the guerrilla leader of the Farabundo Martí National Liberation Front (FMLN), in *New York Times*, February 9, 1982. In the interview, Carpio—who broke with the Communist Party of El Salvador when he was not elected secretary general in 1970 and the party chose to pursue elections rather than armed revolt as he advocated—said: "Our program is for a democratic, revolutionary government, not for a Socialist government." See also "Marxist Attempts to Allay American Fears," *Washington Post*, March 8, 1982, pp. A1, 16. For a good account of what the guerrillas say in Cuban and Mexican newspapers, see Gabriel Zaid, "Enemy Colleagues: A Reading of the Salvadoran Tragedy," originally published in the Mexican monthly *Vuelta* and republished in *Dissent* (Winter 1982), pp. 13–40.

20. "Excerpts from Interview with Secretary of State," *New York Times*, February 8, 1982.

21. Adm. Bobby R. Inman, deputy director of the Central Intelligence Agency, introduced John T. Hughes, deputy director for intelligence and external affairs for the Defense Intelligence Agency, before the assembled reporters at the State Department: "We're privileged to have with us today to present the evidence [of Nicaragua's military build-up] John Hughes. John has been in the intelligence business now for slightly over 30 years. He is the premier photo interpreter in the U.S. intelligence community. And those of you with a historical interest may recall in 1962 when John Hughes briefed the evidence, from photography, of the introduction of missiles into Cuba." "Transcript of Statements at State Department on the Military Buildup in Nicaragua," *New York Times*, March 10, 1982.

22. See Abraham F. Lowenthal, "The United States and Latin America: Ending the Hegemonic Presumption," *Foreign Affairs* 55, no. 7 (October 1976), pp. 199–213.

23. Jeane Kirkpatrick, "U.S. Security and Latin America," *Commentary* 71, no. 7 (January 1981), pp. 29–40. I, and a dozen others, responded to Kirkpatrick's argument on U.S. policy toward Nicargua in the April 1981 issue of *Commentary*.

24. "Statement of José Napoleón Duarte," Subcommittee on International Organizations and on Inter-American Affairs of the U.S. House of Representatives Committee on International Relations, *The Recent Presidential Elections in El Salvador: Implications for U.S. Foreign Policy*, 95th Congress, 1st sess., March 17, 1977, p. 61.

25. "Excerpts from Testimony by Haig Before House Panel," *New York Times*, March 3, 1982, p. A12. Haig's views had surfaced the month before in an extensive interview he gave to the *New York Times*. See Bernard Gwertzman, "Haig, Rejecting Vietnam Parallel, Refuses to Bar Force in Caribbean," *New York Times*, February 8, 1982, pp. 1, 12.

26. In response to a question whether "U.S. involvement in El Salvador" was looking more like that of Vietnam, 61 percent of the American people agreed in March 1981 and 71 percent agreed in March 1982. Louis Harris, "Public Opposes Deeper U.S. Involvement in El Salvador," April 1, 1982, syndicated for the *Chicago Tribune*.

27. See Robert Pastor, "Migration in the Caribbean Basin: The Need for an Approach as Dynamic as the Phenomenon," in M. M. Kritz (ed.), *U.S. Immigration*

and Refugee Policy: Global and Domestic Issues (Lexington, Mass.: D. C. Heath, 1983).

28. Ibid.

29. "Hispanic Gains in Suburbs Found," *New York Times*, June 28, 1981, p. 1. Also "'80 Census Shows Sharp Rise in Blacks, Hispanics in U.S.," *Washington Post*, February 24, 1981, p. A3.

30. These are estimates of the Immigration and Naturalization Service. Robert Lindsey, "Salvadorans' Status At Issue on Coast," *New York Times*, June 26, 1982, p. 9.

31. Leon Bouvier, "U.S. Immigration: Effects on Population Growth and Structure," in Kritz, *U.S. Immigration and Refugee Policy*.

32. "Census Report Shows Gains in Education and Housing," *New York Times*, April 20, 1982, pp. 1, B6.

33. For a more extensive discussion of the Caribbean Basin initiative and its relationship to the Simpson-Mazzoli bill on immigration, see Robert Pastor, "Sinking in the Caribbean Basin," *Foreign Affairs* 60, no. 5 (Summer 1982), pp. 1038–1058.

34. For a detailed negotiating scenario, see Robert Pastor, "Winning Through Negotiation," *The New Republic*, March 17, 1982.

35. For more specific recommendations on this lesson and those that follow, see Robert Pastor, "The Target and The Source: U.S. Policy Toward El Salvador and Nicaragua," *Washington Quarterly* 5, no. 3 (Summer 1982), pp. 116–127.

13
The "Cuban Threat" in Central America

Carla A. Robbins

In mid-March 1982 the Reagan administration held a press briefing to present evidence that Nicaragua, with Cuban and Soviet backing, was assembling the largest military force in Central America. This buildup, according to administration officials, far exceeded Nicaragua's defensive needs and posed a major threat to the stability of the entire Central American region. The briefing was to be the first in a series that the administration said would present "overwhelming" and "irrefutable" evidence of communist subversion in Central America.

Charges of Cuban-backed subversion are not new for the Reagan administration. What was unusual about this presentation was the fact that it was conducted by high-level members of the U.S. Central Intelligence and Defense Intelligence agencies. The decision to unleash the intelligence agencies, traditionally used only in times of grave crisis (the photo interpreter chosen was John T. Hughes, the man who briefed the press during the Cuban missile crisis two decades earlier), was a testimony to how important the Reagan administration considers the issue of Cuban subversion and how concerned it is about the American public's increasing skepticism about such charges. Adm. Bobby R. Inman, deputy director of the Central Intelligence Agency, introduced the briefing saying, "I'm here this afternoon because I'm concerned and because I'm angry." Concerned, he said, about ensuring that the U.S. public understood the "military buildup in Nicaragua and what it portends for this country." Angry, he went on to say, because the public had become skeptical of such charges. "I've watched, over the past couple of weeks, public servants trying to grapple with the difficulty of conveying information while protecting critical intelligence sources and methods and finding that they're standardly greeted with 'How can we believe you unless you show us all the evidence.' "[1]

For the administration Cuban subversion is not only the primary cause for the spiraling violence in Central America, it is also the only possible justification to a war-wary American public for making a major economic and military commitment to the region. Despite its best efforts, the administration has had a terrible time proving the existence of a significant Cuban threat in Central America. The White Paper on communist subversion in El Salvador was soundly debunked not long after it was issued.[2] And less than a week after the March 1982 briefing the administration was internationally embarrassed when a young Nicaraguan guerrilla captured in El Salvador and brought to Washington to prove the existence of Cuban-trained guerrillas in El Salvador announced that he had been acting completely on his own. He said that he had only claimed to have been trained in Cuba to avoid further torture.[3] The promised follow-up briefings to present further irrefutable evidence never materialized.

In the aftermath of these public-relations debacles, critics of the administration are asking, if the Cuban and Nicaraguan involvement in El Salvador is so extensive, why has it been so difficult to prove?

In the end the administration has been forced back to *ad hominem* and atavistic arguments about the Cuban threat. Nowhere was this clearer than in the October 1981 "telegram" on renewed Cuban subversion in the hemisphere.[4] Unlike the earlier White Paper, this report contained absolutely no documentary evidence to support its charges of hemisphere-wide Cuban subversion. Instead for proof it relied solely on a detailed rendition of Havana's earlier history of violence and subversion in the hemisphere. The logic in this report, and the logic the administration has been forced to rely on time and again when its evidence has proved unsatisfactory, is not more sophisticated than: they did it once, therefore they *must* be doing it again.

What Did the Cubans Really Do During the 1960s and 1970s?

The common perception is that the Cubans spent all of the 1960s and a good deal of the 1970s trying to subvert legitimate regimes around the world. Although the Castro regime is best remembered for revolutionary rhetoric like Fidel Castro's pledge to "turn the Andes into the Sierra Maestra of Latin America" and Ernesto ("Che") Guevara's call to create "two, three, many Vietnams," the export of revolution was only one brief and comparatively limited phase of Cuban foreign policy.

During the early years the Castro regime devoted a majority of its energies to building normal diplomatic relations with its hemispheric neighbors. Cuban leaders visited all the major capitals and regularly attended meetings of the OAS. At a 1959 meeting of OAS ministers Castro even proposed a plan for regional economic development in which the United States would underwrite the Latin American economies with a grant of thirty billion dollars over the next ten years.[5] According to one observer close to Castro, the Cuban leader was "very enthusiastic about his private Alliance for Progress scheme." At the time Castro was seriously considering "staying on the American side of the fence as the sponsor of this [plan] and as the leader of a Nasser-type revolution."[6]

It is also true that during these early years the Castro regime provided safe haven and some aid to a number of Caribbean exile groups. In 1959 Cuban-based exiles launched attacks on Haiti, Panama, and the Dominican Republic—all failed. But it must be emphasized that Havana's support for these adventures was very limited. It must also be recognized that giving aid to revolutionaries seeking to overthrow dictatorships is a long-standing tradition for Latin America's democratic left. Costa Rica's Figueres, Guatemala's Arévalo, even Venezuela's Betancourt—Washington's number-one ally in the Alliance for Progress—all played similar roles during the late 1940s era of the Caribbean Legion.[7]

The breakdown of Cuba's diplomatic relations in the hemisphere was due to a variety of factors including Havana's diplomatic bumbling, a limited amount of Cuban subversion, strong pressures from Washington, and a right-wing turn in the hemisphere. By 1963 every major state in Latin America except Mexico had turned against the Castro regime. It was at this time that Havana turned its full energies to the export of revolution. What had earlier been a temperamental and ideological commitment now became essential to the republic's survival.

Even then Cuba's actual military commitments to continental revolution remained extremely limited. According to a 1967 study made for the House of Representatives, only "four instances of direct Cuban support to insurgent groups in Latin America" could be proven—in total no more than two hundred Cuban guerrillas and several tons of weapons for the entire decade.[8] Cuba's on-island training for Latin American revolutionaries was comparably small. According to Defense Intelligence Agency testimony in 1971, only an estimated twenty-five hundred Latin American leftists were trained in Cuba during the entire 1961–1969 period.[9] This was a far cry from the 1960s estimates of fifteen hundred to twenty-five hundred a year. It must also be recognized that Havana's attempts to export revolution were not only small, they were also utterly ineffective. Not one Cuban-inspired, -backed, or -trained guerrilla group ever succeeded in taking power. The Cuban threat during the 1960s never lived up to either Havana's claims or Washington's fears.

Given the strength of Havana's ideological commitment to the export of revolution, the question must be asked, why were Cuba's actual efforts so limited? The Cubans suffered from some very real material constraints: The Cuban economy was weak; there was very little foreign exchange; Cuba had no armaments industry and only very limited transport capability. Finally, Moscow opposed Havana's attempts to export revolution. Conditions in Latin America were not ripe for revolution, the Kremlin's theorists argued. Moreover by the late 1960s Moscow was more interested in opening diplomatic and trading relations with the Latin American regimes than overthrowing them. Without Soviet support Havana simply did not—and does not—have the resources to export revolution on the scale suggested by its ideological commitments.

After 1968 Havana abandoned even this limited support for the Latin American guerrillas. Military defeat after military defeat, culminating with Che's death in Bolivia in late 1967, convinced the Cuban leadership that the strategy of armed struggle was not working. At the same time the Cubans were feeling increasingly strong pressures from their Soviet allies to abandon their adventurist policies. By the late 1960s the Cubans could also no longer afford an independent foreign policy—even one as limited as the mid-1960s efforts to export revolution.

Failures in its domestic development programs demanded the republic's full resources and Castro's complete attention. Finally, with the appearance of a leftist-oriented military junta in Peru in 1968 and the election of Salvador Allende in Chile two years later, new policy options became available. These developments placed a new premium on the issue of national sovereignty. It was one thing for Havana to ignore the sanctity of national boundaries when it had no diplomatic relations to maintain. But with a growing number of states seeking to normalize relations, Havana had to respect conventional international behavior.

By mid-1969 Havana had forsworn the export of revolution and was again expressing interest in renewed diplomatic and trading relations with its Latin American neighbors. Where once Castro had condemned Soviet overtures to Venezuela and Colombia as collusion and betrayal of internationalist solidarity, the newly pragmatic leader had come to consider links to Latin America a necessity if Cuba were ever to overcome its dependence on the Soviet Union and its underdevelopment.

It appears that Havana's new commitment to diplomacy was accompanied by a cutoff of aid to the Latin American guerrilla movements. Given the limited amount of aid sent to begin with, this was, of course, difficult to document. Nevertheless a Senate Foreign Relations Committee report issued in 1971 described Cuban support for Latin American insurgency at the time as "minimal."[10] Perhaps a better indicator of the shift in Cuban policies is the response of Havana's previous allies. Early in 1970, Venezuelan guerrilla leader Douglas Bravo attacked Castro by name and accused the Cubans of abandoning the continental revolution in favor of their own selfish concerns about economic development.[11]

Bravo's charges notwithstanding, Havana's decision to abandon the export of revolution did not mean Cuba had abandoned all interest in the region. If anything, after 1970 Cuban aid to Latin America actually increased. The difference was that Cuba's new aid programs were predominantly humanitarian rather than military, and they were directed to official state governments rather than guerrilla movements. Cuba sent earthquake relief to Peru, Nicaragua, Honduras, and Guatemala. By the mid-1970s, Cuban technical advisers, as well as hundreds of doctors, teachers, and construction workers, were involved in development programs in Jamaica, Guyana, Grenada, and St. Lucia.

Even with all these humanitarian gestures, the image of the Cuban guerrilla was not easily shaken. With time, however, and repeated promises from Havana that no Latin American government had anything to fear from the Cuban military, these efforts to woo their neighbors began to pay off. One by one Havana's earlier enemies abandoned the OAS sanctions and reopened diplomatic and trading relations with the Castro regime. By the summer of 1974 even the United States, under the leadership of Henry Kissinger, began to make overtures toward rapprochement with the Castro regime. To all observers it looked as if the days of guerrilla warfare were finally over.

The commitment of some fifteen thousand Cuban troops to Angola by mid-1976 caught everyone by surprise. The Ford administration immediately broke off negotiations, saying the Cubans had obviously lied about wanting readmission to the arena of normal diplomacy. Although Havana's links to the MPLA could be traced back to the days of the mid-1960s, Washington was wrong when it claimed that the Angolan involvement was a return to the export of revolution. In Angola the Castro regime was not trying to subvert a sovereign state. Instead it was supporting a movement that, if not yet sovereign, was recognized as legitimate by a good number of liberal European states and the mainstream Organization of African Unity (OAU).

Even more important, most of Havana's newfound allies did not think of the Angolan involvement as a return to the export of revolution.[12] Instead of undercutting Havana's international standing, it actually improved it. In the aftermath of the Cuban-backed victory of the Movimento Popular de Libertação de Angola (MPLA), Cuba was elected chairman of the Nonaligned Movement. The Ethiopian involvement in mid-1977 was also not a return to the export of revolution. Instead of intervening in another state's affairs, Cuba was helping defend a sovereign state against an intervention from Somalia. The Cuban involvement in Ethiopia again received the endorsement of the OAU, although soon afterward several states began to express concern about the continued presence of some thirty-five thousand Cuban troops in Africa.

The revolution in Nicaragua offered Havana a new set of opportunities and a new set of dilemmas. The Castro regime's enmity toward the Somoza dictatorship can be traced back to the 1961 Bay of Pigs invasion when Luís Somoza Debayle—brother of Anastasio Somoza Debayle—lent his ports for the launching of the anti-Castro exiles. During the mid-1960s Havana had tried to return the favor by giving training and a limited amount of arms to the fledgling Sandinistas. Thus both history and emotion bound the Castro regime to the Sandinista cause. But by 1978 there was also good reason for Cuba to exercise restraint. The Castro regime was on record as having abandoned the export of revolution to Latin America. Should there be even a hint of Cuban subversion in Nicaragua, Cuba could well jeopardize a decade's worth of hard-won diplomatic gains.

As a result the Cubans played only a limited role in the Sandinista revolution. According to a CIA report issued in May 1979, Havana sent the Nicaraguans only two to three planeloads of light weapons.[13] The Cubans sent no troops to fight in the civil war. During the last months of the final offensive the Castro regime may have escalated its commitment, sending both military advisers and several large arms shipments. It must be remembered, however, that at the time Cuba's backing for the Sandinistas was far outweighed by the amount of support provided by such liberal regímes as Venezuela, Costa Rica, and Mexico. Cuba's diplomatic standing in the hemisphere did not suffer.

By the end of the decade—with thirty-five thousand troops stationed in Africa, another ten thousand civilian advisers stationed worldwide, the chairmanship of the Nonaligned Movement, correct diplomatic relations with almost every state in the hemisphere, and victories in Angola, Ethiopia, and Nicaragua—the Castro regime had achieved an international reach it could only have dreamed of during the days of revolutionary export. All this had been attained with a careful eye toward diplomatic conventions and international opinion. Whatever their role during the radical days of the mid-1960s, the Cubans were no longer revolutionary outlaws.

What Are the Cubans Really Doing in Central America?

In February 1981 the new Reagan administration issued its White Paper on El Salvador.[14] In it the administration charged that the spiraling violence in El Salvador was the result of Cuban-sponsored insurgency rather than genuine popular resistance to El Salvador's military-dominated regime. Specifically the White Paper charged the Cubans with providing arms, political and strategic direction, military training, and sophisticated propaganda support to the guerrillas—all intended to "widen and intensify the conflict" in El Salvador, "greatly increasing the suffering of the Salvadoran people and deceiving much of the world about the true nature of the revolution." The White Paper further asserted that El Salvador's was not an isolated case of communist subversion in the Third World. It called the events in El Salvador "strikingly familiar" and part of a "pattern we have seen before, to be specific in Angola and Ethiopia."

It is difficult to determine the extent of Cuba's actual involvement in the Salvadoran civil war. The Castro regime at first denied the Reagan administration's charges of Cuban subversion, calling them "absolute lies," and leveled countercharges of its own that Washington was using the Cuban threat as a pretext for hostile actions in El Salvador and against Nicaragua and Cuba. Subsequently a high-level Cuban official admitted that Cuba had sent a limited amount of arms during the winter 1980 final offensive.[15] There is good reason to be skeptical of the Castro regime's denials since Havana denied its participation in the Angolan, Ethiopian, and Nicaraguan conflicts with equal vehemence. Yet, despite the importance of the issue, there is little evidence to support either the Reagan administration's charges of widespread Cuban subversion or Havana's denials.

The Reagan administration was right to suggest there are precedents of Cuban overseas involvements that could shed some light on Cuban policies in El Salvador. The administration was wrong, however, when it pointed to the Cuban involvements in Angola and Ethiopia as the appropriate precedents. In neither Angola nor Ethiopia were the Cubans involved in "a well-coordinated, covert effort to bring about the overthrow of [an] established government and to impose in its place a Communist regime with no popular support," as the White Paper described Cuba's efforts in El Salvador. It must be remembered that in Angola, the established government—the Portuguese regime—withdrew *voluntarily*, and Cuban military support was used by the MPLA to help defeat alternative guerrilla groups vying for power and their foreign backers from South Africa and Zaire. In Ethiopia the communist coup came three years *before* Cuban troops were ever committed, and Cuban military aid was used to repulse an invasion from neighboring Somalia. Neither of these experiences fits the White Paper's charges or the situation in El Salvador. A much more appropriate precedent would be Cuba's participation in the Nicaraguan civil war. In Nicaragua, covert Cuban military aid as well as Cuban political, military, and strategic advice helped bring about the overthrow of an established—if illegitimate—

regime and helped impose in its place a socialist, if not traditionally communist, regime.

The similarity between the White Paper's charges and the Nicaraguan situation, however, ends there. The Nicaraguan revolution was not the result of Cuban or any other externally sponsored insurgency. It was a grass-roots struggle against a repressive and increasingly illegitimate regime that received military aid, advice, and political support from a large number of political actors—both communist and noncommunist—including Mexico, Venezuela, Panama, Costa Rica, and Cuba. Furthermore, Cuban material commitments to Nicaragua were nowhere near the level of massive arms shipments described in the White Paper.

According to the May 1979 CIA report on Nicaragua, the Cubans did not make more of a commitment to the Nicaraguan civil war because of their fear that any greater involvement would lead to a confrontation with Washington and jeopardize their already delicate political relations in Latin America.[16] There is little reason deductively and very little evidence to suggest that Havana would significantly alter its *modus operandi* in El Salvador. If anything there were more reasons for *restraint* in El Salvador. Washington under Ronald Reagan was obviously much more hostile to the Castro regime and the Salvadoran opposition and thus much more likely to take any suggestion of Cuban involvement in El Salvador as cause for confrontation. Cuba's Latin American allies would also be much less tolerant of a Cuban involvement in El Salvador. Unlike the Nicaraguan civil war, in which every major liberal regime supported the Sandinistas, the Salvadoran civil war split the region's ranks with Mexico and Panama unofficially backing the opposition and Costa Rica and Venezuela strongly backing the junta.

Finally, the Salvadoran opposition is a less likely candidate for extensive Cuban support. In Nicaragua Havana was very cautious about extending aid to the Sandinistas, requiring that they overcome internal political problems, form a united front with members of the Nicaraguan business and landowning communities, and build a broad base of popular support before it would endorse a military struggle and send any military aid. The Salvadoran opposition is today in a much greater state of political disarray and much less assured of solid popular support than the Sandinistas during their final offensive. If the Cubans are following the pattern established in Nicaragua, they would counsel the Salvadoran guerrillas to hold back until they are better organized and assured of greater popular support before launching their final offensive. Cuban arms would be withheld until Havana determined that the time was right for the Salvadoran revolution.

This is not to suggest that the Cubans are not sending some aid to the Salvadoran guerrillas. There is no doubt that Havana is strongly committed to the Salvadoran opposition and has given advice and training to its leaders over the years. Certainly Havana's self-image as the vanguard of the Latin American revolution, as well as the personal leanings of its revolutionary leadership, would require as much. And it is likely that extraordinary circumstances have forced Havana to overcome its recently acquired natural caution and send arms to support the Salvadoran opposition, even if it considered the situation in El Salvador somewhat premature. Castro was apparently persuaded by the Salvadoran opposition's arguments that this is their last chance for victory, given the Reagan election and the massive increase in U.S. arms deliveries to the Salvadoran junta.

But even if Havana has sent, and is sending, military aid to the Salvadoran guerrillas, logic, the available evidence, and the Nicaraguan precedent suggest that the Reagan administration is wrong when it describes the Salvadoran civil war as a "textbook case of indirect armed aggression by Communist powers through Cuba." The Castro regime can no more create the conditions for civil strife in El Salvador than it can guarantee the Salvadoran opposition ultimate victory. The Castro regime learned two important lessons in the late 1960s. First, revolutions cannot be exported, they can only be aided and abetted. Second, for the sake of its own survival, Cuba must be very careful about which movements it supports and under what conditions.

How Should the United States Respond?

A review of Cuban policy over the past two decades suggests that Cuba is not and never has been a major cause for revolution in the hemisphere. The Castro regime was never committed to indiscriminate subversion or violence. And in recent years Havana has been more interested in maintaining good diplomatic relations than in fomenting revolutions. Over the last decade the majority of its overseas commitments have been overt, humane, and constructive.

Even when Havana has decided to support or export revolutions it has never had the means in terms of money, arms, or transport to define the outcome—at least not alone. Washington consistently overestimates Havana's capabilities. In twenty-two years the Castro regime has suported only two successful revolutions: Angola and Nicaragua. Both these revolutions received a significant amount of international support from a wide variety of mainstream, even liberal, states.

Finally, those revolutions that have succeeded with Cuban backing have not turned immediately into Cuban or Soviet pawns. Despite our worst fears, the MPLA victory in Angola has not been that costly to the United States: Southern Africa has not gone communist; Angola has not turned into a military base for the Soviets; Gulf Oil rigs continue to produce in Cabinda while Cuban troops stand guard.

It is still too early to determine the costs from the Nicaraguan revolution. Nevertheless, before the Reagan administration started threatening the Sandinista government, Managua seemed quite interested in maintaining correct and even cordial relations with Washington. The Cubans even urged their Nicaraguan allies to maintain their economic and political ties with the West in general and the United States in particular. It is not that Havana has suddenly become pro–United States. It has not. Rather, Cuba's repeated economic failures and crushing dependence on the Soviets have made the Castro government realistic about the alternatives open to small states. These states, Havana has been saying, cannot afford the luxury of opposing the United States.

Havana has even been urging a negotiated settlement in El Salvador. In late March 1982, senior Cuban officials began to express publicly a strong interest in improving relations with the Reagan administration and finding a solution to the conflict in El Salvador based on negotiations and the exercise of mutual restraint.[17]

After more than a year of repeated and, at times, vehement denials, the Castro government admitted sending arms to the Salvadoran guerrillas. The officials insisted, however, that direct Cuban aid to the guerrillas had stopped almost fourteen months before, soon after the failure of the January 1981 "final offensive," and that in recent months Cuba had ceased to transport arms from third countries. Cuba, they said, was now exercising self-restraint in Central America and was ready to play a "positive role" in resolving disputes and reaching a negotiated settlement of the problems in El Salvador. Havana's overtures seem sincere. And if the United States wants to end the killing in El Salvador—as it claims—it should accept the offer. At the very least, if the Cubans are not sincere, the United States will get the propaganda benefit from calling their bluff.

But before the United States sits down at the bargaining table, it must be clear about what negotiations can and cannot accomplish.[18] In the past, negotiations with Havana failed because Washington overestimated its bargaining strength and asked for too much: specifically, that the Cubans forswear any and all future overseas involvements. Each time the Cubans refused. Beyond the issue of national sovereignty, the Cubans are not going to let *anyone*, not even the Soviets, tell them what they can and cannot do in their foreign policy. They have derived too many benefits from their overseas involvements: international prestige, Soviet payoffs, domestic pride.

The Reagan administration has little to offer the Castro government to offset those benefits. Certainly the Cubans want the embargo lifted, and they want access to American technology in order to diversify their trading partners and lessen their dependence on the Soviets. But, at the same time, the Castro government is realistic about what it can and cannot expect from the United States. So long as Cuba remains socialist, the Soviet Union will be its mentor, protector, and major trading partner. Cuba's foreign exchange will be severely limited. Its ability to take advantage of U.S. markets will be no less limited. For limited access to U.S. markets the Cubans are not going to give up their presence in Angola and Ethiopia or cede all discretionary control over future forays into Central America or elsewhere.

But the Cubans have offered to exercise restraint in El Salvador in return for similar U.S. promises. This offer, although not as spectacular as a promise for a full Cuban *démarche,* should not be minimized. If the United States really wants the Salvadorans to have the freedom to resolve their own problems without outside interference, having the Cubans withdraw from that conflict is a major victory.

Such a quid pro quo agreement with Havana would get the United States out of what has become an increasingly difficult situation in El Salvador. The Reagan administration claims that it must stay in El Salvador to offset Cuban subversion. However, the right-wing coalition that it is protecting there embodies few of the United States' principles. And it has proved difficult to control. Popular and congressional opposition to U.S. involvement in El Salvador has not abated. If the Cubans were to withdraw from the conflict, the Reagan administration would gain a much-needed opening to get out of El Salvador as well.

Havana's stated willingness to negotiate on El Salvador should be a hopeful sign for the rest of Central America. If the Cubans really thought they could win in El Salvador, they undoubtedly would continue to ship arms, train insurgents, and do whatever else they could to ensure a socialist victory. They evidently believe that such a victory is now impossible. There are several reasons for the Castro government's willingness to negotiate. In addition to their doubts about socialism in El Salvador, the Cubans fear that any further commitment to the conflict will bring them into a direct confrontation with the United States. Havana is also painfully aware that its own international prestige and diplomatic contacts have suffered as a result of its role in El Salvador. The specter of renewed Cuban subversion in the hemisphere is not taken lightly by Cuba's neighbors. For all these reasons, the Castro government can be expected to exercise only a very limited role in future Central American conflicts. The United States thus can afford to relax its vigilance toward the "Cuban threat" and begin to search for real and lasting solutions to the problems in Central America—solutions that address the true causes for the current instability: poverty, underdevelopment, and repression.

Notes

1. *New York Times,* March 10, 1982.

2. Jonathan Kwitney, "Apparent Errors Cloud U.S. 'White Paper' on Reds in El Salvador," *Wall Street Journal,* June 8, 1981; and Robert Kaiser, "White Paper on El Salvador Is Faulty," *Washington Post,* June 9, 1981.

3. *New York Times,* March 13 and 14, 1982.

4. "Cuba's Renewed Support for Violence in the Hemisphere," paper presented to the Subcommittee on Western Hemisphere Affairs, U.S. Senate Foreign Relations Committee, December 14, 1981.

5. Fidel Castro, *Discursos Pronunciados por Comandante Fidel Castro Ruz en tres Capitales de América Latina: Buenos Aires, Montevideo, Rio de Janeiro* (Havana: Minfar, 1959).

6. Javier Pazos, "Cuba—Was a Deal Possible in '59?" *The New Republic,* January 12, 1963.

7. For a history of the democratic expeditionary groups known as the Caribbean Legion, see Charles D. Ameringer, *The Democratic Left in Exile* (Coral Gables, Fla.: University of Miami Press, 1974), pp. 59–110.

8. "Communist Activities in Latin America," Report of the Subcommittee on Inter-American Affairs, U.S. House of Representatives Committee on Foreign Affairs, July 1967.

9. "Soviet Naval Activities in the Caribbean," Hearings before the Subcommittee on Inter-American Affairs, U.S. House of Representatives Committee on Foreign Affairs, 1971, pt. 2, p. 16.

10. "United States Policy Toward Cuba," Hearings before the U.S. Senate Committee on Foreign Relations, May 1971, p. 4.

11. For left-wing disillusionment with Castro's alleged sellout to the Soviets, see K. S. Karol, *Guerrillas in Power* (New York: Hill and Wang, 1970).

12. On Cuba's often rocky relations with the Third World, see Carla Anne Robbins, "Looking for Another Angola: Cuban Policy Dilemmas in Africa," The Wilson Center Latin American Program, Working Papers 38 (Washington, D.C.: Woodrow Wilson International Center for Scholars, 1979).

13. *New York Times,* July 4, 1979.

14. U.S. State Department White Paper, "Communist Interference in El Salvador," Special Report no. 80, February 23, 1981.

15. Leslie H. Gelb, "Those Nice Noises from Cuba Could Be a Signal or Just Static," *New York Times,* April 18, 1982.

16. *New York Times,* July 4, 1979.

17. *New York Times,* April 6, 1982; Leslie H. Gelb, "Those Nice Noises from Cuba-"; and private talks with Cuban diplomats in Havana.

18. For a further discussion of U.S. policy options toward Cuba and in Central America, see Carla A. Robbins, *The Cuban Threat* (New York: McGraw-Hill, 1983).

14
The Socialist Countries and Central American Revolutions

Henrik Bischof

This chapter deals first with Moscow's Latin American policy during the period from Fidel Castro's assumption of power in Cuba in the late fifties until the victory of the Sandinista revolution in Nicaragua in the late seventies, with special emphasis on the Central American region. Second, it focuses on East European assistance to Nicaragua. Third, it analyzes the prospects of Soviet influence in the area in the light of revolutionary developments in El Salvador, Guatemala, and Honduras.

Any serious analysis of the Soviet Union's attitude toward Central America must inevitably take into consideration both Washington's policy in its traditional "backyard" and the existing power structures in the region including the problems resulting from them. Any other approach to the subject would boil down to a mere propaganda effort.

The present crisis in Central America is manifest in various dimensions, and its solution depends on a number of internal and external factors. Among the former is an acute social conflict, to which there seems to be no solution by peaceful means as long as traditional patterns of power structure prevent the implementation of urgently required reforms to solve fundamental problems of development and bring about some kind of social justice. Consequently, the growing repression on the part of the ruling oligarchy inevitably leads to clashes with the ever-widening section of the underprivileged. If these internal factors had been allowed to operate without outside interference, they might have produced some kind of solution to this internal conflict, resulting in the establishment of a more liberal and just social system. External forces have, however, aggravated the situation.

As most Central American states are relatively small and potentially weak, different power blocs and supraregional political forces have been trying to influence developments in the region. The global East-West conflict dominating present-day international relations—with the two great powers, the United States and the USSR, trying mutually to safeguard and expand their spheres of influence—complicated developments in the region. As Washington considers Central America part of its own sphere of influence, it took measures to protect the region from Soviet intrusion. Totally ignoring the prevailing social problems, which are a typical outgrowth of the North-South conflict, things were twisted to fit into the pattern of East-West conflict. The complex social and economic problems of the region and its power mechanisms were oversimplified by dividing its exponents up into advocates of "communism" on the one hand and defenders of "freedom" on the other. Simultaneously, the Soviet Union was blamed for all the trouble in the area. Washington maintained that Moscow was wielding unlimited power and enjoying unrestricted opportunities to establish a permanent foothold in the Western Hemisphere. Soviet opportunities to attack U.S. strongholds in Central America are, however, limited to the same extent as are U.S. options to encroach upon established Soviet positions inside the Soviet orbit, for instance, those in Poland or Afghanistan.

One inevitable consequence of Washington's self-imposed policy of viewing the Central American crisis from an exclusive East-West angle—that is, communism versus freedom—has been the necessity to side with the repressive regimes in order to protect their outdated power structures. Simultaneously, the political forces that spearheaded the resistance movement against the oppressive rulers and seized power in some Latin American countries were left as a plaything to Soviet political ambitions. Thus Moscow was offered the chance to assume the role of sponsor of the national liberation movement and of defender of the underprivileged against their oppressors. Following a trend already evident in Africa and Asia in recent years, events in Central America showed that Soviet inroads on established positions in the Western Hemisphere were not so much a consequence of Moscow's own initiative as of Western miscalculations.

Soviet Policy in Central America: From Castro's Triumph to the Victory of the Sandinistas

Even the most astute study of Soviet Latin American policy would fail to provide a clue to any Soviet initiative aimed at the implementation of "communism" in Central America.[1] During the period between World War II and the early fifties the USSR displayed, in fact, only a very limited interest in Latin American affairs, not to mention Central America. During that period of cold war, Soviet and U.S. spheres of influence were clearly defined. The USSR saw no chance for any penetration into the Western Hemisphere. Though Moscow succeeded in establishing diplomatic relations with Nicaragua and Honduras in 1944 and 1945, respectively, those relations were soon suspended in the wake of the cold war. Even during the following years of detente Moscow was not able to set up diplomatic missions in El Salvador, Guatemala, Honduras, and Nicaragua. Until the late sixties East European presence in the area was restricted to nonresident Polish and Yugoslav ambassadors in Honduras and Nicaragua, respectively.

Soviet interest in Latin American affairs was only stimulated after the victory of Fidel Castro in Cuba. In fact the triumph of the Cuban revolution took the Soviets by surprise. The Soviet bloc and the Communist party of Cuba had actually had no share in the developments that led up to this event. Fidel Castro's 26th of July Movement had been considered as "petit bourgeois" in Moscow, and it took more than one year, in fact until 1960–1961, for the Soviets to start to cash in on the situation.

A Policy of Restraint

The unrestrained Latin American ambitions of the Khrushchev leadership came to an abrupt end, however, with the Cuban missile crisis in 1962. It took another few years, in fact until the mid-sixties, before the Brezhnev-Kosygin administration adopted a more flexible attitude and designed a rather long-term Latin American strategy. Since that time Soviet policy in Latin America has been focused on efforts to restrain U.S. influence in the area. From the Soviet point of view this does not require the establishment of "socialist" regimes. Soviet political objectives would rather be promoted through pro-Western and anticommunist regimes, such as the governments of Mexico and Argentina, taking a nationalist stand on certain issues. The following methods reveal the main features of Soviet Latin American strategy: political propaganda to support Latin American nationalism in order to reduce dependence on the United States, promotion of popular fronts, electoral alliances and similar peaceful action designed to seize power through peaceful means, establishment of political and cultural relations both on an official government basis and on a semiofficial level, and, last but not least, expansion of economic and commercial ties.

Since the late sixties this policy has achieved some success in a number of Latin American countries. Soviet diplomatic presence, economic relations with COMECON (Council for Mutual Economic Aid) countries, and communist-inspired popular fronts were, however, unsuitable options as far as Central American countries like El Salvador, Guatemala, Honduras, and Nicaragua were concerned, if one leaves aside a certain amount of Soviet trade with El Salvador in the years between 1972 and 1977—though the bilateral trade agreement signed in 1974 has never been ratified—and Soviet imports worth $5.8 million from Guatemala in 1973. As far as the other East European countries are concerned, a small trade turnover has been registered since 1976 between Czechoslovakia (Ceskoslovenska Socialisticka Republika—CSSR) on the one hand and Guatemala and Honduras on the other and between Hungary and El Salvador, Guatemala, Honduras, and Nicaragua respectively. Soviet indifference toward Central America is also illustrated by the fact that Soviet analysts and Latin American experts failed to submit any monograph or other analysis on the subject until the early seventies.[2]

Moscow's restraint was further prompted by the fact that the pro-Soviet Communist parties of El Salvador, Guatemala, Honduras, and Nicaragua were among the smallest Communist parties in Latin America in terms of membership and, in addition to this, banned in all four countries. Their leaders' main occupation was to attend Soviet Communist party congresses in Moscow and to score "deviationists" from the Soviet line. Party splits and factionalism caused by Trotskyism, the Soviet-Chinese conflict, and Cuba's support of guerrilla warfare—as opposed to the "peaceful parliamentarian" road to power advocated by the Soviets—provided an additional heavy burden to those small Central American Communist parties. According to the U.S. State Department, the pro-Soviet Communist parties of El Salvador and Nicaragua both had an estimated membership of 200 in the years between 1965 and 1970, whereas membership of the Communist parties of Guatemala and Honduras declined from about 1,000 in 1965 to 750 and 300, respectively, in 1970.[3] There is good reason to believe that the Communist Party of El Salvador had, in fact, a strength of no more than 50 members and the Guatemalan Communist party was restricted to the central committee members at that time.

Throughout the sixties Communist party conferences in Central America, Mexico, and Panama usually ended up with vows of loyalty to the Soviet Union. During all those years, when Moscow's "Chilean model" was confronted with Cuba's strategy of "rural guerrilla," with the Soviet standpoint eventually prevailing under the impact of the electoral victory of the Chilean "Unidad Popular" in 1970, Communists in Central America remained in a deplorable situation. When Moscow came up with a revised Latin American conception in the seventies—completely abandoning the theory of noncapitalist development, emphasizing the progressive role of Latin America's bourgeoisie and military, and supporting nationalist governments—pro-Soviet Communists in El Salvador, Guatemala, Honduras, and Nicaragua had to face the bitter fact that preconditions for Moscow's new strategy were practically nonexistent in their countries.[4]

The Central American Communist Parties

In Guatemala, where the pro-Soviet Communist party (Partido Guatemalteco del Trabajo—PGT) had been able to play an active political role during a brief period from 1952 to 1954, the Communists wore themselves out in the bickering between advocates of the Soviet line of nonviolence on the one hand and exponents of the Cuban strategy of rural guerrilla warfare on the other hand. Though the PGT during the sixties was not disinclined to support armed action as one form of struggle on the road to power, it simultaneously rejected Fidel Castro's theories. As a result of this ambiguous attitude, the guerrilla organization Fuerzas Armadas Rebeldes (FAR), which was founded in 1963, broke away from PGT control in February 1968. Although the PGT leadership set up a rival FAR organization (Fuerzas Armadas Revolucionarias), neither the party nor the guerrilla forces has ever recovered completely from that conflict.[5]

The pro-Soviet Communist Party of El Salvador (Partido Comunista de El Salvador—PCES) was most outspoken in its opposition to Cuban-type guerrilla warfare and eventually maneuvered itself into hopeless isolation among the country's left-wing forces. The PCES opposed the growing influence of both "petit bourgeois revolutionists" and "right-wing deviationists" in its own labor organization (Federación Unida de Sindicatos Salvadoreños—FUSS). Castroist guerrilla warfare was practically nonexistent in El Salvador during the sixties and seventies.[6]

In Honduras the Communist party (Partido Comunista de Honduras—PCH), worn out by a series of splits started in 1971, strictly rejected armed struggle, although the party leadership admitted in 1972 that the situation in Honduras ruled out any possibility of achieving revolutionary targets through peaceful means. This contradictory position prevented the party from establishing a foothold in the labor and peasant movements, and the PCH did not consider it worthwhile to establish its own organizations within these movements. An attempt to join the electoral alliance of the opposition in 1971—toeing the new Soviet line—also failed. Though the situation did not change during the following years, the new party platform announced in May 1977 still claimed that it was possible to seize power through nonviolent action.[7]

In Nicaragua the insignificant Communist party (Partido Socialista Nicaragüense—PSN) was unable to follow Moscow's instructions to form a united front with other groups. Though some PSN members joined the Frente Sandinista de Liberación Nacional (FSLN) established in 1961, which attracted general attention through spectacular guerrilla action in 1967–1968, the PSN dismissed the FSLN as "ultra-left" and its actions as "premature." Even though the PSN admitted that armed struggle was the only way to overthrow the Somoza dictatorship, it maintained as late as the early seventies that the revolutionary situation required for such action did not yet exist in Nicaragua.[8]

A revolutionary situation did, however, exist in Nicaragua. Once again, as in the case of Cuba back in 1959, the pro-Soviet Communists misinterpreted the situation. Consequently, Nicaragua's revolution bypassed Moscow and the PSN, without giving the latter much chance to have any influence on it. The FSLN, which was not given much credit either by Moscow or Western experts, had indeed—like Fidel Castro in Cuba—learned a lesson from the ill-fated rural guerrilla activities of the sixties. Resuming guerrilla actions in the seventies, the FSLN made allowance for local conditions. Opening itself to different political currents and recruiting its members from all strata of the population, including the all-important middle class, the FSLN grew into what can be described as a new type of guerrilla organization. It successfully bridged the gap between the revolutionary ideas of young intellectuals on the one hand and the workers' and peasants' movement on the other. Of the three different FSLN tendencies—Prolonged Popular War, Proletarian, and Tercerista—the latter, which included quite a number of non-Marxist elements and advocated a united front of all Somoza opponents, eventually prevailed. After a spectacular operation by an FSLN commando in Managua in December 1974, FSLN guerrillas were already fighting on four fronts by 1976 and were able to launch large-scale operations against the Somoza regime by 1977. In 1978 the FSLN became the coordinating and catalyzing force of a national uprising, which swept away the Somoza regime in July 1979. The characteristic feature of this new type of guerrilla force that has emerged in Nicaragua is that it obtained its legitimation from the incorporation of all sectors of society, including the church, which joined forces in an upsurge of mass struggle.[9]

Misled by the propaganda of the Somoza regime, most Western experts misjudged the FSLN until the end of 1978 as a pro-Soviet communist organization. On the other hand, Moscow too was mistaken. A fundamental analysis published by Soviet Latin America experts in July 1978 made no mention of Nicaragua. Its main line was that Moscow-oriented parties in Latin America continued to be confronted with extremists who were claiming the Communists were "opportunist" and "compromising" and advocating premature action by bringing pressure to bear on the working class and aiming at an immediate seizure of power.[10]

Having openly dismissed the FSLN, which adopted the ideas and strategies of the Nicaraguan nationalist hero Augusto César Sandino, as "petit bourgeois" and "nationalistic," the PSN had no chance to claim a share in the victory of the Nicaraguan revolution. The actions of leading PSN party members, who supported the FSLN toward the end of the civil war but were subsequently exposed as agents of Somozist organizations, discredited the pro-Soviet Nicaraguan Communists even further.[11] Six months before the overthrow of Anastasio Somoza Debayle, at the beginning of 1979, the PSN was still a member of the moderate opposition alliance Frente Amplio de Oposición (FAO), which was gradually losing influence at that time. Following its usual opportunist line, the PSN also joined the left-wing alliance Movimiento Pueblo Unido (MPU), the political arm of the FSLN. This enabled PSN to climb on the bandwagon before the FSLN's victory in July 1979. Tactical considerations guided the PSN when it offered to dissolve the party and incorporate the PSN into a united Sandinista party in September 1979. The Sandinistas have so far not accepted that offer. In the fifty-one-member State Council (Consejo de Estado), the PSN held only one seat in 1981 and the PSN-controlled trade union, the Confederación General del Trabajo (CGT), two seats.

The pro-Soviet PSN has ever since remained insignificant and without influence. If the nationalist Sandinista leaders should eventually be forced to abandon their original targets—establishment of a specifically Nicaraguan social system, mixed economy, political pluralism under the guidance of the Sandinistas, political and educational mobilization of the masses, and nonaligned foreign policy—the reasons for such a development will not have to be sought among internal but rather among external factors. Above all, it is the mounting pressure from Washington and the obvious U.S. policy of destabilizing Nicaragua that prevent the Sandinistas from taking a national road to socialism within the framework of the capitalist system instead of choosing the Cuban road and seeking Soviet protection. Forecasting developments in the light of the present situation, it can easily be predicted that Soviet-bloc assistance to Nicaragua is bound to increase in the long run. As U.S. pressure is driving Nicaragua into the arms of the Soviets, any further radicalization of the regime can only be prevented by a fundamental change in Washington's policy. It is, in fact, up to the United States—as protective power of the region—not only to permit but even to guarantee vis-à-vis the Soviet Union that Nicaragua will be able to set up its self-chosen sociopolitical system.

East European Aid to Nicaragua

The Communist countries granted diplomatic recognition to the new government in Nicaragua within a few days after the overthrow of the Somoza regime in July 1979. The Soviet Union was, however, among the last few Communist countries to establish diplomatic relations on an ambassadorial level with Managua—on the eighteenth of October, 1979. Until the end of 1979 the East European countries did not offer any financial assistance to Nicaragua. After the United States had suspended its economic aid to Nicaragua on January 23, 1980, and eventually canceled a US$15 million credit offer on March 2, 1980, the Sandinistas took their first step in the direction toward Eastern Europe. A high-ranking FSLN delegation concluded a number of agreements with the Soviet Union, Czechoslovakia (CSSR), East Germany (GDR), and Bulgaria in March and April 1980. Another visit of FSLN leaders to the USSR, CSSR, Bulgaria, and Hungary in November and December 1980 was intended to prevent further economic and political isolation of Nicaragua. Members of the Nicaraguan State Council, who visited Prague in April 1981, stressed that East European economic commitments to Nicaragua were a consequence of the cancellation of U.S. aid.

When Washington suspended even a US$9.6 million credit for wheat purchases in the first half of 1981, the Soviet Union donated twenty thousand tons of wheat to Nicaragua, and Bulgaria donated ten thousand tons. The GDR provided fifty thousand tons of grain by mid-1981. Still, only 17.4 percent of the foreign-credit total offered to the FSLN government by the end of 1981 came from Communist sources. Substantial amounts of Soviet credits were not provided until about two years after the change of government in Nicaragua, when junta leader Daniel Ortega Saavedra visited Moscow in May 1982. Since then the Soviet Union has become one of Nicaragua's main donor countries, besides Mexico, Libya, Cuba, and Venezuela. Altogether Nicaragua received credits worth US$216.8 million and grants amounting to US$31 million from the Soviet Union during the period from 1980 to 1982. Further credits were extended by Bulgaria (US$67 million), the GDR (US$56 million), the CSSR (US$30 million), and Hungary (US$5 million).

A whole set of agreements has since been concluded between Nicaragua and East European countries: consular agreements with the USSR and Hungary; air-traffic agreements with the USSR and the GDR; agreements on economic, scientific, and technical cooperation with the USSR, the GDR, and Bulgaria; agreements on scientific and technical cooperation with the CSSR, Yugoslavia, and Hungary; and cultural agreements with the USSR, CSSR, GDR, and Hungary.[12]

In the party-political field the FSLN has so far arranged cooperation programs with the ruling Communist parties of the USSR, GDR, Bulgaria, and Hungary. The Sandinist trade-union federation (Central Sandinista de Trabajadores—CST) accepted assistance from the East German trade-union federation for the training of CST cadres as far back as 1979. In 1981 the CST signed an agreement with Czechoslovakia's trade union.

The Soviet trade-union federation donated a bus and two other motor vehicles to the CST in June 1981, and in the same month the CST joined the Communist-controlled World Federation of Trade Unions. In 1982 the Soviet trade unions donated goods worth US$300,000 to flood victims through the CST. The Sandinist youth organization signed cooperation agreements with the youth organizations of Poland, Hungary, and the GDR; the Nicaraguan journalists' union (Union de Periodistas Nicaragüenses—UPN) entered into cooperation agreements with the East German journalists' federation and joined the Communist-controlled International Organization of Journalists (IOJ). The official Nicaraguan press agency ANN (Agencia Noticiosa Nicaragüense) signed agreements on the exchange of news broadcasts with the Soviet news agency TASS (Telegrafnoje Agentstvo Sovetskovo Sojusa), the East German ADN (Allgemeiner Deutscher Nachrichtendienst), Czechoslovakia's CTK (Ceskoslovenská tiskova kancelář), and Bulgaria's BTA (B'lgarska telegrafua agencija). Agreements on cooperation in the field of radio and television were signed with the USSR, GDR, and Hungary. Military delegations from Nicaragua visited the GDR in 1980 and 1982 and the Soviet Union in 1981.

Nicaragua's trade with Eastern Europe, intended to reduce the country's dependence on U.S. markets, developed at a very slow rate. In September 1979 the first commercial contract on coffee exports to the Soviet Union was signed. Since then the GDR, CSSR, Hungary, Bulgaria, and Yugoslavia have become markets for Nicaraguan coffee. Long-term trade agreements providing for most-favored-nation treatment and payments in convertible currency were concluded with the USSR, CSSR, GDR, and Bulgaria in March and April 1980, and a trade agreement with Hungary was signed later on. A series of commercial contracts provided for the supply of such items as 800 lorries, 150 trailers, small trucks, plant-protection equipment, and pesticides as well as medical apparatus from the GDR; 261 dump trucks for road building, 159 tractors, 30,000 tons of iron, 60,000 tons of urea, and 10,000 tons of ammonia from the Soviet Union; and pharmaceuticals from Bulgaria. The Soviet Union also donated Nicaragua 200 tractors.

Through November 1, 1981, Nicaragua had contracted Soviet aid for the following projects:

- feasibility study and construction of a 350 Mw hydro-power station on the Rio Grande near Matagalpa
- construction of a 160 Mw hydro-power station on the Rio Grande and Pequino and Tuma rivers

- construction of a 400-bed hospital and a polyclinic in Managua and provision of a 20-member Soviet medical team for a period of three years
- construction of a 100-bed hospital in Chinandega (a donation) and dispatch of a 140-member Soviet medical team for three months
- mineral exploration covering an area of 4,000 square kilometers
- evaluation of the gold reserves of the La India mine
- opening up of the Limón gold mine
- utilization of the scrap material of the Siana gold mine
- setting up a training center for gold-mining technology near Quima and provision of twelve Soviet experts for a two-year period
- establishment of an experimental station for cotton growing covering an area of 200 hectares
- setting up a mining-industry training center for two hundred students
- setting up a fishing-industry training center for two hundred students
- drawing up a topographical map of Nicaragua at a scale of 1:50,000 and assistance to the geodetical and topographical services of the country
- technical-aid grant for the review, analysis, and evaluation of Nicaragua's national energy-development plan
- construction of a satellite ground station for the intersputnik system near the Najapa lagoon and of a radio transmitter-receiver network in the northeastern part of Nicaragua
- building a floating dock for the repair of fishing vessels and warehouses in the port of San Juan del Sur, with service personnel being trained at the expense of the USSR
- survey of Nicaragua's gold and silver mines carried out by ten Soviet experts in the period from August to November 1980
- dispatch of eight Soviet research vessels from August 1980 to May 1982 for the investigation of oceanographic resources at Nicaragua's Atlantic and Pacific coasts
- deployment of two Soviet experts as managers for the national fishing industry in the port of Bluefields starting August 1980
- technical aid for Nicaragua's fishing industry (scholarship grants for Soviet fishery colleges, repair of fishing vessels, investigation of fishing resources in inland waters)
- equipment of a scientific laboratory at the National Autonomous University of Managua
- increasing the transmitting power of two broadcasting stations
- equipment of a polytechnical school at Managua

- equipment of a training center for the electrotechnical industry in León
- equipment of a training center for the repair of agricultural machinery in Matagalpa
- technical aid for a cultural program comprising the reorganization of Nicaragua's higher educational system and the establishment of cultural centers throughout the country
- the loan of two Soviet transport helicopters for a six-month period starting April 1981 and training of Nicaraguan pilots to fly them

The GDR promised Nicaragua it would build textile mills and provide fifty school laboratories as well as technical aid for economic planning and management. Czechoslovakia's commitments include the construction of a cotton-spinning mill and a hosiery factory, supply of two thousand telephone apparatuses, and donation of 600 kilometers of cable. Hungary dispatched experts for the health service and for regional planning.

Bulgaria pledged aid for about thirty projects, among them:

- construction of a 30 Mw hydro-power station at the Rio Ye-Ye to supply the mining regions of Bonanza, Siuna, and Rosita
- expansion of nine substations in Los Brasiles, Masaya, and La Oriental
- establishment of a transformer repair shop
- reconstruction of the El Betulio mine
- geological research
- production sharing in the pharmaceutical sector
- establishment of a mixed trading company
- technical aid for the excavation of the Rio Escondido and the Los Mares river
- supply of fifty freight elevators
- expansion of the ports of El Bluff and Puerto Cabezas
- establishment of seventy-five telephone exchanges in rural areas
- donation of one hundred buses
- reconstruction of a fruit-tinning factory in Granada
- building a fruit-tinning factory in Sebaco
- building a baby-food factory

Special mention has to be made of Eastern Europe's assistance in the field of education. At the end of 1980 the Soviet Union provided 100 scholarship grants for the instruction of agrarian and mechanical engineers, 150 for vocational training, 15 for postgraduate studies, and 30 for the training of technical assistants. The USSR also offered scholarship grants for such specialized subjects as monument conservation, library science, record production, and theatrics. By September 1982, seven hundred Nicaraguan students were studying in the USSR on Soviet scholarships. For its "alphabetization campaign" Nicaragua received a Soviet donation comprising 2 helicopters, 10 Land Rovers, 500,000 pencils, 500,000 copybooks, 30,000 pairs of shoes, 1,000 radio sets, and 10,000 spectacles by the end of 1980. In 1981 the Soviet Union contributed US$8 million to the alphabetization campaign.

The first group of seventy Nicaraguans to study in the GDR arrived in September 1981. A Hungarian scholarship program for Nicaraguan students was agreed upon in February 1981.

In the health sector the East European countries provided multifarious aid. Fifty-eight heavily injured Nicaraguans received free treatment in GDR hospitals. East Berlin also supported the rehabilitation center for amblyopes in Managua. The USSR since October 1979 has provided more than one million doses of vaccine to support the Nicaraguan government's campaign against measles, whooping cough, and tuberculosis and has donated equipment to a hospital in Chinandega. Bulgaria provided on a grant basis nine medical doctors, who worked in Nicaragua from March 1980 to March 1981, and sent medical equipment worth US$500,000 in July 1980. A health cooperation agreement was also signed with Hungary.

Relief assistance (medicines, blankets, tents, food, vaccines, blood plasma, clothes, writing utensils, surgical instruments, motor vehicles, office equipment, and so on was provided in the period from August 1979 to December 1982 by the USSR (worth US$70 million), the GDR (US$60 million), Bulgaria (US$11 million), the CSSR (US$5 million), and Hungary (US$0.5 million).

The simple fact of increased Communist aid, however, does not necessarily lead to the establishment of a communist regime. Quite a number of developing countries—for example, Algeria, Iraq, Iran, India, and Turkey—have received ten times the amount of Communist development aid granted to Nicaragua without turning communist. What actually induces Nicaragua increasingly to seek Communist support is above all the permanently growing pressure from the United States to destabilize the regime as well as the indifference of Western Europe. In mid-1982 FSLN leader Tomás Borge still insisted: "We have our own revolution, with its own style, personality, and profile. If there is concern that we will establish a regime like that of the USSR, our answer is no; like Cuba, we say no, because a true revolution does not mimic others."[13]

Perspectives for Soviet Influence

After the Soviet Union had displayed little interest in the Nicaraguan revolution from 1979 to 1981 and—in consideration of Washington's interests—had carefully avoided the impression of seeking a foothold in the region, the situation changed in 1982. Several developments, such as Washington's attitude toward Poland, U.S. assistance to repressive regimes in El Salvador and Guatemala, mounting U.S. pressure on Costa Rica and Panama, the new political situation in Latin America resulting from the Falklands/Malvinas conflict, and, last but not least, the declaration of bankruptcy by a number of Latin American countries, encouraged the Soviet Union to expand its influence on the Latin American continent.

Soviet Latin America analysts immediately recognized the international significance of the successful popular uprising in Nicaragua and its potential repercussions on developments in neighboring countries.[14] Early Soviet analyses of 1979 gave credit to "Latin American communists" for events in Nicaragua,[15] but this untenable theory was abandoned in 1981. Since then the Soviet Union has provided full backing to the FSLN and paid rapturous tribute to the Sandinistas' achievements, trying to exploit their victory in the interest of Soviet policy in Latin America. Recent analyses no longer praise the "revolutionary role" of Nicaragua's Communists and do not even mention the pro-Soviet PSN.[16] Thus the Soviet Union and its allies performed a dramatic *volte-face* and posed as the sponsors and protectors of the Nicaraguan revolution.[17]

Belatedly, the Soviets even published excerpts of a book by Tomás Borge on FSLN activities in the sixties, a period when there was only negative comment from Moscow on the Sandinistas' guerrilla efforts.[18] The importance presently attached by the Kremlin to events in Central America is also emphasized by the priority given to the "popular-democratic revolution" in Nicaragua and the "struggle of patriots" in El Salvador over problems like Chile and the Middle East, as revealed in the list of CPSU (Communist Party of the Soviet Union) slogans issued on the occasion of the sixty-fifth anniversary of the Soviet October Revolution in 1982.[19]

After having neglected Central America for years, Soviet experts on Latin America recently dedicated a complete issue of their special periodical to this subject.[20] Communist parties of El Salvador, Guatemala, Honduras, Costa Rica, and Panama met in 1982—in the absence of Nicaragua's Communists—to discuss U.S. policy in the area.[21] A conference on "general and special features of revolutionary processes in Latin America and the Caribbean" attended by twenty-two Communist parties and thirteen "other revolutionary organizations" of the region was convened in Havana.[22] The conference, which illustrated Moscow and the local Communist parties' reassessment of the situation under the impact of the Nicaraguan revolution, registered a remarkable upswing in the "anti-imperialist popular liberation movement" in Central America.

After the triumph of the Nicaraguan revolution the armed struggle of different guerrilla organizations in El Salvador assumed the proportions of a civil war, assigning the role of a bystander to the Soviet-oriented Communist Party of El Salvador (PCES), which had failed to mobilize the popular masses. Rival left-wing Marxist mass organizations—independent of Moscow—such as the Bloque Popular Revolucionario (BPR) and the Frente Acción Popular Unida (FAPU), whose leaders considered the pro-Soviet communists as "traitors," came into existence in 1978. The Ejército Revolucionario del Pueblo (ERP) guerrilla organization, which had broken away from the PCES in 1975, and the other leading Salvadorean guerrilla organization, the Fuerzas Populares de Liberación (FPL), were blamed in 1978 by PCES secretary general Jorge Shafik Handal for their "nihilistic programmes."[23] Upon instructions from Moscow the PCES, however, changed its attitude in 1980, admitting self-critically its errors and describing the "armed struggle as the only means to seize power under given circumstances."[24] In no time the PCES founded its military arm (Fuerzas Armadas de Liberación—FAL), which so far has failed to launch any major guerrilla action. PCES also joined the united guerrilla movement, the Frente Farabundo Martí de Liberación Nacional (FMLN). Secretary General Handal became an FMLN leader and has since been busy granting interviews to the East European press.[25] An FMLN delegation headed by PCES politburo member Rubén Sanchez visited Eastern Europe in 1982, and PCES central committee member Jaime Barrios poses as the permanent representative of the FMLN in Eastern Europe. Through this channel Moscow is trying to establish contacts between Communists and opposition in El Salvador, to emphasize the share of the PCES in the resistance movement and to exert influence on the FMLN.

Similarly, Moscow has come round to a positive reassessment of the armed struggle in Guatemala, although the most important Guatemalan guerrilla organizations—the Ejército Guerrillero de los Pobres (EGP) operating since 1975, the Organización del Pueblo en Armas (ORPA) operating since 1979, and the Fuerzas Armadas Rebeldes (FAR) of the sixties, which resumed operations in 1978—do not assign a leading role to the pro-Soviet Partido Guatemalteco del Trabajo (PGT). In 1980 these three guerrilla groups entered into an alliance with the PGT–Núcleo de Dirección Nacional (PGT-Núcleo), a faction split off the PGT; in February 1982 these four groups formed the Unidad Revolucionaria Nacional Guatemalteca (URNG) on the model of the Salvadorean FMLN.

Political backing for the URNG comes from two mass organizations, the Frente Democrático contra la Represión (FDCR) and the Frente Popular 31 de Enero (FP-31), which both have the support of broad sections of the population and of different political currents. The URNG's five-point program guarantees the preservation of small- and medium-sized farm holdings, equal rights for Indians and *mestizos* (people of mixed blood), and a nonaligned foreign policy.

The URNG joint declaration of February 1982 also called upon the pro-Soviet PGT to give active support to the armed struggle instead of paying only lip service to it.[26] This suggests that the PGT, which is split into three factions at least, was at that time not yet prepared to give unreserved support to the guerrillas. Speaking at a conference in Havana in 1982, a PGT delegate deplored the fact that although the PGT had officially endorsed the strategy of armed struggle at its fourth party congress in 1969, the party had so far been unable to translate this attitude into practical action.[27] The East European countries were less reserved in this respect; their press gave extensive coverage to the activities of Guatemala's guerrilla organizations—regardless of the PGT's tactical reservations.[28] In spring 1982 the first URNG delegation visited the Soviet Union and Eastern Europe.[29]

Encouraged by developments in El Salvador and Guatemala, which offered Moscow a chance to weaken U.S. positions, communism has started to cash in on the situation resulting from increased guerrilla activities in Honduras. Again, as in the case of Guatemala and El Salvador, the Soviets make the national guerrilla forces, which split off from the pro-Soviet and pro-Chinese Communist parties, a cat's paw. In mid-1982 five Honduran guerrilla groups—the Movimiento de Liberación Popular "Chinchonero" (MLP) founded in 1980, the Fuerzas Populares Revolucionarias "Lorenzo Zelaya" (FPR) founded in 1981, the Frente Morazanista de Liberación de Honduras (FMLH) founded in 1968 and revived in 1980, the Juan Rayo commandos, and the Froilán Turcios commandos (the latter two formed in 1982)—declared their readiness to enter into discussions on the formation of a united front. The pro-Soviet Partido Comunista de Honduras (PCH) kept aloof from this development (its second party congress in 1972 had strictly rejected guerrilla warfare).[30] Since then the new party leadership elected in 1979 has shown some flexibility—approving "all forms of struggle," but still rejecting an "immediate armed uprising" in Honduras as "political adventurism."[31]

Notes

1. See Henrik Bischof, "Einige Aspekte der sowjetischen Lateinamerika-Politik," in *Politik in Lateinamerika,* ed. Klaus Lindenberg (Hannover: Verlag Politik und Zeitgeschichte, 1971), pp. 176–190.

2. See J. Gregory Oswald (ed.), *Soviet Image of Contemporary Latin America: A Documentary History* (Austin: University of Texas Press, 1970).

3. See "World Strength of the Communist Party Organizations," in *Annual Reports* (Washington, D.C.: Bureau of Intelligence and Research, 1965 and 1970).

4. Concerning the situation of individual Communist parties in Central America, see *Yearbook on Latin American Communist Affairs*, ed. William E. Ratliff (Stanford: Hoover Institution Press, Stanford University, 1971).

5. See Huberto Alvarado, "Einige Lehren der Revolution in Guatemala im Lichte Leninscher Ideen," in *Probleme des Friedens und des Sozialismus* (Prague), no. 12 (1970).

6. See Roque Dalton's critical contribution in *Tricontinental* (Havana), March/April 1969.

7. Milton Paredes, "Programm der Partei, Programm für die Massen," in *Probleme des Friedens und des Sozialismus* (Prague), no. 7 (1978), p. 916.

8. See R. Perez in *Probleme des Friedens und des Sozialismus* (Prague), no. 4 (1972), pp. 477–478.

9. See Thomas W. Walker (ed.), *Nicaragua in Revolution* (New York: Praeger, 1981).

10. Ju. A. Antonov and M. F. Kudačkin, "Osobennosti sovremennovo položeniya v stranakh Latinskoy Ameriki i taktika kompartiy," in *Voprosy istorii KPSS* (Moscow), no. 7 (1978), pp. 44–54.

11. See Joseph K. Skinner, "Somocistas on Trial," in *Monthly Review* (London), May 1982, p. 51.

12. For data listed in this section see *Aussenpolitik kommunistischer Länder und Dritte Welt* (Bonn: Forschungsinstitut der Friedrich-Ebert-Stiftung, 1979, 1980, 1981).

13. *El Nuevo Diario* (Managua), June 23, 1982.

14. A. Shulgovsky, "The Social and Political Development in Latin America," in *International Affairs* (Moscow), no. 11 (1979), p. 56.

15. *Pravda* (Moscow), September 29, 1979.

16. See I. M. Buličev, "Uspekhi i problemi sandinistskoy revolucii," in *Latinskaya America* (Moscow), no. 7 (1981), pp. 26–41; M. L. Čumakova, "Nicaragua: kurs na nezavisimost, neprisoedinenie i sotrudničestvo," in *Latinskaya America* (Moscow), no. 7 (1982), pp. 72–85; and Hans-Dieter Leh, "Nicaragua: Kampf der FSLN für den Zusammenschluss aller antiimperialistichen und demokratischen Kräfte," in *Deutsche Aussenpolitik* (East Berlin), no. 8 (1982), pp. 47–57.

17. See TASS statement of March 11, 1982; *Neue Zeit* (Moscow), no. 37 (1982), pp. 14, 15; and *Neues Deutschland* (East Berlin), July 27, 1982.

18. *Latinskaya Amerika* (Moscow), no. 10 (1982), pp. 108–126.

19. Radio Moscow, October 16, 1982.

20. *Latinskaya Amerika* (Moskow), no. 7 (1982).

21. *Probleme des Friedens und des Sozialismus* (Prague), no. 5 (1982), pp. 605–612.

22. *Probleme des Friedens und des Sozialismus* (Prague), no. 9 (1982), pp. 1223–1240.

23. *Latinskaya Amerika* (Moscow), no. 1/2 (1978).

24. *Probleme des Friedens und des Sozialismus* (Prague), no. 9 (1982), p. 1237.

25. See *Horizont* (East Berlin), no. 10 (1982), p. 12; *Rabotničesko delo* (Sofia), June 30, 1982; and *Latinskaya Amerika* (Moscow), no. 9 (1982), pp. 44–56.

26. Joint Proclamation of URNG in *El Día* (Mexico City), February 22, 1982.

27. *Probleme des Friedens und des Sozialismus* (Prague), no. 9 (1982), p. 1237.

28. See *Berliner Zeitung* (East Berlin), January 12, 1982; *Horizont* (East Berlin), no. 41 (1982), pp. 14, 15; and *Neue Zeit* (Moscow), no. 35 (1982), pp. 25, 26.

29. *Latinskaya Amerika* (Moscow), no. 9 (1982), pp. 57–61.

30. *Probleme des Friedens und des Sozialismus* (Prague), no. 4 (1972).

31. *Probleme des Friedens und des Sozialismus* (Prague), no. 5 (1982), p. 609.

15
Venezuelan Policies Toward Central America

Demetrio Boersner

Venezuela, together with Colombia, Central America, and Mexico, is a part of the continental rim of the Caribbean subregion.[1] Because of its geographic localization in the eastern half of that subregion, Venezuela tends to devote somewhat greater attention to the West Indian islands and the Guianas than to Central America. The eastern Caribbean constitutes Venezuela's gateway to the outside world and its "natural" area of presence and of interest.[2] This does not mean, however, that the evolution of Central America leaves Venezuela indifferent. The Central American nations are linked to Venezuela by many ethnic, cultural, social, and political affinities. Moreover, Venezuela's security and well-being are affected by changes taking place in the isthmus. All the developing countries of the larger Caribbean area are permeable and interdependent as regards their respective sociopolitical models and the external influences that they accept and reflect. Therefore Venezuela today is very conscious of its interest in playing a role in the shaping of Central America's future. The fact that Venezuela has "discovered the Pacific," through membership in the Andean Pact and increasing trade with Japan, tends to heighten its consciousness of Central America's importance.

I basically agree with Wolf Grabendorff that Venezuela is one of the Latin American "regional powers,"[3] together with Argentina, Brazil, Colombia, Cuba, and Mexico. Its economic importance as a petroleum exporter and political prestige as a relatively stable democracy have transformed Venezuela into one of the various "models" that compete for the favor of the less-developed or weaker nations of Latin America and particularly of the Caribbean–Central American subregion. I am also in agreement with Grabendorff that Venezuela's policy toward Central America until now has been discontinuous and moved mainly by short-term considerations, but that the country generally tends to align itself with a middle-of-the-road, reformist alliance of forces, as against the defenders of the status quo and the revolutionaries.[4]

In this chapter an attempt will be made to trace the evolution of Venezuelan policy toward the Central American area mainly from 1974 to the present. Nevertheless, a few words must be said, for the sake of historical continuity, about the period preceding 1974. The events from 1974 on are grouped in two sections, one dealing with the presidency of Carlos Andrés Pérez (1974–1979), the other with the period of Pres. Luis Herrera Campins (1979–1984). In a final section, a few ideas are suggested in regard to future prospects or possibilities.

Venezuela and Central America Before 1974

During Spanish colonial times, Venezuela had links with the island Caribbean through the *audiencia* (the Spanish administrative unit) of Santo Domingo, but virtually none with the Central American isthmus. During the independence struggle and its immediate aftermath, however, Venezuela was brought into contact with Central America. As the greatest personal representative of the emerging Spanish American people and their socioeconomic and intellectual elites, Simón Bolívar went forth from Venezuela to liberate and organize Colombia (with Panamá), Ecuador, Perú, and Bolivia. Venezuela, Colombia including Panamá, and Ecuador were united in the republic of Greater Colombia. Thereafter, Bolívar—the Liberator—embarked on his grand design of creating a Latin American confederacy for joint defense, constant political consultation, and growing economic integration. As a matter of course he invited the United Provinces of Central America (independent and united in a single federal state since 1824) to participate in the Congress of Panamá that was held in 1826 to bring about the planned confederacy. The Central Americans attended the congress and were signatories, jointly with Greater Colombia, Mexico, and Perú, of the remarkable instruments of union and integration that the Liberator had conceived.

It soon became evident, however, that no socioeconomic and psychological basis existed as yet for Latin American unity or even for the continuing cohesion of some of the existing states. Bolívar's dream was unrealizable in an agrarian, precapitalist setting without adequate means of communication and with political power in the hands of military *caudillos* who based their might on semifeudal regional rule, resisting centralization and national integration. Both Greater Colombia and the Central American federation fell apart. For seventy years the underdeveloped, divided subcontinent would be dominated by British trade and influence and thereafter by the ever-growing might of the United States.[5] From 1830 to 1899, Venezuela was torn by civil strife and ruled by a succession of dictators. As a weak and backward debtor country, it was an object and not a subject within the international system. Venezuela had no coherent foreign policy during this period.

With the rise of the dictator Cipriano Castro in 1899, and especially under his successor Juan Vicente Gómez (1908–1935), the country entered a period of changes. Petroleum replaced coffee and cocoa as the main export product. With oil money, the Venezuelan autocratic state paid its debts, created a modern army, crushed the regional warlords, and built the first highways linking the west and the east of the nation with the center. Even though in a rudimentary way, the formation of a modern middle class and working class began.

Gómez died in December 1935, and January 1936 marked the entry of Venezuela into the twentieth century. Trade unions and political parties arose. Under presidents Eleazar López Contreras (1936–1941) and Isaías Medina Angarita (1941–1945), political liberalization progressed greatly, together with modernization and urban growth.[6]

During the entire Gómez era, as well as under the governments of López and Medina, there existed no contact with Central America beyond formal diplomatic relations and sporadic human rapports. And yet, Venezuelan readers were aware of the struggles of Augusto César Sandino as well as the rise and fall of dictators in the isthmus, and the name and poetry of Rubén Darío were revered as everywhere in Latin America and the Spanish-speaking world.

In October 1945 Medina was overthrown by a revolutionary coup, undertaken jointly by discontented junior officers and the social-democratic Acción Democrática party, largely representative of the lower middle class and urban and rural workers. The "revolutionary junta" headed by Rómulo Betancourt (1945–1947) and the constitutional government of Pres. Rómulo Gallegos (1948) launched a foreign policy that had as its main priorities the liberation of Latin America from right-wing dictatorships and the search for greater equality in political and economic relations between the two Americas. The attempts to strengthen the democratic cause in the subcontinent and to weaken the dictatorial regimes brought Venezuela into conflict with the rightist despots of the Caribbean and Central America, particularly with Rafael Leónidas Trujillo of the Dominican Republic and Somoza I (Anastasio Somoza García) of Nicaragua.

In November 1948 the Venezuelan social-democratic regime was overthrown in a rightist coup by the very military leaders who in 1945 had brought it to power. The coup was a part of the general reactionary wave that swept over Latin America as a consequence of the cold war and U.S. pressures in favor of "anticommunism." Ideological alliances were reversed: Venezuela became a friend of dictators and cooled or broke relations with the Latin American democracies. Measures to reduce the economic hegemony of U.S. corporations were abandoned, and new oil concessions were granted. Relations with Central America were not intensive, but there was political agreement and harmony with Somoza and other dictators, while sharp enmity arose between the Caracas regime and the social-democratic governments of Costa Rica.[7]

Democracy returned to Venezuela—this time solidly and with the backing also of the upper classes—in January 1958. The international situation favored democratization in Latin America: post-Stalin detente, the beginning of the rise of the Third World and acceptance of the import-substitution model within the existing international division of labor.

Betancourt was returned to power in the elections held at the end of 1958. This time he decided to proceed cautiously, first consolidating political democracy with the support of the entrepreneurial sectors and the army, before embarking on any eventual attempts to change the social order.

Venezuelan foreign policy from 1958 to 1968, under Presidents Rómulo Betancourt and Raúl Leoni, of the Democratic Action party (Acción Democrática—AD), had as its main priority the defense of democracy throughout Latin America. By encouraging democracy and discouraging dictatorships abroad, Venezuela hoped to strengthen its own democratic system. The policy was based on the Betancourt Doctrine (the contention that the "effective exercise of representative democracy" is compulsive for OAS members, and nonrecognition of de facto regimes resulting from coups against elected governments).

Since it was directed not only against authoritarian governments of the extreme right but also against the regime of Fidel Castro (who since 1961 had supported Venezuelan leftist rebels), the Betancourt Doctrine brought its adherents in line with U.S. foreign policy in some of its aspects and determined a definite "East-West" perception of international problems by the decision makers in Caracas. Obviously a foreign policy based on the Betancourt Doctrine brought Venezuela into political contact and interaction with the Central American subregion, either in a friendly and cooperative spirit or in one of coldness and hostility.[8]

By 1968, when Rafael Caldera Rodríguez and the Christian Democratic party Copei were elected to power, both the world situation and that of Venezuela had changed. Detente was advancing strongly. The international system was no longer bipolar: At least three autonomous decision centers had arisen among the superpowers. The Third World was on the rise, in search of a global North-South dialogue and a new economic international order. In Venezuela, political democracy was consolidated and socioeconomic issues loomed large.

President Caldera therefore embarked on a new foreign-policy orientation. The Betancourt Doctrine was abandoned; stress was laid on Latin American integration and the "pluralist unity" of the subcontinent in search of greater autonomy vis-à-vis the United States and other dominant centers. The cause of "international social justice" (a fairer distribution of wealth and power among nations) was announced to be Venezuela's main concern. The East-West perception of the international reality was largely replaced by a North-South perception.

The Caldera government launched a program of financial and technical cooperation with the Caribbean. This was mainly directed at the island states and the Guianas, but studies were made and missions sent out with the aim of extending the "Venezuelan presence" to Central America, regardless of the type of government of its various countries.[9]

Venezuela and Central America from 1974 to 1979

In December 1973, Carlos Andrés Pérez and his Democratic Action party were elected to power by a large majority of votes. The new president had been Betancourt's minister of the interior and was considered right wing within the social-democratic realm. He was determined, however, to demonstrate that this perception was untrue. Riding the tide of Venezuelan and OPEC (Organization of Petroleum Exporting Countries) power derived from the world energy crisis, President Pérez put into effect a left-of-center policy and became one of the leading figures of the Socialist International and the Third World.

The rise of world oil prices trebled the Venezuelan government's income. This enabled President Pérez to raise external financial assistance. At the same time, the switch of international leverage power from the industrialized centers to the oil exporters made it possible to nationalize the Venezuelan petroleum industry, as well as the extraction of iron ore.

During 1974 and 1975, the Pérez government reestablished relations with Cuba and initiated a foreign policy generally oriented toward the greater union of Latin America in the cause of a struggle for more equitable North-South relations. The new fiscal wealth of Venezuela was used in part to strengthen all external financial cooperation programs with the Caribbean, Central America, and Latin America at large. Aside from common economic concerns, Pérez also sought to promote greater solidarity in defense of Latin American political aspirations: Largely because of his efforts, support for Panama and its struggle for the canal became more potent and effective.[10]

Pérez very much believed in the importance of personal presidential diplomacy. Often he bypassed his foreign ministry by directly contacting foreign heads of state, meeting them informally, and thus establishing the overall frames of reference for the country's external relations.

On January 1, 1976, the oil industry was definitely nationalized, fulfilling an old Venezuelan dream. State ownership and direct control over the country's petroleum resources opened wide new possibilities for influence and "leadership" abroad. It might be said that on January 1, 1976, Venezuela truly took the step toward greater autonomy and toward becoming a "regional power" or "middle power" in the Western Hemisphere.[11]

The Pérez government abstained wisely, however, from assuming unilateral and unconsulted "leadership" attitudes. The president's personal talks with foreign heads of state or government became more frequent. Within OPEC, Venezuela was the main proponent and mover of the decision to create and develop an aid fund for the Third World, thereby showing practical solidarity and counteracting the dominant centers' attempts to portray OPEC as the poor countries' "exploiter" and the factor responsible for world inflation.[12]

In the Caribbean and Central America, the Pérez government established special understandings, based on political and ideological affinity, with certain national leaders: Gen. Omar Torrijos of Panama, Pres. Daniel Oduber of Costa Rica, Prime Minister Michael Manley of Jamaica, and, north of the Central American subregion, Pres. Luis Echeverría Alvarez of Mexico. Personal and political friendship and understanding between Pérez and Echeverría were particularly good and provided a framework for cooperation of two Latin American "regional powers" that have much in common in terms of internal organization and foreign-policy interests. The latter might be summed up as involving the desire for greater autonomy vis-à-vis the United States and leadership for stable, reformist progress in the Caribbean and Central America, as well as the maintenance of a *modus vivendi* with Cuba and radical revolutionary forces. The creation of the Latin American Economic System (SELA) was Echeverría and Pérez's main common initiative.[13]

Pérez was highly aware of the positive value of participation in the Socialist International (SI) by the governing Democratic Action party. The party took part in all important meetings of the SI and paid high membership fees and voluntary contributions to international solidarity causes. A good rapport developed between President Pérez and Willy Brandt, who was elected president of the SI in 1976, at the Geneva congress that Pérez attended. A meeting of world social-democratic leaders was held in Caracas in May 1976 at the invitation of the Venezuelan party. At that meeting, the principle of cooperation between international social democracy and emerging forces of the Third World was stressed and approved.[14]

The "advanced" social democrats such as Willy Brandt agreed with enlightened Third World leaders such as Carlos Andrés Pérez that the cause of pluralist democracy vis-à-vis the communist challenge is best served by constructive competition for the adherence of the uncommitted liberation forces, rather than by repressive attitudes in alliance with conservative factors. Even certain movements that had already joined the Marxist-Leninist camp might eventually be swayed towards "Titoist" formulas.

In accordance with this view, Venezuela between 1974 and 1979 sought to draw Fidel Castro back into the Latin American community.[15] On several occasions, the Cuban president took part in informal top-level meetings organized by Carlos Andrés Pérez. Bilaterally, Cuba and Venezuela reached an unwritten but binding agreement: In return for the former's abstention from seeking to export its revolutionary model to Venezuela and its Caribbean neighborhood, the latter would (and did) provide oil on favorable terms and try to persuade the United States to soften the economic and diplomatic blockade against the Castro regime.[16]

In Central America, Venezuela not only supported Torrijos in the Panama Canal problem and cooperated with democratic Costa Rica, but sought to persuade Anastasio Somoza Debayle and other dictators to liberalize their regimes. When the Sandinist revolt began in Nicaragua, at first Pérez tried to persuade Somoza to yield voluntarily and to turn power over to a liberal provisional government of some sort. In 1978, the revolutionary struggle within the country had turned dramatically sharp, with liberal middle-class sectors joining the revolt after the assassination of the journalist Pedro Joaquín Chamorro. The Venezuelan government agreed with the Carter administration that it would be desirable for Somoza to leave power quickly, in favor of a democratic coalition regime, before the Sandinists gained full and exclusive control over the revolutionary movement. Pérez never left any doubt in regard to his basic adherence to the values of Western representative democracy and his rejection of radical one-party models. But he went much farther than the U.S. liberals and agreed with Willy Brandt, Olaf J. Palme, and other "advanced" leaders of international social-democracy that, even in those cases where a liberation movement in the Third World had acquired radical characteristics and fallen to some degree into the Marxist-Leninist temptation, such a trend was not irreversible. By aiding such a liberation movement, the progressive sectors of the West stood a chance to gain the favor of the rebels involved and to dissuade them from joining the Moscow camp. In any case, such an approach was more likely to be successful than that of repressive and reactionary warfare.

In conformity with such thinking, and intending to fight *both* Somoza's semifascism *and* the eventual rise of Soviet-Cuban influence in Nicaragua, Carlos Andrés Pérez began actively to aid the Sandinists, once it became evident that Somoza had no intention of resigning. Venezuela and Panama were instrumental in helping the Nicaraguan revolutionaries to win their civil war and at the same time were able to encourage and strengthen noncommunist socialists within the Sandinist Front, as against the completely pro-Cuban elements.[17]

Thus, Venezuela's policy toward Central America from 1974 to 1979 had a basically "autonomist" character, seeking to turn the subregion, with intensified Venezuelan assistance and leadership, into a conscious part of the Third World, without, however, forgetting the indispensable ties to the United States and the West. The Socialist International and Western Europe were looked to as allies in this policy. The aim was not complete independence from the West, but rather a larger degree of autonomy in what might be regarded as the "left wing" of the noncommunist world.

Pérez's Central American and global policy in many ways was the continuation of that of Caldera. The Third World orientation, however, was ideologically and propagandistically strengthened. The petroleum factor was successfully used, together with dynamic presidential diplomacy, to earn prestige for Venezuela and its chief of state throughout the Third World, in international social democracy, and among the forces of the revolutionary left—without losing the basic trust of the Jimmy Carter administration in the United States.

Venezuela and Central America from 1979 to 1982

The election of Luis Herrera Campins and the Christian Democratic (COPEI) party to succeed Carlos Andrés Pérez and AD in the Venezuelan government disrupted the continuity of the country's foreign policy.

As has been shown in the previous sections, the Venezuelan democratic governments at first adopted a foreign policy aimed mainly at the strengthening of democracy against both the extreme right and the extreme left. That policy tended to align Venezuela with the West in the East-West confrontation. Subsequently, Venezuela switched toward a new foreign-policy perception, stressing autonomy and the search for a new economic order through North-South dialogue and South-South cooperation. With Luis Herrera Campins at the helm, the pendulum at first swung back from "autonomism" to "occidentalism." This tendency lasted until the first quarter of 1982, when the South Atlantic crisis (the Falklands/Malvinas conflict) appeared to usher in a new switch toward the "left."

Reasons for the Shift in Foreign Policy

Several factors impelled the new Venezuelan administration to move away from pronounced "autonomism" toward greater cooperation with the United States in regard to Central America and other areas. In the first place, there was the mere wish to "punish" and reject Carlos Andrés Pérez and his adherents by abandoning his policies and doing the opposite, wherever this was feasible.[18]

Second, COPEI had the feeling, based on its electoral experiences, that the United States generally tended to favor AD more than the Christian Democrats and that this had strongly influenced the result of the 1973 elections that had brought the social democrats back to power after Caldera's administration. It was necessary and convenient, according to COPEI leaders, to establish a solid rapport with the U.S. political and economic establishment, defining areas of cooperation and alliance.[19]

Third, Luis Herrera Campins came to power with the reputation of being a leftist within the Christian Democratic ranks. The Venezuelan business community regarded him with a certain amount of distrust. Right wingers within his own party were openly critical of him. In order to strengthen his position within the country and in his party, the new president decided to turn rightward in several important domains. One of them was economic policy: "monetarist," antiinflationary, and stressing the role of the private sector. The other was to be foreign policy.

Fourth, the Christian Democratic International felt itself threatened by the victorious advance of the Socialist International in Latin America as well as in other parts of the world. From 1976 on, the Socialist International's line of alliance with Third World liberation movements had been basically successful, and the prestige of world social democracy (associated with the personality of Willy Brandt) was extremely great. By aiding the Sandinists and enrolling various Central American parties and movements in its ranks, the SI had established its influence in the subregion, as well as also in the island Caribbean with social-democratic bases in Jamaica and the Dominican Republic. The Venezuelan Christian Democratic leader Arístides Calvani, who had been Caldera's foreign minister, was now the general-secretary of the Christian Democratic Organization of America (ODCA). He and his associates conceived a strategy consisting of an alliance with the United States to fight both Marxism and social democracy in Latin America and to place Christian Democratic and "centrist" parties in power wherever possible. In conformity with this view, an alliance was concluded between Latin American Christian Democratic and U.S. conservative forces, on the occasion of a seminar sponsored by the Konrad Adenauer Foundation and the American Enterprise Institute, held in Washington, D.C., in May 1980.[20]

Another reason for President Herrera Campins's move to the "right" in foreign policy was the state of Venezuela's finances. During the years of high oil prices and great OPEC leverage, the Venezuelan government had been inclined to overspend and to overexpand its commitments. By 1979, world recession was definitely setting in, demand for energy resources had fallen, and oil-exporting countries found themselves in difficulties. Clearly realizing this, President Herrera's advisers favored an improvement of relations with the world's dominant financial centers.

The increasingly conservative mood in the United States and Western Europe also was taken into account. The star of Ronald Reagan was clearly rising after 1979. A U.S. administration headed by such a man was likely to be intolerant toward policies of an "autonomist" type. The developing countries had to make allowances for the conservative (and repressive) mood in the North.

All these factors were parts of an overall picture of growing recession and of renewed cold war between the superpowers. The Third World had lost strength and no longer offered a solid basis of support, as had been the case a few years earlier.

Results of the Shift in Foreign Policy

In 1980, the change in Venezuelan foreign policy, particularly in regard to Central America and the Caribbean, showed itself in the first place by the cooling and subsequent freezing of relations with Cuba.[21]

Although basically the Cuban and the Venezuelan "models" are no doubt contradictory, and on a world scale detente was deteriorating, the Cuban government tried to maintain the good relations that had prevailed with Venezuela during the Carlos Andrés Pérez period. Between March and September 1979, Fidel Castro assured Venezuela that he did not intend to implant his presence in Grenada against the will or wishes of the Caracas government and that he would refrain from any interference in the internal affairs of the Netherlands Antilles, located in the close vicinity of the Venezuelan coast. At the sixth nonaligned summit in Havana in September 1979, the Cubans took pains to be particularly courteous and friendly toward the Venezuelan delegation.[22] It was Caracas, and not Havana, that took the basic decision to cool and even freeze the relations between the two countries.

Incidents that occurred when Cuban nationals tried to force their way into the Venezuelan Embassy in Havana in search of asylum were magnified by Venezuelan government statements and by the press. In "reprisal" for Cuban police surveillance of the Venezuelan mission in Havana, truly intolerable measures were taken against the freedom of movement of the Cuban diplomats in Caracas.[23]

On the other hand, the anti-Castro activists suspected of blowing up the Cuban civilian airplane over Barbados in 1976, whom Carlos Andrés Pérez had promised to punish severely if their guilt was proved, suddenly began to receive friendly treatment from the Venezuelan authorities. In September 1980, the military prosecutor who previously had tried to prove them guilty suddenly stated that he believed them innocent.[24] Highly incensed, Fidel Castro let it be known that, if the accused were set free, he would formally break off diplomatic relations with Venezuela.[25] That point was never reached: Apparently the intention in Caracas was to freeze but not to break.

The second manifestation of the change in foreign policy came when Venezuelan government officials, from the beginning of 1980 on, began to express in an ever more insistent manner their alarm over a supposed "encirclement" of Venezuela by "Soviet-Cuban expansionism."[26]

The Venezuelan initiative that most strongly impressed foreign observers, however, was that of joining the United States in an unconditional policy of support for the Salvadorean junta headed by the Christian Democrat José Napoleón Duarte. COPEI leaders sought to belittle reports of rightist atrocities in the beleaguered Central American country and joined the Americans in vehement propaganda against the Democratic Revolutionary Front (the FDR). When France and Mexico issued their call for the recognition of the Salvadorean rebels as legitimate belligerents and for negotiations in search of a "Zimbabwe-type" solution, the Venezuelan government emitted shouts of rage and did not hesitate to join some of Latin America's most discredited right-wing dictatorships in a common statement against Mexico and France.[27]

The freezing of relations with Cuba and the joint action with the United States in El Salvador to raise the Christian Democrats to power no doubt were in keeping with the general strategy of U.S.–Christian Democratic alliance discussed at the aforementioned conference held in Washington, D.C., in May 1980. In regard to Nicaragua, however, the government of President Herrera has followed a course differing from that of the United States. Whereas the Reagan administration showed a constantly hardening hostility toward the Sandinist regime and took measures to isolate and destabilize it, Venezuela even during the 1980 and 1981 period aided Nicaragua economically and exerted discreet, nonoffensive pressures on the country in the sense of preserving its internal pluralism and granting a portion of influence to persons of Christian Democratic leanings.[28]

In spite of the strongly anti-Marxist and pro-U.S. content of Venezuelan foreign policy during the years 1980 and 1981, the Caracas government signed the San José agreement with Mexico in August 1980, to provide oil energy resources to Central America and the Caribbean under favorable conditions.[29] The Mexican-Venezuelan cooperation in this domain was not affected by the acute political disagreements between the two countries in regard to El Salvador and Cuba. Furthermore, both governments agreed to keep these disagreements within limits and to seek areas of concord and joint action. In April 1981, Luis Herrera Campins and José López Portillo issued a joint statement in Mexico, which expressed common ideas without entering too much into details.[30] Within the "Nassau group" formed by the United States, Canada, Mexico, and Venezuela (later Colombia) to aid the Caribbean area, the Mexicans and the Venezuelans agreed in the defense of a multilateralist methodology, with the public sectors exerting leadership over the private sectors, as against Reagan's insistence on unilateralism and primacy of the private sector.[31] Likewise, at the North-South meeting at Cancún in October 1981, Venezuela supported all the Third World criticisms of the U.S. position.[32]

It would therefore be untrue to define the Venezuelan policy toward Central America and the Caribbean in 1980 and 1981 as one of unconditional subservience to the United States. Rather, it was a policy of reasoned alliance for the achievement of certain common purposes accompanied by areas of disagreement.

Foreign Policy Since 1982

A second phase of Luis Herrera's foreign policy—an autonomist phase, critical of the United States and leaning toward the Third World—began in April 1982. Ostensibly it was provoked by the South Atlantic crisis: shock and indignation at seeing the United States and Western Europe join Britain in support of an armed imperial intervention against a Latin American country and its cause that, no matter how badly served, was anticolonialist and supported by UN resolutions.[33] There were, however, other reasons perhaps more decisive than the Falklands/Malvinas conflict, which served as a welcome pretext.

One of these motives was disappointment at the outcome of joint U.S.-Venezuelan initiatives in Central America. The Christian Democratic Organization of America and the Venezuelan government had been sure that somehow the United States would exert pressure to ensure the victory of José Napoleón Duarte in the Salvadorean election of March 28, 1982. The results were a blow to Christian Democratic ambitions: The parties of the right and the extreme right won decisively and Roberto D'Aubuisson—of sinister reputation—emerged as the leading political figure. Duarte was ousted from the presidency and replaced by Alvaro Magaña. A feeling of bitterness ran through the Latin American Christian Democratic ranks. At the various signs of U.S. satisfaction over the Salvadorean election results, the Christian Democrats felt that they had been used and were now being discarded as no longer of interest. In part, the Venezuelan leftward switch in foreign policy probably reflected that reaction.

In addition to this, there were domestic considerations. Because of the policy of economic austerity, the Herrera government and the COPEI party had become extremely unpopular, as was shown by various public opinion polls. The new foreign policy was partly intended to gain the sympathy and support of Venezuelan left-wing forces, with a view to the elections to be held in December 1983.

Finally, there was still another important reason for the policy switch. The Herrera government had allowed the frontier controversy with Guyana to reach unduly huge proportions in foreign-policy priorities and in public opinion. Ever since Venezuela decided in 1981 not to renew the agreement "freezing" its claim to more than half of Guyana's present territory, a sharp diplomatic struggle has continued between the two countries, and the Georgetown government was able to marshal the support of much of the Third World. To counter such a strategy, the Venezuelan side decided to compete for Third World sympathies. Reconciliation with Cuba was initiated from May 1982 onward, partly in order to gain Fidel Castro's support for Venezuela's demand that Guyana resume negotiations about the frontier issue. And the Caracas government at the same time announced its intention to apply for full membership in the Nonaligned Movement, instead of the present observer status. These moves automatically required a more conciliatory attitude toward revolutionary movements in Central America and a more critical position vis-à-vis the United States.

Future Prospects

As we have seen in the preceding sections, Venezuelan policy toward Central America was marked during the first decade of the democratic regime (1958–1968) by the desire to consolidate and strengthen political democracy and to isolate dictatorships both rightist and leftist. It was therefore strongly influenced by the "East-West" perception of international affairs. During the second decade of Venezuelan democracy (1969–1979), the emphasis changed from an East-West to a North-South view. Greater autonomy vis-à-vis the United States, and growing integration of Latin America and unity of the Third World for the attainment of a new international economic order, were stressed as the most important objectives. The Herrera government was more contradictory and unpredictable than its predecessors. In a four-year span, it repeated in some ways the two phases that Venezuelan foreign policy had gone through in the previous two decades. From 1979 to March 1982, the attitudes toward the outside world and particularly toward Central America and the Caribbean were conservative and "occidentalist," whereas from April 1982 on the emphasis was switched to "autonomism" and support to Third World causes. As we have seen, this sudden change probably was due to some motivations of a tactical, rather than an ideological or fundamental, nature.

The overall trend in the future is likely to be reformist and autonomist rather than conservative and strongly "western." Venezuela will thus return to the general line it followed from 1969 to 1979.

One of the reasons for this assumption is that the winner of the Venezuelan elections of December 1983, the AD candidate Jaime Lusinchi, is a representative of the "advanced" democratic-socialist tendency within his party and agrees with former president Pérez on the desirability of a Third World type of policy.

Another reason lies in the fact that Venezuela's vast untapped oil resources—in the bituminous layer of the Orinoco valley—will continue to provide it for a good many years with a minimal basis of economic prosperity, sufficient to permit a certain measure of independence from the United States and other dominant centers in the field of international politics.

Continuing conflicts of economic interest between the developing countries and the industrialized world will also tend to keep Venezuela in an autonomist position in its behavior toward Central America and other regions. As long as the recession lasts, the United States will certainly maintain a relatively hard and negative line in regard to the North-South dialogue, and antagonisms between the industrialized centers and OPEC countries are not likely to lessen. This will probably have the effect of driving Venezuela into continuing the search for Third World solidarity and for greater bargaining power vis-à-vis the Americans.

Venezuela's feeling of vulnerability, in case Central America should explode into generalized warfare, will continue impelling it to try to still the troubled waters and to join Mexico in seeking Central American stability through reform and negotiations.

Notes

1. For the definition of the Caribbean subregion in terms of a "basin" made up of islands and rimlands united by their condition of "developing" areas, see: Michael Manley, *La política del cambio* (México: N.p., 1976), p. 140; and Gonzalo Martner, "La cuenca del Caribe: Futuro centro del desarrollo latinoamericano," *Nueva Sociedad*, Caracas, no. 24 (May–June 1976), pp. 33–54.

2. Demetrio Boersner, *Venezuela y el Caribe: presencia cambiante* (Caracas: Avila, 1978).

3. Wolf Grabendorff, "The Role of Regional Powers in the Central American Crisis: A Comparison of Mexico, Venezuela, Cuba, and Colombia (typewritten draft, used with permission from the author), 1982.

4. Ibid., p. 15.

5. Demetrio Boersner, *Relaciones internacionales de América Latina: Una breve historia* (México: Nueva Imagen, 1982), pp. 75–117.

6. José Luis Salcedo-Bastardo, *Historia fundamental de Venezuela*, 8th ed. rev. (Caracas: Universidad Central de Venezuela, 1979), pp. 403–412, 554–560.

7. Arístides Calvani, "La política internacional de Venezuela en el último medio siglo," *Venezuela moderna: Medio siglo de historia*, ed. Ramón J. Velásquez et al., 2d ed. (Caracas: N.p., 1979), pp. 450–457; and Boersner, *Venezuela y el Caribe*, pp. 45–59.

8. Rómulo Betancourt, *Hacia América Latina democrâtica e integrada* (Caracas: Ed. Senderos, 1967).

9. Calvani, "La política internacional," pp. 461–467, 473–474, 479–480, 487–488, 490–495.

10. Robert D. Bond, "Venezuela's Role in International Affairs," in Robert D. Bond (ed.), *Contemporary Venezuela and Its Role in International Affairs* (New York: New York University Press, 1977), pp. 227–262; and Franklin Tugwell, "The United States and Venezuela: Prospects for Accommodation," in Bond, *Contemporary Venezuela*, pp. 199–226.

11. John D. Martz, "Venezuelan Foreign Policy Toward Latin America," in Bond, *Contemporary Venezuela*, pp. 165–175.

12. *El Nacional*, Caracas, November 18, 1975; and Martz, "Venezuelan Foreign Policy," p. 169.

13. Martz, "Venezuelan Foreign Policy," pp. 171–173.

14. *El Nacional* and *El Universal*, Caracas, May 22–26, 1976.

15. Alfredo Peña, *Conversaciones con Carlos Andrés Pérez*, vol. 2 (Caracas: N.p., 1979), pp. 272–284.

16. Author's talks with Venezuelan, Cuban, and Mexican diplomatic and journalistic sources.

17. Peña, *Conversaciones con Carlos Andrés Pérez;* and Michael Manley, *Jamaica; Struggle in the Periphery* (London: Third World Media, 1981), p. 178.

18. Author's talks with Christian Democratic foreign-policy planners at various times in 1979.

19. Ibid.

20. "American Enterprise Institute and Konrad Adenauer Stiftung Conference on the Present and Future Status of Christian Democratic and Centrist Parties in Latin American and the Caribbean, Washington, 21–23 May 1980" (mimeographed doc.), quoted by Gregorio Selser, "Christdemokratie: Speerspitze der USA in Lateinamerika," in Tilman Evers et al. (eds.), *US-Intervention und kapitalistische Gegenrevolution*, Lateinamerika, 6 (Berlin: Olle und Wolter, 1982), pp. 76–77.

21. Such a development was foreseen as a possibility by Martz, "Venezuelan Foreign Policy," p. 192.

22. Personal impressions of the author at the Havana conference.

23. *El Nacional, El Universal, El Diario de Caracas,* and *Zeta,* Caracas, March–July 1980.

24. Alicia Herrera, *Pusimos la bomba, y qué?* (Valencia, Venezuela: N.p., 1981), pp. 113–229.

25. Verbal reports of diplomats and journalists, Caracas, May 1980.

26. *El Nacional, El Universal, El Diario de Caracas,* March 1980–May 1981.

27. *Le Monde,* Paris, September 1, 1981; *New York Times,* September 3, 1981; and *El Nacional,* September 4, 1981.

28. Nevertheless, former president Carlos Andrés Pérez accused COPEI and the Christian Democratic International of having delayed the fall of Somoza in 1979, by insisting on persons of their ideology being included in the subsequent provisional government and suspending aid to the democratic revolutionary movement. *El Nacional,* June 22, 1981.

29. *El Diario de Caracas,* August 3, 1980.

30. *El Nacional,* April 9, 1981.

31. Efe News Agency, Madrid, July 7, 1981; Simón Alberto Consalvi, "Notas del Viernes," *El Nacional,* July 10, 1981; Efe, Nassau, July 10, 1981; Associated Press (AP), Nassau, July 11, 1981; and *El Nacional,* July 13, 1981.

32. United Press International (UPI), AP, Efe, *El Nacional,* October 21–26, 1981.

33. President Herrera's criticism of the U.S. position was expressed most harshly during his visit to Nicaragua on the occasion of the third anniversary of the Sandinist revolution. UPI, Masaya, July 19, 1982.

16
Mexico in Central America: The Limits of Regional Power

Bruce Michael Bagley

Over the course of Pres. José López Portillo's *sexenio* (1976–1982), Mexico emerged from the ranks of the minor actors in hemispheric affairs to assume the status of a major regional power. Prior to López Portillo's presidency, Mexico had consistently pursued an antiimperialist, antiinterventionist foreign policy that was rhetorically at odds with that of its dominant northern neighbor, the United States: for Arbenz in Guatemala in the 1950s, against the Organization of American States' economic and diplomatic sanctioning of Cuba in 1962 and 1964, against the United States' Dominican intervention in 1965, and for Allende in Chile in the early 1970s. But despite the consistency of their foreign-policy pronouncements, before the triumph of the Sandinista revolution in Nicaragua in 1979 the Mexicans had never underwritten their foreign policy with the economic resources needed to give it real meaning.

In post-Somoza Nicaragua, however, Mexico has proven both willing and able to provide substantial levels of aid, and it has done so despite U.S. hostility toward the Nicaraguan revolution and explicit U.S. efforts to isolate the Sandinista regime both economically and politically. It is this demonstrated capacity to back rhetoric with resources that differentiates current Mexican foreign policy from earlier phases and marks Mexico's transformation from a minor actor in hemispheric affairs into a regional power. Not surprisingly, given the turmoil in the subregion and its geographical proximity to Mexico, Central America has been the primary arena in which Mexico has sought to exercise its influence.

Mexican Foreign Policy in Central America

Mexico's rise to regional-power status and its attendant foreign-policy autonomy forced the López Portillo administration to make some fundamental foreign-policy choices over the last few years. Beginning with the 1979 decision to withdraw official recognition from the Somoza dictatorship, through its August 1980 joint oil facility with Venezuela, its August 1981 joint communiqué with France on El Salvador, and its February 1982 mediation efforts on behalf of Cuba and Nicaragua, the López Portillo government consistently adopted positions at variance with those of the United States and especially of the Reagan administration. The conflicts were most intense over alternative Central American and Caribbean policies—U.S. hostility toward Nicaragua, Grenada, and Cuba and U.S. military support for the Salvadoran government—but were by no means limited to that set of issues.[1]

Two basic reasons appear to account for the differing approaches to the Central America crisis pursued by Mexico and the United States over the late 1970s and early 1980s. First, the Reagan administration has insistently argued that the problems in Central America derive primarily from Soviet-Cuban, and more recently Nicaraguan, subversion in the area.[2] The López Portillo administration, in turn, consistently rejected this East-West interpretation of the Central American crisis and emphasized instead the economic inequalities, social injustice, and political repression that have sparked broad-based opposition movements in countries like Nicaragua, El Salvador, and Guatemala. Second, the Reagan administration believes that Mexico is the final domino in a chain of falling Central American dominoes that began with Nicaragua. The López Portillo government dismissed the idea that Mexico is likely to become a target of subversion for revolutionary groups based in Central America, either now or in the future, as many U.S. conservatives have claimed.[3]

President López Portillo forcefully reiterated his country's rejection of the East-West view of the Central American crisis in his February 21, 1982, address in Managua, Nicaragua:

> The distinguishing feature which marks the destiny of the Central American and Caribbean peoples today is their struggle for a thorough transformation in the age-old social, economic and political conditions which have been imposed on them by poverty, tyranny and oppression. Anyone who does not understand this will be unable to understand the dramatic upheaval that is shaking the area. In the same way in which entire nations of Africa and Asia waged difficult battles during the post-war period to attain their independence and put an end to the colonial era, today Central America and the Caribbean are fighting to change internal and external structures very similar to the colonial system that prevailed on those continents. Just as most of those Asian and African struggles could not be injected by force into the terrible East-West or capitalism-socialism dichotomy, the Central American revolutions of our time are refusing such manichean classifications. . . . The Central American and Caribbean revolutions which

are under way are primarily struggles of poor and oppressed peoples to have a better life and be freer. To claim that they are something else, and to act as if they were, is counterproductive.[4]

Reasoning in the López Portillo administration on the question of Mexico's internal stability ran directly counter to prevailing thinking in the United States on several different grounds. First, Mexican policymakers see any effort to "prop up" the basically illegitimate regimes of countries like El Salvador and Guatemala through massive military assistance not only as doomed to fail but also as bound to involve tremendous human suffering, population displacement, and economic disruption throughout the region. The civil war in El Salvador alone has already generated hundreds of thousands of refugees, tens of thousands of whom are now in Mexico. Rising levels of conflict and violence in Guatemala have resulted in streams of Guatemalan refugees flooding into Mexico as well.[5] Rather than a solution to the Central American crisis, the López Portillo administration viewed the Reagan "military" approach as directly destabilizing for Mexico itself: As long as violence continues in Central America, Mexico will continue to be beset with economic and political refugees it can ill afford to receive, and its own internal political order will be increasingly threatened. From this perspective, Reagan's arming of the generals in Central America will only prolong the inevitable at great cost to the entire region and to Mexico specifically.[6]

Second, the López Portillo government was convinced that by befriending revolutionary forces and governments in Central America, Mexico would be able to purchase a kind of "insurance policy" against the export of revolution. The argument was that if the revolutionary Central American regimes were economically indebted to Mexico and in need of continued economic and technological support, it was unlikely that they would permit hostile acts against Mexico to be launched from their territory. The López Portillo government also believed that the chances of moderating the subsequent behavior of these regimes would be greater if a cooperative strategy was pursued.[7] This belief reflected Mexico's past foreign-policy experience with Cuba and its traditional approach to internal stability.

Finally, the Mexican authorities are aware that Mexico, unlike other Latin American countries, has an "institutionalized" political left—made up mostly of intellectuals, journalists, students, some union leaders, and the left parties—that they must take into account, particularly in the area of foreign policy.[8] Although the Reagan administration seems unaware of it, for any Mexican president to align himself with Reagan's hard-line policy in Central America would provoke intense internal opposition. Mexico's sympathetic attitude toward the Sandinistas in Nicaragua and the Frente Democrático Revolucionario in El Salvador is in part due to the strength of the limited but vociferous sectors of Mexican public opinion in favor of these groups. López Portillo, like his predecessors, used a progressive foreign policy to defuse domestic opposition to PRI rule, and his successor Miguel de la Madrid Hurtado finds himself constrained to maintain similarly progressive policies for the same reasons.

There is, of course, room to maneuver, for Mexican presidents enjoy great autonomy, particularly in foreign affairs. Mexico under de la Madrid has assumed a lower rhetorical profile in the region as he focuses his attention on Mexico's internal problems. But any major reversal of Mexican policy toward Central America would undoubtedly provoke stinging domestic criticism. More important, it would be disastrous for Mexico, whose own internal political stability is intimately connected to the successful resolution of the region's conflicts. This is true not because Mexico is likely to be seriously threatened by guerrilla groups from outside, but because a regionalization of the conflict in Central America would force the nation's civilian elite to grant larger budgets and increasing decision-making power to the armed forces. In view of this fundamental reality, it was unlikely that President de la Madrid would significantly reduce his country's involvement in the Central American crisis. Indeed, he was seeking from the beginning of his *sexenio* to promote negotiated settlements along the lines initiated by López Portillo in order to moderate U.S. policies as well as those of Cuba and Nicaragua and thereby facilitate the restoration of peace throughout the region.[9]

Mexican Economic Interests in Central America

At the outset of any discussion of Mexico's role in Central America, it is necessary to dispel the myth that Mexico is motivated by a desire to replace U.S. economic hegemony in the subregion with its own influence—that its Central American policies conceal imperialist designs. In fact, despite geographical proximity and cultural and linguistic affinities, Mexican economic involvement in Central America has never been substantial. Indeed, the lack of complementarity between Mexico and the Central American economies makes it more appropriate to view them as rivals or competitors than as potential partners. This is particularly true in the realm of trade in manufactured goods, for those few industrial products that Mexico could reasonably hope to export to Central America at competitive prices are precisely those that the Central

American nations have sought to produce locally through Central American economic integration.[10]

Two key economic indicators—trade and investment—reveal the reduced levels of interaction between the Mexican and Central American economies. In 1973, after a decade of Mexico's efforts to cultivate trade with Central America in order to diversify its own levels of relations, total Mexican exports to the subregion amounted to only US$52 million. In 1977, they had risen to US$111 million, largely because of the favorable export climate created by the 1976 devaluation of the Mexican peso. As of 1980, mostly on the strength of Mexican oil shipments, exports had reached US$228 million. In relative terms, however, the 1980 figure represented only 1.5 percent of all Mexican exports, an actual decrease from the 1969 total of 1.8 percent.[11]

Mexican imports from the Central American countries have been even less impressive. Between 1973 and 1980 the absolute figure rose from US$6.8 million to US$32 million. In view of the substantial increase in total Mexican imports over the period, however, the 1980 sum actually represented a relative decline from 0.18 percent to 0.16 percent of all Mexican imports.[12] For comparative perspective, it is worth noting that in 1980 Mexican exports to Central America equaled only 3.6 percent of total Mexican exports to the United States, while Mexican imports from Central America were the equivalent of only 0.4 percent of total Mexican imports from the United States.[13] The trade relationship with the United States is clearly of overwhelming importance, whereas commercial linkages with Central America are of minor significance.

In terms of investment, in 1972, after a major campaign had been launched by Pres. Gustavo Díaz Ordaz (1964–1970) to encourage Mexican direct private investment in Central America, the total amounted to only US$89 million. Moreover, over the 1970s these investments were sold off to Central American business people and governments, thereby reducing Mexican investment to negligible sums and ending an important, although unsuccessful, experiment in Mexican economic diversification.[14]

The future of Mexican trade and investment in Central America appears no more promising than the past. The lack of complementarity remains the critical factor. This basic obstacle has been exacerbated recently by economic turmoil in Central America resulting from civil war, oil-price hikes, and world recession. Only Mexican exports of oil to the subregion can be expected to expand significantly over the 1980s, and these are likely to respond more to political than economic considerations.[15]

Rather than trade or direct private investment, Mexico's economic linkages with Central America today fall primarily into the category of aid. Petroleos Mexicanos (PEMEX), the state-owned oil company, has become a key conduit for Mexican economic and technical assistance. It is currently exploring for petroleum in Costa Rica, Panama, Nicaragua, and Cuba. Furthermore, on August 3, 1980, Pres. López Portillo met with Pres. Luis Herrera Campins of Venezuela in San José, Costa Rica, where they jointly established the Mexico-Venezuela Agreement on Energy Cooperation for Central America and the Caribbean. This joint oil facility provides for the sale of oil to nine Central American and Caribbean countries (including Nicaragua, Guatemala, El Salvador, Honduras, and Costa Rica) in quantities up to 160,000 barrels per day distributed in equal parts by Mexico and Venezuela at market prices. Although no special price concessions were made, both governments agreed to extend credits of 30 percent of total sales to each country on five-year terms at 5 percent interest. If the recipient countries use the oil purchased under the facility for energy-related development projects, credits can be extended for twenty years at 2 percent interest. In 1981, the total value of this facility had reached approximately US$700 million, split evenly between Mexico and Venezuela.[16]

This sizable aid commitment is not motivated primarily by altruism, Third World solidarity, a search for international prestige, or a desire to exercise regional influence, although such factors should not be discounted altogether. The most basic reason is self-interest. Mexico's leaders believe that Mexico's own internal political stability would be negatively affected by economic turmoil and instability in Central America and the Caribbean. The 1979 oil-price hikes placed a crushing new burden on the already hard-pressed economies of the region, thereby threatening the entire area with economic breakdown and chaos. The oil facility was designed to help ward off such an eventuality and thereby safeguard Mexico's own domestic order.[17]

Mexico's Relations with Central American States

Nicaragua

Mexico's assertion of regional influence in Central America has found its most forceful expression in the context of revolutionary Nicaragua. Politically, Mexico actively sought the ouster of the Somoza regime and the assumption of power by the Sandinistas over 1978 and 1979 in the hope of creating a stable and legitimate political system in that country. Since the Sandinista triumph in July 1979, Mexico has consistently supported, both diplomatically and economically, the consolidation of the Nicaraguan revolution. Along with Venezuela and the Andean Pact countries, in 1979 Mexico played a key role in blocking a U.S. initiative in the OAS to create a multinational peacekeeping force that would have prevented a Sandinista victory in Nicaragua.[18] In a move replete with diplomatic symbolism, in May 1979 Mexico broke diplomatic relations with the Somoza regime and recognized the Sandinista revolutionaries, thereby lending considerable international legitimacy to the Sandinista movement.[19] Following the revolution, Pres. José López Portillo and Foreign Minister Jorge Castañeda of Mexico frequently reiterated their country's solidarity with Nicaragua despite the open hostility of the United States.

In an effort to create a political counterweight to the hostile United States and generate additional international support for the Sandinistas, in 1979 Mexico's governing party—the Partido Revolucionario Institucional (PRI)—founded the Permanent Conference of Latin American Political Parties (Conferencia Permanente de Partidos Políticos de América Latina—COPPPAL) made up of centrist and leftist parties from Latin America. Although Mexico itself is not a member of the Socialist International, some COPPPAL members are and the two organizations generally have pursued policies favorable to the Sandinistas in Nicaragua and negotiated settlements elsewhere in Central America.[20]

Mexico has been particularly active in providing economic and technical assistance to Nicaragua since the triumph of the Sandinista revolution. In 1980, a binational state enterprise for the exploration of forest products was established and joint projects were also undertaken in areas ranging from mining through geothermal energy, fishing, communications, transportation, health, housing, and food distribution. It is estimated that Mexico provided 16 percent of the total financial aid received from abroad by the Sandinista government between 1979 and early 1981, more than twice the amount given by any other Latin American government. As of April 1982, Mexico had provided economic assistance to Nicaragua totaling almost US$200 million. During 1981, Mexican assistance was partially eclipsed by the extension of a credit line of US$100 million to the Sandinistas by the Libyan government, but there is little doubt that the Mexicans continue to be an important source of economic aid and technical expertise for the Sandinista regime.[21]

Since 1979 Mexican political and economic support for the Sandinistas has been directed toward moderating the Nicaraguan revolution and facilitating the emergence of a stable political regime. In view of the growing hostility of the United States toward the Sandinistas, especially over the first two years of the Reagan presidency, this has generally meant that Mexico's efforts have been concentrated on preventing the diplomatic and economic isolation of the Sandinistas. It is in this context that the multiple pledges by Pres. López Portillo to the effect that "Mexico will defend the cause of Nicaragua as its own" and its various "peace plans" for the region should be understood.[22]

Less frequently noticed or understood is the fact that Mexico has also brought its influence to bear on the Sandinistas in an effort to moderate the internal dynamics of the Nicaraguan revolution. For example, when Secretary of State Alexander M. Haig visited Mexico City in November 1981, the Mexicans indicated a willingness to express to the Sandinistas, through private diplomatic channels, their concern over Nicaragua's military buildup and the restrictions on political freedoms imposed by the regime.[23] In a February 1982 COPPPAL meeting held in Managua, Nicaragua, the PRI delegates encouraged the Sandinistas to publicly reaffirm their commitment to political pluralism, a mixed economic model, and nonalignment and their willingness to sign nonaggression pacts with all of Nicaragua's neighbors in Central America.[24] On February 21, 1982, in an address delivered in Managua in which he proposed a comprehensive peace plan for Central America, Pres. López Portillo declared that if the proposed nonaggression pacts were put into effect, it would be possible for Nicaragua to halt its military buildup, even though this statement produced considerable consternation within the Sandinista leadership.[25]

Pres. Miguel de la Madrid Hurtado has continued to pressure the Sandinistas behind the scenes to moderate their behavior in order to bring about a regional peace settlement. U.S. support for covert action from Honduras into Nicaragua is, in the context of this strategy, viewed as counterproductive, for it can only bring about greater internal radicalization of the Nicaraguan revolution and undercut the possibilities for creating a stable peace. Even if the United States and the anti-Sandinista opposition were successful in toppling the Sandinista regime in Managua sometime soon, a very unlikely prospect, it is obvious that Nicaragua would be wracked with violence and instability for years to come, for at least fifty thousand Sandinista army and militia members would undoubtedly resort to prolonged guerrilla warfare against the U.S.-backed regime.

El Salvador

In El Salvador, the López Portillo administration actively worked toward securing a negotiated settlement of the current civil war. Its policies were characterized by antipathy toward the Salvadoran military, the right-wing parties, and the Christian Democrats and obvious sympathy toward the revolutionary left.

Reflecting this posture, López Portillo frequently deplored the massive human-rights abuses taking place in that country.[26] His government also prevented the Salvadoran Christian Democrats from joining COPPPAL and in mid-1980 recalled its ambassador from El Salvador.[27] Furthermore, it also allowed the Salvadoran opposition to set up its headquarters in

Mexico City. Even more revealing, on August 28, 1981, Mexico joined with France to present a declaration before the UN Security Council that recognized the Frente Democratico Revolucionario (made up of the guerrillas' mass organizations and various leftist parties) and the Farabundo Martí National Liberation Front (composed of five guerrilla groups) as a "representative political force" legitimately entitled to negotiate with the incumbent Salvadoran civilian-military junta headed by Christian Democrat José Napoleón Duarte.[28]

The Mexicans also consistently criticized the process that led up to the March 28, 1982, Salvadoran elections, because it did not provide sufficient guarantees to the left. In fact, Mexico, along with France, Sweden, Holland, Denmark, Greece, Yugoslavia, Nicaragua, and Algeria, jointly sponsored a United Nations General Assembly Resolution on December 16, 1981, that denied that conditions for free elections existed in El Salvador. This resolution also recognized the legitimate right of the FDR/FMLN to participate in shaping the future of the country, called for negotiations among all parties to the conflict, and requested that all nations withhold further military assistance to the government of El Salvador. Despite intense lobbying by U.S. ambassador to the UN Jeane Kirkpatrick, the resolution was adopted by a vote of seventy to twenty-two. In the wake of the elections, the López Portillo government refused to recognize the results of the elections as a "solution" to the on-going civil war as the Reagan administration seemed to believe.[29] Although Mexico distanced itself from the Salvadoran government through such policies, it did not break diplomatic relations with El Salvador as it had done with the Somoza regime in Nicaragua. In its joint communiqué with France, for example, Mexico used the "representative political force" formula rather than declaring a "state of belligerency," because the former approach did not obligate it to assume a position of neutrality vis-à-vis both parties or to sever its relations with the Salvadoran regime as the latter necessarily would have required. In explaining his country's strategy, Foreign Minister Castañeda noted that the "representative political force" formula was more appropriate because the Salvadoran guerrillas did not control any territory.[30] Behind such legalisms, however, it appears that both the Mexican government and the Salvadoran left wanted relations to be maintained in order to allow Mexico to continue to play a mediating role in El Salvador, a role that would have been impossible had relations been broken altogether.[31]

It is also important to note that through the joint oil facility with Venezuela, Mexico has continued to provide sorely needed economic assistance to the debilitated Salvadoran economy. This tactic dovetails with Mexico's other efforts to maintain at least a modicum of leverage in El Salvador. It also appeared to be part of an implicit arrangement with Venezuela's Pres. Luis Herrera Campins in which Mexico "trades off" assistance to El Salvador and other relatively conservative governments in Central America and the Caribbean (e.g., Costa Rica, Guatemala, Honduras, and Jamaica) in exchange for a continuance of Venezuelan aid to Nicaragua. Finally, it allows Mexico to project an image of "even handedness" in its diplomacy in the region that has helped to forestall international criticism of its campaign for a negotiated settlement to the Salvadoran civil war and other conflicts in the area.

Guatemala

Mexico's relations with Guatemala have been cool and distant for years. Historically, the strains derive from territorial disputes between Mexico and Guatemala over Chiapas and from Guatemala's long-standing fears of Mexican economic and political dominance. Over the last decade or so, Mexican support for Belizean independence and territorial integrity has been a source of considerable friction as well.[32]

In the early 1980s these traditional tensions were exacerbated by opposition to the dictatorship of Fernando Romeo Lucas García and the rising tide of violence and civil strife in Guatemala that has sent tens of thousands of refugees across the border into Mexico.[33] President López Portillo's indefinite postponement of his scheduled visit to Guatemala in 1980 symbolized the diplomatic distance that has characterized Mexico's relations with Guatemala.

In 1980 Mexico invited a number of high-ranking Guatemalan military officers to observe major Mexican military maneuvers carried out in the country's southern states bordering on Guatemala. At least one U.S. analyst has cited this event as evidence of "a cooperative spirit" between the two nations' armed forces.[34] While there may have been some element of "cooperation" in this invitation, a more balanced interpretation would necessarily characterize it as, at very least, a two-edged sword. In effect, the Mexican military was also demonstrating to its Guatemalan counterparts that the Mexican armed forces were capable of a major show of force in the south and that any Guatemalan military incursion across the border would be met with a Mexican response. It also may have been intended to indicate that the Mexicans were able to control their own borders and to allay Guatemalan fears that Mexican territory would be used by guerrilla forces to launch attacks on Guatemala.

As the Lucas García regime prepared for "democratic" elections in Guatemala in mid-March 1982, the López Portillo administration remained skeptical and aloof. The fraudulent nature of these elections, which provoked bitter criticisms from even the right-wing parties that participated in them, and the subsequent coup that brought Gen. Efrain Rios Montt to power on March 23, 1982, bore out Mexico's skeptical attitude. While the Reagan administration at first endorsed the elections and then the Rios Montt government, Mexico's relations with Guatemala continued to deteriorate. In July, 1982, the Rios Montt regime began a vigorous pacification campaign against the guerrillas that has been criticized by international human-rights organizations as "brutal" and "despotic."[35] As a result of this antiguerrilla drive, the stream of Guatemalan refugees into Mexico has become an increasingly severe problem in Mexico.[36] As part of its counterinsurgency campaign, the Guatemalan military has crossed over, or fired, into Mexico on several occasions.[37] Foreign Minister Castañeda has protested these incursions and requested that "clear and absolute instructions be given to Guatemalan troops and para-military forces that operate in the frontier zone to respect scrupulously Mexican territory and to abstain from entering it or firing at persons on the Mexican side of the frontier."[38] He also requested official Guatemalan clarification of the disappearance—and apparent murder—in September 1981 of a Mexican vice consul stationed in the Guatemalan border town of Malacatan.[39]

Despite these protests, however, it is apparent that Mexico has maintained a lower diplomatic profile with regard to Guatemala than it has concerning Nicaragua or El Salvador. When asked if the Mexican government had "forgotten" about Guatemala, Castañeda responded:

> What has occurred is that there has not been an international situation that merits or permits actions similar to those adopted in other cases. The conditions are different. In El Salvador there was already a civil war . . . , countries were taking different sides and it seemed desirable to call for negotiations. Mexico did so because it was appropriate. We were unsuccessful but it was worth the effort, it seemed right to us. . . . If the same situation were to occur again, we would do the same thing. To date, the Guatemalan case has not presented a similar situation. We maintain scrupulously normal relations with the Guatemalan government, particularly with regard to the principle of non-intervention. We have not helped either side, just as in El Salvador we have not given a single pistol to anyone. Our attitude has been exemplary.[40]

Even though it is true that the guerrillas are not yet as strong in Guatemala as they were in Nicaragua or they are in El Salvador, it is also true that Mexico's national interests are more directly exposed in Guatemala than elsewhere in Central America. Hence, it would appear disingenuous to claim as Foreign Minister Castañeda has that Mexico's "scrupulous" diplomacy with regard to Guatemala is only a function of the lower level of guerrilla struggle in that country. Indeed, the levels of official violence and indiscriminate repression are, if anything, more intense and the military threat to Mexico more immediate in Gautemala than in other Central American countries where Mexico has expressed disapproval of the incumbent regimes.

Despite public statements to the contrary there can be little doubt that Mexico's leadership is concerned that the violence in Guatemala could spill over into Mexico, particularly into the border areas and its vulnerable southern oil fields. The military modernization programs undertaken by the López Portillo administration in 1980 was at least in part a response to such fears.[41] The October 1982 decision not to send troop reinforcements into the border areas, despite repeated incursions by the Guatemalan military, was prompted by a desire to minimize the risk of military clashes with Guatemala and to avoid the worsening of political tensions in Mexico.[42] The López Portillo government's efforts to remove refugees from camps along the Guatemalan border in October appeared to be motivated by a similar desire to discourage the Guatemalan military from moving into Mexican territory in pursuit of suspected guerrillas.[43]

The situation in Guatemala is deteriorating very rapidly. Rios Montt's antiguerrilla campaign, despite the scorch-and-burn tactics employed, is more likely to intensify the civil war than to pacify the country. The numbers of refugees crossing into Mexico are likely to increase, and Guatemalan military incursions will probably continue. Under these circumstances, it would seem that Pres. Miguel de la Madrid will have little alternative but to pursue a negotiated settlement of the civil war in Guatemala. Mexico's own internal political order requires it.

Mexico's Search for Negotiated Settlements in Central America

The López Portillo administration did not seek the installation of radical, Marxist regimes in Central America, despite claims by U.S. conservatives to the contrary.[44] In fact, its policies in Central America have been designed to modify the virulence of the Sandinista revolution in Nicaragua and the leftist opposition in Salvador and to prevent the regionalization of the conflicts in the area. The Mexicans' preferred outcome throughout Central America would be "left-wing PRIs," that is, regimes similar to Mexico's one-party dominant system: moderately revolutionary, moderately pluralist, unaligned with either superpower, and tolerant of mixed economies. Confronted with the choice between right-wing military regimes like the Somoza dictatorship in Nicaragua or the civilian-military junta in El Salvador, the Mexicans have consistently favored negotiations with the left-wing opposition over the perpetuation of repressive military dictatorships. Such policies are not adopted lightly in Mexico, nor are they the result of momentary flashes of anti-Americanism, sudden surges of *machismo* (manhood and strength), or mere sops to the Mexican left. Among the limited choices available, López Portillo opted for the alternatives that he believed would promote long-term stability in the region at the least cost to Mexico. The preferred mechanisms for settling the current conflicts and restoring peace have been negotiations, not victories on the battlefield.[45]

Both López Portillo and Miguel de la Madrid have declared that Mexico will continue to pursue negotiations even in the face of U.S. indifference or hostility to such efforts.[46] Indeed, over the last few years the López Portillo government actively promoted mediation over confrontation despite the chilly reception its various initiatives received in Washington. The current Mexican strategy appears to be to enlist the support of other countries behind its proposals for negotiated settlements and thereby bring additional pressure to bear on the Reagan administration to moderate its hard-line approach to the problems of the region, while simultaneously urging moderation on Cuba and Nicaragua. Reactions in Latin America to Mexico's August 1981 joint declaration with France calling for negotiations in El Salvador to end the civil war were roundly negative, as the United States and at least a dozen Latin American and Caribbean nations proceeded to denounce the initiative publicly as "interference" in the internal affairs of El Salvador.[47] López Portillo's offer, made on February 21, 1982, in Managua, Nicaragua, to facilitate direct discussions between the United States and Cuba and the United States and Nicaragua also proved unproductive when then Secretary of State Alexander M. Haig let it be known that the United States did not need or want Mexican mediation.[48]

In the wake of the Falklands/Malvinas conflict, however, Mexico's hopes of finding Latin American allies for its peace initiatives in Central America seemed to have improved somewhat, as its joint diplomatic note with Venezuela calling on Honduras, Nicaragua, and the United States to negotiate their outstanding conflicts rather than resort to force seemed to indicate.[49] The subsequent Panamanian endorsement of the Mexican-Venezuelan proposal, which laid the groundwork for the founding of the Contadora Group on January 9, 1983, reinforced this impression, as did the request from a bipartisan group of 106 members of the U.S. House of Representatives urging President Reagan to "respond positively" to the joint initiative.[50]

Of course, U.S. willingness to cooperate in these or any other proposed negotiations in Central America remains the key to their ultimate success, as the Mexicans are well aware. Indications are that the Reagan administration will not enter into such negotiations unless Nicaragua first meets the "preconditions" set by the United States. In response to the

Mexican-Venezuelan proposal, President Reagan revealed that he had sent letters to both Mexico's López Portillo and Venezuelan Pres. Luis Herrera Campins expressing his "great interest" in their "very constructive" recommendations for a negotiated settlement of the Nicaraguan-Honduran problem.[51] But in subsequent "clarifications," State Department officials made it abundantly clear that the United States felt that the Mexican-Venezuelan plan dealt with "only one aspect of the regional problem." They also revealed that the Reagan administration preferred the "verifiable and reciprocal" regional accord outlawing arms trafficking, subversion, and foreign military and security advisers in the entire area put forward by a group of Caribbean Basin countries in San José, Costa Rica, a few weeks after the Mexican-Venezuelan proposal.[52]

The basic objection of the Reagan government to the Mexican-Venezuelan plan is that it does not address the "root problem" of Nicaraguan "subversion" in Central America or Cuban and Soviet bloc involvement in such activities. Reagan's advisers also contend that the joint proposal does not address the Sandinistas' growing "totalitarianism," that is, their refusal to permit "moderate" opposition political leaders to participate in the governance of the country. The Reagan administration's endorsement of the San José proposal is justified on the grounds that "any meaningful attempt to address the problems of Central America must be within a regional context that achieves 'democratic pluralism' and an 'end to support for terrorist and insurgent groups' in other countries of the region."[53]

Neither President Reagan's warm but essentially noncommittal response to the Mexican-Venezuelan proposal nor his government's endorsement of the San José plan represents any real change in the basic approach of the United States to the conflicts in the region or its determination to "turn back" what it views as a wave of communist-inspired subversion in Central America. Reagan did not reject the Mexican-Venezuelan plan out of hand, because his government has felt increasing pressure, both domestic and international, to adopt a more flexible attitude toward negotiated settlements. The Reagan administration maintains that the "door is open" to negotiations with Nicaragua, but only if the Sandinistas first alter their "unacceptable behavior" within and outside Nicaragua's borders.

Sandinista leader Daniel Ortega Saavedra endorsed the Mexican-Venezuelan proposal and agreed to a meeting with Pres. Roberto Suazo Córdova of Honduras to seek a solution to the conflicts between their countries. But the Sandinistas have steadfastly rejected the preconditions the United States has attempted to impose. Their position is that they are willing to discuss all outstanding issues with the United States "any time, any where" but without preconditions on either side.[54]

In view of this apparent impasse, the Reagan administration is unlikely to agree to direct negotiations with the Sandinistas any time soon, and the Hondurans, after consultations with the United States, have been reluctant to accept direct talks.[55] Much more probable is a continuation of the present "war of attrition"—some have described it as a "slow-motion Bay of Pigs" operation—currently being conducted against Nicaragua by opposition groups based in Honduras.[56] Covert CIA support for these anti-Sandinista forces is an open secret as are current U.S. efforts to build up the Honduran military.[57] The extent of direct Honduran governmental involvement in these destabilization efforts remains undetermined, although some degree of complicity is obvious for the camps of *contras* (guerrillas fighting against the Sandinistas) continue to operate on Honduran soil unimpeded and no arrests or captures have taken place.[58]

Rather than negotiations, the logic of the Reagan administration's position calls for the intensification of current hostilities toward Nicaragua in order to force the Sandinistas to accept negotiations on U.S. terms or to overthrow the Sandinista regime altogether.[59] The United States will doubtless continue to endorse negotiations publicly, for politically it cannot afford to do otherwise. But few results can be expected unless a formula for direct negotiations between the United States and Nicaragua is devised. In the absence of such a formula, present U.S. policies would appear to run a high risk of precipitating a major war between Honduras and Nicaragua and the extension of armed conflict throughout the region.

Constraints on Mexican Foreign Policy

In its recent Central American policies Mexico has demonstrated a considerable degree of autonomy vis-à-vis the United States, but the limits of that autonomy have proven in practice to be rather narrow. Mexico's dependence on oil exports to finance domestic growth and to underwrite its foreign-policy commitments constitutes the most basic of the international constraints. The 1981–1982 world oil glut produced dramatic declines in oil revenues, leading to economic crisis in Mexico. Worsening domestic economic conditions—devaluation, high inflation, declining exports, a multi-billion-dollar trade deficit, 40 percent under- and unemployment, an eighty-one-billion-dollar foreign debt, and the need for emergency economic aid from the international community—have limited the funds Mexico can dedicate to its foreign-policy objectives without severely shortchanging domestic priorities.[60]

A second major constraint limiting Mexico's independence in the foreign-policy field is its relative economic and military weakness vis-à-vis the United States and the overwhelming importance of its bilateral relations with its dominant northern neighbor. In the extreme case of direct U.S. military intervention in Central America, the Mexicans would doubtless condemn the United States in all available international forums, but they would be unable to do much else. Militarily they are incapable of a response, although they could become a center of gunrunning into the region and a haven for political opposition groups.[61] They certainly could not afford to retaliate economically by cutting back petroleum sales to the United States, further restricting trade, or limiting investment; ultimately, Mexico would be the bigger loser. Despite growing interdependence, Mexican influence over U.S. foreign policy is even more limited than U.S. influence over Mexico's international behavior. At best, the Mexicans can continue to offer to serve as mediators among the contending parties while attempting to bring pressure to bear on the Reagan administration by enlisting the support of other nations behind proposals for negotiated settlements.

The third and final set of constraints on Mexican foreign policy derives from the domestic political system rather than the international environment. On the one hand, Mexico's well-developed sense of nationalism and the presence of an "institutionalized left" require Miguel de la Madrid Hurtado to pursue a foreign policy in the Caribbean and Central America similar to that of his predecessor. On the other hand, the progressive policies adopted by López Portillo in Central America produced significant dissent in conservative sectors of Mexican society, particularly among business people, some elements of the military, and the right-wing parties.[62] De la Madrid must therefore be careful not to strain unduly the traditional consensus surrounding Mexican foreign policy by undertaking controversial Central American policies. In this context, Guatemala represents an especially knotty problem because widespread sympathies in Mexico for the Guatemalan insurgents and antipathy toward the Guatemalan military suggest one strategy, whereas security concerns require that Mexico take steps to ensure that its southern border does not become a staging ground for Gautemalan revolutionaries.

Conclusion

Over the López Portillo *sexenio,* Mexico emerged as a major independent actor in the Caribbean Basin. Yet Mexico's influence in the region remains tenuous. Fluctuations in the international petroleum market and domestic economic collapse have combined to limit the resources the country is able to marshal to back its foreign-policy initiatives. In view of the overriding importance of its bilateral relationship with the United States, it is virtually unthinkable that Mexican authorities would resort to economic reprisals against the United States over foreign-policy issues, even if the Reagan administration were to undertake a unilateral intervention somewhere in Central America. Nevertheless, Mexico has both the opportunity and the motivation to play a role as political mediator in the region and President de la Madrid has continued his predecessor's search for negotiated settlements despite U.S. resistance. Without U.S. cooperation, however, the chances for success are slim indeed.

Notes

1. In his fifth State of the Union Address on September 1, 1981, President López Portillo harshly condemned the U.S. decision to produce the neutron bomb, lamented the demise of the Second Strategic Arms Limitation Treaty talks (SALT II), and decried the growing arms race between the two superpowers. Many of these same criticisms were repeated and amplified in his sixth and final State of the Union Address on September 1, 1982. For the texts of these addresses, see *Excelsior,* September 2, 1981, pp. 1, 14; and *Comercio Exterior* 32, no. 9 (September 1982), pp. 919–947.

2. "Haig's ultimate fear is that the entire region, from Mexico to Panama, might fall into the Soviet orbit, which would not only threaten America's vital security interests, but would also show the world that the U.S. is unable to contain the spread of communism even in its own backyard." *Time,* March 22, 1982, p. 19. For the Reagan administration's analysis of the extent of Soviet-Cuban involvement in subversive activities in the region, see U.S. Department of State, "Cuba's Renewed Support for Violence in Latin America," Washington, D.C.: Bureau of Public Affairs, Special Report no. 80, February 23, 1981; Thomas O. Enders, "The State of Danger in the Caribbean Basin," informal remarks by Assistant Secretary Enders at the Pan-American Society, New York, January 13, 1982, 7 p.; T. O. Enders, "Building the Peace in Central America," Washington, D.C.: Bureau of Public Affairs, Current Policy no. 414, August 20, 1982, 4 p.; U.S. State Department, "Cuban Armed Forces and the Soviet Military Presence," Washington, D.C.: Bureau of Public Affairs, Special Report no. 103, August 1982, 5 p.; and T. O. Enders, "The Central American Challenge," *AEI Foreign Policy and Defense Review* 4, no. 2 (1982), pp. 8–12.

3. For examples of conservative fears about Mexico, see Constantine Menges, "The Second Arc of Crisis—Panama to Mexico, 1980–83," Washington, D.C.: The Hudson Institute, 1980, 21 p.; C. Menges, "Central America and the U.S.," *SAIS Review,* no. 2 (Summer 1981), pp. 13–35; and C. Menges, "The United States and Latin America in the 1980s," in P. Gifford, ed., *The National Interests of the United States* (Washington, D.C.: The Wilson Center, 1981), pp. 53–72. One of the best examples of this line of thinking is provided by a 1981 *Washington*

Post editorial entitled "Mexico's Dangerous Indulgence . . . ," which said, "Something is missing from the Common Mexican prescription. It is bound to become more noticeable as the crisis in Central America, and Mexico's oil-fed appetite for a larger international role both grow. The missing factor is Mexico's own vulnerability to precisely the sort of revolutionary tendencies it is now encouraging in El Salvador and elsewhere." *Washington Post,* January 26, 1981, p. A16. For the Mexican dismissal of its vulnerability see *Excelsior,* June 24, 1982, pp. 1, 15.

4. *El Dia,* February 22, 1982, p. 8.

5. Alan Riding has reported the flight of more than forty thousand Guatemalan refugees into Mexico over the last year. *New York Times,* September 28, 1982, p. A4. On the refugee problem in Guatemala, see *New York Times,* September 12, 1982, p. E3; September 15, 1982, p. A2; October 6, 1982, p. A2.

6. The unleashing of a generalized armed struggle in the region could force a new Mexican vision of the problem; that is, the need to resort to an armaments policy with all that implies for the objectives of her own development. In economic terms it would signify a diversion of resources from productive areas that are urgent for the consolidation of the economy; in political terms it would signify the weakening of the traditional political class which would be increasingly forced to share the strategies of development with the military sector. Furthermore, a development policy openly joined to U.S. notions of security would lead to the failure of the present government's effort to incorporate political pluralism into the political system. The efforts carried out in recent years to incorporate greater political openness by institutionalizing the participation of diverse ideological forces in the electoral process would become useless. Security considerations would wind up dominating those of domestic political modernization. The social crisis predicted for Mexico by supporters of the domino theory, among others, would shortly become reality, but for different reasons. A policy of political strife would spoil the efforts of democratization and could bring on critical confrontations in Mexican society.

René Herrera Zúñiga and Mario Ojeda, "Mexican Foreign Policy and Central America," in R. E. Feinberg, ed., *Central America: International Dimensions of the Crisis* (New York: Holmes and Meier, 1982), pp. 167–168.

7. "The Mexicans see their policy essentially as one of open communication that ultimately, though perhaps incidentally, may actually help the United States by defusing potential confrontations in the area and leaving the door ajar to moderation through persuasion rather than coercion." Christopher Dickey, "Oil-Rich Mexico Sets Its Sights on Independent World Role," *Washington Post,* September 4, 1980, p. A19.

8. On the linkage between domestic politics and foreign policy, see Olga Pellicer de Brody, *Mexico y la Revolucion Cubana* (Mexico: El Colegio de Mexico, 1972); O. Pellicer de Brody "Tercermundismo del capitalismo mexicano: Ideología y realidad," *Cuadernos Politicos,* no. 3 (1975), pp. 52–59; Yoram Shapira, "La politica exterior de Mexico bajo el regimen de Echeverria: Restrospectiva," *Foro Internacional* 19, no. 1 (July–September 1978), pp. 62–91; and Wolf Grabendorff, "Mexico's Foreign Policy—Indeed a Foreign Policy?" *Journal of Interamerican Studies and World Affairs* 20, no. 1 (February 1978), pp. 85–92.

9. I am indebted to Réne Herrera Zúñiga of El Colegio de Mexico for comments on an earlier draft of this chapter in which he emphasized that Mexico's efforts have been intended to moderate not only U.S. policies but also those of Cuba and Nicaragua.

10. René Herrera and Mario Ojeda, "The Policy of Mexico in the Caribbean Basin," Mexico: El Colegio de Mexico, September 1982 (Mimeographed), pp. 5–6.

11. Herrera and Ojeda, "Mexican Foreign Policy and Central America," p. 173.

12. Ibid.

13. Robert L. Ayres and Cathryn Thorup, *Central America: The Challenges to U.S. and Mexican Foreign Policy* (Washington, D.C.: Overseas Development Council, 1981), p. 12.

14. Ibid.; and Herrera and Ojeda, "The Policy of Mexico in the Caribbean Basin," p. 6.

15. Herrera and Ojeda, "Mexican Foreign Policy and Central America," p. 174.

16. Ibid., p. 176; and *Latin America Regional Reports: Mexico and Central America,* December 3, 1982, p. 8.

17. Herrera and Ojeda, "Mexican Foreign Policy and Central America," pp. 174–179.

18. Edward J. Williams, "Mexico's Central American Policy: Revolutionary and Prudential Dimensions," in H. Michael Erisman and John D. Martz, eds., *Colossus Challenged: The Struggle for Caribbean Influence* (Boulder, Colo.: Westview Press, 1982), p. 154.

19. Ibid.

20. Karl-Ludolf Hübener, "The Socialist International and Latin America: Problems and Possibilities," *Caribbean Review* 11, no. 2 (Spring 1982), p. 40.

21. A. T. Bryan, "Mexico and the Caribbean: New Ventures into the Region," *Caribbean Review* 10, no. 3 (Summer 1981), pp. 4–7, 36; Williams, "Mexico's Central American Policy," pp. 154–159; and *El Tiempo,* April 3, 1982, p. 2E (Bogotá).

22. For an example of López Portillo's promises to defend the Nicaraguan revolution see *Barricada,* May 8, 1981, pp. 1, 7. On the logic behind Mexico's peace efforts see René Herrera Zúñiga, *La politica exterior Mexicana en Centroamerica: Factores coyuntrales, intereses nacionales y la geopolitica regional,* Occasional Papers Series, Dialogue no. 11 (Miami: Florida International University, Latin American and Caribbean Center, October 1982), 29 p.

23. *Washington Post,* November 25, 1981, p. A16.

24. *Libertad,* week of February 26 to March 4, 1982, p. 8 (Costa Rica).

25. Although the Sandinistas' negative reactions were not widely publicized, I have been told by a reliable source that they were concerned that López Portillo's proposal would obligate them to disarm unilaterally and thereby leave Nicaragua vulnerable to future attacks launched against the revolution from neighboring countries or to destabilization efforts initiated by a hostile United States. Many of the Sandinistas interpreted these proposals as an indication that Mexico was no longer a reliable ally.

26. Williams, "Mexico's Central American Policy," p. 155.

27. Ibid.; and John F. McShane, "Emerging Regional Power: Mexico's Role in the Caribbean Basin," in E. G. Ferris and J. K. Lincoln, eds., *Latin American Foreign Policies: Global and Regional Dimensions* (Boulder, Colo.: Westview Press, 1981), pp. 200–201.

28. The French-Mexican communiqué was the product of weeks of consultations between France and Mexico, including direct talks between Mexican foreign minister Jorge Castañeda and French foreign minister Claude Cheysson. In effect, the declaration came as close as possible to recognizing a state of belligerency without actually doing so. Both France and Mexico have continued diplomatic relations with El Salvador. *Washington Post,* August 29, 1981, p. A17. Nicaragua and Cuba lauded this initiative as a "very positive" step toward the peaceful settlement of the Salvadoran civil war. *Washington Post,* September 6, 1982, p. A31, and *Miami Herald,* September 1, 1981, p. 13A. But reactions in most of Latin America were quite negative, as revealed by the backing received by a joint Colombian-Venezuelan statement that expressed "great concern" over Mexico and France's decision to "intervene in the internal matters of El Salvador" in support of "subversive extremist groups which by violence seek to twist the democratic and free determination of the Salvadoran people." *San Francisco Chronicle,* September 3, 1981, p. 14. Both the governing military-civilian junta in El Salvador and the United States flatly rejected any proposal to negotiate with the guerrillas. *Washington Post,* September 5, 1981, p. A22.

29. *New York Times,* November 25, 1981, p. A10; December 17, 1981, p. A11.

30. *Washington Post,* August 29, 1981, p. A17; and Williams, "Mexico's Central American Policy," p. 158.

31. Williams, "Mexico's Central American Policy," p. 159; and Olga Pellicer de Brody, "Mexico's Policy Towards Central America," Mexico: CIDE, 1981, pp. 14–17.

32. McShane, "Emerging Regional Power," p. 201.

33. *Washington Post,* May 23, 1981, p. A22; and *Unomasuno,* January 22, 1982, p. 1.

34. Williams, "Mexico's Central American Policy," p. 157.

35. *New York Times,* September 12, 1982, p. E3; September 15, 1982, p. A2; October 6, 1982, p. A2.

36. *San Francisco Chronicle,* July 27, 1982, p. 12; and *New York Times,* October 9, 1982, p. 4Y; October 29, 1982, p. A8.

37. *New York Times,* September 28, 1982, p. A4.

38. Ibid.

39. Ibid.

40. *Excelsior,* June 24, 1982, p. 15.

41. *New York Times,* October 5, 1980, p. A3; and Stephen J. Wagner, "The Modernization of the Mexican Military and Its Significance for Mexico's Central American Policy," paper prepared for the Military Policy Symposium on "Mexico, the United States, and Central American Revolutionary Change," Strategic Studies Institute, U.S. Army War College, Carlisle, Pa., November 1982, 16 p.

42. *San Francisco Chronicle,* October 18, 1982, p. 11.

43. Ibid.

44. Herrera and Ojeda, "Mexican Foreign Policy and Central America," pp. 165–170; Herrera, "La politica exterior Mexicana en Centroamerica"; and Olga Pellicer, "Mexico's Policy Towards Central America," p. 17.

45. Herrera and Ojeda, "Mexican Foreign Policy and Central America," pp. 169–170; and Caesar D. Sereseres, "The United States and Mexico: Divergent Approaches to Resolving the Central American Conflict," paper prepared for the U.S. Army War College Symposium, "Mexico, the United States, and Central American Revolutionary Change," Carlisle, Pa., November 1982, 8 p.

46. *Unomasuno,* June 30, 1982, pp. 1, 6; and *Latin American Weekly Report,* October 15, 1982, p. 2.

47. *San Francisco Chronicle,* September 3, 1981, p. 14; and *Miami Herald,* September 1, 1981, p. 13A.

48. For the complete text of López Portillo's offer to facilitate "dialogue" between the contending parties in Central America, see *El Dia,* February 22, 1982, p. 8. López Portillo proposed three basic steps: (1) U.S. rejection of any threat or use of force aimed against Nicaragua, (2) a balanced reduction of arms and military troops in the area, and (3) a series of nonaggression pacts between Nicaragua and the United States and Nicaragua and its Central American neighbors. López Portillo also offered Mexico's good offices to establish talks between Cuba and the United States.

The initial U.S. reaction was quite cool because the Reagan administration wanted to keep international attention focused on the upcoming March 28, 1982, elections in El Salvador. The principal objection voiced by the United States was that the Mexican proposal did not address the questions of Nicaraguan support for the guerrillas in El Salvador. The Mexican effort was, however, endorsed by Nicaragua, Cuba, the USSR, and the Salvadoran guerrillas. See *Wall Street Journal,* March 15, 1982, p. 2; *New York Times,* March 18, 1982, p. A16; and *Washington Post,* March 19, 1982, p. A18.

The positive reactions that Mexico's diplomatic initiative elicited from the U.S. Congress and press as well as from Europe over early March 1982 apparently led the Reagan administration to alter its approach toward the Mexican proposals. First on March 7, and then again on March 14, Secretary of State Haig met in New York with Foreign Minister Jorge Castañeda of Mexico to discuss the Mexican peace plan. Following the March 14 meeting, it was announced that Mexico had received a "go-ahead" from the United States and that Castañeda would soon travel to Cuba and Nicaragua to "communicate" the U.S. position. *Washington Post,* March 15, 1982, pp. A1, A20; March 19, 1982, p. A19.

When U.S. conservatives strongly condemned this announcement—expressing fears that the United States was about to concede a role to Cuba and the Soviet Union in shaping the future of Central America—the Reagan administration moved quickly to dispel the idea that Mexico had been empowered to negotiate with these countries on behalf of the United States. On March 15, Secretary of State Haig declared that "there are no plans at this time for high-level U.S. talks with either Cuba or Nicaragua, and he described the proposals given to Castañeda as a reiteration of a plan offered to Nicaragua last year and rejected by the revolutionary government there." *Washington Post,* March 16, 1982, pp. A1, A16. In fact, Secretary of State Haig had met secretly with Vice-President Carlos Rafael Rodríguez of Cuba on November 23, 1981, in Mexico City prior to López Portillo's February 21, 1982, speech in Managua, and Ambassador-at-large Gen. Vernon D. Walters had met with Fidel Castro in Cuba in early March 1982 before the Haig-Castañeda meetings. Castañeda's effort in late March to schedule further meetings between the United States and Cuba during April 1982 in Mexico City never materialized, and by May it had become clear that Mexican hopes for further "dialogue" had faded completely. *New York Times,* November 25, 1981, p. A7; *Unomasuno,* January 30, 1982, p. 17; and *New York Times,* May 18, 1982, p. A12.

As a Reagan administration official subsequently acknowledged to Alan Riding of the *New York Times,* "as you know, we were cool to the initiative from the beginning, but we were effectively ambushed by Congress and public opinion. We had to agree to negotiate or appear unreasonable." *New York Times,* May 10, 1982, p. A12. In effect, the Reagan administration went along with the Mexican initiative in order to defuse public criticism of its hard-line policies toward the Central American crisis and to buy time for the Salvadoran elections. In the wake of these "successful" elections, the Reagan administration made "no secret of its desires to eliminate Mexico as an intermediary in the region." *New York Times,* May 10, 1982, p. A12.

49. The Mexican-Venezuelan proposal was sent to President Reagan in the form of a letter on September 15, 1982. *New York Times,* October 7, 1982, p. A7.

50. *Washington Post,* October 2, 1982, p. A25; October 7, 1982, p. A24.

51. *New York Times,* October 7, 1982, p. A7.

52. Ibid.

53. Ibid.; and *Latin American Weekly Report,* October 15, 1982, p. 2.

54. *Washington Post,* October 8, 1982, p. A28; *New York Times,* October 7, 1982, p. A7; and *Boston Globe,* September 26, 1982, p. A23.

55. Pres. Roberto Suazo Córdova responded that he was "too busy" to attend a meeting with Nicaragua's Daniel Ortega Saavedra set for October 13, 1982, in Caracas, Venezuela, "raising the question whether he now opposed the idea of direct negotiations with Nicaragua or whether he merely found the proposal date inconvenient." *New York Times,* October 10, 1982, p. A6. In subsequent conversations held in the United Nations under the auspices of Secretary General Javier Pérez de Cuellar, the foreign minister of Honduras, Edgardo Paz Barnica, and the foreign minister of Nicaragua, Miguel D'Escoto Brockman, agreed that their respective defense ministers would hold direct talks in an effort to settle their outstanding disputes. It was also reported that Honduran president Suazo Córdova had agreed "conditionally" to meet with Sandinista leader Daniel Ortega Saavedra if the "foreign ministers from the countries [of Mexico, Venezuela, Nicaragua and Honduras], the rest of Central America and the leading Caribbean countries agree first on an agenda." *New York Times,* October 12, 1982, p. A4.

56. See Lynda Schuster, "Latin Hotspot: Honduras Becoming a New Battle-ground for Central America," *Wall Street Journal,* September 28, 1982, pp. 1,

14; and Washington Office on Latin America, "Nicaragua: Is War with Honduras Inevitable?" *Update Latin America* 7, no. 5 (September–October 1982), pp. 1–2. The Nicaraguans claim that there are at least seventeen "antisandinistas" camps currently located in Honduras. *Unomasuno,* July 22, 1982, p. 12.

57. T. S. Montgomery, "Reagan's Honduras," *New York Times,* October 1, 1982, p. A32; Wayne Smith, "Wrong Central American Policy," *New York Times,* October 12, 1982, p. A29; and *Washington Post,* October 17, 1982, pp. A1, A12.

58. *Washington Post,* October 15, 1982, pp. A1, A21; October 16, 1982, pp. A17, A21. *Unomasuno,* July 21, 1982, p. 6; July 23, 1982, p. 12.

59. On the logic of the Reagan administration's Central American policies, see Piero Gleijeses, *Tilting at Windmills: Reagan in Central America* (Washington, D.C.: Copublication of the Caribbean Basin Studies Program and the Foreign Policy Institute, The School of Advanced International Studies, The Johns Hopkins University, 1982), 40 p.

60. How limiting the current Mexican economic crisis will be is necessarily a matter of speculation. The Mexicans have already agreed to an extension of their joint oil facility with Venezuela for nine Caribbean Basin countries through August 1983, and President Miguel de la Madrid Hurtado repeatedly promised continuity in Mexican foreign policy toward the region. It is, however, unlikely that the new president will be willing or able to commit significant levels of additional resources to foreign policy, at least in the first years of his *sexenio.*

61. Mexican spending on defense in 1981 amounted to only about 2.5 percent of the national budget, one of the smallest outlays in the entire hemisphere. Over the past three years, the army has grown by 25 percent to about 125,000 (versus over 200,000 in the Cuban armed forces). On the basis of projected petroleum revenues, the country has undertaken a military modernization program that includes the purchase of at least twelve F-5E jet fighters from the United States. It has also been reported that the López Portillo government began training a 4,000-member "quick-reaction" force in 1981 designed to defend the country's southern border and oil fields against a possible spillover of guerrilla warfare from Central America. *Washington Post,* February 18, 1982, pp. A1, A24.

On the modern Mexican military, see Jorge Alberto Lozoya, *El Ejército Mexicano (1911–1965)* (Mexico City: El Colegio de Mexico, 1970): David F. Ronfeldt, "The Mexican Army and Political Order Since 1940," in Abraham Lowenthal, ed., *Armies and Politics in Latin America* (New York: Holmes and Meier, 1976), pp. 291–312; Edward J. Williams, "Mexico's Modern Military: Implications for the Region," *Caribbean Review* 10, no. 4 (Fall 1981), pp. 12–21, 45; William S. Ackroyd, "The Military in Mexican Politics: The Impact of Professionalization, Civilian Behavior, and the Revolution," paper presented at the twenty-eighth meeting of the Pacific Coast Council on Latin American Studies, San Diego, Calif., October 14–16, 1982, 30 p.; and Stephen J. Wagner, "The Modernization of the Mexican Military."

62. The rightist PAN (Partido de Acción Nacional) presidential candidate, Pablo Emilio Madero, was especially critical of López Portillo's foreign policy toward Central America during the country's recent electoral campaign. *Uno-*

masuno, June 25, 1982, p. 3. Rumors of possible dissent within the Mexican military were reported in the *Washington Post,* September 23, 1982, p. A29. Mexican business people opposed López Portillo's policies toward the region on the grounds that Mexico's opposition to the United States will make the U.S. government and U.S. commercial banks less cooperative in helping Mexico out of its current financial difficulties.

17
West European Perceptions of the Crisis in Central America

Wolf Grabendorff

West Europeans generally have been stunned by the development of the Central American crisis. This is not only because of the political violence but also because of the intentions of the Reagan administration to use El Salvador to test the willingness of the West European allies to join in drawing a line against communist interventions in the U.S. "front yard."[1]

West European countries were both uneasy and surprised about this "linkage" between Atlantic alliance problems and the revolutionary process in a small Central American country. They felt uneasy because recent events in Central America had been greeted with some understanding, if not satisfaction, by the rather large constituency for Third World problems in most West European countries. They felt surprise because even those who generally favored a containment policy against Soviet global expansion did not consider Central America the most urgent place to press such a policy. Obviously the West Europeans lacked adequate understanding of U.S. sensitivities—in the country at large and among the decision makers of the Reagan administration in particular—with regard to this region so close to home.

This chapter addresses some of the factors that have contributed to different perceptions among political groups and governments in Western Europe, on the one hand, and among policymakers and others in the United States, on the other. It should be emphasized, however, that important conservative political groups in Western Europe share the dominant views in the United States about the causes of and remedies for the crisis in Central America.

There are many reasons why West European perceptions and reactions to Central American developments since the late 1970s have differed from U.S. perceptions and reactions. Geographical distance is not the least important among them, but a fear that the East-West conflict could be intensified by the emergence of new areas of great-power rivalry in the Third World also plays a role. It is therefore important to contrast the different views about the causes of the Central American crisis before analyzing the real or perceived political implications of the crisis on Western Europe.

The first section of this chapter examines the global setting for revolutionary developments in Central America. The second section summarizes the instruments and strategies of various European actors in Central America; this section is intended to explain the West European role in that region without detailing the political or economic involvement of various West European countries.

This chapter also briefly considers policy options and outlines scenarios for international cooperation to contribute to more peaceful regional developments of Central America.

Internal and External Origins: A North-South Problem or East-West Rivalry?

The origins of the Central American crisis have been fiercely debated not only in the United States but also in Western Europe. Advocates of a "regional" solution to the political violence blame the problems on the extreme social injustice, illegitimate political systems, and continuing repression of popular participation in countries like Guatemala, Honduras, and El Salvador and in Nicaragua prior to its revolution. This group maintains that change in Central America is inevitable and that any attempt by Western powers to preserve the status quo in that area will only lead to more radicalization and violence—and increase the tendency in the area to turn to the socialist bloc for help.[2] According to this group, the longtime association of the United States and Western countries in general with the "old order" has spurred "antiimperialism" among people who favor a change in government. Previous Western policies make it very difficult for outsiders to try to mediate these basically socioeconomic conflicts in Central America. Because the internal and regional political processes have gone beyond the moderate reformist stages, any efforts to "modernize" political systems in Central America are believed to be doomed.

The advocates of a global solution do not deny the internal problems but stress the importance of external, radical forces—communist inspired if not communist directed—in the breakdown of the old order.[3] This group finds the authoritarian regimes in the region rather stable and their socioeconomic systems not at all repellent because "such societies create no refugees."[4] Since the representatives of the old order were "friendly," noncommunist elites, their weakening has almost automatically led to a decline of U.S. influence in the region.

This group views the ability of Marxist influence to destabilize Central American societies in the context of the East-West power struggle. Containment of communism and the Soviet influence in the Western Hemisphere is of decisive importance for all Western countries; therefore the dissolution of the old order in Central America has to be stopped. The "Globalists" prefer authoritarian governments to possible totalitarian societies (such as what they fear is developing in Nicaragua). From this group's perspective, it would be in the best interest of the Central American societies themselves as well as of the West in general if the breakdown of regimes could be stopped and the external influence ended. Once the left had been cut off from external support, reform could be initiated to lead these countries toward more democratic systems. In short globalists concur that a return to the status quo ante is not only possible but even desirable; it can be achieved by concerted efforts to defeat communist—that is, Soviet and Cuban—influence.

Both regionalists and globalists have influenced West European perceptions of the Central American crisis. Generally, the regionalist approach seems prominent among the Social Democratic parties and governments, whereas the globalist approach is more representative of their Christian Democratic counterparts.[5] But this generalization is simplistic. The German Christian Democrats, for example, are well aware of both the importance of the internal origins and of the North-South dimensions of the conflict. The Social Democrats and Christian Democrats differ more over the direction and instruments of change in Central America than over the causes of recent upheaval.

Throughout Western Europe, the regional approach to the Central American crisis has definitely taken priority over the global approach. The general view in Western Europe is that internal socioeconomic and political conditions must be improved before any stabilization of the region will become feasible. A return to the old order in Nicaragua and El Salvador or a continuation of it in Guatemala and Honduras is viewed as neither possible nor desirable. In both cases such a return would very likely involve extremely high political costs that would be a burden not only for the United States but also for Western Europe, specifically with regard to relations with the Third World.

Political Implications and Economic Interests: Atlantic Alliance Cohesion or Third World Accommodation?

The political implications of the Central American crisis for Western Europe have to be seen in three contexts: the East-West conflict, the

Atlantic alliance, and West European relations with the Third World. There can be little doubt that in all three areas West European interests are highly vulnerable. Therefore West European reaction to developments that touch on all three areas will necessarily be strong but by no means united.

Most West European parties and governments believe that any Third World conflict involving one of the superpowers is likely to become an East-West issue. Afghanistan is one such case, and Central America could become another if the United States should become convinced that only military intervention could preserve its national interest. Such a development would seriously strain the Atlantic alliance, since Western Europe is unlikely to view possible changes of political systems in Central America as a threat to the security of the United States.

Many West Europeans who have come to accept the ever-present missiles on the other side of the iron curtain as a fact of life find it hard to understand the "Cuba trauma" that has haunted U.S. policymakers since the Cuban missile crisis and that seems to be of special importance to the Reagan administration. Many West European analysts also question whether every socialist system established in Central America will automatically become a Soviet ally and base for offensive sophisticated weapons. The security-related preoccupations of the United States with regard to Central America are regarded by many Europeans as inconsistent with the U.S. position as a superpower.[6] There is a general fear about dramatic domestic as well as international repercussions of a U.S.-sponsored intervention in Central America.

The argument of the U.S. government—that outside interference in Latin America in general and in the Caribbean Basin in particular must be viewed as a threat to the U.S. global position—is based on the geopolitical concept of zones of influence.[7] West European policymakers well understand this concept, but some do not share it. Some of them fear that once criteria based on zones of influence are accepted, the Soviet Union might use them to defend its own aggressive policies in what it considers its zone of influence. If the United States views a change of government from a friendly, oligarchic, free-enterprise system to an unfriendly, socialist system with a centrally planned economy as incompatible with its role as superpower, Europeans wonder whether that U.S. view will infringe the sovereign rights of Third World countries to determine their own forms of government.

Some West European countries find it hard to preserve political unity within the Atlantic alliance with respect to Central America.[8] Those who view the conflict in North-South terms are unwilling to back U.S. policies because they feel that their own economic cooperation with the Third World should not be jeopardized by unreasonable U.S. opposition to any political change. Even Europeans who view the Central American crisis as an evolving East-West issue doubt whether this region really is the most important one in which to "stand up against Soviet expansion." Many Europeans who generally support a policy of getting tough with the Soviets consider the stakes much lower in Central America than in the [Persian/Arabian] Gulf or Africa. France has been in the forefront of that position. Mitterrand's initiatives toward the Central American crisis (the French-Mexican declaration on El Salvador, the arms sale to Nicaragua, the diplomatic mission to Cuba) are meant to offer a Western alternative to the hard-line position of the Reagan administration.[9]

Another reason for the mixed reaction to the Reagan administration's appeal for European support of its policies was that prior consultation was minimal.[10] Christian and Social Democratic parties have had close contacts in Central America for more than a decade, so some European politicians were stunned when the United States failed to use these channels but instead asked West Europeans to support a policy they find hardly convincing—and only after the policy had already been established.

Policymakers on both sides of the Atlantic have deplored the lack of a unified Western policy toward Central America, but a unified policy was hardly possible because of the differing views about the origins of and possible remedies for the upheaval in the region. Nevertheless, the basic interests of all partners in the Atlantic alliance remain the same:

- to prevent the Central American countries from adhering to the socialist bloc
- to avoid regional and internal instability due to interstate or intrastate violence
- to guarantee economic cooperation through the support of free-market economies
- to further economic development and social justice through bilateral and multilateral aid programs

The differences among the West Europeans themselves as well as between them and the Reagan administration lie mainly in the choice of instruments and strategies to achieve these goals and in the establishment of priorities. The U.S. government—influenced by domestic political factors—seems to favor short-terms solutions, whereas the West Europeans tend to accept some short-term instability in the interests of reaching long-term stability in the region.

Instruments and Strategies: Party Diplomacy or National-Security Diplomacy?

Responding to the Need for Social Change

Most Third World societies are, by definition, societies in change; as the old order in these countries crumbles, dealing with their political representatives becomes increasingly difficult. This is especially true in Central America. Maintaining relations only with the ruling forces in these countries has proved inadequate: Such action excludes contacts with the forces who not only may be more responsive to the needs of the majority of the population but also are very likely to be the governments of tomorrow. As a result of the deficiencies in the pattern of bilateral relations and in response to the needs of various political and pressure groups in Central America countries, West European nonstate, transnational activities have dramatically increased during the past decade. The churches and the trade unions have been in the forefront of such activities, but the political parties and some professional groups have followed their lead. The Christian and Social Democratic parties of West Germany—largely because of the expertise and efficiency of their respective political foundations (Konrad-Adenauer-Stiftung and Friedrich-Ebert-Stiftung)—have become the most active West European groups in Central America.[11] This has been supplemented during the last few years by the close cooperation of other West European political leaders in the Christian Democratic World Union and the Socialist International.[12] During the late 1970s, both organizations used their long-term relationships with a number of Latin American parties to advance democracy in the region. Their presence in Latin America, however, dates back to the 1960s, when Chile's Eduardo Frei had a close relationship with West Europeans.

External political and financial support are not new to Latin American regimes. Some Central American regimes have had very close links with U.S. administrations and business interests. Christian and Social Democratic groups in Central America found it quite logical, and to a certain extent necessary, to seek outside support, given the adverse outlook for democratic development in their countries and the frequent exclusion of these groups from privilege and power. Many times the initiative for closer party relations was taken in Central America rather than in Rome, Bonn, or Brussels. Some of the West European party leaders who had suffered extended periods of persecution and exile during the 1930s and 1940s had a strong moral commitment to help Central American victims of authoritarian governments or military dictatorships.[13] This commitment helped unite people who held different views about the methods and goals of political development in their respective countries.

The existence of extreme social injustice in all Central American countries except Costa Rica and the blocking of all reform measures for generations by the ruling elites spurred a strong commitment in the ranks of Christian and Social Democratic parties in Europe to social and political change in Central America. The Social Democrats particularly understood the reasoning behind the radicalization of the democratic left in Nicaragua, El Salvador, and Guatemala. They feared that these political groups would be forced into closer cooperation with Cuba and the socialist bloc if the Western democracies did not support their aspirations for revolutionary change in their countries.

Through transnational party cooperation, therefore, internal political struggles have indeed become internationalized. The question is, however, given the intransigence of the ruling elites, did the antiregime elements in these countries have any other course? U.S. support for the regimes had been—with some exception during the Kennedy administration—uninterrupted until the advent of the Carter administration. When the Carter administration finally tried to shift some U.S. support toward the more reformist elements in some countries, it found the domestic political costs to be high and the local political environment in Central America no longer receptive to such initiatives.

Some West European politicians believe this experience proves that unless democratic groups have been prepared to cope with the problems of change of power, a shift of official policy among states cannot effect social change in Central America. Elections alone also are no remedy for societies torn by violence, especially since in most Central American countries elections historically have been fraudulent or the results have been annulled by the military. Many times the elections—like the ones in 1982 and 1984 in El Salvador—serve no purpose other than to try to legitimize the government internationally and to stabilize the status quo internally. All groups who have a stake in social change and political participation see defeat of the military and a change of the power structure as their only hope to achieve their goals.

Responding to Threat Perceptions

Transnational party cooperation grows out of an assumption that the main causes of civil strife in Central America are internal. When outside military intervention threatens, "national-security diplomacy" comes into play.[14] The United States' preoccupation with national-security considerations must be seen in the context of Caribbean Basin geopolitics and superpower global credibility. For its part, a recipient country like El Salvador or Guatemala seeks not only sufficient arms and training to defeat insurgent forces,[15] but also endorsement for its policies and help in achieving token reforms that might again—internally—buy time and—externally—legitimize the government. Both sides aim to address a real or perceived security threat without investigating the reasons why such a threat evolved or is seen to have evolved.

A national-security–oriented policy toward Central America, which was evolving during the last year of the Carter administration and has become the centerpiece of the Reagan administration policy toward all of Latin America, can be successful on a short- to medium-term basis. The political costs, however, are high. The short-term stability that might be achieved can succeed only through continuing the alliance with the forces within Central America that are associated with repression and persecution of all popular forces, including moderate political leaders. In any country an alliance with a weak political system tends to strengthen the military as opposed to civilian component of society.[16] The recent history in Latin America has demonstrated that there is no easy way to have security first and democracy later.

None of the structural problems of the Central American socioeconomic systems can be solved by strengthening the security apparatus. The willingness to accept a political compromise—not a typical characteristic for Latin American military establishments anyway—will be further eroded as a side effect of national-security diplomacy. But the high political price to be paid for such a relationship is not confined to the effects on the Central American countries' development. If the United States becomes too closely identified with a certain Central American regime—be it El Salvador's or Guatemala's—the United States will become, to a certain extent, hostage to that regime's policies. Criticism within the United States and from its allies will increase as military cooperation increases.[17] The United States will pay the highest price in its future relationship with the Third World.[18] If the United States' evolving relationship with Central America can be viewed as a model of U.S. relations with Third World countries in general,[19] a national-security–oriented policy might turn out to be a major long-term failure. As mentioned previously, it is over this point that Western Europe and the United States have their sharpest policy differences, since the Western concepts of democracy and development could suffer irreparable damage in the Third World.

To avoid further internal as well as international polarization in Central America, some West European parties have tried to help find a political solution to the problems in El Salvador and to avoid an international isolation of Nicaragua. Neither effort has been very successful so far, partly because of the unwillingness of the groups in power in El Salvador to cooperate and partly because the United States did not want itself or third parties to participate in such efforts.[20] The German Social and Christian Democrats have been especially active in the search for a political solution in El Salvador, since both have exceptionally good connections either with the government or the opposition. There is little doubt in Western Europe that elections will not end the civil war and that mediation will take a very long time. But a negotiated settlement seems to be the only way out of the bloody war that neither side seems able to win.[21] Obviously, revolutionary groups must be included in the mediation process, but no political settlement is likely to accommodate both extremes of the political spectrum, for which exile may be the only way out.

Many political groups in Western Europe have viewed the Nicaraguan revolution with great sympathy, but their willingness to aid the process of building a new society in Nicaragua will depend greatly on the extent to which political pluralism is able to survive there. This preoccupation should not be misunderstood as insistence upon a specific political model for Nicaragua. In general Europeans have not endorsed the U.S. response to the Nicaraguan revolution, especially since the advent of the Reagan administration. The Europeans fear that a policy of isolation of Nicaragua will hardly serve Western interests and believe that only cooperation with Western countries will give Nicaragua a chance to fulfill the goals of the Sandinist revolution. Given the history of Nicaragua's relations with the United States, U.S. pressure on Nicaragua might prove counterproductive. For the time being, therefore, even though it looks as if some West European countries will try to ease the pressure on Nicaragua rather than to follow the example of the United States, that might become more difficult once Nicaragua loses its political support from some Latin American states.

From a West European viewpoint, such differences between the United States and its European allies are not necessarily crucial. The United States has had little experience to equip it to compromise with alien political forces and concepts in Central America. Inside the United States no strong leftist movement has ever challenged the political system; outside the country no forceful neighbor has ever required the United States to get used to living alongside a political or economic system not to its liking. Both experiences abound for many West European states, and their willingness to accept such situations may have contributed to the general postwar political stability in Europe. By counseling political compromise, Western Europe has tried to help avoid serious policy failures in Central America, where obviously neither the traditional hegemonic role nor the position of strength of the United States seems to be helping to reduce internal or international tensions.[22]

Outlook

The events in Central America and the varying responses from other states and transnational actors demonstrate the changing power relationship within the international system. Small, minor countries in other parts of the Third World have become catalysts for major crises, if one or both superpowers chose to use them as a test of their relations with each other, their allies, or the Third World in general. Not since the Cuban missile crisis over twenty years ago have such developments affected Latin America.

No wonder that the countries concerned and their neighbors wanted to avoid becoming the center of international attention. New regional powers might offer the only long-term answer to the regional crises that evolve from power changes in some countries. Many Third World countries view with increasing skepticism the keen interest of the superpowers to impose their own ideological preferences on Third World countries once the old order has been overcome. Political systems like Mexico's might indeed serve as better examples for postrevolutionary society in Central America than do either West or East European models. Furthermore, Central American countries are likely to gain more maneuverability from a nonaligned foreign policy than from close relations with any of the superpowers.

The United States may need to become accustomed to increasingly independent, but not necessarily hostile, countries in its immediate neighborhood. For the United States as well as for Western Europe, the crisis in Central America could turn out to be a test of adaptability of Western policies to necessary changes in the Third World. The willingness of the United States and Western Europe not only to tolerate but to facilitate structural socioeconomic changes to benefit the underprivileged in Third World countries would help avoid future upheavals in Central America—and elsewhere.

Notes

1. See also the author's earlier version of this chapter, "Western European Perceptions of the Turmoil in Central America," in Richard E. Feinberg (ed.), *Central America: International Dimensions of the Crisis* (New York: Holmes and Meier, 1982), pp. 201–212; and Heinrich-W. Krumwiede, "Centroamérica vista desde Europa Occidental," in Donald Castillo Rivas (ed.), *Centroamérica: Más allá de la crisis* (Mexico, D.F.: Ed. SIAP, 1983), pp. 407–423.

2. Addressing the eleventh German-American Conference in Princeton on March 21, 1981, the deputy chairman of the German Social Democratic party, Horst Ehmke, drew attention to that fact: "We have for such a long time helped

to defend outmoded structures that we should not be surprised that the revolutionary movements seek help wherever they are able to get it . . . and that the Soviet Union and Cuba are taking advantage of that situation" (author's translation).

3. Department of State Special Report no. 80, February 23, 1981,"Communist Interference in El Salvador," mentions "another case of indirect armed aggression against a small Third World country by Communist powers acting through Cuba" and "the gravity of actions of Cuba, the Soviet Union, and other communist states who are carrying out what is clearly shown to be a well-coordinated, covert effort to bring about the overthrow of El Salvador's established government and impose in its place a Communist regime with no popular support" (p. 1).

4. Jeane Kirkpatrick, "Dictatorships and Double Standards," *Commentary* 68, no. 5 (November 1979), pp. 34–45.

5. "La posición demócrata-cristiana alemanacoincide en gran parte con la política estadounidense en el área." "Alemania y EE.UU. en divergencia," *América Latina: Informe Semanal,* August 22, 1980. See also the article by a leading Latin American specialist of the Christian Democratic Konrad-Adenauer-Stiftung, Josef Thesing, "Krisenherd Mittelamerika," *Politische Meinung,* no. 24 (November 1979), pp. 64–72, in which he says: "It is also remarkable that the United States government today is willing to assign the Christian Democratic parties (especially in El Salvador and Guatemala where they are strong) an important role in resolving the conflicts in Central America" (author's translation) (p. 72).

6. This view is shared by some of the most prominent Latin American specialists in the United States; see, for example, Jorge I. Dominguez, "The United States and Its Regional Security Interests: The Caribbean, Central, and South America," *Daedalus* 109, no. 4 (Fall 1980), pp. 115–133: "The Soviet Union and Cuba, therefore, do not pose a conventional threat, and pose a declining unconventional threat to the United States or other countries of the region. To the extent that a conventional threat is potential, the United States has sufficient force to meet it" (p. 122).

7. Viron P. Vaky, "Hemispheric Relations: 'Everything Is Part of Everything Else,'" *Foreign Affairs: America and the World* 59, no. 3 (1980), pp. 617–647, describes this veiw: "The problem which most Americans have in thinking about Latin America, in fact, is that they have come to consider the dominant U.S. position in the world and the overwhelming hegemony the United States exercised in the Hemisphere in the 20 years following World War II as the normal state of affairs" (p. 639).

8. The most vocal have been France, Holland, Denmark, and Sweden. See "M. Cheysson en Amérique Centrale," *Le Monde,* August 4, 1981; and "Joergensen greift Washington an—Reagans Politik ist eine Belastung," *Frankfurter Allgemeine Zeitung,* February 11, 1982.

9. See "Apoyamos a Nicaragua—Entrevista exclusiva con Cheysson," *Barricada,* August 5, 1981; "Declaración Conjunta Mexicano-Francesa sobre El Salvador," *Revista Internacional y Diplomática,* September 1981, p. 8; "France Will Send Mission to Cuba to Test Chances for Better Ties," *International Herald Tribune,* February 5, 1982; and "France Confirms Sale of Rockets to Nicaragua," *Washington Post,* February 1, 1982.

10. Pierre Schori, the international secretary of the Swedish Social Democratic party, wrote: "We find it curious and unfortunate that instead of querying and counteracting the involvement of European social democracy the U.S. does not make positive use of it. Our purposes are not extremist or even extreme. We believe, like Mexico for example, that it is unrealistic to try to exclude from a solution armed resistance against the regime." "Central America Dilemma," *Socialist Affairs,* no. 1 (1981), p. 37.

11. For a critical review, see "Bonn's Tilt Leftward in Central America Worries U.S.," *Washington Post,* September 1, 1980.

12. For the Central American activities of the Socialist International, see Schori, "Central American Dilemma"; Daniel Waksman Schinka, "La I.S. en América Latina," *El Día,* April 8 through 11, 1980; and Klaus Lindenberg, "Die Sozialistische Internationale verstärkt ihr Engagement in Lateinamerika und der Karibik," *Neue Gesellschaft,* February 1980, p. 168. For the position of the Christian Democrats, see Mario Solorzano, "El papel de la Democracia Cristiana en la actual coyuntura centroamericana," *Nueva Sociedad,* no. 48 (May/June 1980), pp. 22–33.

13. This is even recognized by Jeane Kirkpatrick, "U.S. Security and Latin America," *Commentary* 71, no. 1 (January 1981): "Both the Socialist International and the radical Catholics conceive themselves as specialists in political rectitude, and their participation in Central America politics has enhanced its moralistic content at the same time that Cuban/Soviet participation has enhanced its violence" (p. 34).

14. I have borrowed this term from Alexandre S. C. Barros, who uses it for a different purpose in "The Diplomacy of National Security: South American International Relations in a Defrosting World," in Ronald G. Hellman and H. Jon Rosenbaum (eds.), *Latin America: The Search for a New International Role* (Beverly Hills, Calif.: Sage Publications, 1975), p. 131.

15. "When aid and comfort from the U.S. in the form of money, arms, logistical support, and the services of counterinsurgency experts are no longer available, governments like those of Nicaragua, El Salvador and Guatemala are weakened." Kirkpatrick, "U.S. Security and Latin America," p. 35.

16. "Everybody knows—though it is passed over in silence—that a concentrated rollback in El Salvador and Nicaragua would set back the development of democratic parties and structures by many years" (author's translation). Horst Bieber, "Aufs Falsche Pferd gesetzt," *Die Zeit,* February 13, 1981, p. 12.

17. "The Socialist International has repeatedly made clear its support for revolutionary change in El Salvador. . . . The Socialist International calls on all foreign governments and outside forces to halt any support direct or indirect to the Duarte regime." *Socialist International Press Release,* no. 1/81, January 23, 1981.

18. "The consequences of military aid to such a government for the long-term interests of the United States must be weighed with the utmost care. Rejecting the strong opposition of democratic allies in the region to U.S. military involvement places us on a path toward self-imposed regional isolation." Statement by Sen. Edward M. Kennedy in the hearings "U.S. Policy Toward El

Salvador," March 5 and 11, 1981, Senate Subcommittee on Inter-American Affairs, p. 98.

19. "Our actions vis-à-vis Latin America may well hold the key to our future relationship with all the Third World." Ronald Reagan, "The Canal as Opportunity: A New Relationship with Latin America," *Orbis,* Fall 1977, p. 563.

20. See "Gespräche über El Salvador in Bonn," *Neue Zürcher Zeitung,* March 5, 1981; and "Die Amerikaner halten wenig von Europäischer Vermittlung in El Salvador," *Frankfurter Allgemeine Zeitung,* March 6, 1981.

21. "We believe that both sides in the conflict will have to compromise, that a new deal will have to be made. For as things now stand, both blocs are powerful. They appear capable of continuing the conflict for a long time to come. Neither side can be conclusively defeated." Schori, "Central American Dilemma," p. 38.

22. "Chances for major United States policy successes will be virtually nonexistent, while the risks of failure, embarrassment and even humiliation will grow in direct proportion to the extent of American commitments to maintaining at least the image of regional hegemony." Richard Millett, "Can We Live with Revolution in Central America?" *Caribbean Review,* Winter 1981, p. 53.

About the Contributors

Cynthia J. Arnson, Associate Fellow of the Institute for Policy Studies in Washington, is a doctoral candidate at Johns Hopkins University, School of Advanced International Studies. She has written widely on U.S.–Central American relations, U.S. arms sales, and military assistance and has written *El Salvador: A Revolution Confronts the United States* (1982).

Bruce Michael Bagley, Assistant Professor of Comparative Politics and Latin American Studies at the School of Advanced International Studies (SAIS), Johns Hopkins University, received his Ph.D. from the University of California at Los Angeles. He is currently the associate director of the Latin American Studies Program at SAIS. He was awarded a Tinker Foundation postdoctoral grant to carry out research in Colombia and Venezuela during 1983. His many publications include "United States–Mexcian Relations: A U.S. Perspective," in *Proceedings of the Academy of Political Science,* vol. 32, no. 1, 1981, and "Mexican Foreign Policy in the 1980s: The Emergence of a Regional Power," in *Current History,* November 1981.

Henrik Bischof, Research Associate at the Research-Institute of the Friedrich Ebert Foundation in Bonn, has been the editor-in-chief of the journals *Entwicklungspolitische Aktivitäten kommunistischer Länder* and *Aussenpolitik kommunistischer Länder und Dritte Welt* published by the Friedrich Ebert Foundation. He has written numerous articles about the relations of communist and Third World countries.

Demetrio Boersner, Professor of International Relations at the Universidad Central de Venezuela, received his Ph.D. from the University of Geneva. He has been visiting professor at the University of Geneva, the University of Liverpool, and the University of the West Indies as well as an adviser to the Venezuelan ministry of foreign affairs. He has published numerous books and articles in various languages, including

Venezuela y el Caribe: Presencia cambiante (1978) and *Relaciones Internacionales de América Latina* (1982).

Donald Castillo Rivas, Professor of Economy at the Universidad Nacional Autonoma de México, received his Ph.D. from the University of Barcelona. He has held previous appointments at various universities in Chile, Argentina, and Mexico and has also been a consultant to numerous international organizations. His many publications include *Acumulación de Capital y Empreseas transnacionales en Centroamérica* (1980) and (as editor) *Centroamérica: mas allá de la crisis* (1983).

Margaret E. Crahan, Henry R. Luce Professor of Religion, Power, and Political Process at Occidental College in Los Angeles, received her Ph.D. from Columbia University. She is also a member of the Department of History at Herbert H. Lehmann College, City University of New York. She has served on the Executive Council of the Latin American Studies Association, as vice-president of the Latin American Foundation, and on the Board of Directors of the Washington Office on Latin America. Her numerous articles and books include (as editor) *Human Rights and Basic Needs in the Americas* (1982) and (as coeditor with Franklin W. Knight) *Africa and the Caribbean* (1979).

Richard E. Feinberg, Director of the Foreign Policy Program and Senior Fellow at the Overseas Development Council, received his Ph.D. from Stanford University. He served as the Latin American specialist on the Policy Planning Staff of the Department of State from 1977 to 1979. Presently he is also an adjunct professor at the Georgetown University, School of Foreign Service. He has written numerous articles and books on U.S. foreign policy, Latin American politics, and international economics, including (as editor) *Central America: International Dimensions of the Crisis* (1982); *Subsidizing Success: The Export-Import Bank in the U.S. Economy* (1982); and *The Intemperate Zone: The Third World Challenge to U.S. Foreign Policy* (1983).

Piero Gleijeses, Adjunct Professor of American Foreign Policy and Latin American Studies at the School of Advanced International Studies, Johns Hopkins University, received his Ph.D. from the Graduate Institute of International Studies in Geneva, Switzerland. He was a fellow at the Lehrman Institute (1979–1980) and has been a visiting lecturer at the State Department's Foreign Service Institute (1980–1981). His publications include *The Dominican Crisis: The 1965 Constitutionalist Revolt and American Intervention* (1978) and *Tilting at Windmills: Reagan in Central America* (1982).

Wolf Grabendorff, Senior Staff Member at the Stiftung Wissenschaft und Politik, Research Institute for International Affairs in Ebenhausen, West Germany, has been the Latin American correspondent for the German National TV System ARD as well as a visiting fellow at the Center of Brazilian Studies, School of Advanced International Studies, Johns Hopkins University. He has written numerous articles and books on the politics and foreign relations of Latin American states, including *A donde Latinoamérica?* (1979) and (as editor) *Lateinamerika—Kontinent in der Krise* (1974).

Harald Jung, Representative of the Friedrich Ebert Foundation in Santo Domingo, Dominican Republic, received his Ph.D. from the University of Kassel. He has also been a research fellow at the University of Oxford. He has written numerous articles about Central America and is the author of *Nicaragua: Bereicherungsdiktatur und Volksaufstand* (1980).

Heinrich-W. Krumwiede, Assistant Professor of Political Science at the University of Mannheim, received his Ph.D. from the University of Mannheim. He has recently been a John F. Kennedy Memorial Fellow at Harvard University. He has published numerous articles on the role of the church in Latin America and on Central American politics. He is the author of *Politik und Katholische Kirche im gesellschaftlichen Modernisierungsprozess: Tradition und Entwicklung in Kolumbien* (1980).

Richard L. Millett, Professor of History and Chairman of the Latin American Studies Committee of Southern Illinois University at Edwardsville, received his Ph.D. from the University of New Mexico. He has written numerous articles on Central American and Caribbean politics. His books include *Guardians of the Dynasty: A History of the U.S. Created Guardia Nacional de Nicaragua and the Somoza Family* (1977) and (as editor with W. Marvin Will) *The Restless Caribbean: Changing Patterns of International Relations* (1979).

Robert A. Pastor, Faculty Research Associate at the School of Public Affairs, University of Maryland, College Park, received his Ph.D. from Harvard University. He was a guest scholar at the Brookings Institution, and from 1977 until 1981 he served as the senior staff member responsible for Latin American and Caribbean affairs on the National Security Council of the White House. He also served as executive director of the Linowitz Commission on U.S.–Latin American Relations and taught at Harvard University. Aside from numerous articles he is the author of *Congress and the Politics of U.S. Foreign Economic Policy* (1980).

Carla A. Robbins, Staff Editor at *Business Week,* received her Ph.D. from the University of California at Berkeley. In addition to numerous articles she is the author of *The Cuban Threat* (1983).

Jörg Todt, Research Associate for Latin America at the Research Institute of the Friedrich Ebert Foundation in Bonn, received his Ph.D. from the University of Bochum.

Edelberto Torres-Rivas, Professor of Sociology at the Instituto Centroamericano de Administración Publica in San José, Costa Rica, has been a fellow at the Wilson Center in Washington recently. His numerous publications include *Crisis del poder en Centroamérica* (1981) and (as editor) *Centroamérica hoy* (1975).

Index